World Environmental HISTORY

BERKSHIRE 宝库山
ESSENTIALS

World
Environmental
HISTORY

宝库山精选：世界环境历史

William H. McNeill

David Christian, J. R. McNeill,

Jerry H. Bentley, Ralph C. Croizier,

Heidi Roupp, and Judith P. Zinsser

Editors

Brett Bowden

Associate Editor

山 BERKSHIRE
A global point of reference

Digital editions

World Environmental History is available through most major e-book and database services (please check with them for pricing).

For information, contact:
Berkshire Publishing Group LLC
122 Castle Street
Great Barrington, Massachusetts 01230
www.berkshirepublishing.com
Printed in the United States of America

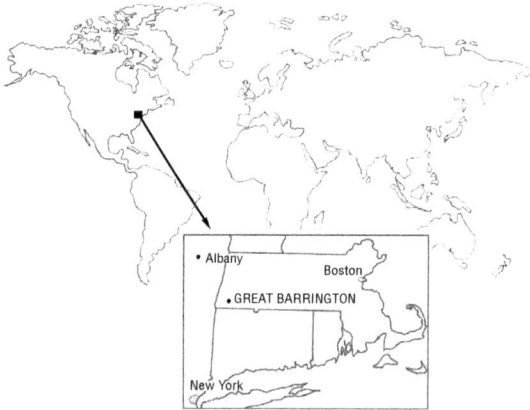

Library of Congress Cataloging-in-Publication Data

World environmental history / William H. McNeill ... [et al.], editors ; Brett Bowden, associate editor.
 p. cm. – (Berkshire essentials)
 Summary: Environmental articles from the Berkshire encyclopedia of world history, 2nd ed.
 Includes bibliographical references.
 ISBN 978-1-933782-96-6 (pbk. : alk. paper) — 978-0-9743091-9-4 (e-book)
 1. Ecology—History. 2. Human ecology—History. 3. World history. 4. Ecology—Study and teaching. 5. Human ecology—Study and teaching. I. McNeill, William Hardy, 1917- II. Bowden, Brett, 1968- III. Berkshire encyclopedia of world history.
 QH540.8.W66 2011
 333.72–dc23
                    2011023179

THE **BERKSHIRE** ESSENTIALS SERIES

From the *Berkshire Encyclopedia of World History, 2nd Edition*:

- *Africa in World History*
- *Art in World History*
- *Big History*
- *Religion and Belief Systems in World History*
- *War, Diplomacy, and Peacemaking*
- *Women's and Gender History*
- *World Environmental History*

Distilled for
the classroom
from Berkshire's
award-winning
encyclopedias

BERKSHIRE ESSENTIALS from the *Berkshire Encyclopedia of China*
and the *Berkshire Encyclopedia of Sustainability* also available.

Contents

About this "Berkshire Essentials" Volume

For more than a decade Berkshire Publishing has collaborated with an extraordinary worldwide network of scholars and editors to produce award-winning academic resources on cutting-edge subjects that appeal to a broad audience. With our Berkshire Essentials series—inspired by requests from teachers, curriculum planners, and professors who praise the encyclopedic approach we often use, but who still crave single volumes for course use—we at Berkshire have designed a series that "concentrates" our content.

Each Essentials series draws from Berkshire publications on a wide-ranging topic—world history, Chinese studies, and environmental sustainability, for starters—to provide theme-related volumes that can be purchased alone, in any combination, or as a set. (For example, individual volumes of the Essentials in World History series take a global approach to Africa; art; big history; religion and belief systems; war, diplomacy, and peacemaking; women's and gender studies; and of course, with this volume, world environmental history.) Teachers will find the insightful, illustrated articles indispensable for jump starting classroom discussion or independent study. Individuals—whether students, professionals, or general readers—will discover the articles invaluable when exploring a new line of research or an abiding interest.

As Shepard Kretch III, J. R. McNeill, and Carolyn Merchant explain in the introduction to this volume, "world environmental history not only considers the whole world but is also a worldwide undertaking" that encompasses a variety of approaches by scholars in a number of disciplines. (One approach, which considers biological and physical processes as integral parts of history, sees "biotic actors" such as mammals, birds,

Various aspects of farming in ancient Egypt are depicted in the Tomb of Nakht, on the West Bank of Luxor.

plants, bacteria, and viruses playing important roles. So do geological formations and disruptions (such as deserts, mountains, islands, tsunamis, and earthquakes), and human interventions (including oil spills, deforestation, and urbanization). We at Berkshire have cultivated an impressive network of environmental scientists, botanists, ecologists, sociologists, anthropologists, archaeologists, and naturalists whose research and writing (on these topics and more) we bring together for this book.

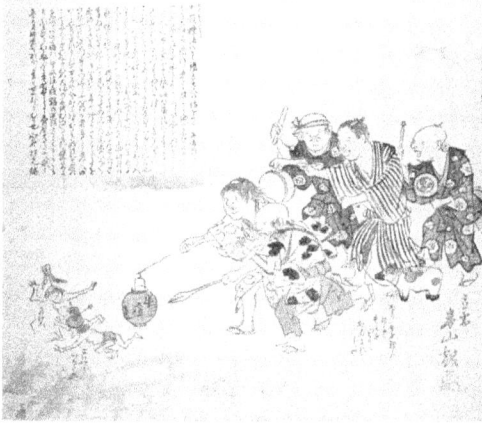

This print by Matsukawa Hanzan enlightened viewers about the importance of the smallpox vaccine and the work of Kōan Ogata, a Western-trained doctor who vaccinated three thousand people in 1849 at his clinic in Osaka, Japan.

World Environmental History's rich content includes coverage of theories and practices inherent to the study of human–environmental interaction—such as carrying capacity, based on Thomas Malthus's 1798 assertion that "the power of population is indefinitely greater than the power in the Earth to produce subsistence for man," and ecological imperialism, the process during which colonizers brought plants, animals, and diseases of their homelands to conquered lands and indigenous populations. The renowned world historian David Christian, a regular contributor to Berkshire publications, discusses the enormous changes that have affected our relationship to the biosphere since 1800, just about the time we began to depend heavily on fossil fuels. As a result, some geologists believe the Earth left its natural geological epoch, the Holocene, and entered a warmer, stormier, and less biodiverse epoch, the Anthropocene. In a related article, "Climate Change," Anthony N. Penna draws on scientific studies and historical data to present a comprehensive survey of global "freezes and thaws" and the three major post–Industrial Revolution factors that continue to contribute to abrupt weather-pattern changes and warming—energy exchanges between the oceans and the atmosphere, fossil-fuel emissions, and solar energy. And yet, Penna writes, these factors "possess such complex and unpredictable characteristics that to date the most advanced computer and global climate models have been unable to predict future climate events."

Taking precautions and proactive measures to ensure a sustainable future is, of course, one of the most crucial aspects of world environmental studies. This volume includes coverage of environmental movements beginning in the late eighteenth and nineteenth centuries, many years before the term environmentalism was coined. Alexander M. Zukas takes a close look at the Green Revolution that began in the 1960s, a contested "development" in agriculture with economic, political, and social ramifications. The Green Revolution's basic goal was to produce higher-yielding strains of corn and wheat. Big business, especially in chemicals and seeds, considered it a boon to production and profit, as well as a giant step in the direction of guaranteeing food safety; small farmers, ecologists, and community activists, however, argued that it harmed the environment, obliterated indigenous cultural and agricultural practices, and created unsustainable debt for developing countries whose output would largely go to feed the developed world. "Ethnobotany," on the other hand, explains how—based on cultural practices and needs throughout history—the human management and manipulation of plants and landscapes have helped create species and habitat diversity.

We at Berkshire appreciate comments and questions from our readers. Please send suggestions for other Essential volumes you'd like to see in this world history–themed series. And do check our website for news about our other Essential volumes on China and environmental sustainability.

Karen Christensen
CEO and Publisher
Great Barrington, Massachusetts

Introduction—World Environmental History

Human struggles have always occurred within the framework of the natural world, and that framework has, always and everywhere, been in flux—sometimes rapid, sometimes slow. Wildlife, soils, climate, and disease are just some of the hundreds of factors in the natural world that have always constrained and conditioned the human experience. For its part, human action has increasingly affected the natural world and its evolution. Human society coevolves with nature; human history unfolds within a broad natural context even as it helps shape that context.

The emergence of environmental history as a field of scholarship is part of a broad shift in the way we understand our environment. Centuries ago, at least in most cultures, the stars and the planets were thought to be immutable fixtures of the heavens. The Earth, too, was generally understood as everlasting, and life on Earth, even if in some versions created all of a piece, included a fixed number of species which had been there from the start and would remain until the finish. But since the 1830s geologists have offered a picture of Earth's history that is truly historical. Biologists since the 1860s have increasingly agreed that life on Earth is always in flux, that species come and go. More recently astronomers and cosmologists have concluded that the universe itself is not timeless but instead historical. It is perhaps 13 to 14 billion years old, still expanding, and the stars, galaxies, and planets within it come and go. Increasingly, static or even equilibrium models of how everything works have given way to dynamic, historical models. The field of environmental history chronicles and analyzes the dynamics of life on Earth.

World environmental history not only considers the whole world but is also a worldwide undertaking. Although historians in the United States were the first to refer to themselves as environmental historians and first formed an organization explicitly devoted to environmental history, scholars elsewhere had long been interested in the same sorts of questions, historical geographers foremost among them. Indeed, drawing a distinction between the interests and methods of historical geographers and those of environmental historians is difficult. Nevertheless, from roughly the 1980s, scholars choosing to call themselves environmental historians have set to work around the world. In Europe the most active communities developed in Germany, Sweden, Finland, Spain, and Britain. In Africa, where political and economic instability are huge obstacles to scholarly work, environmental historians have emerged since the mid-1980s, especially in South Africa, but in eastern Africa too. India has had a particularly active group of environmental historians since about 1985, as has Australia, and, more recently, New Zealand. Since 1990 or so a small but determined group of environmental historians has emerged in Latin America, mainly in Brazil and Mexico. By and large, environmental history has few practitioners in Russia, China, Japan, and the Arab world, although foreigners have explored themes of environmental history quite successfully for China and Japan. There are signs, moreover, that these pioneering efforts are attracting followers and inspiring new research. As environmental historians in those areas catch up to their colleagues in India, Germany, or the United States, we shall have a richer, deeper command of the world's environmental history.

Perspectives and Approaches

Environmental history encompasses a variety of approaches to analyzing human interactions with the natural world. By viewing physical and biological processes as integral parts of history, the natural world becomes a subject for historical investigation. Mammals, birds, plants, bacteria, and viruses constitute biotic actors that play important roles in the unfolding of history. Abiotic constituents and processes—climatic change, soil composition, hydraulic forces, and atmospheric compounds, for example—are also important in the eyes of environmental historians. In the human realm, economic systems, population sizes, consumption patterns, political institutions, attitudes toward race and gender, and ideas about nature affect our interaction with natural systems.

Cultural perspectives on nature vary widely around the globe. Indigenous peoples, Eastern philosophers, nineteenth-century Romantics, and environmental scientists all had or have differing views of what nature is and how the natural world arose. People have used stories, myths, dance, art, photography, and religion to express their perceptions of nature as a gift of the gods or a collection of resources to be used for human benefit, and to craft guidelines for ethical behavior. A narrative approach sets up overarching story lines of progress in subduing and controlling nature or of the loss of pristine nature and the decline in species and environmental quality. Whatever the approach, the complexity and unpredictability of nature and human societies are inescapable themes in environmental history. Environmental history is thus of growing interest and value to many other disciplines, to policy makers, restoration ecologists, and a variety of cultures and societies around the world.

Environmental History and the History of Science

World environmental history draws on numerous sciences and their histories. Ecology, botany, zoology, bacteriology, medicine, geology, physics, and chemistry all bear directly on environmental history. Perhaps the most fundamental and encompassing science is ecology. Climate, rainfall, and average annual temperatures set limits to the vegetation and related animal life in a given region. Soil types may vary greatly over short distances, as may water availability. Depending on the array of conditions present, the region will either be attractive for human settlement or challenging to it. A given culture's extraction of such resources as plant and animal foods, fossil fuels, or minerals for trade affects local ecological conditions and hence the potential for continued settlement or the necessity of migration. The science of ecology therefore aids environmental historians in interpreting the ways in which a culture interacts with the land and surrounding peoples. But environmental historians are also aware that ecology as a science continues to evolve, and that the history of ecology is relevant to how environmental history is written. Ecological concepts such as plant succession, biodiversity, the balance of nature, and the unpredictability of weather are reassessed and modified over the years, influencing the way world environmental history is written and revised.

The history of disease and medicine is equally important for environmental historians. The susceptibility or immunity of a population to an introduced disease is critical to the success both of colonizers and indigenous populations. Much of world environmental history can be interpreted in the light of epidemics of diseases such as smallpox, measles, bubonic plague, tuberculosis, influenza, and viruses that European colonizers brought to the New World. Outbreaks of cholera and yellow fever associated with contaminated or stagnant water, and black and brown lung diseases associated with the mining and manufacturing industries are also influential disease patterns in environmental history. Knowing the history of epidemiology, virology, and toxicology can therefore be critical to the way environmental historians interpret their subject matter.

Another approach to environmental history is through the history of the environmental and earth sciences. How a culture understands geology, climatology, and mineralogy influenced the ways in which it extracts minerals, processes them, and attaches importance to them—and that understanding changes with time. Whether a society uses coal, iron, gold, or silicon as a resource depends not only on the availability of the resource but also on how it is conceptualized at a given historical moment and how it fits into a society's material infrastructure and interpretation of nature. For example, whether it is acceptable to mine for metals may depend on whether metals are thought of as living or dead, as well as on the technologies available to extract and process them and the importance of metal products to material culture and personal wealth.

Finally, the histories of physics, biology, and chemistry help environmental historians understand the ways in which a society thinks about the natural world. Newtonian mechanics, Darwinian evolution, thermodynamics, atomic theory, and the periodic table of elements are frameworks both for technological development and for aesthetic, ethical, and religious appreciation of the natural order and humanity's place within it. All branches of the history of science, then, are integral parts of world environmental history.

Environmental History and Gender

Gender is important to world environmental history because the nature of male and female interactions with the natural world has changed over time and differs from culture to culture. Gathering, hunting, fishing, and horticulture—all activities that affect environmental quality and resource availability—often have sex-specific components. In some cultures men are primarily responsible for hunting larger game animals while women may participate in hunting smaller animals and in meat processing. In some cultures women are primarily responsible for gathering and shifting horticulture (using digging tools), while in others men may assume responsibility for horticulture and for settled agriculture when large draft animals are used in plowing. Fishing likewise is often differentiated along gender lines, with men setting nets and weirs or fishing from boats and women gathering shellfish or fishing with hooks and lines.

The ways in which such gendered production systems use, exploit, or conserve resources are relevant to the production systems' sustainability over time and their adaptability to new environments. Environmental historians study such systems on a

"A Man & Woman of the Naudonessie" [sic], an illustration from *Travels through the interior parts of North-America in the years 1766, 1767, and 1768.* New York Public Library.

case-by-case basis. For example, during the period of European colonization, agricultural systems in which men used draft animals and plows in large fields for grain production while women worked in vegetable and herb gardens, tended poultry, and processed food spread rapidly around the temperate regions of the globe, supplanting indigenous systems based on gathering, hunting, fishing, and horticulture. While the colonizing systems may have been more efficient than the indigenous systems in exploiting soils and forests for subsistence and profit, they may also have wasted resources—at least initially, until resource degradation stimulated agricultural improvement and forest conservation. Of interest to environmental historians is the interaction between women and men in traditional systems and between cultures during colonization. Environmental historians ask whether any generalizations can be made or patterns discerned regarding the roles of the sexes in conserving or exploiting resources.

Environmental historians are also interested in how women and men responded to the need for resource conservation and environmental improvement during the era of industrialization at the beginning of the nineteenth century and the era of environmentalism at the end of the twentieth century. Women played major roles in lobbying for the conservation of forests, parks, and wildlife, often seeing themselves at odds with the interests and activities of men, which they perceived as exploitative and wasteful. Similarly, women also challenged the men of their communities to clean up polluted air and water and to institute street cleaning and garbage collection. During the environmental movement of the 1970s and subsequent decades, which was sparked in large part by Rachel Carson's 1962 book *Silent Spring*, women pressed for wilderness preservation, clean air and water legislation, pesticide controls, and the cleanup of toxic landfills and chemical incinerators. Women around the world became leaders in conservation, environmental, and antitoxic movements both in industrialized and developing nations, from the local to the international level.

A third issue is the relationship between gender and metaphor in depicting nature in myth, religion, science, literature, and art. Whether nature is viewed as created and directed by a male god, a goddess, a female nature acting through God's direction, a raven, a grandmother spider, or a set of gender-neutral processes can be relevant to the ways in which humans approach and use nature. Images of nature—such as a mother to be revered, a virgin to be raped, or a witch who brings on bad harvests and human ailments—can influence human ethical behavior and ritual practice. Some rituals may encourage the conservation of resources while others may have little practical consequence but may nevertheless set up a framework of reverence and respect for the natural world. Conversely, rituals may encourage exploitation and waste. Analyzing the gendered meanings found within a given culture's icons and narratives can thus provide clues to attitudes that may reinforce particular practices or provide inspiration for changing those practices.

Environmental History and Anthropology

For well over a century anthropologists have posed many of the same questions as environmental historians. As their discipline took shape in the nineteenth century, a number of anthropologists were concerned with the relationship between humans and the environment; specifically, the determining or constraining influence of geography, environment, or climate on human society and culture. Their arguments (now discredited) suggested that extremes in climate or latitude, or barrenness of land, hindered the development of culture and mental disposition, while temperate climates were believed to favor the development of what theorists perceived as human capacity.

Nineteenth-century anthropology was swept along by evolutionism, which brought to the discipline a continuing focus on human adaptations in different environments. At first, evolutionary interest centered on grand unilineal schemes: evolution of the family, religion, or human society. Reaction to these speculative designs was sharp at the outset of the twentieth century, which saw the beginning of an era of anti-evolutionist (and anti-environmental-determinist) fervor, but in the 1930s and 1940s anthropologists returned to evolution with greatly lowered sights in a succession of fields called cultural evolution, cultural ecology, ecological anthropology, and historical ecology. Their theories about the static or dynamic relationship between humans and the environment tended to be grounded in specific historical and cultural contexts and have been important for the unfolding relationship between anthropology and environmental history.

Cultural Evolution and Cultural Ecology

Cultural evolution and cultural ecology, premised on the theory that humans adapt to natural and social environments by cultural means, were popular fields in anthropology for decades. Anthropologists explored the relationship between technology, population, control of energy, and social complexity. Many considered technology and the instruments and modes of production, as well as certain natural characteristics (for example, the environmental circumscription of societies with expanding populations), important determinants of culture and human behavior. A modified geographical determinism linked these schemes to those of the nineteenth century, but it was almost always tempered by the interplay of environment and technology. The focus almost always remained on human society, however, not on the environment, although clearly evolution played out in unfolding relationships between human societies and their environments.

Ecological Anthropology and Historical Ecology

In the 1960s, anthropological interest in the human-environmental relationship matured as ecological anthropology—which explores the application in human societies of the concepts of ecosystem, ecological niche, habitat, and adaptation—came into its own. The most famous work of ecological anthropology suggested that ritual was the regulatory mechanism balancing the ratio of human and pig populations to the carrying capacity of the land in New Guinea. Other works explored the adaptations and human-land relations of hunter-gatherers, pastoralists, or agriculturalists under changing circumstances (including the encroaching presence of global economic systems). The challenges of applying the concepts of function, adaptation, and system at both the level of the individual and the group have been constant in both ecology and anthropology.

The most recent iteration of the anthropological interest in human-environment relations is historical ecology, defined as the study of ecosystems of the past through change in landscapes. For many of its proponents, historical ecology emerged not merely because scholars wished to understand past human-environment relationships but also out of a desire to guide humanity to a sustainable future.

Anthropological Archaeology

The commitment of anthropological archaeologists to exploring ecological and evolutionary questions has remained particularly constant through the years. Many have been deeply influenced by cultural ecology; others focus on individual decision making and still others on more systemic processes in environmental change (insofar as either is revealed in the archaeological record).

Recent archaeological contributions to our understanding of the impact of humans on ancient environments around the world have been substantial. They include studies of the impact of predation, fire, increases in population size and density, the domestication of plants and animals, urbanism, intensification of production, and crowd diseases. A growing number of archaeologists are interested in large-scale histories of past societies. For example, they have investigated the impact of climatic fluctuation or volcanic eruptions in the American West, the impact of farming in the Mediterranean, the connections, if any, between the demand for trees, deforestation, and human population dispersal. When people migrate they transport their landscapes (both mental models and physical icons) with them, and anthropological archaeologists are increasingly interested in the impact of such movements and changes.

Social and Cultural Anthropology

Social and cultural anthropologists contribute to environmental history through ethnography and historical analysis. Their interests are remarkably varied. Some study indigenous peoples' extensive knowledge of the natural world, made sense of culturally and organized in taxonomies that both overlap with and depart significantly from Western scientific schemes. Others focus on the cultural construction of nature, the demographic and environmental impact of epidemic disease, anthropogenic landscapes, the impacts of pastoralism and agrarianism, long-term adaptations and the possibilities of sustainability, the cultural construction of environmental values, the ethnography of environmentalism, the politics of environmental issues, and environmental justice. It is a varied and rapidly expanding field, one no doubt enhanced by the realization that the relationship between humans and the environment will present some of the most critical challenges of the twenty-first century.

Environmental History and Natural History

The links between natural history—the descriptive, systematic and, ultimately, scientific study of the natural world—and environmental history are varied. In the West, the roots of the discipline of natural history can be traced to Aristotle and to certain early-modern thinkers, whose taxonomies reflected the importance of the perceived relationship between the natural world and humans. Not surprisingly, ideas about the natural world reflected thoughts about human emotions, aesthetics, morality, society, and culture. In the sixteenth through eighteenth centuries—a period of Western expansion of geographical and descriptive knowledge of the natural world—more detached perspectives on nature entered natural history through exploration and the return of specimens to cabinets of curiosities even as religious explanations of nature remained essentially intact.

In some ways the eighteenth century was a high point for natural history. During that century Carl Linnaeus, Georges Buffon, and others published significant works of natural description and classification, governments sponsored the study of natural history, botanical decoration and illustration became popular, and people celebrated arcadian harmony. A

Intricate display of glass recreations of plants from the Ware Collection of Blaschka Glass Models of Plants. The collection was created in the 19th century to serve as a teaching collection—it is renowned for its beauty and for the botanical accuracy of the plant models. Collection of the Harvard Museum of Natural History. Photo by Anna Myers.

benign, holistic relationship between man and nature was posited, and there was a significant rise in concern for the environment.

In the nineteenth century natural history's emphasis on morphological study of life forms continued but theoretical energy shifted to newly emergent disciplines, all of which were increasingly (after mid-century) affected by evolutionary thought. By the early twentieth century biology, physiology, ecology, and other fields of scientific inquiry had pushed natural history aside, relegating it in the minds of many to an antiquarian pursuit confined to museums. Many regarded ecology in particular as the new natural history.

Yet natural history continued, both as a descriptive and taxonomic pursuit and in the nature essays of such writers as John Burroughs, John Muir, Aldo Leopold, and many others whose humanist, aesthetic, or spiritual awe mediated their experience of nature as much as did science. It may be in the nature essay, traceable to the eighteenth-century British clergyman and naturalist Gilbert White, that natural history has seen its most consistent overlap with environmental history. Today's nature writers continue to stress the importance of combining in their narratives close descriptive, systematic knowledge of the natural world with empathy and reflection.

But natural history remains highly visible to the public not just in natural-history essays but through the existence of major museums whose names proclaim dedication to assemblages of facts about the natural world, to scientific description and taxonomy. As the outgrowth of cabinets of curiosities, museums of natural history emerged in the eighteenth century and proliferated in the nineteenth and twentieth. Today they educate millions of visitors in the Western world about the natural world and, increasingly, about environmental history.

A Global Approach

Pursing the study of environmental history on the global scale has never before been so logical or so crucial. The ongoing accumulation of carbon dioxide in the atmosphere, sulfur dioxide moving with the winds to fall as acid rain far from its point of origin, the overharvesting of the sea's richest fishing grounds, salt accumulation in irrigated lands—these, and many biosphere-threatening processes like them, are global (or nearly global) in scale. So were biosphere-friendly movements such as the late-nineteenth-century establishment of national parks and the late-twentieth-century emergence of popular environmentalism.

In the twenty-first century people increasingly see themselves as part of a global community, and as its citizens feel they must take action (whether within an organization, a grassroots group, or individually), to protect the environment from further damage. Environmental civil disobedience—protests that often begin on a local level in the form of a tree sit to protest deforestation, for instance, or, as Al Gore suggested in 2008, a blockade of bulldozers at an excavation site where a coal-fired power plant is scheduled to be built—attract media attention that can spark public discussion and serve as an agent of change.

Ultimately rather few subjects in environmental history are truly local because, as the naturalist John Muir noted, in nature everything is always hitched to everything else. The arenas in which the events of environmental history have been played out are of various sizes and are often overlap. The discipline of world environmental history thus aims to make a signal contribution toward the biosphere by putting human history into its broadest context.

Shepard KRECH III
Brown University

J. R. McNEILL
Georgetown University

Carolyn MERCHANT
University of California Berkeley

Anthropocene

Human activities have become so pervasive and profound that they rival the great forces of nature and are pushing the Earth into planetary terra incognita. Some geologists believe that that the Earth has now left its natural geological epoch—the interglacial state called the Holocene—and is rapidly moving into a less biologically diverse, less forested, much warmer, and probably wetter and stormier state, the Anthropocene.

In 2000, and then more formally in the journal *Nature* in 2002, Paul J. Crutzen, a Dutch Nobel Prize–winning atmospheric chemist, argued that in about 1800 the world entered a new geological epoch, the Anthropocene. This was the era in which our own species, without intending to do so, and without even understanding what was happening, became not just a significant force for change within the biosphere, but perhaps *the most important single force* for change within the biosphere.

Impressed by these arguments, several geologists have proposed that the Anthropocene be formally recognized as a new geological period. At present, we live in the Holocene epoch, which began in 10,000 BP (before present). If the new proposal is accepted, the Holocene era will be designated as having ended in 1800 CE, and the Anthropocene will be designated as the epoch to follow. The date 1800 is an appropriate starting point for the Anthropocene; that is when the global concentration of major greenhouse gases—carbon dioxide and methane—began to rise significantly. It is no accident, therefore, that the new epoch coincides with the invention and spread of the improved James Watt steam engines, and with conventional dates for the beginnings of the Industrial Revolution. From an ecological point of view, the beginning of the Anthropocene offers a powerful marker for the beginnings of the modern era of human history.

In a controversial 2005 study, the paleoclimatologist William Ruddiman proposes a different periodization. He argues that through deforestation and the spread of domesticated livestock and wet rice farming, humans may have been shaping the atmosphere on global scales for as long as 8,000 years by raising atmospheric levels of carbon dioxide and methane. He suggests that these changes prevented the early return to a new Ice Age and allowed the great agrarian civilizations of human history to flourish. In other words, human activity created the global climatic conditions that allowed the world's major agrarian civilizations to flourish during the last 5,000 years. Ruddiman's arguments may be overstated, but even so, they suggest that the Anthropocene is not just a byproduct of modernity, but had roots many millennia in the past.

The idea of the Anthropocene (like its conceptual partner, the *anthroposphere*) has much to offer world historians. First, it highlights the remarkable fact that our species, *Homo sapiens*, is the first single species in the history of the entire planet to have had a significant impact on the biosphere as a whole. Earlier in the planet's history, large groups of organisms such as early photosynthesizing bacteria created the Earth's oxygen-dominated atmosphere. But as far as we know, no single species has ever had such a profound impact on the biosphere. The idea of the Anthropocene therefore highlights our uniqueness as a species, and the power of our capacity for sustained ecological innovation.

The idea of the Anthropocene also offers a powerful tool for thinking about some of the dominant features of modern world history. It highlights the astonishing scale of the changes that have transformed our relationship to the biosphere in the last two hundred years, and the many contemporary challenges those changes have created. And by doing so it suggests that there is an objective basis for the claim that world history did indeed enter a new era at about 1800, the time of the fossil fuels revolution. Finally, the idea of the Anthropocene highlights the profound importance of environmental history to world history in general.

David CHRISTIAN
Macquarie University, Sydney
Ewha Womans University, Seoul

See also Anthroposphere

Further Reading

Crutzen P. J. (2002, January 3). The Anthropocene. *Nature 415*, 23.

Climate Change 2007—The Physical Science Basis. (2007). Contribution of Working Group I to the Fourth Assessment Report of the IPCC. Retrieved January 29, 2010, from http://www.ipcc.ch/ipccreports/ar4-wg1.htm

Ruddiman, W. (2005). *Plows, plagues, and petroleum: How humans took control of climate.* Princeton, NJ: Princeton University Press.

Will, S., Crutzen P. J., & McNeill, J. R. (2008, December). The Anthropocene: Are humans now overwhelming the great forces of nature?" *Ambio, 36*(8).

Zalasiewicz, J., et al. (February 2009). Are we now living in the Anthropocene? *Geological Society of America, 18*(2), 4–8.

Anthroposphere

The *anthroposphere*—we humans together with our environment—addresses the degree to which we, as opposed to other life forms, have impacted and penetrated the biosphere. The concept, introduced in the late twentieth century, proposes that monopolies of human power throughout history, such as agrarian and industrial regimes, have deeply affected the relations between humans and the nonhuman world.

The concept of *anthroposphere*, like the concept of *biosphere* from which it derived, was first introduced in the natural sciences in the late 1980s and early 1990s. The term refers to that part of the biosphere that is affected by humans—just as the part of the biosphere that is affected by elephants could be called *elephantosphere*. Such terms are all predicated on the idea that there is a two-way relationship between every living species and the environment in which it lives. All life is part of an ecosystem, all ecosystems together constitute the biosphere—the total configuration of living things interacting with one another and with nonliving things. Every form of life continuously affects, and is affected by, its ecosystem—and human life is no exception.

Anthroposphere is an open concept, containing suggestions for research and reflection, sensitizing us to the problem of how far and how deeply the impact of human activity has penetrated into the biosphere. By reminding us that human societies are embedded in ecosystems, the concept helps to bridge the gap between the natural sciences and the social sciences and humanities. Moreover, it can be used to formulate and elucidate the simple but far-reaching proposition that many trends and events in human history, from its earliest beginnings to the present day, can be seen as functions or manifestations of the expanding anthroposphere.

Extensive and Intensive Growth

The anthroposphere emerged with the evolutionary transition from hominids to humans. Initially, expansion must have been very slow and replete with regressions. In the long run, however, the human population grew in numbers from modest beginnings to 6.79 billion in 2010, and it spread from its origins in northeastern Africa over increasingly more territory, until it was a significant presence on every continent except Antarctica. Together these two forms of expansion represent extensive growth. *Extensive growth* can be defined as sheer extension of biomass, physically and geographically. It is a matter of proliferation: more of the same, reaching farther and farther—like rabbits in Australia or cancer cells in a human body.

In the expanding anthroposphere, extensive growth has always been accompanied, and in all likelihood even driven, by intensive growth. If extensive growth can be defined in terms of more and more, intensive growth refers to the emergence of something new. In the case of the anthroposphere, it arises from the human capacity to find new ways of exploiting energy and matter by collecting and processing new information. If the key word for extensive growth is proliferation, the key word for intensive growth is differentiation—its primary effect always being to add new and different items to an existing stock or repertoire. Once an innovation has been accepted, it may then be copied in multiple forms and grow extensively. Thus intensive growth and extensive growth intermingle. (Like the concept of anthroposphere and other central concepts used in this article, such as agrarianization and industrialization, the concepts of intensive and extensive growth are intended not to express any value judgments.)

Learning as a Source of Power

Human life, like all life, consists of specific combinations of matter and energy structured and directed by information. Two particular features distinguish human life from other forms of life and hence are important in understanding the anthroposphere. First, humans rely much more strongly on learned information than any other species. Second, most of the information that human individuals learn comes from other individuals: it is information that has been pooled, shared, transmitted—it is, in a word, *culture*.

The most important vehicle for human communication is language, composed of symbols. Symbols therefore constitute a vital dimension of the anthroposphere. Information conveyed in symbols can be handed down from generation to generation and used to aggregate and organize matter and energy in the service of human groups, thus strengthening the position of those groups in the biosphere. The development of language made it possible for humans to adopt new forms of behavior that made them increasingly different from other animals. A strong reason for maintaining the new forms of behavior must have been that they gave humans the advantage of greater power over those other animals.

This seems to be one of the clues for understanding the course of the long-term development of the anthroposphere. Again and again, innovations occurred, like mutations in biological evolution, and again and again, of those innovations, those tended to be retained that helped increase the power of the groups that maintained them. As humans increased their power through such innovations as language and the mastery of fire, other animals inevitably declined in power. Some became extinct, while all surviving species had to adjust their ways of life to the newly gained superiority of human groups. At later stages,

similar shifts in power relations occurred within human society itself, compelling defeated groups to adjust to the dominance of more successful groups. Many innovations in the history of human culture were adjustments to power losses.

Differentiation: Regimes

The domestication of fire culminated in the establishment of what may be called a monopoly—a monopoly of power that was held by the human species and in which eventually all human communities of the world shared. The formation of this monopoly affected the relations between humans and the nonhuman world so deeply that we may call it the first great ecological transformation brought about by humans, which was followed much later by two similar transformations—generally known as the agricultural and industrial revolutions, and more precisely characterized by the long-term processes of agrarianization and industrialization.

Each of the three transformations marked the formation of a new socioecological regime (that is, a form of social organization and a way of life attuned to a specific level of control over matter and energy): the fire regime, the agrarian regime, and the industrial regime, respectively, marked by the utilization of fire and elementary tools, the rise and spread of agriculture and animal husbandry, and the rise and spread of large-scale modern industry. The later regimes did not make the earlier regimes obsolete; rather, they absorbed them and, in so doing, transformed them.

With each new regime, new monopolies of human power were formed, opening up new opportunities for control, security, comfort, and wealth. All these benefits, however, involved costs. This was already evident when the fire regime exerted pressure on people to collect fuel and to tend their hearths; it became even more evident when the strains of the agrarian and industrial regimes were added to the fire regime.

Four Phases of Human History

The most convenient backdrop for writing history is undoubtedly chronology. When it comes to dealing

"It's a question of discipline," the little prince told me later on. "When you've finished washing and dressing each morning, you must tend your planet." • **Antoine de Saint-Exupéry (1900–1944), from *The Little Prince***

with such encompassing long-term processes as the expansion of the anthroposphere, however, one can also speak fruitfully in terms of broad phases. By taking as benchmarks the successive formation of the three major socioecological regimes, we can distinguish four phases in human history:

1. The phase before the domestication of fire. In this phase all human groups subsisted on foraging; there were no groups with fire or cultivated fields or factories.
2. The phase when there were at least some groups with fire, but none yet with fields or factories.
3. The phase when all human groups had fire and some also had cultivated fields, but none had factories.
4. The phase we have reached today, when all human societies have fire but are also using products of fields and factories.

Of course, it would make a great deal of difference for a group of foragers whether it found itself living in the first, second, third, or fourth phase, as in the first it would come in contact only with other groups that had basically similar skills. In any of the subsequent phases, however, it might come in contact with groups whose skills made them more powerful than the foragers. As a further elaboration of this simple model of four phases, we may subdivide each phase into three subphases: a phase when there was no group with the defining technology (fire, agriculture, or industry), a phase when there were both groups with and groups without the defining technology, and a phase when there were only groups with the defining technology. Making these finer gradations in the four phases raises the intriguing problem of how to account for the transitions from one subphase to the next. How was a particular regime first established, how did it spread, and—most intriguing—how did it become universal?

The last question in particular brings out the world-historical import of the phase model. Besides being applicable to the three major socioecological

regimes, the questions also apply to the adoption of other innovations, such as metallurgy, writing, and the development of cities.

Agrarianization

The history of the past ten thousand years may be read as a series of events accompanying the agrarianization of the anthroposphere—a process whereby human groups extended the domain of agriculture and animal husbandry all over the world, and in so doing made themselves increasingly more dependent upon this very mode of production.

The agrarian way of life was based on a new human monopoly—the monopoly of control over pieces of territory (fields)—in which people more or less successfully subjected vegetation and animal life to a human-directed regime. The result was twofold: elimination of competing species (parasites and predators) and concentration of resources and people in ever-greater densities. Although agrarian regimes sometimes suffered decline, their overall tendency was to expand.

Expansion did not take place in a uniform and even fashion. In fact, the unevenness of its development was a structural feature of agrarianization. From its very beginnings, agrarianization was marked by differentiation—initially between people who had adopted agriculture and people who had not. Eventually, in the phase of industrialization, the last nonagrarian peoples vanished, and with them this primary form of differentiation.

Still, various forms of differentiation within the agrarian (or, rather, agrarianizing) world continued. Some agrarian societies went much further than others in harnessing matter and energy for human purposes, for example, by means of irrigation or plowing. In societies that grew accustomed to higher yields of agrarian production, competition to control the wealth thus generated usually led to social stratification—the formation of different social strata marked by huge inequalities in property, privilege, and prestige. Another closely related form of differentiation typical of this phase was cultural diversification. In Mesopotamia, the Indus Valley, northeastern China,

Egypt, the Mediterranean basin, Mexico, the Andes region, and elsewhere, agrarian empires developed that are still known for their distinct cultures, each with its own dominant language, system of writing, religion, architecture, dress, methods of food production, and eating habits. In the heyday of agrarianization, the anthroposphere was marked by conspicuous differences in culture or civilization—differences resulting to a large extent from the interplay of gains in power by some groups and accommodation to power losses by others.

Industrialization

Around 1750 the immense deposits of fuel energy that had lain virtually unused by any living species began to be exploited for human purposes. A series of innovations provided the technical means for tapping these supplies and for using them to generate heat and mechanical motion. No longer were people completely dependent on the flows of energy that reach the Earth from the sun and that are partly converted into vegetation by means of photosynthesis. Just as at one time humans had been able to strengthen their position in the biosphere by learning to control fire, they now learned the art of using fire to exploit the energy contained in coal, oil, and gas.

These innovations stimulated great accelerations in extensive growth. According to a rough estimate, the total human population must have reached 1 million at some time in the Paleolithic, 10 million at the time when agrarization began, 100 million during the first stages of urbanization, 1,000 million at the beginning of industrialization. The next tenfold increase, to 10 billion, is expected to be completed within a few generations. Along with the increase in human numbers, networks of production, transport, and communication have grown worldwide so that the anthroposphere is now truly global. Universal acceptance of a common system of time measurement, based on Greenwich Mean Time, is a telling example of how common standards of orientation are spreading all over the world. At the same time, the inequalities between and within human societies that arose as structural features of advanced agrarian regimes persist in industrial society. Those inequalities now also exert disturbing global pressures, as do imminent ecological problems such as global warming, which are generated by the way in which the anthroposphere is currently expanding.

Toward a Synthesis

In the eras of agrarianization and industrialization, the anthroposphere gave rise to social regimes that were only indirectly related to the natural environment. The money regime and the time regime may serve as illustrations. Both exemplify how people turned their attention away from the natural environment, and from ecological issues, toward a more purely social aspect of the anthroposphere, represented by the clock and the calendar or the purse and the bank account. Those regimes thus supported the illusion that the anthroposphere is autonomous. That illusion was furthered by the concomitant intellectual tendency to separate the social sciences from the natural sciences and to cultivate discrete and seemingly autonomous social-science disciplines, such as psychology and sociology.

Today there is a growing awareness that as the anthroposphere encroaches upon ever larger portions of the biosphere, it absorbs more and more nonhuman elements. The notion of ecological interdependence is gaining ground. A classical theme in the social sciences has been the interweaving of planned actions and unplanned consequences. All human activities have unintended consequences; recognition of that fact is now being combined with the insight that the anthroposphere (itself the product of unplanned evolutionary processes) has become an agent in the evolution of the biosphere. Human life has become a formidable co-evolutionary force. Sociocultural processes are channeling and steering the course of biological evolution.

Without using the word *anthroposphere*, the world historians William H. McNeill and J. R. McNeill, the ecological historian Alfred Crosby, the biologist Jared Diamond, and several others have shown that it is possible to write about the history of the anthroposphere. Further theoretical inspiration can be drawn from the traditions of sociology and anthropology inaugurated by Auguste Comte and Herbert Spencer and continued by such scholars as Norbert Elias and Marvin Harris, in combination with the geological and biological study of the biosphere as launched by Vladimir Vernadsky in the early twentieth century and taken up again by Lynn Margulis and James Lovelock from the 1970s onward. The names mentioned are but a few among many authors whose works contribute to our understanding of the history and dynamics of the anthroposphere.

Johan GOUDSBLOM
University of Amsterdam

See also Anthropocene

Further Reading

Baccini, P., & Brunner, P. H. (1991). *Metabolism of the anthroposphere*. Berlin, Germany: Springer Verlag.

Bailes, K. E. (1998). *Science and Russian culture in an age of revolutions: V. I. Vernadsky and his scientific school, 1863–1945*. Bloomington: Indiana University Press.

Crosby, A. W. (1986). *Ecological imperialism. The biological expansion of Europe, 900–1900*. Cambridge, U.K.: Cambridge University Press.

Christian, D. (2004). *Maps of time: An introduction to big history*. Berkeley and Los Angeles: University of California Press.

De Vries, B., & Goudsblom, J. (Eds.). (2002). *Mappae Mundi: Humans and their habitats in a long-term socio-ecological perspective*. Amsterdam: Amsterdam University Press.

Diamond, J. (1997). *Guns, germs and steel. The fates of human societies*. New York: Random House.

Elias, N. (1991). *The symbol theory*. London: Sage.

Elvin, M. (2004). *The retreat of the elephants. An environmental history of China*. New Haven: Yale University Press.

Fischer-Kowalski, M., & Haberl, H. (2007) *Socioecological transitions and global change. Trajectories of social metabolism and land use*. Cheltenham, U.K. and Northampton, MA: Edward Elgar.

Goudsblom, J. (1992). *Fire and civilization*. London: Allen Lane.

Goudsblom, J., Jones, E. L., & Mennell, S. J. (1996). *The course of human history: Economic growth, social process, and civilization*. Armonk, NY: M. E. Sharpe.

Margulis, L., Matthews, C., & Haselton, A. (2000). *Environmental evolution: Effects of the origin and evolution of life on planet Earth*. Cambridge, MA: MIT Press.

McNeill, J. R. (2000). *Something new under the sun: An environmental history of the twentieth century*. New York: W. W. Norton & Company.

McNeill, J. R., & McNeill, W. H. (2003). *The human web. A bird's-eye view of world history*. New York: W. W. Norton & Company.

McNeill, W. H. (1976). *Plagues and peoples*. Garden City, NY: Doubleday.

Niele, F. (2005). *Energy. Engine of evolution*. Amsterdam: Elsevier.

Richards, J. F. (2003). *The unending frontier. An environmental history of the early modern world*. Berkeley: University of California Press.

Samson, P. R., & Pitt, D. (Eds.). (1999). *The biosphere and noosphere reader: Global environment, society and change*. London: Routledge.

Sieferle, R. (2001). *The subterranean forest. Energy systems and the industrial revolution*. Cambidge U.K.: The White Horse Press.

Simmons, I. G. (1996). *Changing the face of the earth: Culture, environment, history* (2nd ed.). Oxford, U.K.: Blackwell.

Smil, V. (1997). *Cycles of life: Civilization and the biosphere*. New York: Scientific American Library.

Trudgill, S. T. (2001). *The terrestrial biosphere: Environmental change, ecosystem science, attitudes and values*. Upper Saddle River, NJ: Prentice Hall.

Vernadsky, V. I. (1998). *The biosphere*. New York: Copernicus. (Original work published in Russian in 1926)

Wright, R. (2000). *Nonzero. The logic of human destiny*. New York: Random House.

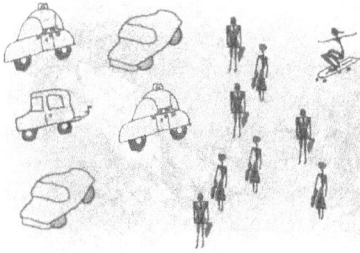

Biological Exchanges

With few exceptions, the spread of plants, animals, and diseases was limited to geographically bound regions for much of the Earth's history. Humans facilitated biological exchange, intentionally and accidentally carrying species across natural borders. As opportunities for human travel increased, so did the opportunities for biological exchange, often with dramatic consequences.

During most of the history of life on Earth, geographic barriers such as oceans and mountain ranges divided the planet and inhibited migrations of most kinds. Only birds, bats, flying insects, and good swimmers consistently bucked the trend. A few other species did so occasionally, thanks to sea-level changes and land bridges or to chance voyages on driftwood. However, for most species most of the time, biological evolution took place in separate biogeographical provinces.

Intracontinental Biological Exchange

This long phase of separation ended when human beings began their long-distance migrations. Deep in prehistory hominids (erect bipedal primate mammals) walked throughout Africa and Eurasia, occasionally bringing a plant, seed, insect, microbe, or rodent to a place it would not have reached on its own. With plant and animal domestication ten to twelve thousand years ago, people began to transport such things on purpose and more frequently. Most of the plants and animals susceptible to domestication lived in Eurasia, and those sensitive to

climate or day length (several flowering plants take their cues to bloom from day length) spread most easily along the east-west axis of that continent. The sets of domesticated plants and animals on which Eurasian and North African agriculture and herding are based spread almost instantaneously by the standards of the past, although in fact the spread took a few millennia. This process of spreading no doubt proved highly disruptive biologically as local biogeographic provinces were invaded by alien creatures spread by humanity. It also proved highly disruptive historically, obliterating peoples who did not adapt to the changing biogeography, the changing disease regimes, and the changing political situations brought on by the spread of farmers, herders, and eventually states. Out of this turmoil of Afro-Eurasian biological exchange emerged the great ancient civilizations from China to the Mediterranean. They all based their societies on intersecting but not identical sets of plants and animals.

Biological homogenization within Afro-Eurasia had its limits. The links between northern Africa, say, and eastern Asia before 500 BCE were slender. Varying topography and climate also checked the spread of species. The process presumably accelerated when interregional contacts flourished, for example, when empires created favorable conditions for the movement of goods and people. The era of the Han dynasty (206 BCE–220 CE) in China and the Roman Empire, for example, when the trans-Asian trade route called the Silk Roads was a well-beaten path, unleashed a small flood of biological exchanges. The Mediterranean acquired cherries at this time, and possibly smallpox and measles, too; sorghum made its way from east Africa to India to China, and grapes, camels, and donkeys arrived in China from southwest Asia and northern Africa.

Within Eurasian history two more moments of heightened biological exchange occurred. The next moment occurred during the early Tang dynasty (618–907 CE) in China. The Tang rulers came from various ethnic and cultural traditions and for a century and a half showed keen interest in things foreign: trade, technology, culture (e.g., Buddhism), and plants and animals. The court imported exotica: curious creatures, aromatic plants, ornamental flowers. Much of this exotica was inconsequential in social and economic terms, but some of it, such as cotton (imported from India), was not. The Tang were culturally receptive to strange plants and animals, but political conditions helped too: their political power on the western frontier, and the geopolitical situation generally before 750, promoted the trade, travel, and transport that make biological exchange likely.

For roughly a century and a half (600–750 CE) the numerous political organizations of Central Asia were frequently consolidated into only a few, simplifying travel by lowering protection costs. A handful of large empires held sway throughout Central Asia, making the connections between China, India, and Persia (modern-day Iran) safer than usual. These geopolitical arrangements fell apart after 751, when Muslims defeated Tang armies, and after 755, when rebellion shook the Tang dynasty to its foundations. Thereafter, both the stability of the geopolitical situation and the receptivity of the Tang to things foreign changed, waning more often than waxing, and the opportunities for biological exchange grew scarcer.

Another moment of heightened biological exchange within Eurasia occurred with the Pax Mongolica (Mongol Peace) of the thirteenth and fourteenth centuries. By this time most of the feasible exchanges of plants and animals had already taken place. However, the heightened transport across the desert-steppe corridor of Central Asia may have brought carrots and a species of lemon to China and a form of millet to Persia. Quite possibly this transport also allowed the quick diffusion from Central Asia of the bacillus that causes bubonic plague, provoking the famous Black Death, the worst bout of epidemics in the recorded history of western Eurasia and northern Africa. Plague may also have afflicted China during these centuries, although the evidence is ambiguous.

Although this process of Eurasian (and North African) biological exchange never truly came to an end, it slowed whenever political conditions weakened interregional contacts. It also slowed in general after around 200 CE, with the erosion of two eras of peace—the Pax Romana (Roman Peace) and Pax Sinica (Chinese Peace), which had encouraged long-distance travel and trade within Eurasia. By that time sugarcane had taken root in India, spreading from its New Guinea home. Wheat had spread widely throughout most of its potential range, as had cattle, pigs, horses, sheep, and goats. Less and less was left to do even when political and economic conditions encouraged biological exchange.

Meanwhile on other continents, similar, if smaller-scale, processes of biological exchange and homogenization were in train. In the Americas maize spread both north and south from its Mesoamerican home (the region of southern North America that was occupied during pre-Columbian times by peoples with shared cultural features), slowed, it seems, by difficulties in adapting to different day lengths at different latitudes. In Africa the Bantu migrations of two thousand years ago probably diffused several crops throughout eastern and southern Africa and possibly brought infectious diseases that ravaged the indigenous, previously isolated, populations of southern Africa. These events in Africa and the Americas, too, must have been biologically and politically tumultuous, although the evidence is sparse.

In biological terms the process of human-promoted biological exchange selected for certain kinds of species, those that co-existed easily with human activity: domesticates, commensals (organisms that obtain food or other benefits from another without damaging or benefiting it), and plants that thrive on disturbed ground, most of which we usually call "weeds." These species prospered under the new regimes of expanded human migration and interaction; for them, history had taken a favorable turn. Indeed, humanity was in a sense working for them, spreading their genetic footprints far and wide within the continents and into the future.

Biological Exchange and Biological Invasion

Intercontinental biological exchange also has a long pedigree. The first people to migrate to Australia may have accidentally brought some species with them forty thousand to sixty thousand years ago. About thirty-five hundred years ago, later migrants to Australia purposely brought the dingo (a large dog), the first domesticate in Australian history. The dingo quickly spread to all Aboriginal groups outside of isolated Tasmania and also formed feral packs. It proved an effective hunting dog and led to the extinction of some indigenous mammals. The dog (not the dingo) was also the first domesticated animal in the Americas, brought across the Siberian-Alaskan land bridge with some of the first settlers during the last Ice Age. Here dogs probably played a significant role in reducing the populations of large mammals, many of which became extinct soon after humans arrived in North and South America. Initial human settlement of unpopulated islands also wrought major ecological changes throughout the southwest Pacific and Polynesia, including numerous extinctions, from about four thousand years ago until the colonization of New Zealand roughly seven hundred or one thousand years ago.

All of these instances were invasions of "naive" lands—continents and islands that had no prior exposure to humanity and its fellow travelers or to the intensified fire regimes that human presence normally brought. This fact helps to explain the dramatic effects, particularly the rash of extinctions that followed upon human settlement of Australia, New Zealand, and the Americas.

Eventually people began to transport animals, plants, and pathogens from one human community to another across the seas. In many cases the only evidence for such transfers is the existence of the imported species. The sweet potato, a native of South America, somehow arrived in central Polynesia by 1000 CE and subsequently spread widely throughout Oceania (lands of the central and southern Pacific). It is a delicate crop and could not survive a driftwood voyage: no one doubts that people transported it, although no one knows just when, how, or even who. It eventually became a staple food in the western Pacific, highland New Guinea, and to a lesser extent the eastern Asian archipelagoes and mainland.

A second mysterious transoceanic crop transfer took place across the Indian Ocean some time before 500 CE. Somebody brought bananas, Asian yams, and taro to eastern Africa. These crops had much to recommend them because they do well in moist conditions, whereas the millets and sorghum that Bantu expansion brought into central and southeastern Africa were adapted to dry conditions. Plantains, of which bananas are one variety, had existed in the wild from India to New Guinea. Linguistic and genetic evidence suggests they arrived on the east African coast as early as three thousand years ago and reached the forest zone to the west of Africa's Great Lakes around two thousand years ago, just about the time of the Bantu migrations. Quite possibly the success of Bantu speakers, often attributed to their use of iron, owed something to their successful adoption of these exotic crops. As relative newcomers to eastern and southern Africa, they had less invested in prevailing ecological patterns and fewer disincentives to experiment. Bananas, taro, and yams were probably introduced to eastern Africa more than once and almost surely were brought again in the settlement of Madagascar that took place not long before 500 CE. These Asian crops assisted in the epic (but unrecorded) colonization of central Africa's moist tropical forests by farmers, as well as in the settlement of Madagascar.

Several other significant intercontinental biological transfers took place before 1400 CE, mainly between Africa and Asia, a route that posed minimal obstacles to sailors. Africa's pearl millet, derived from a western African savanna grass, is the world's sixth-most-important cereal today. It was introduced into India three thousand years ago and today accounts for about 10 percent of India's cereal acreage. East

African sorghum entered India at about the same time and eventually became India's second-most-important grain after rice. Sorghum stalks were also useful as fodder for India's cattle. Finger millet, also from Africa, arrived in India only around one thousand years ago. It became the staple in Himalayan foothill communities and in far southern India. The transfer of African crops to south Asia mainly provided India with drought-resistant dryland crops, opening new areas to settlement and providing a more reliable harvest where water supplies were uncertain. These examples suggest a lively world of crop exchange—and probably weeds, diseases, and animals, too—around the Indian Ocean rim from about three thousand to fifteen hundred years ago. The regular monsoon winds of the Indian Ocean helped make this region of the world precocious in its maritime development and hence biological exchange.

Whereas south Asia received new crops from Africa, it sent new crops to the Middle East and the Mediterranean. Facilitated by the relative peace supervised by the Abbasid dynasty (749/750–1258), between the tenth and thirteenth centuries Arab trading networks brought sugar, cotton, rice, and citrus fruits from India to Egypt and the Mediterranean. These plants, and the cultivation techniques that came with them, worked a small revolution on the hot and often malarial coastlands of northern Africa, Anatolia in Turkey, and southern Europe. They caused many coastal plains to be brought under cultivation on a regular basis, often for the first time since the Roman Empire. Sugar and cotton could flourish with unskilled and unmotivated slave labor; their introduction may have quickened the slave raiding that kept Mediterranean and Black Sea populations anxious for centuries. Keeping an army of laborers at work on deadly malarial coasts—in the Levant (countries bordering on the eastern Mediterranean), Egypt, Cyprus, Crete, Sicily, Tunisia, and Andalusia in Spain, to mention a few centers of sugar production—required constant topping up from poorly defended peasantries. This quest took slave merchants and raiders to the Black Sea coasts but also across the Sahara Desert and along Africa's Atlantic coast. Saadian Morocco, a state originally based on plantations in the Sous and Draa River valleys, brought sugar and African slaves together in a profitable mix that would soon be transplanted to Atlantic islands such as the Canaries and Madeira and then to the Americas.

A second avenue of exchange linked the Mediterranean basin to western Africa. Although this exchange was not genuinely intercontinental, the Sahara Desert for several millennia functioned somewhat like a sea, as the Arabic term for "shore" (*sahel*) for the western African desert edge implies. One thousand years before Christopher Columbus crossed the Atlantic, some unknown soul crossed the Sahara, reuniting the Mediterranean and the *sahel*, which the increasingly arid Sahara had divided since about 3000 BCE. Trans-Saharan trade developed in salt, slaves, and gold. However, this reunification no doubt included a biological dimension. Large horses seem to have made their debut in west Africa via trans-Saharan trade. Linguistic evidence suggests they came from the Maghreb region in the north. Horses eventually became a decisive element in a military revolution in the *sahel*, creating a mounted aristocracy who by the fourteenth century built imperial states. The Jolof, Mali, and Songhai empires of west Africa depended on horse cavalry, which underwrote their military power and, via slave raiding, their economies. When ecological conditions permitted, these empires bred their own warhorses, and when conditions did not permit, the empires had to import them, usually from Morocco. In any case, the social, economic, and political history of west Africa took a new direction with the arrival of large horses.

These events show that long before the great age of oceanic navigation, the links of trade and colonization in the Pacific Ocean, in the Indian Ocean, and across the Sahara Desert brought biological exchanges that powerfully influenced the course of history. The further exchanges attendant upon the voyages of Columbus, the Portuguese navigator Ferdinand Magellan, the British sea captain James Cook, and others extended this process, wrenchingly, to lands formerly quite separate in biological (as in other) terms.

Biological Globalization

After 1400 CE mariners linked almost every nook and cranny of the humanly inhabitable Earth into a biologically interactive unit. The world's seas and deserts were no longer isolated biogeographical provinces. The world became one without biological borders as plants, animals and diseases migrated wherever ecological conditions permitted their spread, although how soon and how thoroughly they did so often depended on patterns of trade, production, and politics.

Columbus inaugurated regular exchanges across the Atlantic whereby the Americas acquired a large set of new plants and animals as well as devastating diseases that severely depopulated the Americas between 1500 and 1650. Simultaneously, Africa and Eurasia acquired some useful crops from the Americas, most notably potatoes, maize, and cassava (manioc). Ecosystems and societies in the Americas were remade with new biologies and new cultures. The same thing was true, however, even if less catastrophically, in Africa and Eurasia. The new food crops fed population growth in Europe and China and possibly in Africa, too (no firm evidence exists). Maize and potatoes changed agriculture in Europe, as did maize and sweet potatoes in China, allowing more intensive production and allowing lands not suited to wheat, barley, rye, or rice to come into production. In Africa maize, cassava, and peanuts became important crops. Today 200 million Africans rely on cassava as their staple food. Many of the rest, mainly in the south and east, rely on maize.

These modern biological exchanges had political meanings and contexts. European imperialism, in the Americas, Australia, and New Zealand, simultaneously promoted, and was promoted by, the spread of European (or more usually Eurasian) animals, plants, and diseases. Europeans brought a biota (the flora and fauna of a region) that worked to favor the spread of European settlers, European power, and Eurasian species and thereby to create what Alfred Crosby, the foremost historian of these processes, called "neo-Europes"—including Australia, New Zealand, most of North America, southern Brazil, Uruguay, and Argentina.

Beyond the neo-Europes, in the Americas something of a neo-Africa emerged. More than 10 million Africans arrived in the Americas in slave ships. In those same ships came yellow fever and malaria, which profoundly influenced settlement patterns in the Americas. The ships also brought African rice from the west coast, which became the foundation of the coastal economy in South Carolina and Georgia during the eighteenth century and was important in Suriname in South America as well. Other African crops came, too: okra, sesame, and (although not in slave ships) coffee. African biological impact on the Americas did not cease with the end of the slave trade. Much later African honeybees imported into Brazil crossbred to create an "Africanized" bee that since the 1950s has colonized much of the Americas.

The age of sail brought the continents together as never before. But sailing ships did not prove hospitable carriers to every form of life. They filtered out a few, those that could not for one reason or another survive a long journey or that required conditions that sailing ships could not provide. The age of steam and then the age of air travel broke down yet further barriers to biological exchange, adding new creatures to the roster of alien intruders and accelerating the dispersal of old and new migratory species alike.

The advent of iron ships toward the end of the nineteenth century, for example, opened a new era in biological exchange involving species of the world's harbors and estuaries. After the 1880s iron ships began to carry water as ballast. Soon special water ballast tanks became standard, and thus, for example, a ship from Yokohama, Japan, bound for Vancouver, Canada, would suck up a tankful of water and, more than likely, a few marine species from Japanese shores, cross the wide Pacific, then release its Japanese water and sea creatures in Puget Sound before taking on a Canadian cargo. During the 1930s Japanese clams hitched such a ride and upon arrival began to colonize the seabeds of Puget Sound, creating a multimillion-dollar clam fishery in British Columbia and Washington State. A jellyfish that devastated

Black Sea fisheries came from the East Coast of the United States in about 1980. The zebra mussel, a Black and Caspian seas native, colonized the North American Great Lakes and river system from a beachhead established near Detroit in 1985 or 1986. It has cost the United States and Canada billions of dollars by blocking water intakes on city water systems, factories, and nuclear power plants.

A more recent invader of the North American Great Lakes is the fishhook flea, a crustacean that is a native of Caspian and Black sea waters. It first appeared in Lake Ontario in 1998 and is now in the all the Great Lakes and New York's Finger Lakes, menacing sport and commercial fisheries and disrupting the lakes' food web. The failures of Soviet agriculture and the expanded grain trade from North America during the 1970s and 1980s created a new pattern of ship traffic that quickly brought disruptive biological exchanges. Nowadays thirty-five thousand ocean-going ships and three thousand marine species are in transit at any given time, linking the world's harbor and estuarine ecosystems as never before. The exchanges via ballast water are but a single variety of the swirl of biological exchange going on in modern times. Transport, travel, and trade take place on such a scale now and with such rapidity that a vast homogenization of the planet's flora and fauna is under way.

Perspectives

From the Olympian height that allows a view of all life on Earth over its entire history, the last ten thousand years appear as an instantaneous homogenization of ecosystems, a new era in Earth history. Humankind has connected formerly distinct spheres of life through trade and travel, reprising in the blink of an eye what previously happened through continental drift. Some 300 to 250 million years ago the world's continents fused to form a single supercontinent, called "Pangaea." Creatures formerly kept apart from one another now rubbed shoulders. Large numbers of them became extinct by about 220 million years ago, perhaps in part on account of this new familiarity (although other theories exist). Reptiles inherited the Earth,

spreading throughout the globe. During the last few millennia the human species has once again fused the continents, and to some extent the seas, and is probably provoking (through this and other means) the sixth great extinction spasm in the history of Earth.

From a less Olympian height, other vistas present themselves. The process of biological exchange is much influenced by the technology of transportation. The invention of ships, of ocean-going ships, of ballast tanks, of railroads and airplanes all led to changes and surges in the pattern of biological exchange. Transport technology provides one rhythm. Another rhythm is political.

Some states and societies showed great eagerness to import exotic species. Monarchs of ancient Egypt and Mesopotamia buttressed their prestige by maintaining gardens and zoos filled with exotic plants and animals. The Tang dynasty, as noted, showed a similar enthusiasm. Thomas Jefferson tried his best to establish rice and silkworms in Virginia. Later, the U.S. government employed an army of plant prospectors, who scoured the globe for potentially useful species and brought tens of thousands to the United States. During the nineteenth century Australia and New Zealand featured "acclimatization societies," which imported species that met with their approval (usually from Britain). Nowadays the United States, Australia, New Zealand, and many other countries spend vast sums trying to prevent the importation of unwanted species, hoping to forestall biological invasions rather than foment them. Altogether, biological invasions now cost the United States more than all other natural hazards combined, including floods, hurricanes, tornadoes, earthquakes, and so forth.

Beyond the disposition that any society might have toward exotic species, the changing nature of geopolitics also affected biological exchange. Trade and travel—and presumably biological exchange—expanded in times of peace and contracted in times of war, brigandage, and piracy. Probably eras of imperial unification provided the best political environment for biological exchange, when a single power enforced a general peace. Anarchic systems of competing states probably checked biological exchange by slowing trade and travel, notwithstanding the effects of mobile armies and navies. Furthermore, imperialism also seems to have inspired, as well as eased, the process of collection: botanical gardens and the like. Kew Gardens outside of London proved a crucial link in transferring rubber seeds from Brazil to Malaya at the end of the nineteenth century, starting a new plantation economy in southeast Asia. The swings between moments of consolidated imperialism and anarchic struggle established another rhythm governing the history of biological exchange. This rhythm, of course, was influenced in turn by biological exchanges, as in the case of horses on the African savanna.

One can only postulate such patterns in the history of biological exchange. Demonstrating their validity would require quantitative evidence beyond what one can reasonably hope to find. Yet, one may be sure that time and again during the past ten millennia biological exchange has altered history. The next ten millennia will be quite different: fewer exchanges of existing species will take place because so many already have. Newly engineered species will occasionally depart from their creators' scripts, however, fashioning unpredictable biological dramas. Some of these surely will help shape the future.

J. R. McNEILL

Georgetown University

See also Columbian Exchange

Further Reading

Burney, D. (1996). Historical perspectives on human-assisted biological invasions. *Evolutionary Anthropology, 4,* 216–221.

Carlton, J. H. (1996). Marine bioinvasions: The alteration of marine ecosystems by nonindigenous species. *Oceanography, 9,* 36–43.

Carney, J. (2001). *Black rice: The African origins of rice cultivation in the Americas.* Cambridge, MA: Harvard University Press.

Cox, G. W. (1999). *Alien species in North America and Hawaii.* Washington, DC: Island Press.

Crosby, A. (1972). *The Columbian Exchange: Biological and cultural consequences of 1492.* Westport, CT: Greenwood Press.

Crosby, A. (1986). *Ecological imperialism: The biological expansion of Europe, 900–1900.* New York: Cambridge University Press.

Curtin, P. (1993). Disease exchange across the tropical Atlantic. *History and Philosophy of the Life Sciences, 15,* 169–196.

Dodson, J. (Ed.). (1992). *The naive lands: Prehistory and environmental change in Australia and the southwest Pacific.* Melbourne, Australia: Longman Cheshire.

Groves, R. H., & Burdon, J. J. (1986). *Ecology of biological invasions.* Cambridge, U.K.: Cambridge University Press.

McNeill, W. H. (1976). *Plagues and peoples.* Garden City, NJ: Anchor Press.

Mooney, H. A., & Hobbs, R. J. (Eds.). (2000). *Invasive species in a changing world.* Washington, DC: Island Press.

Watson, A. (1983). *Agricultural innovation in the early Islamic world: The diffusion of crops and farming techniques.* Cambridge, U.K.: Cambridge University Press.

Carrying Capacity

The growth of a population in a given environment is theoretically limited by the availability of resources and susceptibility to disease or disaster, thus the maximum number or density of organisms an area can support is called the *carrying capacity*. The threshold for humans is unknown, because they respond to scarcity by moving to new areas, adopting new resources, or inventing technologies to increase capacity.

Carrying capacity is the theoretical limit on the size of a population of any organism that a given environment of defined size can support indefinitely. The limit is usually stated in terms of the food supply, but density-dependent diseases have probably been the most important factor in limiting many animal and human populations through most of history. Other limiting factors may have included specific nutrients or water, or even physiological responses to the psychological stresses of high population density. The "law of the minimum" suggests that the limit will be set by whichever resource is in shortest supply or is activated at the lowest population density.

If food is the limiting resource, as is usually assumed, any population of food consumers is limited by the regenerative capacity of its food supply. If the consuming animal eats only the amount regenerated, (if, for example, wolves eat only as many sheep as are born each year, or the sheep eat grass only as fast as it can regenerate), the consumers and the food supply can theoretically coexist forever in equilibrium (unless the environment itself changes). The equilibrium may be static or may involve interrelated fluctuations in the size of the two populations, as when, for example, wolves deplete the sheep population and then

decline in numbers themselves, which then permits the sheep to regenerate. If the consumer continues to eat more of its prey than the prey can regenerate, the population of prey and therefore of consumers will be reduced conceivably to extinction. Exceeding carrying capacity may result either in excessive mortality among consumers, in reduced fertility from malnutrition or disease, or in both. Density-related social dynamics among the consumers may also affect both mortality and fertility. The same principles apply to specific isolated human populations subsisting on limited resources (as in the Arctic or extreme deserts) where there is nowhere else to go, no alternative resources, limited ability to move food, and limited ability of the human group to enhance the growth of its resources.

Carrying Capacity Applied to Human Beings

How important carrying capacity has been in human history is a matter of debate. A Malthusian perspective implies the importance of carrying capacity by arguing that human populations are—and by inference have been—limited by food-related technology that expands only through fortuitous human invention. Thomas Malthus (1766–1834) argued that the human population cannot expand indefinitely because it will inevitably outstrip its food supply. Humans will eat beyond Earth's technologically enhanced carrying capacity, with dire consequences.

Although Malthus may be right about the long-term future, he was clearly wrong about much of human history to date and for the near future. The carrying capacity concept clearly has not applied overall and in

Buffalo berry gatherers in Mandan. Photo by Edward S. Curtis (1868–1952). Any population of food consumers is limited by the regenerative capacity of its food supply. Library of Congress.

the long run to the growth of our species as a whole (although it has almost certainly applied locally and in the short run).

People are omnivores who eat an extraordinarily wide (and still expanding) range of foods. We respond to shortage by expanding the breadth of our diets. (Few human populations consume all of the edible resources within range until forced to do so by hunger.) We also can increase the range of environments we occupy, and we can move food from place to place. Most important, we have demonstrated an enormous capacity to increase food supplies by investing additional effort in obtaining and processing them.

A controversy exists about the relative importance of supply and demand as determinants of human food supplies in human history. Many scholars believe that Malthus profoundly underestimated the ability of growing populations themselves to force changes in food choices, technology, and related behaviors. Throughout history, the human population has made adjustments that have ultimately resulted in the adoption (more than invention) of new technology. If demand can push supply, the meaning of carrying capacity as a fixed limit must be questioned.

Evidence for the importance of economic demand in human history comes in many forms. New foods eaten have often been less palatable, less nutritious, and harder to obtain that those they supplemented—and therefore unlikely to have been adopted just because they had been discovered or new technology invented. Many new environments colonized were clearly not preferred (deserts, tropical rain forests, and the Arctic) and would not have been colonized voluntarily. Many new technologies or steps taken to improve food supplies resulted in declining quality of food or declining efficiency of food-getting techniques. Much of the history of evolving economies seems to have involved diminishing returns, particularly in the quality of human health and nutrition.

Carrying Capacity for Foraging Peoples

Between 100,000 and about 12,000 years ago the human population consisted of foragers, small populations of whom survived into recent centuries and even into the present in forms modified by outside contact. These groups are mobile, live at low population density, and eat fresh wild foods. Malnutrition is quite rare among modern foragers and appears to have been rare among foragers in the past, but becomes increasingly important as populations grow and "progress" to new food resources and new technologies. Ancient and historic foragers also have been relatively disease-free, because low population densities and periodic movement prevent many infectious diseases from spreading or minimize their impact. The disease burden has clearly increased with increasing population density through human history. Major epidemic diseases such as smallpox are clearly of relatively modern origin. Modern peasants and the poor enjoy nowhere near foragers' standard of nutrition and health.

Various studies show that large game is among the highest quality and most easily exploited of resources

Pieter Brueghel the Younger, *A Village Landscape with Farmers* (1634). Oil on panel. Humans respond to scarcity by moving to new areas, adopting new resources, or inventing technologies.

when available. But large game occupies large territories and is depleted easily. Early human foragers' diets apparently included a relatively high proportion of large game; human hunters may have hunted many large mammals to extinction before falling back on secondary resources.

Early in prehistory population growth was extremely slow, absorbed mostly by territorial expansion. The slow growth probably resulted mostly from low fertility or birth control (since the life expectancy of such groups equaled that of later populations that grew much faster). As population densities increased, the role of infectious disease as a limit to populations increased. Malthusian constraints resulting from food shortages may also have been operating in specific times and places, but hunger and starvation may actually have increased in frequency and severity in later, non-foraging populations. Slow growth might also have been the result of population mechanisms geared not so much to the ultimate carrying capacity of natural resources as to the "carrying capacity" of choices defined by preferred labor inputs and food choices, or even of personal space.

As populations grew increasingly in the last 20,000 years, the territory available to each group declined, and large mammals became scarce, to the point where groups were ultimately forced to broaden their diets to include a wider range of more prolific resources (a wider range of vegetable foods, birds, small mammals, fish, and shellfish), resulting in an increase in the carrying capacity of each unit of land. But the new resources were apparently less desirable foods, less nutritious, and more difficult to exploit, thus commonly consumed only as preferred resources were exhausted. Our ancestors probably adopted, rather than invented, new technologies such as fish hooks, grindstones, and arrows suitable for exploiting smaller game that were obvious or long-known but unused until needed rather than being confined by the limits of fortuitous economic invention independent of need.

Wild small seeds, including cereals, were apparently very low on the list of preferred foods. They raise the carrying capacity of each unit of land but are not particularly nutritious and are very difficult to convert to food. (Even today, cereal grains and tubers

Population, when unchecked, increases in a geometrical ratio. • Thomas Robert Malthus (1766–1834)

are staples primarily for the poor, because they are plentiful and cheap.)

Carrying Capacity after the Adoption of Agriculture

Agriculture and the domestication of plants, first adopted about 10,000 years ago, are usually considered major inventions that further raised the productivity of land and permitted groups to become sedentary. They apparently resulted in a slight increase in the rate of population growth, probably not from increased life expectancy but from greater fertility and or altered birth control choices. But they, too, may have been a concession to increased population density. They clearly further lowered the quality of nutrition and may have increased labor demands.

On the one hand, sedentism and the ability to store food may have helped smooth out seasonal fluctuation and bottlenecks in the food supply; on the other, storage anchored populations to the vicinity of their stores, perhaps making those populations more vulnerable to crop failure, especially as domesticated crops modified for human use are often less suited to natural survival than their wild ancestors and hence more vulnerable to disease and pests. The concept of storing foods restricted diets to storable resources, but stored foods lose nutrients during storage, and actual physical losses of stored food (due, for example, to spoilage) threatened the reliability of the whole enterprise. Reliance on stored resources also increased people's vulnerability to expropriation of stored resources by others, while sedentism also exposed populations to increased infection risks.

Common reconstructions hold that among established farmers, the invention of new tools or exploitation of new technologies—the hoe, the plow, draft animals, fertilizers, and irrigation—increased the carrying capacity of land and made labor more efficient. A more controversial thesis holds that methods of farming involving plentiful supplies of

land and low population densities may have been more efficient than the more intensive methods associated with increased population density. Denser populations require increasing the productivity of land by shortening the periods of time that the land lies fallow, which in turn may necessitate the adoption of new tools. It is possible, therefore, that both before and after the adoption of agriculture, demand and labor investment, not technological "progress," may have been the engine of economic growth. The idea of a fixed ceiling on resources modifiable only by fortuitous invention independent of need would then have little explanatory power.

Carrying Capacity in Recent Centuries

Artificial Malthusian constraints on population clearly became important with the emergence of civilization, because ruling classes (a defining feature of civilization) can withhold food from the lower classes and prevent them from generating demand for food. (Demand implies both desire or need and the ability to produce, pay for, or otherwise command food.) Hunger in the modern world among bountiful food supplies results from the inability of the poor to pay for food. Many argue that solutions to world hunger at present relate to the distribution of wealth, not natural Malthusian limits.

Moreover, in recent centuries, the growth of the world population has accelerated markedly. Nor can that growth be attributed to modern medicine's reducing human mortality, as it began well before the advent of modern medicine. Some argue that high growth rates are not a property of so-called primitive groups—that is, groups that depend on a high birth rate to assure their survival—but are a conscious response to the demands of colonial or world systems. If or when new efforts and new technology become necessary to feed the world's population, the implementation of those new technologies will depend on the degree to which the rich concern themselves with the poor. If that is the case, then increases in food technology are indeed independent of population and demand.

Ultimate Human Carrying Capacity of Earth

In the long run, demographers generally estimate the ultimate carrying capacity of Earth at 10–70 billion people (although some estimates are much higher.) The modern world population as of 2010 is approximately 6.8 billion. The variation in those estimates is due in part to different assumptions about the ability and willingness of human populations to exert more effort, employ new technologies, eat new foods, and accept lower standards of living.

But the human carrying capacity of Earth may well ultimately be measured not by food resources but by the limited supply of some other necessary resource. Fresh water is already in short supply, and that supply can be enhanced only at great cost. Carrying capacity might also be defined ultimately by the highest density that a human population can reach before it triggers an unstoppable epidemic of infectious disease—probably the most important limit on population for the foreseeable future. And it may well be defined by the limits of the capacity of social organization to mitigate social and psychological stresses brought on by declining personal space.

Mark Nathan COHEN

State University of New York, Plattsburgh

See also Population and the Environment

Further Reading

Birdsall, N., Kelley, K. C., & Sinding, S. W. (Eds.). (2001). *Population matters.* New York: Oxford University Press.

Bogin, B. (2001). *The growth of humanity.* New York: Wiley-Liss.

Boserup, E. (1965). *The conditions of agricultural growth.* Chicago: Aldine de Gruyter.

Brown, L. R., Gardner, G., & Halweil, B. (1999). *Beyond Malthus.* New York: Norton.

Cohen, J. E. (1995). *How many people can the earth support?* New York: Norton.

Cohen, M. N. (1977). *The food crisis in prehistory.* New Haven, CT: Yale University Press.

Cohen, M. N. (1984). Population growth, interpersonal conflict and organizational response in human history. In N. Choucri (Ed.), *Multidisciplinary perspectives on population and conflict* (pp. 27–58). Syracuse, NY: Syracuse University Press.

Cohen, M. N. (1989). *Health and the rise of civilization.* New Haven, CT: Yale University Press.

Ellison, P. (1991). Reproductive ecology and human fertility. In G. C. N. Mascie-Taylor & G. W. Lasker (Eds.), *Applications of biological anthropology to human affairs* (pp. 185–206). Cambridge, U.K.: Cambridge Studies In Biological Anthropology.

Ellison P. (2000). *Reproductive ecology and human evolution.* New York: Aldine de Gruyter.

Harris, R. M. G. (2001). *The history of human populations, 1.* New York: Praeger.

Kiple, K. (Ed.). (1993). *The Cambridge world history of human disease.* Cambridge, U.K.: Cambridge University Press.

Kiple, K., & Ornelas, K. C. (Eds.). (2000). *The Cambridge world history of food.* Cambridge, U.K.: Cambridge University Press.

Livi-Bacci, M. (2001). *A concise history of human populations* (3rd ed). Malden, MA: Basil Blackwell.

Malthus, T. (1985). *An essay on the principle of population.* New York: Penguin. (Original work published 1798)

Russell, K. (1988). *After Eden: The behavioral ecology of early food production in the Near East and North Africa* (British Archaeological Reports International Series No. 39). Oxford, U.K.: British Archaeological Reports.

Wood, J. (1995). *Demography of human reproduction.* New York: Aldine de Gruyter.

World Watch Institute. (2008). *State of the world, 2008.* New York: Norton.

Climate Change

Fluctuations in global temperatures throughout history have been accompanied by changes in sea levels and altered weather patterns, both of which have been linked to mass migrations, famines leading to disease, the collapse of some civilizations, and the growth of others. These cycles of warm and cold are affected by energy exchanges between oceans and the atmosphere, fossil-fuel emissions, and solar energy.

Many world historians explain changing Earth history in terms of its changing climate. Scientists however focus more directly on the causes for long-term climate change. They are: the exchange of energy by the oceans and atmosphere, fossil-fuel emissions, and solar energy. With global temperatures on the rise since 1860, climatologists predict that they may continue to increase by as much as 2°C during this century. Evidence of global warming appears in a melting Arctic ice cap—a reduction in volume of 3 to 4 percent each decade since the 1970s. As a result, sea levels have been rising since 1900 with the rate of change accelerating in the last half century. Contracting ice sheets and rising sea levels submerge coastal areas that affect the natural migration of some plants, animals, and microbes. According to the United Nations' Intergovernmental Panel on Climate Change (IPCC) report titled *Climate Change 2007*, "Warming of the climate system is unequivocal, as is now evident from observations of increases in global average air and ocean temperatures, widespread melting of snow and ice, and rising global mean sea level." During warming phases in the northern latitudes, migrating forests replace northern tundra and formerly marginal lands may become suitable for cultivation and food production. The costs to millions and possibly billions of people who live near the rising seas, slightly above, at, or below sea level would be devastating as rising temperatures and volatile weather in the tropics and middle latitudes would displace them from their homelands.

Climate fluctuations from warm, temperate, and interglacial to cold, arctic, and glacial can occur rapidly within a century and without much warning. The final collapse of the last Ice Age occurred about 9500 BCE and marked the beginning of the current global warming period. This rapid atmospheric warming, possibly the most significant climate event in the last forty thousand years, caused abrupt rises in global sea levels. Warming and glacial melt at about 7500 BCE flooded the Black Sea basin. The biblical "flood" may have been a reference to this natural catastrophe. Although many gaps exist in our knowledge about climate warming and cooling, efforts to unravel the complexities of the global climate have focused on specific events that trigger changes in the weather.

The Atlantic Circulation Energy Exchange

The world's oceans serve as a heat transportation system absorbing much of the heat from the solar energy penetrating the atmosphere. As rising temperatures increase freshwater snowmelt, the salinity of the oceans decreases, affecting their circulation. Decreasing the volume of heavy salt water disrupts the great Atlantic Deep Water Circulation, which brings warm tropical water across the equator toward the North Pole. These warm waters become the "gulf

Polluted runoff is the greatest threat to U.S. coastal waters; accordingly, fossil fuel emissions are one of the leading causes of long-term climate change.
National Oceanic and Atmospheric Administration.

stream" that warms the New England coast and brings moisture and warmth to the British Isles. Without it, these coastal regions would become several degrees colder, turning fertile soil into permafrost.

Since the oceans transport heat, abrupt small increases in temperature or increases in fresh glacial melt lower the density of the water, namely its capacity to sink, slowing down and in severe instances stopping the circulation. According to some climatic models, turning off or slowing down this current, often called "a huge heat pump," has cooled down the northern temperate regions and been responsible for many of the abrupt climate oscillations during the last 100,000 years.

El Niño

For the past forty years the salt content of the North Atlantic has declined continuously. But recent failures to simulate the relationship of these rapid climate changes to the Atlantic circulation have led scientists to search for another climatic event

that may contribute to either hemispheric or global climate change. They have concluded that the tropical Pacific Ocean and its El Niño episodes in combination with the Atlantic circulation may provide an answer.

As the world's largest ocean, the Pacific covers about 181 million square kilometers, with the widest band along the tropics, where solar energy is converted mostly into heat. Ocean currents and wind velocity serve to distribute this heat. During some years, atmospheric and sea temperatures are abnormally warm for reasons that are not completely understood. These reasons may include sunspot activity, the effects of the Atlantic Deep Water Circulation, and the fact that the world's oceans now consume a larger carbon load caused by fossil-fuel emissions.

Some climatologists believe that these anomalies may trigger El Niño oceanic conditions, meaning that the flow of cold water from South America to the warm Pacific pool decreases or ceases entirely. In the absence of the easterly wind shears that drive the surface cold water to Asia, westerly winds push the warm Pacific pool toward the Americas. Hot and humid air travels with this warm pool, soaking previously arid equatorial islands and the coastal regions of the Americas from Peru to the west coast of the United States with torrential rains. With accelerating westerly winds, precipitation extends into the Western Hemisphere from the Americas and Eurasia to the Russian plains. Drought strikes India, China, Indonesia, and Africa.

The impact of El Niño on the distribution of heat and precipitation around the world is well known. What remains unknown is the relationship between Atlantic and Pacific oceanic events on the global climate. Ocean temperatures and salinity influence circulation. In fact, some North Atlantic deep water may enter the equatorial Pacific and cool the water temperature and the atmosphere as it does in the Atlantic Ocean and in this way defuse the catastrophic climatic effects of El Niño. If the cold water circulation of the Atlantic slows or stops, however, then there exists no known constraint on El Niño's harmful effects.

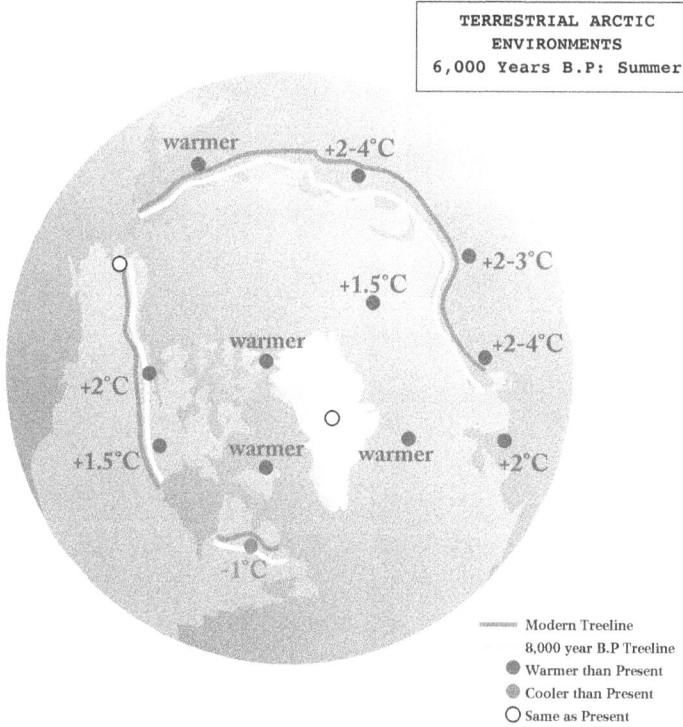

TERRESTRIAL ARCTIC
ENVIRONMENTS
6,000 Years B.P: Summer

warmer   +2-4°C

+2-3°C
+1.5°C

warmer   +2-4°C

+2°C

+1.5°C   warmer   warmer   +2°C

-1°C

Modern Treeline
8,000 year B.P Treeline
Warmer than Present
Cooler than Present
Same as Present

circulation, raised atmospheric temperatures, and created volatile weather.

By 1100 CE the warm period was giving way to the little Ice Age and mega-El Niños were in decline. With less energy transfer to activate the tropical oceans, one last major El Niño reached landfall in northern Peru in 700 CE. These pre-Spanish Conquest El Niños, similar to other major climatic events in world history, caused major political and cultural dislocations in the lives of native people. Floods in coastal areas and drought east of the Andes Mountains forced populations to relocate, rebuild, and adapt to the volatile weather systems that visited South America throughout this warming period.

El Niño's Impact on World History

Prior to the Spanish conquest of the Incas in 1500 CE, advanced civilizations of native farmers and fishermen spread out along the northern Peruvian coast. These Native Americans, called the Moche, built pyramids, crafted pottery, and made gold ornaments to celebrate their spiritual and material achievements. The remains of their irrigated canals and mud-brick buildings attest to their advanced civilization. The sedimentary evidence found in riverbeds, in coastal lagoons, and by examining the fossil remains in these sediments reveals that repeated episodes of El Niño disrupted Moche civilization. Floods and droughts forced the Moche to abandon established sites for newer ones. With more energy from the overheated oceans, mega-El Niños activated water and wind

El Niño in Recent History

Research into the history of the El Niño weather phenomenon stems from the discovery that the El Niños of the 1980s had worldwide effects. Because of drought conditions during that decade, peasants were forced to leave northeastern Brazil, political instability occurred in some sub-Saharan countries, and food shortages became commonplace in India, China, and Japan. El Niño weather systems prove unmistakably the connectedness of the global climate system and its specific effects on biological entities, historical developments, and local and regional weather patterns.

The El Niño events of 1982–1983 reinforce theories and knowledge about the energy exchanges of the world's cold and warm waters, especially in the

El Niño Watch: A satellite image shows the Pacific Ocean stabilizing, 11 July 1998. NASA.

Indian, Pacific, and Atlantic, by absorbing solar energy and releasing heat into the atmosphere. The destructive forces unleashed by El Niño episodes suggest that the world's oceans reach a point of energy overload and need to discharge their accumulated heat. In this way an unpredictable global climate system is brought back into delicate balance.

As we have seen, scientists have identified three basic causes of global climate change—the exchange of energy by the oceans and the atmosphere, fossil-fuel emissions, and solar energy. Much remains to be discovered about its causes and effects, however. Solar energy output has periodic and sometimes irregular patterns of intensity. Periods of high intensity occur during eleven-year cycles and those of low intensity take place about every three and one-half years. Although the similarities in the pattern are not conclusive, some scientists argue that El Niño returns at intervals of high intensity. Finally, no substantial body of evidence points to a relationship between the warming of the Pacific waters in recent decades, a trigger for El Niño, and atmospheric pollution. Since much is unknown about El Niño, it remains an area of great interest for scientists and historians because of its potential effects on the global climate and global population.

The Role of Fossil-Fuel Emissions

Rising global temperatures translate into increased atmospheric water vapor, a greenhouse gas, as more of the world's warming ocean water evaporates, causing more precipitation. Releasing the energy sequestered for millions of years in fossilized plants and animals by burning coal, oil, and gas elevates concentrations of another greenhouse gas, carbon dioxide (CO_2), in the atmosphere. Most of these emissions come from three key sectors: electricity generation,

Due to climate change, sea levels have been rising since 1900 with the rate of change accelerating in the last half century. Researchers from NOAA's National Geodetic Survey conduct a shoreline survey. National Oceanic and Atmospheric Administration.

transportation, and the heating and cooling of residential, commercial, and public buildings. Electric power generation globally contributes 41 percent of all CO_2 emissions. During periods of industralization, the burning of fossil fuels and the process of deforestation have increased the carbon dioxide load in the atmosphere by about 25 percent. Within the last hundred years, 40–50 percent of the world's pioneer forests and uninhabited lands that change CO_2 into oxygen by the process known as photosynthesis have been transformed into agricultural production and commercial and residential construction. Also caused by the burning of fossil fuels, other fast-growing greenhouse gases such as methane (CH_4) and chlorofluorocarbons (CFCs) with greater heat-absorbing qualities than CO_2 have affected atmospheric

temperatures. From 1850 to 2000, the human contribution to the increased concentration of CO_2 by burning fossil fuels, deforestation, and agriculture was about 1.7 trillion tons. About 40 percent of this CO_2 remains in the atmosphere and it is increasing at a rate of about 0.5 percent per year. The life span of CO_2 molecules in the atmosphere is one hundred years, meaning that the emissions from the first Model T automobile that became available to consumers in 1927 and every vehicle built since remains a part of the human-induced global carbon load.

Global warming occurs more rapidly in frigid regions rather than in the temperate and tropical areas because arctic air lacks water vapor. This characteristic makes CO_2 a more important greenhouse gas where the air is cold and dry. In warmer, humid air, water vapor is a more important as a transporter of heat than CO_2. Because warming is unevenly distributed across the planet, what exactly CO_2 contributes to global warming remains debatable.

During the current warming phase one can expect the physical properties of CO_2 to contribute to more rainfall, higher atmospheric and oceanic temperatures, more clouds, and higher wind velocity. The biological effects of CO_2 are noteworthy, contributing to longer growing seasons in the temperate and tropical climates. Arid and semiarid lands mainly unavailable for agriculture may receive sufficient moisture to increase food stocks for a global population whose growth rate will stabilize at between 9 and 12 billion people by 2050. The specific impacts of human population growth on the global climate system remain unknown, however.

The Role of Solar Energy

Two additional forces drive the global climate system. One cited often in the scientific literature but recently challenged is the Milankovitch explanation. The Serbian astronomer M. M. Milankovitch argued that the eccentric orbit of the Earth established its major global climatic cycle of 100,000 years. During that time the planet goes through a full interglacial/glacial cycle. Within this longer pattern, another

41,000-year cycle controls the amount of solar energy reaching the Earth's higher latitudes. It is caused by the tilt of the Earth on its axis.

A much shorter cycle caused by the "wobble" of the Earth on its axis occurs either at 23,000- or 19,000-year intervals and affects the amount of radiation striking the low latitudes and the equator. Milankovitch argued that during the last 800,000 years, Earth experienced eight complete glacial/interglacial cycles. The Ice Ages lasted for 90,000 years followed by 10,000-year periods of warming. Accordingly, the current interglacial phase should be coming to an end.

Since the Milankovitch explanation accounts for only 0.1 percent change in the total solar energy reaching the Earth, however, some climatologists have looked elsewhere for a more coherent driving force behind climate change. They argue that fluctuations in solar energy follow a cyclical pattern of sunspot activity. Using this pattern, they have identified a pattern of eight cycles during the last 720,000 years of the Earth's history. They are ninety thousand years in length, from full glacial with –0.3 percent of solar energy output to full warming with +0.3 percent. Given the dynamic changes in the Earth's history and the gaps in our knowledge about its physical and biological properties however, predictions about future global climate changes remain illusive, despite the existence of this cyclical pattern.

Impact of Climate Changes on World History

A warming phase during the last major ice age from 33,000 to 26,000 BCE may have eased the migration of anatomically modern humans from Africa and southwestern Asia into Europe, replacing the resident Neanderthals. Before rising global sea levels eliminated the passage from Siberia to North America, this warming phase allowed human hunters to cross the frozen Bering Straits. In successive waves, possibly beginning as early as 32,000 BCE but no later than 11,000 BCE, they followed the hunt and populated the Americas.

As the last glacial maximum was ending about 13,000 BCE, a time when rising temperatures on Greenland approximated current ones, the retreat of the glaciers was interrupted by two little ice ages, the Older Dryas at 12,100 BCE and the Younger Dryas at 10,800 BCE. (A dryas is an Arctic flower that grew in Europe during the last Ice Age.) Evidence that the warm water circulation failed to reach the northern hemisphere around 12,700 BCE and inaugurated the Younger Dryas suggests that glacial melt entering the North Atlantic at the end of the last glacial maximum either slowed or stopped the Deep Water Circulation. It transformed the northern temperate regions into a little ice age for the next 1,300 years. The landscape of the British Isles became permafrost, with summer temperatures dropping below 32°C and winter ones below –10°C. Icebergs floated to the Iberian coast and long periods of drought affected Asia, Africa, and the midcontinent of North America. The slowdown of the Atlantic circulation may have been responsible for the changing hemispheric climate.

Climatic Impacts on Indo-European Civilizations

Little ice ages have punctuated world history during these warming phases. As a result of cooling, the once fertile pastoral civilization of the Sahara collapsed, forcing the migration of its inhabitants to the Nile River valley about 5500 BCE. This settlement along the Nile coincided with the millennia-long rise of the ancient Egyptian civilization. Between 5000 and 4500 BCE, the Egyptians established their first empire and within centuries built the great pyramids at Giza. The Harappa civilization in the Indus Valley flourished as well, constructing public buildings and private dwellings of mud and fired bricks and using geometric plans to organize its cities.

From 4500 to 3800 BCE, a "global chill" interrupted human progress with seemingly endless periods of drought. The global climate may have been colder than at any time since the Younger Dryas. As happened during earlier periods of cold and arid

conditions, the human population migrated south, escaping from the most extreme climatic conditions. Farming populations, the descendants of Indo-Europeans who in progressive migrations had brought farming technology into western and northern Europe from Southwest Asia many thousands of years before, were forced by the cold climate to retreat southward. They retreated to warmer regions along the Mediterranean and southeastward to Ukraine, to southwest Asia, India, and into northwest China.

Another protracted cold period brought drought to the irrigation-dependent "fertile crescent" civilizations of the Tigris, Euphrates, and Indus valleys between 3250 and 2750 BCE. In fact, some archaeologists suggest that the lush, naturally irrigated landscape in modern southern Iraq may have been the location of the biblical "Garden of Eden." Recent archaeological research has verified that the collapse of the great agricultural Akkadian Empire in northern Mesopotamia (3200 to 2900 BCE) coincided with a major volcanic eruption and a subsequent climate shift from moist and cool to dry and hot that lasted for more than a century. These concurrent events forced this ancient population to leave the north and migrate into southern Mesopotamia (modern Iraq).

The Rise and Fall of the Mayan Civilization

Another global cold spell that lasted from 2060 BCE to 1400 CE had beneficial effects turning tropical and subtropical regions into cooler and dryer climates. In Central America, the Mayan civilization expanded its agricultural productivity northward into the Yucatan, now part of Mexico, and built pyramids and cities in areas formerly thick with tropical vegetation and malaria-bearing mosquitoes. They remained there for about a thousand years.

Years without rainfall caused a series of collapses in Mayan agricultural productivity. Sedimentary records suggest that droughts began 1200 CE and revisited the region for the next five hundred years. They abandoned some cities in 1240 CE and the remaining ones in 1190 CE, when another severe dry period hit the area. Other causes may have contributed to the demise of the Mayans but the relationship of climate change to the collapse is a compelling one. After this particular global chill ended, the hydrological cycle gained strength as the climate warmed. The tropical forest returned along with the mosquitoes and forced the remaining Mayans to abandon their homes and to migrate southward. The fact that Mayan ruins are discovered now in the dense tropical rain forests of Central America is evidence of more recent global warming.

With the stronger hydrological cycle of the last 150 years, pioneers have cleared forests for agriculture, growing seasons have expanded, and more food has become available for a growing population. The relationships between climate change, the migration of human and animal populations, and the rise and decline of civilizations will require more detailed study before global climate change becomes more accepted as a causal factor in world history.

The Little Ice Age

Evidence from sediments and ice cores reveal that a little ice age (shorter than the typical 80,000 to 90,000 years) of long duration from approximately 1300 to 1850 CE swept across the northern hemisphere. Viking outposts in Greenland populated during the Medieval Warm Period (1000–1300 CE) succumbed to the freeze between 1200 and 1300. Food production plummeted in preindustrial Europe. Even in the best of times, where diets consisted mostly of bread and potatoes, daily food consumption seldom exceeded 2,000 calories. Widespread malnutrition was followed by famine and the outbreak of infectious diseases.

The bubonic plague followed the great European famine in 1400. Between 1100 and 1800, France experienced frequent famines, twenty-six in the twelfth century and sixteen in the nineteenth century. Increasing cold temperatures shortened the growing season by at least one month in northern European countries and the elevation for growing crops retreated about 18 meters. Not all populations suffered equally during this ice age, however. For those living along major rivers and coastal areas, fishing provided the animal protein lacking in the diets of the majority. In New England, 1815 was called "the year without a summer." After 1850 and without warning this little ice age came to an end. Increased solar energy, the impact of industrialization on the atmospheric concentrations of greenhouse gases and changes in the Atlantic Deep Water Circulation have been identified as causes, either alone or in combination.

Climate Change: The Future

Examining climate events in history and reviewing the scientific findings of the present suggest that no single cause can adequately explain significant climate oscillations. The convergence of many changes in the world's oceans, atmosphere, and land causes the disruptions and outbursts that we identify as significant climate events. These events possess such complex and unpredictable characteristics that to date the most advanced computers and global climate models (GCMs) have been unable to predict future climate events.

Despite our fragmentary knowledge of past climate events, knowing what to do in the future presents us with a great challenge. Population growth into coastal areas and onto marginal lands makes catastrophes more likely during periods of abrupt change. Increases in material consumption and energy use will continue to place stress on global ecosystems. The goal of sustainable growth in the developed world and the expectations for the same in the developing world remain elusive. In the words of Vaclav Smil (1990, 23), "If concerns about planetary warming will help to bring some sanity into the craven pursuit of economic growth and personal affluence throughout the rich world, and if they will aid in promoting control of population growth and responsible development policies in the poor world, then a warming trend might actually be an effective catalyst of desirable changes."

Anthony N. PENNA
Northeastern University

See also Ice Ages; Oceans and Seas

Further Reading

Alley, R. B. (2000). Ice-core evidence of abrupt climate changes. *Proceedings of the National Academy of Sciences of the United States of America, 97*(4), 1331–1334.

Caviedes, C. N. (2001). *El Niño in history: Storming through the ages.* Gainesville: University Press of Florida.

Congressional Budget Office. (2003). *The economics of climate change: A primer.* Washington, DC: United States Government Printing Office.

Culver, S. J., & Rawson, P. F. (Eds.). (2000). *Biotic response to global change: The last 145 million years.* Cambridge, U.K.: Cambridge University Press.

DeBoer, J. Z., & Sanders, D. T. (2002). *Volcanoes in human history: The far reaching effects of major eruptions.* Princeton, NJ: Princeton University Press.

Diaz, H. F., & Markgraf, V. (2000). *El Niño and the southern oscillation: Multiscale variability and global and regional impacts.* Cambridge, U.K.: Cambridge University Press.

Durschmied, E. (2000). *The weather factor: How nature has changed history.* New York: Arcade.

Dyurgerov, M. B., & Meier, M. F. (2000). Twentieth century climate change: Evidence from small glaciers. *Proceedings of the National Academy of Sciences of the United States of America, 97*(4), 1406–1411.

Fagan, B. (1999). *Floods, famines, and emperors: El Niño and the fate of civilizations.* New York: Basic Books.

Glantz, M. H. (2001). *Currents of change: Impacts of El Niño and La Nina on climate and society.* Cambridge, U.K.: Cambridge University Press.

Global warming: New scenarios from the Intergovernmental Panel on Climate Change. (2001). *Population and Development Review, 27*(1), 203–208.

Jones, P. D., Ogilvie, A. E. J., Davies, T. D., & Briffa, K. R. (Eds.). (2001). *History and climate: Memories of the future?* New York: Kluwer Academic/Plenum.

Keys, D. (2000). *Catastrophe: A quest for the origin of the modern world.* London: Ballantine.

Ladurie, E. L. (1971). *Times of feast, times of famine: A history of climate since the year 1000.* Garden City, NY: Doubleday.

Lovvorn, M. J., Frison, G. C., & Tieszen, L. L. (2001). Paleoclimate and Amerindians: Evidence from stable isotopes and atmospheric circulation. *Proceedings of the National Academy of Sciences of the United States of America, 98*(5), 2485–2490.

Marotzke, J. (2000). Abrupt climate change and thermohaline circulation: Mechanisms and predictability. *Proceedings of the National Academy of Sciences of the United States of America, 97*(4), 1347–1350.

McIntosh, R. J., Tainter, J. A., McIntosh, S. K. (2000). *The way the wind blows: Climate, history, and human action.* New York: Columbia University Press.

National Assessment Synthesis Team. (2001). *Climate change impacts on the United States.* Cambridge, U.K.: Cambridge University Press.

Novacek, M. J., & Cleland, E. E. (2001). The current biodiversity extinction event: Scenarios for mitigation and recovery. *Proceedings of the National Academy of Sciences of the United States of America, 98*(10), 5466–5470.

Perry, C. A., & Hsu, K. J. (2000). Geophysical, archaeological, and historical evidence supports a solar-output model of climate change. *Proceedings of the National Academy of Sciences of the United States of America, 97*(23), 12433–12438.

Pierrehumbert, R. T. (2000). Climate change and the tropical Pacific: The sleeping dragon wakes. *Proceedings of the National Academy of Sciences of the United States of America, 97*(4), 1355–1358.

Smil, V. (1990). Planetary warming: Realities and responses. *Population and Development Review, 16*(1), 1–29.

Smil, V. (2003). *The earth's biosphere: Evolution, dynamics, and change.* Cambridge, MA: Massachusetts Institute of Technology Press.

Webb, T., III, & Bartlein, P. J. (1992). Global changes during the last 3 million years: Climatic controls and biotic responses. *Annual Review of Ecology and Systematics, 23,* 141–173.

Western, D. (2001). Human-modified ecosystems and future evolution. *Proceedings of the National Academy of Sciences of the United States of America, 98*(10), 5458–5465.

Columbian Exchange

The early exchanges of life forms between Europe and America, which began in earnest with the voyage of Christopher Columbus in 1492, included disease germs, weeds, and vermin as well as medicines, crops, and domesticated animals. The effects were far-reaching for species that had developed in relative isolation on different continents of the Old and New Worlds.

Two hundred million years ago the continents of Earth were massed together contiguously. There was maximum opportunity for terrestrial species to migrate and therefore a higher degree of biotic uniformity than later. Then the continents split, drifted away from each other, and thereafter each continent's species evolved independently. North America and Asia reconnected several times in the far north and so share many species, but there are many contrasts between the two; the Old World, for example, has such native species as nightingales and cobras, which the New World does not share, while the New World has hummingbirds and rattlesnakes, not present in the Old World. Contrasts between South America and the Old World are especially dramatic; in the former one finds nose-waggling tapirs, whereas in the latter one finds nose-waggling elephants.

Old and New Worlds: People, Crops, Animals

Ten thousand years ago the most recent ice age ended, the continental glaciers melted, and sea levels rose, dividing the Old and New Worlds once again. Before that a number of species had passed between the two, the most influential of which was the Old World anthropoid *Homo sapiens*. Thereafter the peoples of the Old World and the Americas evolved separately. The genetic differences that resulted were minor, but the cultural differences were major because the two peoples took different paths in exploiting their different environments.

Both invented agriculture—that is, the domestication of crops and of livestock—but two very different systems of agriculture. The Native Americans probably arrived from Asia with the dog and were therefore familiar with the concept of tame animals, but domesticated few creatures in America, possibly because there were few suitable. Those they domesticated included the llama and alpaca, the guinea pig, and several species of fowl. The Native Americans excelled as farmers, developing one-third or so of all of today's most important food crops: maize, beans of several kinds, the white and sweet potatoes, manioc (cassava), squashes and pumpkins, peanuts, papayas, guavas, avocados, pineapples, tomatoes, chilies, sunflower seeds, and others.

Not surprisingly, Old World indigenes, of whom there were many more than Native Americans and who lived in a wider expanse of land and participated in a greater variety of ecosystems, domesticated more kinds of animals and plants. Horses, donkeys, cattle, pigs, sheep, goats, chickens (today's protagonists of our barnyards and meadows and our chief sources of meat, milk, leather, and animal fiber) are all Old World in origin. The same is true of wheat, barley, rye, oats, rice, peas, turnips, sugarcane, onions, lettuce, olives, bananas, peaches, pears, and many other stock items of our diets today.

Honor sinks where commerce long prevails. • **Oliver Goldsmith (1749–1832)**

Separation of the Old and New Worlds: Disease

The Old World outdid the New as a source of infectious diseases, too. The greater number of people in more varied ecosystems were bound to have a greater variety of diseases, especially because they lived in close contact with their livestock. The intermixing of Old World humans across Eurasia and Africa, and their propinquity with their animals, produced many of the historically most significant diseases. An undoubtedly incomplete list includes smallpox, measles, influenza, malaria, yellow fever, and typhus. Pre-Columbian Amerindians had tuberculosis and treponematosis (having probably brought the latter with them from the Old World) and cultivated, unintentionally, new infections in America, including Chagas Disease, but their indigenous diseases were few and mild compared with those native to the Old World. (Syphilis is often nominated as a distinctively American infection, but that is debatable.)

When Christopher Columbus brought the Old and New Worlds together in 1492, he unleashed the organisms of each on the other. The most spectacular early result of the intermixing was the traumatic spread of Eastern Hemisphere infections among the Native Americans. The European conquest of the Americas was not so much a matter of brutality, though there was plenty of that, as of imported diseases. Smallpox figures significantly in the Spanish conquests of Mexico and Peru, and again and again throughout the Americas. The Native American population fell by as much, claim highly respected demographic historians, as 90 percent before beginning recovery.

On the other hand, Old World plants and animals immensely increased the capacity of America to support in time large human populations. Horses, pigs, and cattle, for instance, went feral from Florida to the Argentine pampa and within a century had propagated into the millions. Old World livestock revolutionized human life and whole ecosystems in the Americas. Meat had been a rare item in the diets of the vast peasantries of the advanced Amerindian societies. After the Columbian Exchange it became common in many regions and in the others, if not common, at least more available than before.

There had been no beasts of burden in the Americas except the dog and the llama. The pyramids and other monuments of the high American civilizations were raised by human muscle. If the burro had been the only domesticated animal brought to Mexico by the invaders, it alone would have revolutionized indigenous societies there.

The impact of the horse on Native American societies was particularly spectacular. Many Amerindians who had been strictly pedestrian became equestrian. From approximately 1750 to 1800, the native peoples of North America's Great Plains (Blackfoot, Sioux, Cheyenne, Comanche, Pawnee, and others) and of South America's pampas (Pehuenches, Puelches, Tehuelches, Ranqueles, and others), all took to the horse.

Old World crops did not at first advance in the New World as rapidly as Old World livestock—they were, after all, not mobile—but also because most of them were temperate-zone plants not suited to Europe's earliest American colonies, which were all in the tropics. But European colonists adjusted, imported suitable species such as sugarcane, for instance, and suitable varieties of homeland crops, and sowed them where the soils and climates were similar to those at home. They discovered that wheat prospered in the Mexican high country, for example. Olive trees and grapes for wine did well in Peru. Within a century of Columbus most of the Old World's important crops were growing in America.

Among the most profitable was sugarcane, the source of a quasi-addictive substance: sugar. The market for sugar in Europe seemed endlessly expansive for centuries, and therefore sugarcane became the single most important crop in the West Indies, Brazil, and other hot, wet regions in or contiguous to the American tropics. The planting, cultivation, harvesting, and processing of the cane required millions of laborers. The Amerindian populations were plummeting, and European immigrants were in short supply. The workers had to come from some untapped source. The single most powerful force driving the Atlantic slave trade was the sugar plantations' need for laborers.

An estimated 12.5 million Africans were commandeered to work American soils, a majority of them, certainly a plurality, to raise an Old World sweet in the New World for Old World consumption.

1492 and the Old World

Amerindian livestock did not revolutionize life in the Old World. Guinea pigs and turkeys have never figured significantly in Europe, Asia, or Africa as food sources, and the llama was so obviously inferior to several Old World animals as a beast of burden that it has never had more than novelty value in the Eastern Hemisphere.

Amerindian crops, however, had enormous effect on the Old World. Most of those which became standard in Old World diets were brought back by the Spanish and Portuguese to Iberia, where they were being cultivated by the sixteenth century; they spread out from there. Some would flourish where Old World crops would not; manioc, for instance, where the rainfall was too much or too little, the soil infertile, and the pests too voracious for traditional staples like rice and yams. Several American foods were more nourishing, more productive, and easier to cultivate and to harvest than traditional Old World crops. Maize became a standard crop in sub-Saharan Africa, in some regions the most important crop.

The white potato, from the high, wet, cool Andes, became one of the most important food sources for the lower classes of northern Europe. In Ireland it became indispensable for the peasantry, and when, in the 1840s, an American fungus, *Phytophthora infestans*, arrived and destroyed the potato crop, a million died of starvation and disease and a million and a half fled the country.

The list of examples of the influence of the Columbian exchange in the Old World diets is a long one; it includes the tomato in Italian cuisine, the chili in Indian recipes, the presence of maize in most sub-Saharan African diets, and so forth. By way of illustrative example, let us consider the story of American food crops in a land usually thought of as resistant to outside influences: China. No Old World people adopted these alien plants faster than the Chinese.

The eagerness with which the Chinese received American foods is related to population pressure. Between 1368 and 1644, the years of the Ming dynasty, the Chinese population doubled at the same time that farmers of the traditional staples, wheat in the north and rice in the south, were running into problems of diminishing returns. They were close to raising as much food as they could on suitable land using existing techniques. The problem may have been especially pressing in the south, where most of the level and near-level land close to markets and sources of water for irrigation was already occupied by rice paddies.

The Spanish and the Portuguese, both with American empires, carried the Amerindian crops to East Asia. The port of Manila, newly Spanish and only a few days' sail from the China coast, played a major role in the transfer of native American crops to China. Sweet potatoes, a calorically rich food, arrived in China some time in the last years of the sixteenth century. This crop did well in inferior soils, tolerated drought, resisted insect pests, and prospered with little care compared with existing staples such as

Mesoamerica developed edible varieties of maize as early as 5000 BCE. When maize arrived in China some 6,500 years later, it was valued as a fast-growing, high-caloric food source. Photo by Clara Natoli (www.morguefile.com).

paddy rice. By 1650 sweet potatoes were common in Guangdong and Fujian provinces and well on the way to becoming the staple of the poorer peasants wherever climate would allow.

Maize arrived in China even before the mid-sixteenth century. It, too, was hardy and required no more attention and strength in weeding and harvesting than children could provide. It produced food faster than most crops and provided high amounts of calories. It soon became a common secondary crop from Shanxi in the northwest to Yunnan in the southwest and eventually a primary crop in several inland provinces.

Peanuts, growing in China at least as early as 1538, have always been considered a novelty food in the West, but became a common item in Chinese meals. Peanuts provide plenty of calories and oil, and as they grow enrich the soil with nitrogen.

According to the demographic historian Ho Ping-ti, "During the last two centuries when rice culture was gradually approaching its limit, and encountering the law of diminishing returns, the various dry land food crops introduced from America have contributed most to the increase in national food production and have made possible a continual growth in population" (Ho 1959, 191–192). That statement applies as well to most of humanity in the Eastern Hemisphere.

Alfred W. CROSBY
University of Texas, Austin

See also Biological Exchanges

Further Reading

Cook, N. D. (1998). *Born to die: Disease and New World conquest, 1492–1650*. Cambridge, U.K.: Cambridge University Press.

Crosby, A. W. (1986). *Ecological imperialism: The biological expansion of Europe, 900–1900*. Cambridge, U.K.: Cambridge University Press.

Crosby, A. W. (1994). *Germs, seeds, and animals*. Armonk, NY: M. E. Sharpe.

Crosby, A. W. (2003). *The Columbian exchange: Biological and cultural consequences of 1492*. Westport, CT: Praeger Publishers.

Denevan, W. M. (1992). *The native population of the Americas in 1492* (2nd ed). Madison: University of Wisconsin Press.

Ho, P. (1959). *Studies on the population of China, 1368–1953*. Cambridge, MA: Harvard University Press.

Kinealy, C. (1995) *The great calamity: The Irish famine, 1845–1852*. Boulder, CO: Roberts Rinehart Publishers.

Kiple, K. F. (Ed.). (1993). *The Cambridge world history of human disease*. Cambridge, U.K.: Cambridge University Press.

Mazumdar, S. (1999). The impact of New World food crops on the diet and economy of India and China, 1600–1900. In R. Grew (Ed.), *Food in global history* (pp. 58–78). Boulder, CO: Westview Press.

Mintz, S. W. (1985). *Sweetness and power: The place of sugar in modern history*. New York: Penguin Books.

Deforestation

Humans have been felling, using, and burning trees for about half a million years, and the forests have receded as human populations have grown and spread. The clearing of woodlands for agriculture has been the leading cause of deforestation, but the harvesting of timber as a raw material and fuel has also played a significant role.

The word *deforestation* is a wide-ranging term to cover the cutting, use, and elimination of trees. Subsumed under it are other activities like fire, domestic heating and cooking, smelting metals, making ceramics, construction of shelter and implements, and the creation of new land for cultivation and grazing. Deforestation is so basic that it is woven into the very fabric of human existence, and hence of world history. Ever since the emergence of *Homo erectus* some 500,000 years ago the quest to provide shelter, food, and warmth has resulted in the use and abuse of the Earth's mantle of forests.

There is much uncertainty about the pace and locale of deforestation during past (and even present) ages. This revolves around the multiple meanings given to three basic questions. What exactly is a forest? What was the extent and density of trees at any past given time? And what constitutes "deforestation"? Pragmatically one may say that a forest can range from a closed-canopy tree cover to a more open woodland, which affects density. *Deforestation* is used loosely to mean any process that modifies the original tree cover, from clear-felling to thinning to occasional fire. It should not be forgotten, however, that forests regrow, often with surprising speed and vigor, and forest regrowth has occurred whenever pressures

on it have been relaxed. This was observed after the Mayan population collapse around 800 CE, after the Great Plague in Europe after 1348, after the initial European encounter with the Americas in 1492, and with agricultural land abandonment in the post-1910 eastern United States and in post-1980 Europe.

Premodern Age (to 1500 CE)

Because crop domestication and the increase and spread of people occurred in largely forested environments, ancient societies everywhere had a cumulatively severe impact on forests. In Europe, Mesolithic cultures (c. 9000–5000 BCE) set fire to the woodland edges to facilitate hunting. The succeeding Neolithic agriculturalists (c. 4500–2000 BCE) had a far greater impact as they felled forests on the fertile loessial soils with stone-and-flint axes to engage in intensive garden cultivation and extensive wheat growing. In order to vary diet, they also ran large herds of pigs, sheep, and especially cattle in woodland and cleared pastures for their meat, milk, blood, and possibly cheese. It was a stable, sedentary society that made full use of the many products of the forest, one calculation being that on average it required 20 hectares of forest land to sustain one person in fuel, grazing, constructional timber, and food.

In Asia, complex and highly organized societies flourished in the forests of the southern and southeastern parts of the continent. Rotational cutting and cultivation followed by abandonment (swiddening) in forests was accompanied by an intensive garden culture for fruit, spices, and vegetables, and the peculiar and highly innovative development of wet rice cultivation (rice paddies), a technique that stopped

In parts of Asia, fertilizers sparked regrowth of local hybrid poplars (*Populus simonigra*) planted in irrigated sandy soil.

erosion and leaching of the soil in the cleared forest in heavy-rainfall areas. Stock, particularly cattle and pigs, were integral to all parts of the economy.

The evidence for similar processes is unfolding for the Americas. Earliest were the swiddens in the equatorial upland rain-forest areas from as early as 12,000 BCE. From the tropical Gulf of Mexico lowland civilizations of the Olmec and Maya to the less organized tribal groups of the Amazon basin, rain forest was being chopped, burnt, and changed or eliminated. Large patches of the Amazon forest were altered irrevocably by the selection and propagation of useful trees and by different cycles of cultivation, so that the mighty rain forest may be one large cultural artifact. In North America, the earliest food-growing settlements (c. 10,000 BCE) were in the rich bottomlands of the continent's rivers in the South and the Southeast. Similar to the practice of the European Neolithics, flood plains and lower river terraces were cleared, and lower slopes altered as intensive cropping expanded, but unlike the Neolithics, hunting loomed much larger in the economy. The vast eastern temperate woodlands were settled later (after c. 800 CE) but the same imprints are evident, resulting in a mosaic of intensively cultivated cleared lands, abandoned fields with early forest succession, and thinned and altered forests. The great difference between the Americas and Eurasia was the absence of grazing animals in the Americas, which had an effect on the Eurasian forests by preventing regrowth and making clearing/firing worthwhile to promote pasture.

Knowledge about deforestation in Africa is sparse, and with the exception of settlement in savanna-woodland and adjacent belts in west Africa, it may not have been very extensive.

The conclusion is that the impact of early humans on the forest was far greater than expected; it may have been one of the major deforestation episodes in history, which left anything but the pristine forest that is such a feature of the romantic imagination of the past and the environmental rhetoric of the present.

The classical world of the Mediterranean basin provides, for the first time, rich literary detail of wood consumption for shipbuilding, urban heating and construction, and metal smelting, but it is tantalizingly silent about clearing for agriculture (always the greatest cause of deforestation) that must have gone on everywhere. This was to be a common story in later ages too. The chopping down of trees as a prelude to farming and providing food was so commonplace that it simply did not warrant a mention, but settlement patterns and crop figures show how extensive it must have been.

The Middle Ages in western and central Europe were entirely different. Here an energetic, inventive, and rapidly expanding population left ample records of forest clearing through charters, rent rolls, court cases, field patterns, and place names. Clearing was motivated by a strong religious belief that humans were helping to complete the creation of a divine, designed Earth and a desire by lay and ecclesiastical lords to expand rental revenues by encouraging settlement on the forest frontier. Also, individuals wanted to achieve social freedom, property, and emancipation by breaking free of the rigid feudal ties.

Undoubtedly three technical innovations helped raise agricultural production. First, the dominant system of two fields with one fallow was replaced by a three-field system, thus a shortening of the fallow period. This was possible because new crops like oats and legumes helped to fertilize the soil and supplemented animal and human nutrition. Second, the development of the wheeled plow with coulter and moldboard allowed cultivation to move from the

A forest worker fells tree at Ellakanda plantation block, a trial cable-logging site at Bandarawela, Sri Lanka.

light soils onto the heavy moist soils that were usually forested. Third, plowing efficiency was improved by the invention of the rigid horse collar and nailed horseshoes, increasing speed and pulling power, thus favoring the horse over the ox. A major underlying driving force was a sixfold increase of population between 650 and 1350 and the need for more food to avert famine.

Cultivation rose from about 5 percent of land use in the sixth century CE to 30–40 percent by the late Middle Ages. The forests of France were reduced from 30 million hectares to 13 million hectares between around 800 and 1300 CE. In Germany and central Europe, perhaps 70 percent of the land was forest covered in 900 CE, but only about 25 percent remained by 1900.

The various elements interlocked to produce what Lynn White, historian of medieval technology, called "the agricultural revolution of the Middle Ages" (1962, 6), which asserted the dominance of humans over nature. It also shifted the focus of Europe from south to north, from the restricted lowlands around the Mediterranean to the great forested plains drained by the Loire, Seine, Rhine, Elbe, Danube, and Thames. Here the distinctive features of the medieval world developed—a buildup of technological competence, self-confidence, and accelerated change—which after 1500 enabled Europe to invade and colonize the rest of the world. In that long process of global expansion the forest and the wealth released from it played a central part.

Massive deforestation must also have happened in China, but the detail is murky. The population rose from about 65–80 million in 1400 CE to 270 million in 1770, and land in agriculture quadrupled. Large swaths of the forested lands in the central and southern provinces were certainly engulfed by an enormous migration of peoples from the north.

Modern World (1500–c. 1900)

During the roughly four hundred years from 1492 to about 1900, Europe burst out of its continental confines with far-reaching consequences for the global forests. Its capitalistic economy commoditized nearly all it found, creating wealth out of nature, whether it be land, trees, animals, plants, or people. Enormous strains were put on the global forest resource by a steadily increasing population (c. 400 million in 1500 to 1.65 billion in 1900) and also by rising demands for raw materials and food with urbanization and industrialization, first in Europe and, after the mid-nineteenth century, in the United States. In the mainly temperate neo-European areas, settler societies were planted and created. Permanent settlement began in earnest by the 1650s after the near elimination of the indigenes by virulent Old World pathogens, like smallpox, measles, and influenza. The imported Old World crops and stock flourished wonderfully. The dominant ethos of freehold tenure, dispersed settlement, "improvement," and personal and political freedom led to a rapid and successful expansion of settlement, although much environmentally destructive exploitation also occurred. Tree growth was considered a good indicator of soil fertility in all pioneer societies, and the bigger the trees the quicker they were felled to make way for farms. The United States was the classic example. The pioneer farmer, through "sweat, skill and strength," (Ellis 1946, 73) was seen as the heroic subduer of a sullen and untamed wilderness. Clearing was widespread, universal, and an integral part of rural life; about 460,300 square kilometers of dense forest were felled by about 1850 and a further 770,900 square kilometers by

1910. "Such are the means," marveled the French traveler, the Marquis de Chastellux in 1789,

> by which North-America, which one hundred years ago was nothing but a vast forest, is peopled with three million of inhabitants. . . . Four years ago, one might have travelled ten miles in the woods . . . without seeing a single habitation. (Chastellux 1789, 29)

It was one of the biggest deforestation episodes ever. A similar process of the pioneer hacking out a life for himself and family in the forest occurred in Canada, New Zealand, South Africa, and Australia. In Australia, for example, nearly 400,000 square kilometers of the southeastern forests and sparse woodland were cleared by the early twentieth century.

In the subtropical and tropical forests, European systems of exploitation led to the harvesting of indigenous tree crops (e.g., rubber, hardwoods), and in time to the systematic replacement of the original forest by "plantation" crops grown by slave or indentured labor. Classic examples of this were the highly profitable crops of sugar in the West Indies, coffee and sugar in the subtropical coastal forests of Brazil, cotton and tobacco in the southern United States, tea in Sri Lanka and India, and later rubber in Malaysia and Indonesia. In eastern Brazil, over half of the original 780,000 square kilometers of the huge subtropical forest that ran down the eastern portions of the country had disappeared by 1950 through agricultural exploitation and mining. In the state of São Paulo alone, the original 204,500 square kilometers of forest were reduced to 45,500 square kilometers by 1952.

Peasant proprietors were not immune to the pressures of the global commercial market. Outstanding was the expansion of peasant cultivation in lower Burma (encouraged by British administrators) between 1850 and 1950, which resulted in the destruction of about 35,000 square kilometers of imposing equatorial (*kanazo*) rain forests and their replacement by rice. Throughout the Indian subcontinent the early network of railways meant an expansion of all types of crops by small-scale farmers, often for cash, that led to forest clearing everywhere.

The Appleton Paper Mills in Wisconsin, circa 1898. Deforestation accelerated in the twentieth century as the demand for paper and wood products boomed, and the need to clear land for factories and cities shrank forests further. Library of Congress.

Uncolonized Asian societies exploited their forests just as vigorously, commercially, and uncaringly as did their European counterparts. There is evidence from, for example, southwestern India and Hunan Province in south-central China from the sixteenth century onward to show that the commercialization of the forest was well established. In the former, permanent indigenous agricultural settlements existed side by side with shifting cultivation, and village councils regulated forest exploitation by agriculturalists. The forest was not regarded as a community resource; larger landowners dominated forest use locally. Scarce commodities such as sandalwood, ebony, cinnamon, and pepper were under state and/or royal control. In Hunan, a highly centralized administration encouraged land clearance in order to enhance local state revenues so as to increase the tax base and support a bigger bureaucracy and militia. State encouragement was also given to migrations into the forested hill country of south China later on. Simply, forests everywhere were being exploited and were diminishing in size as a response to increasing population numbers and increasing complexity of society. In the subtropical world, change was just slower than that unleashed by the Europeans with their new aims, technologies, and intercontinental trade links, but no less severe. Measures of destruction are hard to come by, but between 1860 and 1950 in South and Southeast Asia, 216,000 square kilometers of forest and 62,000 square kilometers of interrupted or open forest were destroyed for cropland.

During these centuries deforestation was also well underway in Europe itself, which was being colonized internally. This was particularly true in the mixed-forest zone of central European Russia, where over 67,000 square kilometers were cleared between around 1700 and 1914.

The insatiable demand in all societies for new land to grow crops and settle agriculturalists has been matched by a rising demand for the products of the forest themselves. For example, the European quest for strategic naval stores (masts, pitch, tar, turpentine) and ships' timbers made major inroads into the forests of the Baltic littoral from the fifteenth century onward and those of the southern United States after about 1700. Alternative construction timbers like teak and mahogany were utilized from the tropical hardwood forests since the beginning of the eighteenth century.

The Last Hundred Years

The pace of transformation increased during the first half of the twentieth century. In the Western world demands for timber accelerated. New uses (pulp, paper, packaging, plywood, chipboard) and relatively little substitution of other materials boosted use, while traditional uses in energy production, construction, and industry continued to loom large. The indispensable and crucial nature of timber in many Western economies gave it a strategic value akin to that of petroleum in economies today. In the tropical world the massive expansion of population by more than half a billion on a base of 1.1 billion resulted in extensive clearing for subsistence, accompanied by an expansion of commercial plantation agriculture. In all perhaps 2.35 million square kilometers of tropical forest were lost between 1920 and 1949. The only encouraging feature in the global picture during these years was the reversion of farmland to forest. This had begun in the eastern United States with the abandonment of "difficult" and hard-to-farm lands in New England in favor of easier-to-farm open grasslands, and continued with the abandonment of some cotton and tobacco growing lands in the southern States. A similar story unfolded in northern Europe with "marginal" farms.

The most publicized deforestation—the deforestation everyone thinks of when the word is mentioned—occurred after 1950. Since then the temperate coniferous softwood forests have about kept up with the demands of industrial societies for supplies of timber and pulp. But the focus of deforestation has shifted firmly to the tropical world. Here, better health and nutrition have resulted in a population explosion and an additional 3.5–4.0 billion people. These are often landless people who have moved deeper into the remaining forests and farther up steep forested slopes. They have no stake in the land and therefore

The unrecorded past is none other than our old friend, the tree in the primeval forest which fell without being heard. • **Barbara Tuchman (1912–1989)**

little commitment to sustainable management. In addition chain saws and trucks have moved felling from the province of the large firm to the enterprising individual. Since 1950 about 7.5 million square kilometers of tropical forests have disappeared, Central and Latin America being classic examples. In addition, the tropical hardwood forests are being logged out for constructional timber at a great rate, while wood is cut for domestic fuel in prodigious quantities in Africa, India, and Latin America. Globally, fuel wood–cutting now roughly equals saw timber extraction—about 1.8 billion cubic meters annually compared to 1.9 billion cubic meters. Cutting wood for fuel is forecast to rise rapidly in line with world population increases.

The Future

The long and complex chronicle of deforestation is a significant portion of world history. It is one of the main causes of terrestrial transformation, whereby humankind has modified the world's surface, a process that is now reaching critical proportions. One thing is certain: with an ever-increasing world population (another 2–3 billion by 2020), many will want to exploit resources and the process of deforestation will not end. Others will want to restrict forest use and preserve it. The tensions between exploitation and preservation will be intense.

Michael WILLIAMS

Deceased, formerly of Oriel College

See also Timber; Trees

Further Reading

Bechmann, R. (1990). *Trees and man: The forest in the Middle Ages* (K. Dunham, Trans.). St. Paul, MN: Paragon House.

Bogucki, P. I. (1988). *Forest farmers and stockholders: Early agriculture and its consequences in north-central Europe.* Cambridge, U.K.: Cambridge University Press.

Chastellux, F. J., marquis de. (1789). *Travels in North America in the Years 1780, 1781, and 1782* (Vol. 1). New York: White, Gallacher and White.

Darby, H. C. (1956). The clearing of the woodland in Europe. In W. L. Thomas (Ed.), *Man's role in changing the face of the Earth* (pp. 183–216). Chicago: University of Chicago Press.

Dean, W. (1995). *With broadax and firebrand: The destruction of the Brazilian Atlantic forest.* Berkeley: University of California Press.

Ellis, D. M. (1946). *Landlords and farmers in Hudson-Mohawk Region, 1790-1850.* Ithaca, NY: Cornell University Press.

Meiggs, R. (1982). *Trees and timber in the ancient Mediterranean world.* Oxford, U.K.: Oxford University Press.

Nielsen, R. (2006). *The little green handbook: Seven trends shaping the future of our planet.* New York: Picador.

White, L., Jr. (1962). *Medieval technology and social change.* Oxford, U.K.: Oxford University Press.

Williams, M. (1989). *The Americans and their forests.* Cambridge, U.K.: Cambridge University Press.

Williams, M. (2003). *Deforesting the Earth: From prehistory to global crisis.* Chicago: University of Chicago Press.

Desertification

Experts disagree over the current rate at which arable land is becoming desert, to what extent human activities are responsible, and whether the process is reversible. Yet events such as the Dust Bowl of the 1930s in the United States are compelling evidence of a link between desertification and human misuse of the land.

Desertification is the process of land becoming desert, as from human mismanagement or climate change. It remains a controversial issue with regard to definition, nature, rate of spread, irreversibility, and causation. Nonetheless, it is a serious example of land degradation in dry lands. Deserts have repeatedly expanded and contracted during the last few millions of years in response to climate changes, but their margins are now being affected by a suite of increasing human pressures that depletes soil and vegetation resources.

Desertification was first used as a term, but not formally defined, by a French forester named "Aubreville" in 1949, and for some years the term *desertization* was defined as "the spread of desert-like conditions in arid or semi-arid areas, due to man's influence or to climatic change" (Rapp 1974, 3).

Different experts have defined *desertification* according to its cause. Some definitions stress the importance of anthropogenic (human-caused) actions. The scientist Harold E. Dregne says, "Desertification is the impoverishment of terrestrial ecosystems under the impact of man. It is the process of deterioration in these ecosystems that can be measured by reduced productivity of desirable plants, undesirable alterations in the biomass [the amount of living matter] and the diversity of the micro and macro fauna and flora,

accelerated soil deterioration, and increased hazards for human occupancy" (Dregne 1986, 6–7).

Other studies acknowledge the possible importance of natural climatic controls but give them a relatively lesser role. In a report for the U.S. Department of the Interior / Bureau of Land Management, *desertification* is defined as "the sustained decline and/or destruction of the biological productivity of arid and semi arid lands caused by man made stresses, sometimes in conjunction with natural extreme events. Such stresses, if continued or unchecked, over the long term may lead to ecological degradation and ultimately to desert-like conditions" (Sabadell et al. 1982, 7).

Other experts are more even-handed with respect to the balance of anthropogenic and natural causes: "A simple and graphic meaning of the word 'desertification' is the development of desert like landscapes in areas which were once green. Its practical meaning . . . is a sustained decline in the yield of useful crops from a dry area accompanying certain kinds of environmental change, both natural and induced" (Warren and Maizels 1976, 1).

Experts are not sure how extensive desertification is or how fast it is progressing. The lack of agreement on the former process makes determining the latter difficult, prompting some to remark, "Desertification will remain an ephemeral concept to many people until better estimates of its extent and rate of increase can be made on the basis of actual measurements" (Grainger 1990, 145).

The United Nations Environment Programme (UNEP) has played a pivotal role in the promotion of desertification as an environmental issue, as is made evident by this statement from *The World*

The name written in the sand by this Mauri man is "Arbweir," the ancient name for Chinguetti. Founded in the tenth century, and considered the seventh holy city of Islam, the old city is now buried by sand. FAO of the United Nations.

Environment 1972–1992: "Desertification is the main environmental problem of arid lands, which occupy more than 40 per cent of the total global land area. At present, desertification threatens about 3.6 billion hectares—70 percent of potentially dry lands, or nearly one-quarter of the total land area of the world. These figures exclude natural hyper-arid deserts. About one sixth of the world's population is affected" (Tolba and El-Kholy 1992, 134).

Some scholars, however, have been critical of UNEP's views on the amount of land that is desertified. They state: "The bases for such data are at best inaccurate and at worst centered on nothing better than guesswork. The advancing desert concept may have been useful as a publicity tool but it is not one that represents the real nature of desertification processes" (Thomas and Middleton 1994, 160).

Despite its critics, UNEP continues to support issues of desertification. UNEP helped established the U.N. Convention to Combat Desertification (UNCCD), which holds an international World Day to Combat Desertification and Drought on 17 June. These worldwide annual events supported by UNEP and the UNCCD seek to raise awareness and promotion of desertification issues. In 2006, UNEP focused the international World Environment Day (held annually on 5 June) on desertification issues with the theme "Don't Desert Drylands."

Rates of Desertification

Experts have conducted relatively few reliable studies of the rate of desert advance. In 1975, the British ecologist Hugh Lamprey attempted to measure the shift of vegetation zones in the Sudan in Africa and concluded that a portion of the Sahara Desert in Sudan had advanced by 90 to 100 kilometers between 1958 and 1975, with an average rate of about 5.5 kilometers per year. On the basis of analysis of remotely sensed data and ground observations, however, other scholars found limited evidence that this ad-vance had taken place (Helldén 1984). One problem is that substantial fluctuations in vegetation production may take place from year to year. Meteorological satellite observations of green biomass production levels on the southern margins of the Sahara Desert have revealed such fluctuations.

The International Soil Reference Center in the Netherlands conducted a global assessment by soil degradation on behalf of UNEP during the late 1980s and early 1990s. The center used a Geographical Information System to analyze data collected through a clearly defined, but largely qualitative, methodology. Despite its flaws, the Global Assessment on Human Induced Soil Degradation (GLASOD) provided a database through which experts could assess susceptible dry land soil degradation in terms of spatial distribution, contributory degradation processes, and relationships to land use.

The GLASOD estimated that during the late 1980s and early 1990s approximately 1 billion hectares, equivalent to 20 percent of the susceptible dry lands, had experienced accelerated soil degradation caused by human activities. Water erosion was identified as the major physical process of degradation in 48 percent of this area and wind erosion in 39 percent.

Chemical degradation (including salinization) was dominant in just 10 percent of the area, and physical changes such as compaction and crusting in just 4 percent. The severity of degradation was described by the GLASOD as strong or extreme in 4 percent of the susceptible dry lands. This figure relates to lands that have had their original biotic (relating to living organisms) functions of the soil destroyed and that are irreclaimable without major restorative measures.

The spatial character of desertification is also the subject of controversy. The spread of desertlike conditions is not, as popularly supposed, an advance over a broad front in the way that a wave overwhelms a beach. Rather, it is like a rash that tends to be localized around settlements. Fundamentally, "the extension of desert-like conditions tends to be achieved through a process of accretion from without, rather than through expansionary forces acting from within the deserts" (Mabbutt 1985, 2). This distinction is important because it influences perceptions of appropriate remedial or combative strategies.

Experts have debated whether desertification is irreversible. In many cases where ecological conditions are favorable because of the existence of such factors as deep, sandy soils, vegetation recovers after excess pressures are eliminated. The speed of recovery depends on how advanced deterioration is, the size of the area that is degraded, the nature of the soils and moisture resources, and the nature of local vegetation. Much desert vegetation is adapted to drought and to harsh conditions and often has inbuilt adaptations that enable a rapid response to improved circumstances.

Nonetheless, long-term monitoring elsewhere tends to reveal that in certain circumstances recovery is so slow and so limited that it may be appropriate to talk of "irreversible desertification." For example, in southern Tunisia tracks made by tanks and wheeled vehicles during World War II are still apparent on the ground and in the devastated and unregenerated vegetation.

Causes of Desertification

The causes of desertification remain controversial. Experts have asked whether it is the result of temporary serious droughts, long-term climatic change,

A man pumps water from an artesian well in North Africa to irrigate the fields. Adequate irrigation in this arid region is necessary for buffalo breeding. Courtesy of the Food and Agriculture Organization of the United Nations.

or human actions degrading the biological environments in arid zones. No doubt severe droughts do take place, and their effects become worse as human and domestic animal populations increase. The devastating drought in the Sahel (the semidesert southern fringe of the Sahara Desert) from the mid-1960s caused greater ecological stress than the droughts of 1910–1915 and 1944–1948, largely because of increasing anthropogenic pressures.

Experts have discredited the concept that climate is deteriorating through postglacial progressive desiccation. However, numerous studies of meteorological data (which in some cases date back as far as 130–150 years) do not allow experts to reach any firm conclusions on systematic long-term changes in rainfall, and the case for climatic deterioration—whether natural or aggravated by humans—is not proven. Indeed, Rapp wrote that after consideration of the evidence for the role of climatic change in desertification his conclusion was "that the reported desertization northwards and southwards from the Sahara could not be explained by a general trend towards drier climate during this century" (Rapp 1974, 29).

Woodcutting is a serious cause of vegetative decline around the area to the south of the Sahara. Many people depend on wood for domestic uses, and the collection of wood for charcoal and firewood is especially serious in the vicinity of large urban centers. Likewise, the recent drilling of wells has enabled rapid multiplication of domestic livestock numbers and large-scale destruction of the vegetation in a radius of 15–30 kilometers around them. Given this localization of degradation, amelioration schemes such as local tree planting may be partially effective, but ideas of planting massive belts as a *cordon sanitaire* (protective barrier) along the desert edge (whatever that is) would not halt deterioration of the land beyond this belt. The deserts are not invading from without; the land is deteriorating from within.

Clearly, therefore, a combination of human activities (e.g., deforestation, overgrazing, and plowing) with occasional series of dry years leads to the presently observed desertification. The process also seems to be fiercest not in desert interiors, but rather on the less arid marginal areas around them. The combination of circumstances particularly conducive to desert expansion can be found in semiarid and subhumid areas—where precipitation is frequent and intense enough to cause rapid erosion of unprotected soils and where humans are prone to mistake short-term economic gains under temporarily favorable climatic conditions for long-term stability.

These tendencies toward bad land-use practices partly result from the imposition of state boundaries on many traditional nomadic societies, restricting their migration routes, or from schemes implemented to encourage the nomads to become sedentary. Some of their traditional grazing lands have been taken over by cash-crop farmers. The traditional ability to migrate enabled pastoral nomads and their stock to make flexible use of available resources according to season and yearly variations in rainfall and to move away from regions that had become exhausted after a long period of use. As soon as migrations are stopped and settlements imposed, such options are closed, and severe degradation occurs.

People have suggested not only that deserts are expanding because of human activity, but also that the deserts themselves were created by human activity. People have proposed, for example, that the Thar Desert of northwest India is a postglacial and possibly a postmedieval creation, and others have suggested that the vast Sahara Desert itself is largely human made (Ehrlich and Ehrlich 1970). This proposal is not accurate. The Sahara, although it has fluctuated in extent, is many millions of years old, predates human life, and is the result of its climatic situation.

Possibly the most famous case of desertification associated with soil erosion by deflation was the Dust Bowl of the 1930s in the United States. In part the Dust Bowl was caused by a series of unusually hot, dry years that depleted the vegetation cover and made the soils dry enough to be susceptible to wind erosion, but the effects of this drought were worsened by years of overgrazing, poor farming techniques, and the rapid expansion of wheat cultivation in the Great Plains. The number of cultivated hectares doubled during World War I as tractors (for the first time) were employed in the thousands. In Kansas alone the wheat area increased from less than 2 million hectares in 1910 to almost 5 million in 1919. After the war wheat cultivation continued apace, helped by the development of the combine harvester and government assistance. Over large areas the tough sod, which had exasperated earlier homesteaders, had given way to friable (easily crumbled or pulverized) soils of high erosion potential. Drought, acting on damaged soils, created the "black blizzards."

Dust storms are still a serious problem in parts of the United States. For example, in the San Joaquin Valley of California a dust storm caused extensive damage and erosion in 1977. More than 22 million metric tons of soil were stripped from grazing land within a twenty-four-hour period. Although the combination of drought and a high wind (as much as 300 kilometers per hour) provided the predisposing natural conditions for the stripping to occur, overgrazing and the general lack of windbreaks in the agricultural land played a more significant role. In addition, broad areas of land had recently been stripped of vegetation, leveled, or plowed up prior to planting. Other quantitatively less important factors included stripping of vegetation for urban expansion, extensive denudation of land in the vicinity of oilfields, and local denudation of land by vehicular recreation. Elsewhere in California dust yield has been considerably increased by mining of dry lake beds and by disturbance of playas (flat-floored bottoms of undrained desert basins that become at times shallow lakes).

A comparable acceleration of dust storm activity occurred in the former Soviet Union. After the "Virgin Lands" program of agricultural expansion during the

1950s, dust storm frequencies in the southern Omsk region increased on average by a factor of 2.5 and locally by factors of 5 to 6.

Desertification is not restricted to heavily populated lands with large agricultural and pastoral populations. As the examples of the U.S. Great Plains and California illustrate, high technology, non-labor-intensive land, and water use can also cause severe degradation.

Human-induced desertification is not new. Although people often focus on the Dust Bowl years of the 1930s and the current degradation of the Sahel, desertification has been the subject of great interest in the Mediterranean area since classical times. Likewise, some evidence indicates that more than four thousand years ago Mesopotamia was suffering from chemical degradation of soils and crop yield reductions as a consequence of the adoption and extension of irrigation. Nevertheless, land degradation is not the inevitable consequence of increasing population densities and land-use intensification, and many techniques are available for desert reclamation.

Andrew S. GOUDIE

St. Cross College

See also Climate Change; Deforestation; Deserts; Salinization; Water; Water Management

Further Reading

Coffey, M. (1978). The dust storms. *Natural History, 87*, 72–83.

Dregne, H. E. (1986). Desertification of arid lands. In F. El-Baz & M. H. A. Hassan (Eds.), *Physics of desertification* (pp. 4–34). Dordrecht, The Netherlands: Nijhoff.

Dregne, H. E., & Tucker, C. J. (1988). Desert encroachment. *Desertification Control Bulletin, 16*, 16–18.

Ehrlich, P. R., & Ehrlich, A. H. (1970). *Population, resources, environment: Issues in human ecology.* San Francisco: Freeman.

Gill, T. E. (1996). Eolian sediments generated by anthropogenic disturbance of playas: Human impacts on the geomorphic system and geomorphic impacts on the human system. *Geomorphology, 17*, 207–228.

Goudie, A. S. (Ed.). (1990). *Desert reclamation.* Chichester, U.K.: Wiley.

Goudie, A. S., & Middleton, N. J. (1992). The changing frequency of dust storms through time. *Climatic Change, 20*, 197–225.

Grainger, A. (1990). *The threatening desert: Controlling desertification.* London: Earthscan.

Grove, A. J., & Rackham, O. (2001). *The nature of Mediterranean Europe: An ecological history.* New Haven, CT: Yale University Press.

Helldén, V. (1984). Land degradation and land productivity monitoring—needs for an integrated approach. In A. Hjort (Ed.), *Land management and survival* (pp. 77–87). Uppsala, Sweden: Scandinavian Institute of African Studies.

Jacobsen, T., & Adams, R. M. (1958). Salt and silt in ancient Mesopotamian agriculture. *Science, 128*, 1251–1258.

Mabbutt, J. A. (1985). Desertification of the world's rangelands. *Desertification Control Bulletin, 12*, 1–11.

Marsh, G. P. (1864). *Man and nature.* New York: Scribner.

Middleton, N. J., & Thomas, D. S. G. (1997). *World atlas of desertification* (2nd ed.). London: Arnold.

Nicholson, S. (1978). Climatic variations in the Sahel and other African regions during the past five centuries. *Journal of Arid Environments, 1*, 3–24.

Rapp, A. (1974). *A review of desertification in Africa—water, vegetation and man.* Stockholm, Sweden: Secretariat for International Ecology.

Sabadell, J. E., Risley, E. M., Jorgensen, H. T., & Thornton, B. S. (1982). *Desertification in the United States: Status and issues.* Washington, DC: Bureau of Land Management, Department of the Interior.

Thomas, D. S. G., & Middleton, N. J. (1994). *Desertification: Exploding the myth.* Chichester, U.K.: Wiley.

Tiffen, M., Mortimore, M., & Gichuki, F. (1994). *More people, less erosion: Environmental recovery in Kenya.* Chichester, U.K.: Wiley.

Tolba, M. K., & El-Kholy O. A. (Eds.). (1992). *The world environment 1972–1992: Two decades of challenge.* London: UNEP Chapman and Hall.

United Nations Environmental Programme (UNEP). (2006). *Don't desert drylands: United Nations environment programme message on world environmental day.* Retrieved December 24, 2009, from http://www.unep.org/wed/2006/downloads/PDF/UNEPWEDMessage06_eng.pdf

Warren, A., & Maizels, J. K. (1976). *Ecological change and desertification.* London: University College Press.

Deserts

Two types of deserts—tropical and temperate —occupy approximately one third of the planet. While thought to be vast areas of limited resources, the usefulness of arid climates throughout history has depended on the social interaction between the climate and a given society. Analyzing hunter-gatherer and nomadic pastoralist societies has given insight to the influence that desert regions have had on human development.

Deserts cover approximately 30 percent of Earth's surface. A rudimentary classification divides them into two broad types: hot deserts (tropical and subtropical deserts) and temperate or midlatitude deserts. Hot deserts, in which temperatures remain high or very high all year round, are found around the tropics in both hemispheres between latitudes 20° and 30° north and south. In temperate deserts, temperatures differ widely between winter and summer (in winter there is often at least one month in which the mean temperature falls below 5°C, and snow may accumulate for several days). Such deserts are found mainly in the interior of Eurasia and in the Southwest of North America. Besides these two broad classes there are other types that in part coincide with tropical deserts, but whose formation is affected by different factors such as cold coastal currents.

Despite their great diversity, the Earth's arid zones share some common characteristics, principally their excessive dryness, which is the result of high temperatures and low, irregular rainfall. The irregularity of rainfall explains another typical characteristic of dry ecosystems: large fluctuations of biomass above and below very low mean values.

Apart from deep subterranean resources, which in most cases remained unexploited until the twentieth century, deserts provide two important kinds of natural resources: scarce but relatively long-lasting water and food resources, and episodic but abundant resources (such as a sudden deluge of rain after which a pasture may develop). In any event, it must be emphasized that it is the interaction, by way of technology and social relations, between a given society and an arid environment that causes certain aspects of a desert to be perceived as either limitations or as resources.

Hunter-Gatherer Societies

Some hunter-gatherer societies of semiarid zones survived into the nineteenth century in America and into the twentieth century in Australia and southwestern Africa. In general these societies had little ability to modify their environment (although they sometimes did so with fire), and they depended on the spontaneous reproduction of spatially dispersed natural resources. They all displayed an astonishing knowledge of their ecosystems and were able to exploit a large variety of ecological niches, which constituted their productive base. They lived in small groups around temporary sources of water. When the water dried up or the resources situated at a short distance from the pool ran out, they were obliged to move away and find another source of water, which means they were constantly on the move. Lack of water was an almost absolute constraint for them; if food was located too far from the water, they could not exploit it and therefore it did not constitute a resource. Different local groups maintained close kinship relations or alliances

Eugène-Alexis Girardet, *Caravan In The Desert*. Oil on canvas. Mobility and the lack of fixed settlements have always given great military advantages to desert peoples.

with neighboring groups in the same or nearby territories. When there was extreme drought or shortage of food, these social relations allowed them to move into territories occupied by their relatives and allies. It has been suggested that the enormous complexity in the kinship systems of some Australian Aborigines, which created strong ties of obligation among different groups, may have been a way of adapting to the uncertain nature of arid environments.

Nomadic Pastoralists

For thousands of years the typical way of life in the deserts of Eurasia and Africa (though not in those of America or Australia) has been that of nomadic pastoralism, a complex, sophisticated mode of subsistence that has played a major role in the history of the Old World. Most researchers believe that nomadic pastoralism arose at the edges of cultivable zones after the Neolithic advent of agriculture and domestication of animals, in regions that were too dry for the development of settled agriculture and cattle raising.

Nomadism specialized in exploiting an ecological niche that the mixed economies (sedentary agriculture and stockbreeding) could not take advantage of. It seems that almost all nomad societies originated directly or indirectly in the Near East. This region, which suffers acute summer droughts or has clearly arid climates, was inhabited by wild animals (goats, sheep, dromedaries) that, owing to their specific characteristics, fulfilled two conditions: they were easily domesticated and were more or less naturally adapted (or could become so, with the help of man) to the arid or semiarid environmental conditions. The other early agricultural and cattle-raising centers of the world, in Asia and America, were not populated with these kinds of animals. Some argue that pastoral nomadism arose independently in the Sahara, but that theory continues to be controversial.

A secondary center of nomadic pastoralism may have had its origin in the steppes of southern Russia, where it would have emerged between the third and second millennia BCE in mixed-economy societies of eastern Europe. In the south of Russia, the horse, domesticated around 3000 BCE, gave herders of sheep and goats (which had originated in the Near East) great mobility. The theory is that the domestication of the Bactrian camel (between the third and second millennium BCE), which is similar to the dromedary but better adapted to cold winters, allowed nomads to penetrate the deserts of central Asia. The discovery of Caucasian mummies, some of them from the second millennium BCE, and of texts written in Indo-European languages in the desert of Taklimakan (in the northwestern Chinese region of Xinjiang) may testify to the extent of this movement.

Analyzing the way nomadic societies interact with the environment helps us to understand the great influence that arid and semiarid regions have exercised on the development of Eurasian and African civilizations. Nomadic pastoralism, as a mode of subsistence, is essentially unstable and expansionist. Herds undergo great fluctuations in size and composition in arid environments. Both ethnographic studies and computer techniques demonstrate the potentially explosive growth of a simple flock of sheep or goats.

The tall Saguaro cacti, pictured here outside Tucson, Arizona, bloom in May and June in the temperate deserts of the southwest United States. Photo by Jane M Sawyer (www.morguefile.com).

Nomadic societies exploit this potential in order to accumulate a lot of animals. From the standpoint of basic units of production, it is an intelligent and adaptive response to environmental fluctuations, but on a regional scale it prepares the way for social and ecological disaster. Assertions that nomads, although they do not consciously attempt to modify their environment, create their own steppes and deserts may contain a certain element of truth. The combination of sudden fluctuations and expansive tendencies gives rise to another of the most well-known aspects of nomadic societies: quick and radical shifts along migratory tracks, which sometimes historically appear as invasions or attacks on settled civilizations. It should be remembered that mobility and the lack of fixed settlements has always given great military advantages to desert peoples.

Nomads exploit their resources in small units of production (households or encampments), but, as with hunter-gatherers, these basic units are linked to each other, generally by means of kinship relations.

It is these links that form the basis of larger units when organizing migratory tracks, regulating rights of access to grazing land, and when facing environmental changes. It is membership in these higher-ranking units that in fact grants rights to territory and its resources. As in many hunter-gatherer societies, among nomads kinship relations have great importance because they operate like economic institutions. The manner in which hunter-gatherers and pastoral nomads relate to nature is very different, however. Whilst the hunter-gatherers exploit a great variety of ecological niches in different places and seasons, the nomads always exploit the same basic resource, pasture (either in different environmental zones or in the same one). Whereas the hunter-gatherer's territorial system is based on moving himself towards the resources, that of the nomad involves moving an entire infrastructure of production, with little regard to the regional availability of microresources (such as small mammals and birds, and wild nuts and fruit, all of which are important to hunter-gatherers). For

As a matter of fact, an ordinary desert supports a much greater variety of plants than does either a forest or a prairie. • **Ellsworth Huntington (1876–1947)**

the hunter-gatherer the great waterless spaces of the desert represent a constraint that prevents him from exploiting resources that are too remote from pools and streams. For the nomad, those spaces only represent a relative limitation, since he can travel long distances transporting water on his animals.

Trading Routes and Oases

From the Atlantic to western China, deserts form a gigantic arid belt that for centuries separated the principal civilizations of the Old World. The nomads, on their constant journeys in search of new pastures, discovered the routes that would allow Chinese silk to travel to Europe across the deserts of central Asia, and that would move gold, ivory, and slaves from tropical Africa to the Mediterranean across the Sahara. They became intermediaries operating between ecologically and culturally different regions, which allowed them to divert surpluses from the agrarian societies of Africa, Europe, and Asia to the arid lands. Thus there emerged, in the oases and at the edges of deserts, fabulously wealthy cities, such as Palmyra, Petra, Samarqand, Timbuktu (Tombouctou), and Almería, in extremely poor environments. The wealth of medieval Islam, which culturally unified the deserts of Asia and Africa, is very much connected with the control of trade between remote civilizations and with the irrigation systems in arid countries.

The oases, like islands in the sea, played a crucial role along the trading routes. But life in these landlocked islands would have been impossible without agriculture, and the main limiting factor for the growth of plants in deserts is water. What characterizes the agriculture of oases is the use of ingenious techniques and complex irrigation systems that permit the extraction and exploitation of water from surface aquifers. The expansion of the Arabs in the Middle Ages helped to spread hydraulic technologies and crops from different regions. The result was the appearance of agricultural ecosystems that were largely freed from the environmental constraints of arid climates, in which man was able to introduce species from different regions. Before the discovery of America the greatest relocation of vegetable species in history occurred precisely across the deserts and oases of Asia and Africa in the medieval Islamic world.

Juan GARCÍA LATORRE
Association for Landscape Research in Arid Zones

See also Desertification

Further Reading

Amin, S. (1972). Sullo sviluppo desiguale delle formazioni sociali. Milan: Terzo Mondo.

Barich, B. E. (1998). *People, water and grain: The beginnings of domestication in the Sahara and the Nile Valley.* (Studia Archaeologica No. 98.) Rome: "L'Erma" di Bretschneider.

Cloudsley-Thowson, J. L. (Ed.). (1984). *Sahara desert.* Oxford, U.K.: Pergamon Press.

Cremaschi, M., & Lernia, S. (Eds.). (1998). *Wadi Teshuinat: Palaeoenviroment and prehistory in south-western Fezzan (Lybian Sahara).* Florence, Italy: C.I.R.S.A.

Cribb, R. (1993). *Nomads in archaeology.* New York: Cambridge University Press.

Evenari, M., Schulze, E.-D., Lange, O. L. ,& Kappen, L. (1976). Plant production in arid and semi-arid areas. In O. L. Lange, L. Kappe, & E.-D. Schulze (Eds.), *Water and plant life* (pp. 439–451). Berlin: Springer-Verlag.

Godelier, M. (1984). *L'idéel et le matériel.* Paris: Librairie Arthème Fayard.

Gumilev, L. N. (1988). *Searches for an imaginary kingdom: The legend of the kingdom of Prester John.* Cambridge, U.K.: Cambridge University Press.

Harris, D. R. (Ed.). (1996). *The origins and spread of agriculture and pastoralism in Eurasia.* Washington, DC: Smithsonian Institution Press.

Howell, N. (1979). *Demography of the Dobe Arca Kung.* New York: Academic Press.

Hunter-Anderson, R. L. (1986). *Prehistoric adaptation in the American South-West.* Cambridge, U.K.: Cambridge University Press.

Jabbur, J. S. (1995). *The Bedouins and the desert.* New York: State University of New York Press.

Khazanov, A. M. (1984). *Nomads and the outside world.* Cambridge, U.K.: Cambridge University Press.

Lee, R. B. (1979). *The !Kung San: Men, women and work in a foraging society.* Cambridge, U.K.: Cambridge University Press.

McNeill, J. (2001). *Something new under the sun: An environmental history of the twentieth century.* London: Penguin History.

Renfrew, C. (1987). *Archaeology and language: The puzzle of Indo-European origins.* London: Jonathan Cape.

Schultz, J. (1995). *The ecozones of the world: The ecological divisions of the geosphere.* Berlin: Springer-Verlag.

Shmida, A., Evenari, M., & Noy-Meir, I. (1986). Hot deserts ecosystems: An integrated view. In M. Evenari, I. Noy-Meir, & D. W. Goodall (Eds.), *Hot deserts and arid shrublands* (Vol. B., pp. 379–387). Amsterdam: Elsevier.

Webb, J. L. (1995). *Desert frontier: Ecological and economic change along the western Sahel, 1600–1850.* Madison: University of Wisconsin Press.

West, N. E. (Ed.). (1983). *Temperate deserts and semi-deserts.* Amsterdam: Elsevier.

Diseases—Animal

Every disease that has caused epidemics and changed the philosophical traditions of societies throughout human history has originated in nonhuman animals and "jumped the species barrier" into humans. There is no meaningful separation between animal and human diseases when discussing the impact of disease on human history.

It is important to emphasize that because humans are mammals, diseases found in other nonhuman animals, especially other mammals, often cross readily into humans. The most important diseases are infectious and highly contagious. Noncontagious diseases have had little or no impact on history. By definition, infectious diseases are capable of spreading rapidly from infected to healthy individuals. Infected individuals either die or recover fully within a short period of time; those individuals who recover typically acquire immunity against further infection by the same illness.

Numerically, the single greatest documented epidemic in human history was an influenza outbreak that killed 40 million people at the end of World War I. The epidemic with the greatest recorded impact was the bubonic plague that killed over 25 percent of the people in Western Europe in the mid-fourteenth century. Despite a lack of documentation, however, the epidemics with the greatest overall impact both on human populations and history were the series of outbreaks that spread through the Americas shortly after contact with Europeans and their domestic animals. These epidemics spread through populations previously unexposed to the diseases of Eurasia, typically causing 90–95 percent mortality, especially within communities suffering from multiple traumas associated with colonialism—violence, slavery, subsistence collapse. Overall these diseases may have killed as many as 100 million people in the Americas.

Prominent examples of infectious diseases that have crossed from other animals into humans include smallpox, cholera, tuberculosis, bubonic plague, and influenza. Although AIDS represents a major potential health problem in the modern world, it is contagious, but neither infectious nor acute. In recent years there have been panics over other animal diseases such as hoof-and-mouth disease, Hanta virus, and so-called mad-cow disease, which may not be a disease in the usual sense at all. These pathological conditions are trivial compared to the impact of the other diseases listed, yet they have received more publicity, perhaps because of ignorance and media-inspired fear, combined with the fact that most people do not understand how various diseases are transmitted.

Most infectious animal diseases that jump to humans are caused by bacteria and viruses whose small size renders them highly volatile and transmissible as aerosols, hence more likely to be transmitted from one individual to another, which is the basis of contagion. A few diseases, such as malaria and sleeping sickness, are caused by protistans, single-celled eukaryotic organisms that are much larger than bacteria or viruses. The larger size of protistans means they cannot be transmitted as aerosols, and hence are transmitted primarily by injection, for example, through insect bites, rendering them much less infectious.

Most infectious disease organisms co-evolve in interactions with other nonhuman species. These

Le Marchand de Mort aux Rats (literally, "the merchant of death to rats," or, more colloquially, "the cat seller"). Rats have historically been carriers of human diseases, such as bubonic plague. Lithograph by Marlet.

nonhuman species have evolved an immune response to the disease-causing organisms, so they are not serious threats either to health or population numbers in their original host species. What renders most of infectious diseases so virulent in human populations is that when first exposed, humans have no evolved immune response to these pathogens; for example, smallpox is related to bovine pox, which causes minor problems in cattle but is often fatal in its mutated form in humans. Similarly, the AIDS virus is closely related to a viral infection that occurs in African primates, where it only causes mild influenza-like symptoms. Other examples include measles, which is closely related to the ungulate disease rinderpest; tuberculosis, which is closely related to a similar disease in cattle; and influenza, which is actually a complex of viral diseases derived repeatedly from similar pathogens occurring in pigs (swine flu) and birds such as ducks and chickens. Recently, malaria was added to this list when it was discovered that the human malarial parasite is closely related to a less virulent form in chimpanzees.

Contagious diseases that manage to cross the species barrier from nonhumans into humans have been a major factor shaping the history of Europe and Asia. A major difference between Europe and Asia as contrasted with the Americas and Africa is that Eurasian cultures domesticated and lived in close association with the animal species that served as the original hosts of these diseases. Domestication of ungulates, especially cattle and swine, set up scenarios whereby humans living on intimate terms with these animals were continually exposed to a wide range of epidemic diseases, which already afflicted the ungulate populations as minor problems. These diseases thrived particularly well in the high densities at which human societies kept cattle and pigs. Farmers are sedentary, living among their own sewage and that of the domestic animals with whom they live in an intimate and symbiotic fashion. In many agrarian societies farmers traditionally took cattle and pigs into their homes at night, both for warmth and to protect their livestock from predators. These conditions both prolong exposure and increase the likelihood of transmission of bacterial and viral pathogens.

Agriculture sustains much higher human densities than the hunting-gathering lifestyles that agriculture replaced. The large concentrations of humans resulting from increased urbanization provided fertile ground for the rapid spread of infectious diseases that originated in other species. Only within the last century did European cities achieve self-sustaining populations, because so many city dwellers died from disease that constant immigration from rural areas was required to sustain urban areas.

The Black Death

Development of world trade routes rapidly increased the dispersal rate of epidemic diseases. By Roman times the populations of Europe, Asia and North Africa had become a giant breeding ground for disease organisms that originated in domestic livestock. Smallpox reached Rome in the second century CE, killing millions of Roman citizens as the Plague of Antoninus. The animal-borne disease with the most profound impact on the course of history in Europe and Asia was bubonic plague. Spread by fleas that pick up the plague bacillus from the fur-bearing mammals that are their normal hosts, plague first appeared in Europe as the Plague of Justinian in 542–543 CE. The most devastating impact of the plague, however, occurred in fourteenth-century continental Europe where it killed as many as 25 million people and became known as the Black Death. In the British Isles alone, plague killed nearly 1.5 million people (25–40 percent of the total population). The main vector for the major outbreak of plague appears to have been furs brought from low-population density areas in central Asia with the opening of trade routes to China in the mid-fourteenth century.

One important, often unappreciated, consequence of the fourteenth-century plague was its profound impact on European philosophy and science. The prevailing European worldview prior to the mid-fourteenth century was mythic and symbolic, rooted in an idea of cyclical time, placing far more emphasis on links between human and nonhuman aspects of the world than did the worldviews that arose after the Black Death.

When plague arrived and began to have devastating impact on local populations, the knowledge base and techniques of this older philosophical tradition were pressed into service, including prayer, medicine based on sympathetic magic, and scapegoating (for example, witch burning). None of these

methods proved effective, and the inability to deal with the resulting death and devastation created both widespread panic and subsequent culture-wide depression. The impact of massive, inexplicable loss of life on a society cannot be overestimated. Belief in spiritual traditions and ways of understanding how the world works are crushed, leading to a sense of spiritual desolation.

The experience of the plague, described by some historians as the "greatest biological-environmental event in history" and the "equivalent of nuclear holocaust" by others, forced Western Europe to develop a new way of organizing its perception of reality. Within Christianity the plague led to loss of faith in a benevolent, heedful Creator, leading to persecution and scapegoating of "heretics," eventually leading to the beginnings of Protestantism and its images of a vengeful, wrathful God.

From a more scholarly perspective, response to the plague experience led to development of an intellectual tradition that separated mind from body, objective from subjective, and human from nature. This led to the beginnings of the Renaissance and development of the Western European "rationalist" scientific tradition, ultimately generating Cartesian dualism, the machine model/metaphor as a way of understanding nonhuman life, and the Baconian-Newtonian worldview. Thus the philosophical and spiritual impact of plague led directly to the "modern" rationalist approach in which experimentation and measurement substituted for observation and experience.

This new way of dealing with reality had numerous positive effects. For example, it led to increased sanitation, which reduced background levels of many contagious diseases. This division of reality into separate spheres of mind and matter provided a powerful methodology for the study and understanding of the "outside" world. It was largely inadequate, however, for understanding inner experience, the human mind, and our relationship with the world of our fellow life forms. Thus, although this dualistic view led to improved sanitation, there was no increased

understanding of the natural cycle of disease or the evolution of immune responses.

Old and New Worlds

The importance of animal diseases in shaping both human history and cultural attitudes toward the environment can be illustrated by comparing the Old World (Eurasia and North Africa) with the New World (North and South America). Many cultures in the Americas developed agriculture, but New World agriculture was based almost exclusively around agronomy, for example, corn, potatoes, squash, and beans, rather than on pastoralism, the herding and domestication of ungulates. The only domestic animals in the Americas were dogs, guinea pigs, guanacos (llama and alpaca), and turkeys. Unlike the domesticated ungulates of the Old World, these New World domesticates were never maintained at high densities, humans did not drink their milk, nor were any of these animals except dogs kept in close proximity to humans, as were livestock in the Old World.

Many New World cultures existed at densities comparable to those found in Europe. The Aztec capital of Tenochtitlán may have been one of the largest cities in the world during its heyday, and there is evidence that in central Mexico human populations surpassed the long-term carrying capacity of the land. Similarly, many other New World communities such as cities of the Mayans, Incas, and the Mound Builder cultures along the Mississippi and Ohio River valleys, lived at densities comparable to those found in European and Asian cultures. Despite high population densities, however, epidemic (crowd) diseases appear to be virtually nonexistent in these indigenous New World cultures; this is almost certainly attributable to the absence of domestic ungulates which have been the source of most epidemic diseases (other than bubonic plague) in Europe, Asia, and North Africa. Despite the apparent absence of epidemic diseases in the New World, such diseases may have played a role in the disappearance of some of the larger city complexes in the Americas, possibly because of poor sanitation.

New World Animal Diseases

One of the greatest ironies of the history of animal diseases is that the absence of nonhuman-derived contagious diseases and associated immune responses in New World humans was almost certainly the major factor in the successful invasion of the New World by Europeans and their worldview, which had been dramatically reshaped by their own experience with contagious disease only a few centuries earlier. Europeans sometimes occupied large parts of Africa and Asia, but without the decimating impact of introduced contagious diseases, they did not significantly reduce the indigenous human populations of these areas. As a consequence, as the age of colonialism draws to a close, the indigenous peoples of Africa and Asia have been able to regain social and political control of their own lands because they have remained numerically dominant in their homelands.

In contrast, the introduction of animal diseases into susceptible human populations in the Americas was much more devastating to indigenous human populations than it was during the plague in Europe. It is estimated that 90–95 percent of the indigenous human population of the Americas perished from introduced diseases.

Contrary to popular mythology this holocaust—referred to as the first, or microbial, phase of the European conquest of the Americas—did not begin with the "discovery of the Americas" by Columbus in 1492; it was initiated some time earlier by Basque whalers, Viking settlers, and English fishermen who began landing along the Atlantic coast of the Americas hundreds of years before Columbus arrived in the Caribbean and before other Spanish explorers (conquistadors) arrived in the New World. There is evidence that some tribes originally living along the Atlantic Ocean retreated inland in an effort to escape epidemics that devastated their populations well before the arrival of Cristóbal Colón at the end of the fifteenth century.

Despite the success of supposed conquistadors like Cortez and Pizarro, it was smallpox that really led to the collapse of the Aztec and Inca empires. Cortez's

The Cow Pock — or — the Wonderful Effects of the New Inoculation! — Vide. the Publications of ẙ Anti-Vaccine Society

"The Wonderful Effects of the New Inoculation!" by J. Gillray. Cow Pox (better known today as smallpox) decimated the indigenous populations of North and South America when European explorers introduced the disease.

initial 1519 foray into the Aztec civilization was much less successful than his subsequent 1520 effort after smallpox arrived in Tenochtitlán. By the early seventeenth century the indigenous population of Mexico had experienced devastation exceeding 90 percent, falling from an estimated 20 million to less than 2 million. The impact of the disease was demoralizing and crushed the ability of the Aztecs to resist Cortez. Similarly smallpox arrived in Inca territory in 1526, setting up the opportunity for Pizarro's successful "invasion" in 1531.

There is recorded evidence that 90 percent or more of the indigenous populations were wiped out by these new contagious diseases that arrived with both Europeans and their symbiotic nonhumans. In one well-documented example, the Mandans, one of the most elaborate of the Great Plains cultures, more than 95 percent of their population died after the arrival of smallpox via a Missouri riverboat in 1837.

Even given these impacts, however, it is likely that New World populations would have rebounded had their land not remained permanently occupied after European invasions and the subsequent continued colonialism that resulted.

The introduction of alien diseases had a devastating impact on the indigenous peoples of the Americas. If the deaths of 20 to 40 percent of local populations in Europe as a result of plague caused restructuring and rethinking of the role of humans in the world, it is difficult to imagine the spiritual, social, and philosophical impact of the loss of 90 to 95 percent of a population, as occurred in many indigenous peoples of the Americas.

Disease is a major factor in limiting rates of population growth; in fact populations free of the impact of diseases typically outstrip those subject to disease. Indigenous Americans appeared relatively free of epidemic disease prior to the arrival of Europeans.

As a consequence indigenous populations had not evolved any immunity to contagious diseases. They did not lack the ability to produce immune responses; instead, the devastation appeared to result from the way in which indigenous populations were exposed to contagion. The major killers of indigenous Americans—smallpox and influenza—were lethal to persons primarily from fifteen to forty years of age, hence the most valuable and productive members of a population, both culturally and demographically. These diseases typically arrived in clusters, punctuated by brief interludes of respite. Thus communities might be ravaged by a series of three or four diseases, followed by a period of remission; communities might subsequently be hit by another bout of a new disease or set of diseases. This combination of periodicity of events with the plurality of the diseases reduced the ability to evolve immune responses.

This pattern generated extreme psychological and spiritual stress. Unable to prevent disease or care for themselves or loved ones, abandoned by kin and other tribal members fleeing the epidemic (and in the process often carrying it to other peoples and communities), many individuals and groups simply gave up hope. Many engaged in activities that only hastened their deaths, such as sweats followed by immersion in cold water. The inability of their traditional holistic methods to treat diseases and control these contagions caused them to lose faith in their healers and medicine people and also to abandon traditional spiritual practices and ceremonies. Because the European invaders had developed some immunity to these diseases, many indigenous peoples assumed that European spiritual and philosophical traditions were superior to their own, which in many cases led to acceptance and adoption of Christianity and its tenets.

The apparent failure of indigenous spiritual traditions, combined with the introduction of new goods and materials, led indigenous peoples to abandon centuries-old traditions of dealing with the natural world, which were based on respect, connection, and conservation. Some peoples may even have blamed the wildlife and the natural world for the epidemics, because it appears that many indigenous peoples associated disease with wildlife and developed cultural traditions that were assumed to minimize the likelihood and impact of disease. For example, the Cherokee assumed that disrespectful treatment of killed deer could lead to crippling illness, such as Lyme disease, which produces crippling effects. The Cherokee blamed the appearance of new diseases on an imbalance in the cosmos caused by failure on their part to perform their rituals correctly. Similarly the Anishinaabe (Chippewa, Ojibway) peoples apparently developed the Mediwiwin healing society and related ceremonies in response to diseases they associated with wildlife, but the diseases were more likely the results of pre-Columbian contact with Europeans.

Affect on Nonhuman Species

Not only humans suffered as a result of the introduction of these diseases. Indigenous peoples depended on many natural populations of animals as sources of food and clothing, including deer, caribou, moose, bison, and beaver, that also experienced massive die-offs from west of Hudson Bay to the Rocky Mountains during the latter part of the eighteenth century. These deaths probably resulted from disease introduced by Europeans through their domestic animals. It is worth noting that these die-offs were primarily among ungulate populations, which would have been most susceptible to the ungulate-borne contagious diseases characteristic of Europe and Asia. New World carnivores, such as wolves and bears, appeared relatively unaffected by these illnesses, but they suffered as a result of the loss of their ungulate food supplies.

In addition to the impact of disease, additional damage was inflicted upon natural populations of animals when indigenous people destroyed animal populations because of an apparent antipathy towards animals, whom were assumed to have broken their covenants with humans by infecting them with disease. Thus one ironic consequence of the introduction of nonhuman-derived diseases was the destruction of cultural traditions based on respect for nonhumans. Most, if not all, indigenous cultures of

North America had philosophical traditions where nonhumans were regarded as creator spirits, and the concept of relatedness was based upon ecological relationships. It has been argued that the devastating impact of introduced disease on these cultures caused them to turn on their nonhuman relatives, allowing some tribes to wipe out local populations of beaver, deer, bison, and wolves, in order to trade furs for European goods and metal.

European Tradition and the Natural World

The invading European tradition, derived primarily from English and Scots cultures, had a very different relationship with the natural world, especially as a result of the Renaissance and the rationalist tradition, which worked to separate itself from any association with the natural world, except as a resource for exploitation. Protestant Christian sects that appeared in western Europe towards the end of the Renaissance (during the Reformation) developed philosophical traditions that offered no encouragement for investigation into the ways of God's creatures. God had given humans "dominion" over nonhumans, providing sufficient justification for any action regarding the natural world.

Europeans regarded mountainous country as unpleasant and dangerous, and forests were considered to be even worse. That these places were wild, hence untamed, was sufficient to trigger terror and hostility in western Europeans. The wild (natural world) was so unreasonably fearsome that encroachment of wild creatures into the human domain was highly alarming. A bee flying into a cottage or a bird rapping at the window was enough to frighten people. The English House of Commons rejected a bill in 1604 because a jackdaw flew through the chamber during the speech of its sponsor.

This difference in response to the nonhuman (natural) world continues to manifest itself today in contemporary responses to animal-borne disease. These responses are often extreme in comparison to the actual threat. The most egregious response in recent years has been the slaughter of hundreds of thousands of farm animals, particularly in the British Isles, in response to minor outbreaks of hoof-and-mouth disease and the sporadic and highly unusual occurrence of so-called mad-cow disease.

In the case of hoof-and-mouth disease, the threat is almost exclusively economic. There is little evidence that hoof-and-mouth disease represents any serious threat to human health. Still the economic threat is deemed sufficient enough to destroy hundreds of thousands of animals, mostly because the possibility exists that they may have been exposed to the disease. Can any moral being imagine such a draconian solution if the animals exposed to a potential contagion were *Homo sapiens*, rather than ungulates? Similarly, wild bison that stray beyond the borders of America's Yellowstone National Park are summarily slaughtered by agents of the state of Montana on the grounds that these animals might act as reservoirs for the cattle disease brucellosis. The irony in this case is that brucellosis is a disease that evolved in Old World bovids and was introduced into America along with cattle. No bison has ever shown the symptoms of brucellosis, yet the fact that a low percentage of bison test positive for exposure to the pathogen is deemed sufficient reason to kill them.

The response to mad cow disease, more properly called bovine spongiform encephalopathy (BSE), is even more absurd. BSE appears to be one of a group of related pathological conditions that may be caused by prions that appear to be protein molecules capable of self-replication. Other diseases in this category are scrapie in sheep and both kuru and Creutzfeldt-Jakob disease in humans. Such pathological conditions impact the central nervous system (CNS) and gradually destroy the brain. The damage to the CNS is what produces the symptoms that have disrespectfully led to this condition being designated with the term *mad cow*. A far better and more accurate term would be *acutely distressed cow*. These apparently prion-based conditions are not directly communicable and can only be passed through consumption of CNS tissue including brain and spinal cord. The only reason these conditions appeared to spread in the United States and

England is because slaughterhouses in those countries use "wastes" remaining after butchering to be ground up and added to cattle feed as a protein supplement.

In humans it is obvious that only through consuming CNS material can humans become infected. Outbreaks of kuru in New Guinea are clearly related to the cultural tradition of consuming the brains of other humans as part of a cannibalistic tradition. In England, BSE-type syndromes have shown up in humans who consumed low-grade commercial hamburgers. It seems obvious that banning the use of the waste products of slaughterhouses in both hamburger for human consumption and in cattle feed could stop any possible outbreak, yet commercial pressures have slowed or prevented such moves. Still, the total number of BSE human victims numbers less than twenty, and there is little likelihood of an outbreak or of a human contracting BSE through eating regular beef in the form of roasts or steaks.

Hanta virus is a rodent-borne viral pathogen. There is actually an entire class of Hanta-like viruses in a variety of murid rodents. The one described as Hanta virus appears to have only one species—deer mice, or *Peromyscus maniculatus*—as its primary host; it does not appear to cause significant health problems in deer mice. In humans, however, this virus causes pneumonia-like symptoms that result in death about 50 percent of the time. This disease is well-known to indigenous peoples of the American Southwest and may be one of the reasons that traditional Diné (Navajo) people destroy a hogan after a person has died in it. In recent years this disease has caused a minor panic in the United States because deer mice are a widespread, common rodent. Hanta does not appear to be transmissible among humans, so it is unlikely to ever become a true epidemic. The number of recorded cases in the United States is less than two hundred since the Center for Disease Control (CDC) has been keeping records.

The major environmental and health-related problems in humans result primarily from close association with domestic animals. This continued proximity has allowed several diseases to jump from their ungulate or avian hosts and cross the species barrier into humans.

Raymond PIEROTTI
University of Kansas

See also Biological Exchanges; Columbian Exchange; Diseases—Overview

Further Reading

Cockburn, A. (1967). *Infectious diseases: Their evolution and eradication*. Springfield, IL: Thomas Press.

Crosby, A. (1972). *The Columbian exchange: Biological and cultural consequences of 1492*. Westport, CT: Greenwood Press.

Diamond, J. (1997). *Guns, germs, and steel*. New York: W. W. Norton & Co.

Dobyns, H.. (1983). *Their numbers become thinned*. Knoxville: University of Tennessee Press.

Gottfried, R. (1983). *The black death: Natural and human disaster in medieval Europe*. London: Robert Hale.

Martin, C. (1978). *Keepers of the game: Indian-animal relationships and the fur trade*. Berkeley: University of California Press.

Sale, K. (1991). *The conquest of paradise*. New York: Alfred Knopf.

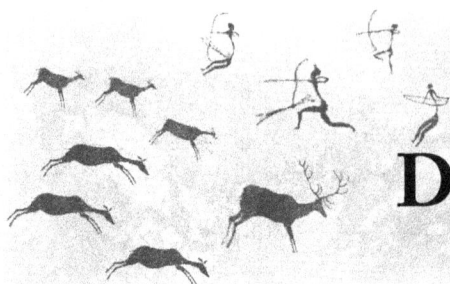

Diseases—Overview

The study and treatment of disease is a never-ending pursuit due to human evolution and our ability to adapt to and resist diseases over time. Research shows that disease increased as foraging stopped and humans began settling together in one place. Only in the twentieth century did epidemiologists recognize that hosts and germs adjust to one another, so symptoms (and medical diagnoses) change.

Disease refers to many kinds of bodily malfunction: some lethal, some chronic, and some merely temporary. Some diseases, like cancer and Alzheimer's disease, increase with age and result from disordered processes within our bodies; others arise from infection by invading germs and afflict children more frequently than adults because we develop immunities after early exposure to them. Symptoms of infectious diseases vary with time and place, owing to changes in human resistance and to evolutionary changes in the germs themselves. Consequently, written descriptions of ancient infections, even when quite detailed, often fail to match up with what modern doctors see. Hence, even when records exist, determining exactly when a particular infection first afflicted people in a given place is often unknowable. And no one can doubt that major disease encounters also took place among peoples who left no records for historians to examine. Nonetheless, and despite all such difficulties, some landmarks in the history of the human experience of disease are discernible from the deeper past, while in recent times the changing impact of diseases and medical efforts to control them are fairly well known.

Diseases among Foragers and Early Farmers

It is safe to assume that our remote foraging ancestors encountered many sorts of parasites, some of which, like the organism that causes malaria, were seriously debilitating. Sleeping sickness, spread by tsetse flies, was so lethal for human hunters that parts of east Africa remained uninhabited until recently, thus preserving vast herds of game animals that tourists now come to see. All the same, it is probable that our early ancestors were tolerably healthy and vigorous most of the time. That, at any rate, is the case among surviving African foragers as observed by modern anthropologists. Probably infectious organisms and their human hosts were fairly well adjusted to one another, having evolved together in tropical Africa; diseases of aging scarcely mattered since their lives were far shorter than ours.

Since many of Africa's tropical parasites could not survive freezing temperatures, infections probably diminished sharply when human bands expanded their range, penetrating cooler climates and spreading rapidly around the entire globe. Leaving African infections behind presumably increased human numbers and helped to sustain their extraordinary geographic expansion.

But infections began to increase again when, in different parts of the Earth, a few human groups began to cultivate the soil and settled down in the same place all year round. That was partly because food production allowed more people to crowd together and exchange infections, and more especially because supplies of water were liable to become contaminated

64

Pieter Bruegel, *The Triumph of Death* (c. 1562). Oil on panel. The painting reflects the social upheaval and terror following the bubonic plague that devastated medieval Europe.

by bacteria from human wastes. This increased exposure to infections of the digestive tract. Moreover, wherever farmers resorted to irrigation, wading in shallow water exposed them to a debilitating infection called schistosomiasis (or bilharzia), which they shared with snails. And whenever cultivators came to depend on a single crop for nearly all their food, dietary deficiencies were liable to set in. A diet of maize, for example, lacks some of the amino acids humans need and provokes a chronic disease called pellagra. Finally, the domestication of animals, though their meat and milk improved farmers' diets, intensified disease transfers back and forth between humans and their flocks and herds. A large array of bacteria and viruses traveled this path.

Yet intensified exposure to such diseases did not halt the increase in farming populations. Instead more people cultivated more ground, producing more food to feed more children. Farming villages therefore multiplied and spread from the regions where they

had initially established themselves, and human beings soon ceased to be rare in the balance of nature, as their foraging ancestors and other top predators, such as lions and tigers, had always been.

All the same, farmers had to labor longer and at more monotonous tasks than foragers did, and they faced famine whenever bad weather or an outbreak of plant disease provoked crop failure. Seizure of stores of food by human raiders was another serious risk that increased wherever grain farmers became dense enough to occupy nearly all suitable farmland. And when raiders became rulers by learning to take only part of the harvest as rent and taxes, farmers faced another drain on their resources and had to work still harder to feed themselves and their new overlords. Life remained short by our standards, so diseases of old age remained exceptional.

Then, beginning about 3500 BCE, rulers and their various hangers-on began to create cities in a few densely inhabited farming regions of Earth, and disease patterns changed again, manifesting diverse and unstable local equilibria. These may be described as regional agrarian disease regimes; they were succeeded after about 1550 CE by an equally unstable global disease regime within which we still find ourselves. The balance of this article will explore these successive disease environments.

Regional Agrarian Disease Regimes

When large numbers of persons began to cluster close together in cities, the problem of waste disposal multiplied as never before. Exposure to new infections multiplied as well, since long-distance comings and goings by soldiers, merchants, seamen, and caravan personnel often crossed disease boundaries and spread infections far and wide. Moreover, when urban populations exceeded a critical threshold, a new class of herd diseases began to afflict humans for the first time. These diseases existed initially among large populations of wild flocks and herds, or dense populations of burrowing rodents and other small animals. A distinguishing characteristic of these diseases was that when they were not fatal, they provoked antibodies in their animal or human hosts, so survivors became immune from a second infection. This meant that the germ could only persist when it found enough newborns to feed upon for a few weeks before death or recovery created another crisis of survival for the infection in question.

Just how large the total host population had to be to permit a chain of infection to continue indefinitely depended on birth rates and how closely in contact potential hosts might be. To move from host to host, many infections depended on airborne droplets, set adrift by breathing, coughing, and sneezing, and therefore they needed close encounters for successful transmission. In the modern era (from about 1750), for example, measles—a viral disease dependent on droplet propagation—required at least 7,000 susceptible individuals within a community of something like 300,000 persons to keep going. Obviously, infections like measles could only persist in urban settings and among villagers in contact with large urban centers.

Some of these, like smallpox and measles, were highly lethal; others like mumps and influenza were milder. No one knows when or where they made good their transfer from animal herds to human hosts, but it is certain that it took place somewhere in Asia, perhaps at several different times and places. It is equally sure that they could do so only in and around cities, thus becoming distinctive new "civilized" diseases.

Their arrival had paradoxical effects. By killing off urban dwellers, they soon made most cities so unhealthful that they needed a stream of migrants from surrounding villages to sustain their numbers. Yet these same diseases also created a new and very powerful advantage for disease-experienced populations in contact with previously unexposed populations. That was because among peoples who lacked acquired immunities, herd infections spread like wildfire, killing adults as well as children. In the modern era, initial exposure to measles or smallpox commonly killed off something like a third of the entire population in a few weeks, leaving survivors dazed and distraught and quite unable to resist further encroachment by the disease-bearing newcomers. The effect was multiplied when successive civilized diseases followed one another in rapid succession. Smallpox, measles, influenza, and even the common cold could all be, and often were, lethal.

Before that drastic pattern could establish itself generally, different centers of civilization had to survive the arrival of these infections from wherever they first started. Everything about the initial spread of herd diseases within Eurasia and Africa remains unknown, but disease disasters that ravaged the Roman Empire between 165 CE and 180 CE, and a second time between 251 CE and 266 CE, probably register the arrival of smallpox and measles in Mediterranean lands, brought back by soldiers returning from Mesopotamia. Written records also show that China suffered unusually lethal epidemics in 161–162 CE and again in 310–312 CE.

It looks, therefore, as though extended contacts within Eurasia, arising from the establishment of the so-called Silk Roads that connected China with Syria,

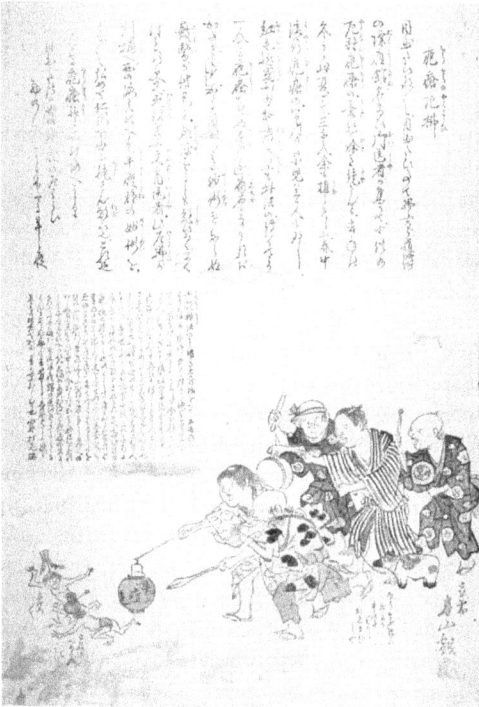

This print by Matsukawa Hanzan enlightened viewers about the importance of the smallpox vaccine and the work of Kōan Ogata, a Western-trained doctor who vaccinated three thousand people in 1849 at his clinic in Osaka, Japan.

allowed highly lethal outbreaks to occur at both extremes of Eurasia at nearly the same time, inflicting severe damage both on the Roman and Chinese empires. But surviving records say little or nothing about lands in between, and guesswork is useless. By contrast, we know that the Americas were exempt from these herd diseases until the Spaniards arrived, and the same was true of other isolated populations around the globe. Consequently, in the sixteenth century, when European seamen began to encounter people lacking immunities to these diseases, massive die-offs regularly ensued

By then the agrarian peoples of Eurasia had another twelve hundred years of disease exchange and exposure behind them. One well-known episode came between 534 CE and 750 CE, when sporadic outbreaks of bubonic plague ravaged Mediterranean coastlands, only to disappear for the next six

centuries. The historian Procopius wrote an exact description of the initial onset of that plague, explaining that it came by ship and originated in central Africa. Other factors were in play; modern studies show that bubonic plague is spread normally by bites of rat fleas, which transfer to humans only after their normal hosts die of the disease. The domestic rats in question were probably native to India, and in 534 CE they were relatively recent arrivals in Mediterranean coastlands.

The infection itself was at home in underground burrows of various species of rodents in central Africa and northern India, where it behaved like a childhood disease among rats and became a lethal epidemic only when it invaded inexperienced populations of domestic rats and, of course, humans. But under those circumstances it was indeed highly lethal.

Procopius says that when the disease first struck in 534 CE, ten thousand persons died daily in Constantinople for forty days. Loss of population and wealth were certainly severe and prevented the Byzantine emperor Justinian (reigned 527–565 CE) from reconquering the richest provinces of the western empire, which he had started to do.

Germanic and northern Europe escaped this bout with plague, probably because rats had not yet established themselves there. But in the so-called Dark Ages other serious epidemics—including smallpox, measles, and influenza—did break out in the north from time to time, and as ships began to travel the northern seas more frequently, all of Europe became more and more tightly tied into the disease pool centered upon the network of Mediterranean cities. Leprosy, tuberculosis, and diphtheria were among the infections that spread more widely during these centuries. But their spread cannot be traced since they did not provoke sudden, massive die-offs as smallpox, measles, and the plague did.

Nothing equally detailed is known about how other centers of civilization in Eurasia and Africa encountered new infections in ancient and medieval times. But two Chinese texts describe an outbreak of bubonic plague along the southern coast in 610 CE, so it looks again as though China's disease history matched that of Europe quite closely. This is not really surprising, since the ships and caravans that moved back and forth among all the Eurasian civilized lands carried infections with them, and invading armies occasionally exposed thousands of inexperienced soldiers to a new infection all at once.

North and East Africa shared in this homogenizing process, while the African interior, Southeast Asia, and northern Eurasia took more sporadic parts and so lagged somewhat behind. But overall, as disease exposures intensified across the entire Old World, resistance to infections increased, and local populations got used to living with heavier disease burdens. The assortment of prevalent diseases always differed from place to place, since climate set limits to many infections. In general, warmer and wetter conditions favored disease organisms; infections that depended on mosquitoes, fleas, or other insects to move from host to host also fared best under those conditions. Winter frost set limits to the spread of many kinds of parasites, and so did desert heat and dryness. In addition, local customs sometimes minimized disease exposures. In southwestern China, for example, where bubonic plague germs were endemic among burrowing rodents, European doctors in the nineteenth century scoffed at superstitious villagers who fled to higher ground whenever they found dead rats in their houses, yet half a century later, after Europeans had learned how the plague was transmitted, they realized that such behavior was an effective precaution against catching the disease. Some customs, on the other hand, intensified infections. Religious pilgrimage is a prime example, as was ritual footwashing in Muslim mosques, where the water in the fountains sometimes contained the organisms that cause bilharzia.

Most disease disasters were soon forgotten, which is why so little is knowable about the spread of infections. But the Black Death was an exception. The heavy die-off provoked when bubonic plague returned to Europe in 1346 continued to haunt folk memory and still colors our common speech. About a third of the population of Europe died of the plague between 1346 and 1350, but what kept the memory of the Black Death alive was the fact that plague continued to break out from time to time in Europe and North Africa down to the present, even after effective antibiotic cures were discovered in the 1940s. We know something about how this came to pass.

First of all, the vast Mongol Empire, extending from China to Russia, permitted rapid, long-range movement throughout Eurasia on a far greater scale than ever before. Plague was only one of several infections that took advantage of this fact to expand their domain. More particularly, a Mongol army invaded the borderland between China and India in 1252, penetrating a region where plague infection was chronic, and seems to have carried the infection back to its homeland in the steppes. At any rate, *Pasteurella pestis* (*Yersinia pestis*), as the bacterium that causes plague is called, somehow found a new home and spread among burrowing rodents of the northern grasslands, where it was discovered by Russian scientists only in the 1890s. This was the reservoir from which the plague of 1346 broke upon Europe and the Muslim world.

Ships spread it swiftly from Feodosiya (or Kaffa) in the Crimea, where it first broke out, to other Mediterranean and north European ports. Then the infection moved inland. Wherever the plague arrived, death came quickly and unpredictably to young and old. More than half of those infected died. In Muslim lands, the disease took a similar toll; China, too, lost about half its population from a combination of plague and warfare by the time the Mongol Empire collapsed and the Ming dynasty took power in 1368.

Plague continued to visit all these lands at irregular intervals thereafter. The population in Europe continued to decline until about 1480, when the accumulated resistances among survivors at last permitted population growth to resume. It accelerated once the plague disappeared from England and northern Europe after a final visit to London in 1665, partly because efforts at quarantining ships coming from plague-infected ports reduced exposure and partly because slate roofs, introduced as protection against fire, created greater

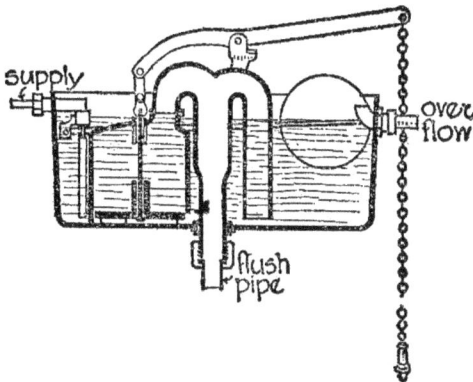

Indoor plumbing and underground sewage systems advanced public health by helping to control the spread of disease in dense, urban centers.

distance between humans and hungry rat fleas than when rats nested overhead in the thatch. In eastern Europe and Asia, plague continued to break out until the twentieth century, but little by little local adaptations reduced its impact everywhere.

Overall, the most enduring change came to the steppes—the Mongol homelands—where nomadic herdsmen found themselves permanently exposed to a very lethal infection. Losses were so heavy that nomads even withdrew from the fertile grasslands of the Ukraine, leaving them vacant for agricultural pioneers to encroach upon, beginning about 1550. This reversed a human tide that had favored nomad expansion ever since the first millennium BCE, carrying first Indo-European and then Turkish languages across Europe and much of Asia.

Other changes in disease patterns accompanied or soon followed the sudden expansion of bubonic plague. The most conspicuous was the retreat of leprosy, emptying thousands of leprosaria that Europeans had built to isolate lepers in accordance with biblical injunctions. Many lepers died of plague during the first onset; but something else must have been at work to overcome the various skin infections that medieval Europeans lumped together and called leprosy. One possibility is Europe's reduced population had a proportionally larger supply of wool with which to clothe themselves, and by wearing long, warm nightclothes and thereby reducing skin-to-skin contact between people, they may have cut

down on the transmission of skin diseases. No one knows for sure.

Ironically, another skin disease, yaws, caused by a bacterium indistinguishable from the one that causes syphilis, may also have been nearly banished from European populations. The epidemic of syphilis that broke out after 1494 may have been the result of the bacterium finding a new path of propagation via the mucous membranes of the sex organs. Again, no one can be sure.

Yet all the mingling and transformations of diseases across Eurasia and Africa before 1500 never erased local differences. Above all, large parts of the Earth remained unaffected by the rising tide of infection among Old World peoples, and they found themselves correspondingly vulnerable when crossing the oceans became routine and a new *global* disease regime began to emerge.

Global Disease Regimes

The first and most overwhelming effect of oceanic navigation was to spread a large array of lethal infections among inexperienced human populations. This process continues in remote Amazon jungles and Arctic shores even today, but by now almost every human population has been at least partially exposed, and the initial shattering effect is past. But when it was new, whole peoples disappeared, and vast landscapes in the Americas and Australia were severely depopulated. Immigrants from Europe and Africa—and subsequently also from Asia—were therefore able to supplant the older inhabitants, creating the mixture of peoples we know today.

Native Americans were the largest population exposed to destruction by the new disease regime. The native population of Hispaniola, where Columbus set up his headquarters, disappeared entirely within a few decades, and within the first fifty years of their exposure to new infections, the much larger populations of Mexico and Peru diminished to about a tenth of what they had been in 1500. Millions died of smallpox and innumerable other infections until immunities accumulating in survivors' bloodstreams checked the die-off. In Mexico and Peru the worst was over by 1650. Gradually population growth began again, though in more isolated parts of the Americas local die-offs continued. Warfare and less organized forms of human violence played a part in destroying Native Americans, but Afro-Eurasian diseases always had the principal role.

Caribbean islands and tropical coastlands of the Americas also proved hospitable to malaria and yellow fever from Africa once the species of mosquito that carried them came across the Atlantic on board slave ships. No exact time horizon for the arrival of malaria in the New World can be discerned, but in 1648 a lethal epidemic of yellow fever in Havana announced the arrival of that disease unambiguously. When it subsequently became endemic, survivors acquired a very potent protection against invading armies, since soldiers from Europe regularly fell ill and died of it within about six weeks of their arrival. This allowed the Spanish to overcome British efforts to conquer the sugar islands in the eighteenth century, doomed Napoleon's attempt to reconquer Haiti in 1801, and persuaded him to sell the Louisiana territory to Thomas Jefferson in 1803. Quite a political career for a virus from tropical Africa!

Elsewhere, inhabitants of Australia, New Zealand, and other isolated communities experienced approximately the same fate as Native Americans did when disease-experienced Europeans arrived among them. Always the newcomers also brought a rich array of other organisms with them: crops and weeds, together with domesticated animals and pests like lice, rats, and mice. The Earth is still reverberating from the ecological upheavals initiated when humans and innumerable other organisms began to cross the oceans, making the biosphere into a single interacting whole as never before.

Disease exchanges ran almost entirely one way, spreading from Afro-Eurasia to other lands. Reverse transmissions are hard to find, though some experts believe that syphilis came to Europe from the Americas. Europeans discovered that disease when it broke out in a French army besieging Naples in 1494, so its connection with Columbus's return in 1493 is indeed possible. But there is no clear evidence of the prior existence of syphilis in the New World, so no one can be sure.

Another disease, typhus, also invaded Europe in 1490; but it came with soldiers from Cyprus and may not have been new, but only newly recognized by doctors of the day. More recently, other infections have also invaded disease-experienced populations of the Earth. AIDS is the most serious and widespread, and it may have been transferred recently from monkeys somewhere in the African interior, or perhaps, like typhus, AIDS is much older and remained unrecognized until increasing sexual promiscuity turned it into an epidemic.

Three other new disease exposures affecting industrialized populations in modern times are also worth mentioning. Tuberculosis (TB), a very ancient infection, gained fresh impetus after about 1780 when new factories, powered by coal and steam, began to crowd people together in industrial towns under unsanitary conditions. Its ravages crested in Europe about 1850, shortly before a German professor, Robert Koch, discovered the bacillus that caused it in 1882, thereby inaugurating a new age for preventive medicine. Yet despite modern medical skills, TB remains the most widespread and persistent human infection worldwide, sustained by the extraordinary growth of cities that had carried more than half of humankind into crowded urban settings by 1950 or so.

Cholera, too, was an ancient disease at home in India, where it flourished among Hindu pilgrims who came to bathe in the Ganges. The cholera bacillus can survive independently in freshwater for considerable periods of time, but it multiplies very rapidly in the human alimentary tract and causes diarrhea, vomiting, fever, and often death within a few hours of its onset. Bodily shrinkage from dehydration and skin discolored by bursting capillaries make the symptoms of cholera especially horrible. So when the disease broke through long-standing boundaries in 1819, spreading to Southeast Asia, China, Japan, East

Africa, and western Asia, it aroused intense fear and panic even though mortality rates remained rather modest—a mere 13 percent of the total population of Cairo, for instance. Between 1831 and 1833 a fresh outbreak carried cholera across Russia to the Baltic and thence to England, Ireland, Canada, the United States, and Mexico. Even more important, cholera established itself in Mecca in 1831, where it infected Muslim pilgrims. They in turn carried it home with them, periodically spreading cholera all the way from Mindanao to Morocco until 1912. Then cholera disappeared from Mecca, and Muslim pilgrims ceased to spread it far and wide; but it lived on in India, where Hindu pilgrims continued to be its principal carriers.

European and American responses to this dread infection were strenuous indeed. Reformers in England set out to reengineer the water supply and sewer systems of London and other cities to assure germ-free drinking water. It took years to build new water systems, but as they spread from city to city, many other sorts of infections diminished sharply. Helped by vaccination against smallpox, dating back to the eighteenth century, cities became far more healthful than before. This sanitary effort involved new laws and medical boards of health with mandatory power to enforce preventive measures. It was the first great medical breakthrough of modern times. Bit by bit, vaccination and sanitation spread around much of the globe, changing human experience of infectious disease so fundamentally that we have difficulty imagining times when infant death was a matter of course and adults died of infections more often than from degenerative diseases of old age.

Yet some diseases were little affected by these preventive measures. The viruses that cause influenza, for example, vary from year to year, and regularly find receptive human hosts whose immunities from previous years are ineffective against the new variants. In 1918–1919 a new strain of the virus proved particularly lethal, killing about 20 million persons as it spread around the world, which made it far more deadly than World War I. Yet, as so often before, survivors soon almost forgot about their encounter with such a lethal epidemic.

That was partly because a second medical breakthrough, comparable to the sanitary successes of the nineteenth century, came after World War II. Suddenly, use of DDT to poison mosquito larvae almost eliminated malaria from many regions of the Earth, while penicillin and other antibiotics became generally available to kill other infections. All at once, instant cures for ancient diseases became a matter of course. On the prevention side, the World Health Organization carried out a successful campaign that eliminated (with the exception of laboratory specimens) smallpox in 1976. Yet these triumphs did not last very long. While effective against mosquitoes, DDT also poisoned so many forms of life that its use was soon abandoned. More generally, infectious agents began to develop resistances to the new antibiotics. As a result, malaria reclaimed some of its old importance, and other ancient infections did likewise.

Then when AIDS was recognized in 1981 and successfully resisted chemical cures, doctors, once so confident of victory over infections, had to admit that their new skills had unexpected limitations. Infections were coming back, and diseases of old age were increasing. All too obviously, and despite all the recent medical marvels, human bodies remain subject to infection and degenerate with age.

Diseases change, and have always done so. Human behavior changes too, affecting how diseases afflict us. Since 1750 or thereabouts, medical knowledge and practice drastically altered the global disease regime and lengthened human life for billions of persons. But all our skills do not change the fact that we remain part of the web of life on Earth, eating and being eaten, everywhere and always.

William H. McNEILL
University of Chicago, Emeritus

See also Diseases—Animal; Diseases—Plant

Further Reading

Cook, N. D. (1998). *Born to die: Disease and the New World conquest, 1492–1650*. Cambridge, U.K.: Cambridge University Press.

Cunningham, A., & Williams, P. (1992). *The laboratory revolution in medicine*. Cambridge, U.K.: Cambridge University Press.

Ewald, P. W. (1994). *The evolution of infectious disease*. New York: Oxford University Press.

Grmek, M. (1989). *Diseases in the ancient Greek world* (L. Muellner & M. Muellner, Trans.). Baltimore: Johns Hopkins University Press.

Kiple, K. (1993). *The Cambridge world history of human disease*. Cambridge, U.K.: Cambridge University Press.

McNeill, W. H. (1998). *Plagues and peoples* (2nd ed). New York: Anchor Books.

Diseases—Plant

The relationship between humans and the diseases that afflict plants is intertwined throughout history. Humans were often the ones who unintentionally introduced or spread certain types of disease among plants, which resulted in food shortages and famine. Thus the study of plant diseases remains crucial; whatever threatens crops threatens the health and survival of humans.

Preliterate peoples as well as some literate peoples believed that spirits cause disease. Greek physicians dismissed this notion and instead insisted that disease had physical rather than supernatural causes. In the fifth century BCE, the Greek physician Hippocrates taught that an imbalance of fluids causes disease in humans, a claim that left the cause of disease in plants both ignored and unexplained. In the nineteenth century, the German botanist Anton de Bary, the German bacteriologist Robert Koch, and the French chemist Louis Pasteur swept aside the ideas of Hippocrates. De Bary, working with the potato, and Pasteur and Koch, working with cattle, demonstrated that pathogens (parasitic microbes) cause disease. The germ theory of disease is the foundation of modern medicine.

The focus on human diseases should not deflect attention from plant diseases. Despite a perception to the contrary, plants suffer from more diseases than humans do and for an obvious reason. Plants colonized the land 410 million years ago, whereas modern humans made their appearance only 130,000 years ago. The pathogens that attack plants have had some 400 million more years to evolve new types by mutation than those that attack humans.

Plants diseases often affected history when they provoked famines, but human actions also affected plants from very early times, when our ancestors learned to control fire and began to burn dry vegetation to help their hunting. Subsequently, humans carried seeds to new locations when they began to plant fields of grain and other food, and eventually they carried favored crops all around the world. They also spread plant diseases unintentionally together with weeds, as well as animals and insect pests. Plants and humankind, in effect, interacted so closely that they began to evolve together. Even as nomadic foragers, humans depended on plants for sustenance. The rise of agriculture in western Asia some 10,000 years ago and its spread throughout the world have wedded the destiny of humans to that of crops (domesticated plants). Whatever has threatened crops has threatened the health and survival of humans.

Diseases of the Staple Grasses

Grasses such as wheat, rice, and rye have been the staple crops that have sustained populations over the centuries; thus the diseases associated with them have great impact on humans, potentially affecting not only food supplies but their health as well.

Wheat Rust

Wheat rust is one of the oldest plant diseases. Some scholars believe that a passage in Genesis records an outbreak of rust in the Levant that caused famine so severe it forced the Hebrews to migrate to Egypt, the granary of the ancient Mediterranean world. If these scholars are right, this text is the earliest written account of a plant disease.

Only in the fourth century BCE did Theophrastus, a Greek botanist and pupil of Aristotle, coin the term *rust* for this disease because of its reddish hue on the leaves and stem of wheat plants. Theophrastus wrote that wheat planted in valleys and other low ground suffered from rust more often and more acutely than wheat planted on high ground, though he could not explain this fact.

That insight came to the Romans. As early as 700 BCE, they identified the reddish hue on wheat plants as the mark of rust. At that time they began to worship Robigus; historians identify Robigus as the god of rust, a fair statement so long as one remembers the Greek rather than Roman origin of the term *rust*. The idea that a god unleashed rust on the Romans underscores their belief that rust had a supernatural cause. Trade with the Greek city-states led the Romans to abandon a supernatural explanation of plant diseases. In the first century BCE, the naturalist Pliny the Elder made the crucial link between moisture and the onset and spread of rust, writing that rust afflicted wheat grown in areas where fog and dew were common in morning and evening. Pliny's insight into the role of water in spreading rust was prescient because rust, like all fungal diseases, spreads in wet environments. The rust fungus needs water to produce the millions of spores that are the next generation of fungi. Two centuries later, the agricultural writer Columella warned farmers against staking their livelihood on wheat. The only protection against rust was to grow a diversity of crops. Columella recommended cultivation of chickpeas and lentils because of their immunity to rust.

Columella had reason to worry: the first three centuries of the Common Era were unusually wet in the lands along the Mediterranean Sea, bringing rust to wheat fields throughout the Roman Empire.

In the seventh and eighth centuries, Arabs brought the barberry bush with them as they swept across North Africa and into Spain. Neither Arabs nor Europeans understood that the bush harbors rust fungi

Close-up of wheat rust, one of the oldest plant diseases. Photo by James Kolmer for the United States Department of Agriculture, Agricultural Research Service.

because the fungi inhabit the bush without harming it, much as the pathogens that cause malaria and yellow fever live in the gut of the female mosquito without harming her. A barberry bush that harbors rust fungi has no symptoms of disease. Only in the seventeenth century did Europeans begin to suspect the bush to be a Trojan horse. In 1660 France enacted the first law to eradicate the bush. Other European nations passed similar laws, as did the American colonies in the eighteenth century.

These measures were not enough to stop the spread of rust. Plant breeders in the nineteenth century began to search for rust-resistant wheat to cross with high-yielding but susceptible varieties; this effort accelerated during that century as England, France, the German states, and the United States poured money into agricultural science. Around 1900 agronomists at the U.S. Department of Agriculture identified an Italian durum wheat suitable for pasta and a Russian emmer wheat suitable for bread. These were the first of innumerable resistant wheat varieties that give humans the best, if incomplete, protection against failure of the wheat crop from rust.

Rice Stunt Disease

Chinese records first mention the cultivation of rice four thousand years ago, though its cultivation began earlier in southeastern Asia. By 500 BCE, farmers grew rice in China, the Korean peninsula, and the swath of land between modern Vietnam and India. By the first century CE, farmers were growing rice in Japan, Indonesia, and the Philippines. The people of these regions were nearly as dependent on rice as the Irish would be on potato in the nineteenth century. True, farmers also grew soybeans throughout Korea and China, and wheat grown along the Indus River reached the people of central and southern India by trade, but soybeans and wheat were minor supplements to a diet of rice.

Roughly forty diseases afflict rice, making difficult the task of sorting among them difficult, as well as among climatic factors, to explain the 1,800 famines that Chinese documents have recorded since 100 BCE and the seventy in India since 33 CE. Because rice needs more water than any other grain to thrive, Chinese and Indian texts often attributed crop failures to inadequate or impure water.

In the sixth century CE, a Japanese text mentions stunted (short or dwarf) rice plants that bore little or no rice. The condition baffled farmers for 1,200 years. In 1733, 12,000 Japanese died of famine when stunt destroyed their rice crop, yet no one was any closer to understanding what stunted rice plants. Unlike Europe, Asia never developed science in its modern form but only gradually assimilated it from Europeans during the eighteenth and nineteenth centuries. The people of Japan and continental Asia did, however, have a tradition of careful observation. This tradition led one Japanese farmer in 1874 to study the feeding habits of leafhoppers on rice plants. He doubted that insect bites alone could arrest plant growth and instead proposed that leafhoppers carried a pathogen that they transmitted to rice plants by bite. The pathogen, not leafhoppers, stunted rice plants.

The idea was as novel as it was correct. Leafhoppers carry within their gut Rice Dwarf Virus just as, one may recall, various species of mosquitoes carry the pathogens for malaria and yellow fever. Rice Dwarf Virus remains virulent throughout a leafhopper's life, and female leafhoppers pass the virus to their offspring, multiplying it with each generation. When the leafhopper population is large, as it must have been in Japan in 1733, the virus becomes widespread enough to cause failure of the rice crop even though the leafhopper is an inefficient flier.

The discovery of insect transmission of a pathogen opened a new field in the study of plant diseases by uniting entomology, the study of insects, with plant pathology. Scientists came quickly to understand that control of insect populations is essential if one hopes to minimize crop damage from an insect-borne pathogen. It was no longer enough for the plant pathologist to understand diseases. He now had to understand the feeding and mating habits of insects and their distribution in areas of disease. The need to combat insects accelerated the study and development of insecticides as a branch of applied chemistry in the twentieth century. The study of insect-borne viruses and the development and use of insecticides would later be crucial in fighting corn diseases in the United States.

Rye Ergotism

The importance of wheat and rice to the sustenance of Europeans and Asians has deflected attention from rye and its diseases. The Germanic tribes that settled the lands that are today France and Germany began growing rye in the second century CE. Wheat always commanded a higher price than rye, making rye bread the staple of the poor until the even cheaper potato spread through Europe between the sixteenth and nineteenth centuries.

The diseases of rye thus afflicted the poor rather than the rich. Particularly serious was ergotism, a fungal disease that fills rye grains with a toxin that in sufficient quantities causes convulsions and death in humans. Unlike most plant diseases, ergot of rye threatens humans by poisoning them rather than by causing famine. The agony of death from ergot toxicity led medieval Europeans to attribute the disease to God's wrath, hence the name "Holy Fire." Medieval chronicles cite the first outbreak of Holy Fire in the eighth century. In 857 CE, thousands died in the Rhine Valley, with smaller outbreaks throughout France and Germany.

One may recall that fungi spread in wet environments. Evidence from dendrology and medieval chronicles suggests that after 1000 CE, Europe's climate turned wet and cool, hastening the spread and severity of ergotism in northern and western Europe. An outbreak in 1039 was the first in a series of virulent outbreaks between the eleventh and eighteenth centuries. Ergotism, along with famine in the early fourteenth century, may explain the high mortality of the Black Death.

Diseases of the Staple Crops Indigenous to the Americas

Like grasses in Europe and Asia, dependence on certain crops can be dangerous—culturally and economically—if they become susceptible to disease.

A drawing from the *Illustrated London News*, 22 December 1849, shows a family affected by famine. The potato blight in the mid-1840s decimated the staple crop of the Irish; one million starved and 1.5 million fled Ireland in the next five years.

Potatoes and corn are two stale crops that have been catastrophically affected.

Late Blight of Potato

The fungus that causes late blight of potato is at the center of a tragedy, the Irish Potato Famine. The tragedy has its roots not in Europe but in the Andes Mountains, where the natives of Peru domesticated the potato. The Spanish conquered Peru in the sixteenth century. In search of gold, they found a more valuable commodity, the potato. From Peru the potato reached Spain by ship around 1570, reaching Ireland before 1650.

By 1800 the Irish, squeezed by their lack of land and high rents, had no choice but to embrace the potato for sustenance because it yielded more food per unit of land than any grain. Reliance on a single crop is always risky, as Columella had emphasized in the first century. The potato posed risks far greater than the Irish could have imagined. The Spanish had brought little more than a few handfuls of potatoes with them. These potatoes were of the same stock and thus genetically uniform. Because the potato propagates by shoots, new potatoes, barring mutation, are genetic equivalents of the parent potato. With all potatoes near carbon copies of one another, any disease that threatens one potato threatens all.

With the potato vulnerable, catastrophe struck in 1845. Six weeks of rain hastened the spread of the blight fungus across Ireland. The plants died and potatoes rotted in the ground. Blight struck again in 1846. Their staple gone, one million starved and 1.5 million fled Ireland in the next five years.

The tragedy galvanized scientists throughout Europe into action. In 1861 Anton de Bary isolated the culprit, a fungus he named *Phytophthora infestans*, and by spreading it on healthy potato plants demonstrated that it caused blight. The Potato Famine had spurred de Bary's discovery, which marked the beginning of plant pathology as a science.

Corn Diseases

As with potato diseases, scientists know little about corn diseases during the pre-Columbian period. What is clear, however, is that corn, unlike potato, is a cross-pollinating plant that produces plants with genetic diversity. Crossbreeding achieves diversity by reshuffling chromosomes in any plant or animal, including humans. This diversity should minimize the occurrence of epidemics, for within a heterogeneous population some individuals, in this case corn plants, should be resistant to disease.

Corn Viruses

Since the 1920s, corn breeders have reduced the genetic diversity by breeding a small number of high-yielding corn plants of roughly uniform genotypes, making corn vulnerable to epidemics. An outbreak of corn stunt disease along the lower Mississippi valley in 1945, reminiscent of the stunt disease that ravaged rice in Asia, presaged corn's vulnerability to an

epidemic. As is true of rice stunt, a virus causes corn stunt disease and is spread by an insect, in this case a species of aphid.

Worse was to follow. A few stunted corn plants in Portsmouth, Ohio, erupted in an epidemic that engulfed the Ohio and Mississippi valleys in 1963 and 1964, costing farmers who had planted on some lands along these rivers their entire corn crop. The culprit was not the corn stunt virus as scientists first thought but two viruses: Maize Dwarf Mosaic Virus (MDMV) and Maize Chlorotic Dwarf Virus (MCDV). The initial confusion among scientists slowed their response, opening the entire Midwest and South to the danger of an epidemic.

The method of virus transmission saved corn growers. A species each of aphid and leafhopper transmits MDMV and MCDV, respectively, by bite. Both feed primarily on Johnsongrass that grows along the Ohio and Mississippi rivers. Both viruses inhabit Johnsongrass, as the ergot fungus inhabits the barberry bush, without signs of disease. But neither insect is a strong flier, and, unlike the leafhopper that carries Rice Dwarf Virus, neither aphid nor leafhopper retains MDMV and MCDV in virulent form more than forty-five minutes, limiting the range of both viruses.

Once scientists had fingered the aphid, leafhopper, and Johnsongrass as culprits, the U.S. Department of Agriculture launched a campaign to kill aphids and leafhoppers by insecticide and Johnsongrass by herbicide in late 1964. The expenditure of chemicals and money ended the threat of these viruses and led scientists to believe they held the upper hand against corn diseases. Success prevented all but a few scientists from questioning the wisdom of growing genetically uniform corn throughout the Midwest and South.

Southern Corn Leaf Blight

Catastrophe struck in 1970 as Southern Corn Leaf Blight, a fungal disease, swept the United States, destroying 710 million bushels of corn, 15 percent of the corn crop that year. From Texas to Georgia and Florida, farmers lost half their corn crop. These losses cost farmers $1 billion, and the collapse of farm commodity prices cost investors billions more. In a single summer, one corn fungus threatened financial ruin.

Plant pathologists identified a single female parent of corn (a type of corn that produced no pollen and so was male sterile) as susceptible to Southern Corn Leaf Blight. By dropping it from the corn pedigree, agronomists bred new varieties of corn resistant to South Corn Leaf Blight, but corn remains as genetically uniform today as it was in 1970.

Future Prospects

The imperative to minimize crop losses from diseases will only intensify in the future as the human population grows exponentially. At their origin 130,000 years ago, modern humans cannot have numbered more than a few thousand. Only around 1800 did the human population number 1 billion. The population doubled by 1940 and again by 1975. Today, more than 6 billion humans crowd the earth, and demographers fear our numbers may swell to upwards of 9 billion by 2045.

To avert famine on an unprecedented scale, farmers must triple food production by then. To fall even 2 percent short of the goal, demographers believe, will condemn some 270 million people to starvation. Only with the highest yielding varieties of potatoes, corn, soybeans, wheat, and rice—the sustenance of humanity—can humans hope to avert widespread starvation. But only a small number of varieties of any crop can yield enough food for a hungry world. The future will only exacerbate the problem of genetic homogeneity. Crops may become more rather than less vulnerable to epidemics.

Christopher M. CUMO

Independent scholar, Canton, Ohio

See also Biological Exchanges; Columbian Exchange; Famine; Population and the Environment

Further Reading

Agrios, G. N. (1997). *Plant pathology* (4th ed). San Diego, CA: Academic Press.

Carefoot, G. L., & Sprott, E. R. (1967). *Famine on the wind: Plant diseases & human history.* London: Angus & Robertson.

Francki, R. I. B., Milne, R. G., & Hatta, T. (1985). *Atlas of plant viruses.* Boca Raton, FL: CRC Press.

Harris, K. F., & Maramorosch, K. (Eds.). (1980). *Vectors of plant pathogens.* New York: Academic Press.

Klinkowski, M. (1970). Catastrophic plant diseases. *Annual Review of Phytopathology, 8,* 37–60.

Littlefield, L. J. (1981). *Biology of the plant rusts: An introduction.* Ames: Iowa State University Press.

Matthews, R. E. F. (1991). *Plant virology* (3rd ed.). New York: Academic Press.

Schumann, G. L. (1991). *Plant diseases: Their biology & social impact.* St. Paul, MN: American Phytopathological Society.

Shurtlett, M. C. (Ed.). (1980). *A compendium of corn diseases* (2nd ed.). St. Paul, MN: American Phytopathological Society.

Smith, K. M. (1972). *A textbook of plant virus diseases.* New York: Academic Press.

Stefferud, A. (Ed.). (1953). *Plant diseases: The yearbook of agriculture.* Washington, DC: Government Printing Office.

Tatum, L. A. (1971). The southern corn leaf blight epidemic. *Science, 171,* 1113–1116.

Thurston, H. D. (1973). Threatening plant diseases. *Annual Review of Phytopathology, 11,* 27–52.

Ullstrup, A. J. (1972). The impacts of the southern corn leaf blights epidemics of 1971–1972. *Annual Review of Phytopathology, 10,* 37–50.

Van Regenmortel, M. H. V., & Fraenkel-Conrat, H. (Eds.). (1986). *The plant viruses.* New York: Plenum.

Vanderplank, J. E. (1963). *Plant diseases: Epidemics & control.* New York: Academic Press.

Webster, R. K., & Gunnell, P. S. (Eds.). (1992). *Compendium of rice diseases.* St. Paul, MN: American Phytopathological Society.

Western, J. H. (Ed.). (1971). *Diseases of crop plants.* New York: Macmillan.

Wiese, M. V. (1987). *Compendium of wheat diseases.* St. Paul, MN: American Phytopathological Society.

Woodham-Smith, C. (1962). *The great hunger, Ireland, 1845–1849.* New York: Harper & Row.

Earthquakes

Earthquakes are experienced as shockwaves or intense vibrations on the Earth's surface. They are usually caused by ruptures along geological fault lines in the Earth's crust, resulting in the sudden release of energy in the form of seismic waves. They can also be triggered by volcanic activity or human actions, such as industrial or military explosions.

Earthquakes can occur almost anywhere in the world, but most take place along particularly active belts ranging from tens to hundreds of miles wide. An earthquake's epicenter is the point on the Earth's surface directly above the source or focus of the earthquake. Most earthquakes are small and cause little or no damage, but very large earthquakes, followed by a series of smaller aftershocks, can be devastating. Depending on the location of the epicenter, these earthquakes can have particularly disastrous effects on densely populated areas as well as the infrastructure that supports them, such as bridges, highways, apartment buildings, skyscrapers, and single-family homes.

Earthquakes can destroy our built-up environments and the essential systems we rely on for our lives and livelihoods. They also have the potential to cause landslides and tsunamis (giant ocean waves that can flood and destroy coastal regions), both of which can have devastating effects on people and communities. The social and economic consequences of earthquakes can be vast, and recovering from them can take many years.

Early Explanations

Humans have come a long way in their understanding of the causes of earthquakes. At first, myths and legends explained processes beneath the Earth's surface. Thinkers from the time of the Greek philosopher Anaxagoras (500–428 BCE) to the German canon and councillor Konrad von Megenberg (1309–1374) in the late Middle Ages believed, with slight variations, that air vapors caught in Earth's cavities were the cause of earthquakes: thus, Thales of Miletus (c. 625–547 BCE), the founder of Ionian natural philosophy, was among the first to attribute earthquakes to the rocking of the Earth on water. The Greek philosopher Anaximenes of Miletus (585–526 BCE) thought that periods of dryness and wetness were responsible for earthquakes. Aristotle (384–322 BCE) described earthquakes as the consequence of compressed air captured in caves; his ideas were used to explain meteorological phenomena and earthquakes until the Middle Ages. Moved by the devastating earthquake at Pompeii and Herculaneum on 5 February 62 (or 63) CE, the Roman statesman and philosopher Seneca (4 BCE–65 CE) backed Aristotle's thinking. Plinius (23–79 CE), the Roman historian and author of *Historia naturalis*, considered earthquakes to be underground thunderstorms.

When classical antiquity was rediscovered by the Christian Occident around 1200, significant parts of Greek ideology were merged with Christian ideas. Albertus Magnus (1193–1280), a German scientist and philosopher, supported the study of the writings of Aristotle and Arabic and Jewish commentators. His own works made an outstanding contribution to the development of the sciences. Georgius Agricola (1494–1555), a German humanist, physician, and mineralogist, believed that earthquakes were the consequence of a subterranean fire ignited by the sun. The long-lasting hypothesis of a central subterranean

79

fire, proposed by the Greek philosopher Pythagoras (570–500 BCE), was revived in the book *Mundus Subterraneus* by German scholar Athanasius Kircher (1601–1680).

During the eighteenth century scientists became increasingly convinced that no natural phenomenon was unexplainable, thus an explanation for earthquakes became a challenge for scientists of the Enlightenment. The English physician William Stukeley (1687–1765) wrote in his *Philosophy of Earthquakes* that earthquakes were caused by electrostatic discharge between sky and Earth, like lightning.

The most catastrophic earthquake of the eighteenth century occurred in 1755, destroying Lisbon, Portugal, killing about sixty thousand people, and initiating great debate about the cause of earthquakes. The following year the German philosopher Immanuel Kant (1724–1804) proposed chemical causes for earthquakes. He rejected mystical and religious explanations and held that the cause is below our feet.

Important Discoveries

The Englishmen John Winthrop (1606–1676) and John Michell (1724–1793) began to reflect not only on the causes but also the effects of earthquakes. Winthrop, a mathematician and natural philosopher, made the important discovery that earthquakes were waves; this discovery would be revived a hundred years later. In 1760, Michell published a study in which he recognized wavelike motions of the ground. With that he anticipated the perception that would lead to an understanding of the cause of earthquakes.

Another significant step was taken by the Irish engineer Robert Mallet (1810–1881) when he began documenting worldwide earthquake occurrences. He compiled a catalog of six thousand earthquakes from which he was able to draw the most complete earthquake map of the world in 1857. The cause of earthquakes was still unknown, but Mallet's research, which led to the understanding of the origin of mountains and continents, supplied the basic approach to answering the question. In 1912, the German meteorologist and geophysicist Alfred Wegener (1880–1930) presented his theory of continental drift, which states that parts of the Earth's crust slowly drift atop a liquid core. Wegener hypothesized that there was a single gigantic continent (Pangaea) 200 million years ago.

Causes

Earthquakes are classified as either natural or induced. Natural earthquakes are further classified as tectonic—the most common (more than 90 percent of all earthquakes are tectonic)—volcanic (occurring in conjunction with volcanic activity), and collapse (for example, occurring in regions with caverns). Induced earthquakes are vibrations of the ground caused by human activities, such as construction of dams, mining, and nuclear explosions. For example, filling a reservoir in Koyna, India, induced a catastrophic earthquake in December 1967 that caused 177 deaths.

Most earthquakes are caused by the movement of tectonic plates, as explained by the continental drift theory of Wegener. Tectonic plates are large segments of the Earth's lithosphere (the outer, rigid shell of the Earth that contains the crust, continents, and plates). The Earth's surface consists of nine major plates: six continental plates (the North American, South American, Eurasian, African, Indo-Australian, and Antarctic plates) and three oceanic plates (the Pacific, Nazca, and Cocos plates). Tectonic plates move in relation to each other and along faults over the deeper interior. Faults are fractures in rock along which the two sides have been displaced relative to each other. An example is the well-known San Andreas Fault in California, which separates the Pacific plate (on which San Francisco and Los Angeles lie) from the North American plate.

When lava is upwelling at midoceanic (mid-Pacific, mid-Atlantic) ridges, rock moves slowly on either side of the ridges across the Earth's surface. New plates are constantly created, while other plates must be

"The Earthquake House" at White City, London. Theories proposed a century apart by the Englishmen John Winthrop and John Mitchell anticipated the modern understanding of the cause of earthquakes. Photo by J. J. Shaw.

absorbed at subduction zones (where the edge of one plate descends below the edge of another).

Earthquakes, volcánoes, mountain building, and subduction zones are generally explained as consequences of steady, large, horizontal surface motions. Most tectonic plates contain both dry land and ocean floor. At present, those plates containing Africa, Antarctica, North America, and South America are growing, whereas the Pacific plate is shrinking. When plates collide, mountain chains such as the Alps and Himalayas arise, accompanied by persistent earthquake activity.

Seismographs and the Richter Scale

Earthquakes are recorded by sensitive instruments called seismographs. Today's seismographs record ground shaking over a band of frequencies and seismic amplitudes. A seismogram (the record created by a seismograph) shows the motions of the Earth's surface caused by seismic waves across time. Earthquakes generate different kinds of seismic waves: P (primary) waves alternately compress and dilate the rock, whereas S (secondary) waves move in a shear motion, perpendicular to the direction the wave is traveling. From a seismogram, the distance and energy of an earthquake can be determined. At least three seismograms are needed to locate where an earthquake occurred. The place at which rupture commences is the focus, or hypocenter, while the point on the Earth's surface directly above the focus of an earthquake is the epicenter. The distance between the focus and the epicenter is the focal depth of an earthquake.

The amount of energy released by an earthquake is measured and represented by its magnitude. One common type of magnitude measurement is the Richter scale, named after the U.S. seismologist Charles Francis Richter (1900–1985). The Richter scale is logarithmic, meaning the seismic energy of a magnitude 7 earthquake is one thousand times greater than that of a magnitude 5 earthquake.

Earthquake Catastrophes

The following examples from different regions provide vivid examples of the kind of devastation earthquakes can inflict on human populations.

1906: San Francisco, California

The 18 April 1906 San Francisco earthquake, with a magnitude of 7.8, remains one of the most cataclysmic in Californian history. The damaged region extended over 600 square kilometers (about 232 square miles). The earthquake was felt in most of California and parts of western Nevada and southern Oregon. The earthquake caused the longest rupture of a fault that has been observed in the contiguous United States. The displacement of the San Andreas Fault was observed over a distance of 300 kilometers (about 186 miles). The maximum intensity of XI, measured on the Modified Mercalli Intensity Scale ratings of I–XII, was based on geologic effects.

The earthquake and resulting fires took an estimated three thousand lives and caused about $524 million in property loss. The earthquake damaged buildings and structures in all parts of the city and county of San Francisco. Brick and frame houses of ordinary construction were damaged considerably or completely destroyed, and sewers and water mains were broken, including a pipeline that carried water from San Andreas Lake to San Francisco, interrupting the water supply to the city. This made it impossible to control the fires that ignited soon after the earthquake occurred, and subsequently those fires destroyed a large part of San Francisco. It was not until 1908 that San Francisco was well on the way to recovery.

1995: Hanshin-Awaji; Kobe, Japan

On 17 January 1995, the Great Hanshin-Awaji earthquake with a magnitude of 6.9 occurred directly under the industrialized urban area of Kobe, Japan, a city of about 1.5 million people. The shock occurred at a shallow depth on a fault running from Awaji Island through Kobe. Strong ground shaking lasted for about twenty seconds and caused severe damage over a large area. More than five thousand people were killed; the total cost of damage and destruction exceeded $100 billion, or

about 2 percent of Japan's gross national product. More than 150,000 buildings were ruined; highways, bridges, railroads, and subways failed; water, sewage, gas, electric power, and telephone systems were extensively damaged.

The city of Kobe—then one of the six largest container cargo ports in the world and Japan's largest—was devastated. Its relative importance as a major hub in Asia declined over the following years, with significant enormous economic consequences. With Japan's having invested heavily in earthquake research, people believed they would be ready for the next earthquake, but their faith was shattered deeply by the Kobe catastrophe.

2003: Bam, Iran

On 26 December 2003, an earthquake occurred below the city of Bam in the southeast of Iran, illustrating again the tragic connection between poor building quality and large numbers of victims. The earthquake had a magnitude of 6.5, and the hypocenter was only 8 kilometers (about 5 miles) below the city. The people of Bam were still sleeping when the earthquake struck. The death toll was estimated at 43,200, with more than 30,000 injured and 100,000 left homeless. The main reason for the large number of fatalities was the generally poor construction quality of buildings, 85 percent of which were damaged. Even though experts had classified the region as a highly exposed zone prior to the earthquake, many of the residences were traditional houses of mud-brick construction, with heavy roofs. Unreinforced masonry holds almost no resistance against the ground motion generated by strong earthquakes.

Preparing for Earthquakes

Increasing population density magnifies the potential damaging effects of earthquakes, especially in urban areas with high seismic activity—for example, San Francisco. For this reason, anti-seismic building codes

We learn geology the morning after the earthquake. • **Ralph Waldo Emerson (1803–1882)**

are important. Appropriate planning and regulation of new buildings and seismic upgrading of existing buildings can safeguard most types of buildings against earthquake shocks. One obstacle to adhering to anti-seismic building codes is high cost; this is true particularly in poorer cities in the developing world, and the effects can be particularly devastating.

Mexico City; Sichuan Province, China; Haiti

The 19 September 1985 Mexico City earthquake, occurred 200 kilometers (about 124 miles) from Mexico City, but the shaking of loose sediments in the city was much stronger than at the epicenter. Nearly ten thousand people died, and the city was heavily damaged as poorly constructed buildings collapsed. The earthquake destroyed as many as 100,000 housing units and countless public buildings.

Hundreds of millions of people live in buildings that would collapse in a strong earthquake, as happened in the mountainous Sichuan Province of China in 2008, when as many as 90,000 people were killed or remain missing, with another 374,000 injured and at least 15 million displaced.

On the afternoon of 12 January 2010, an earthquake with a magnitude of 7.0 devastated parts of Haiti, a nation on the island of Hispaniola in the Caribbean; it was the strongest in the region in over two hundred years. The earthquake occurred at a fault that runs right through Haiti and is situated along the boundary between the Caribbean and North American plates; the epicenter was just 16 kilometers (10 miles) south of the capital, Port-au-Prince, whose population at the time was over 2 million. Aftershocks continued for days, including one a week later registering a magnitude of 5.9. As of late January 2010 the projected death toll ranged from 70,000 to 200,000. The severity of the earthquake

was exacerbated by two factors: the depth of the quake was shallow, meaning that energy released was closer to the Earth's surface and less able to be absorbed by the Earth's crust; and nearly all of the buildings in Haiti were substandard construction, many cinderblock and mortar.

It is anticipated that, in the future, more catastrophes with high death tolls will occur. Owing to the rapid growth of many developing-world metropolises in highly exposed regions, such scenarios are distinctly more probable, despite the possibilities provided by modern earthquake engineering.

As of 2010, the time, location, and magnitude of earthquakes cannot be accurately predicted. Damage and casualties can be minimized, however, if builders adhere to building codes based on the seismic hazards particular to their areas.

Christa HAMMERL
Central Institute for Meteorology and Geodynamics

See also Climate Change

Further Reading

Bolt, B. A. (1976). *Nuclear explosions and earthquakes: The parted veil.* San Francisco: Freeman.

Bolt, B. A. (1993). *Earthquakes.* San Francisco: Freeman.

Ghasbanpou, J. (2004). *Bam.* Iran.

Gubbins, D. (1990). *Seismology and plate tectonics.* Cambridge, U.K.: Cambridge University Press.

Hansen, G., & Condon, E. (1990). *Denial of disaster. The untold story and photographs of the San Francisco earthquake and fire of 1906.* San Francisco: Cameron and Company.

Jones, B. G. (Ed.). (1997). *Economic consequences of earthquakes: Preparing for the unexpected.* Buffalo: State University of New York.

Lay, T., & Wallace, T. C. (1995). *Modern global seismology.* San Diego, CA: Academic Press.

Richter, C. F. (1958). *Elementary seismology.* San Francisco: Freeman.

Ecological Imperialism

Ecological imperialism is the process by which colonizers carried the plants, animals, and diseases of their homeland to new lands, albeit sometimes unintentionally. Changing a new environment to more closely resemble a familiar one was often critical to the establishment and success of the imperialists, most prominently Europeans in the Americas, Africa, and Oceania.

Imperialism is usually considered to be a political and sometimes an economic or religious phenomenon. But it also has an ecological side: imperialists have intentionally, more often unintentionally, and always inevitably carried with them plants, animals, and microlife from their lands of origin to their new lands. Where imperialists have been successful not simply in conquest but also in settlement, they have done so with the indispensable assistance of the life forms they brought with them. The most successful imperialists have been those who have, as much by chance as intention, changed the flora and fauna, macro and micro, of their new environments to be much like their old environments.

Immigrant life forms often have done poorly in their new homes: for instance, attempts to permanently establish the European nightingale in North America have never succeeded. But these immigrants, moving into environments where organisms were not preadapted to prey on or effectively resist them, have often done well indeed.

Examples of Ecological Imperialism

Ecological imperialism is as old as human migration. For example, the ancestors of the Australian aborigines arrived in Australia from the Malay Archipelago fifty or so thousand years ago and some millennia afterward imported their dog, the dingo—the continent's first domesticated animal—which figured importantly in their success there.

The best examples pertain to European expansion because the Europeans were the first to habitually cross oceans, that is to say, to travel between continents with sharply contrasting biotas (flora and fauna). The human invaders' attendant organisms spearheaded alterations in local ecosystems essential for the biological and economic success of the humans. This can be considered under three headings: crops, animals, and diseases.

Crops

Europeans learned to eat the foods of America and Oceania (lands of the Pacific Ocean) but generally preferred their own food, planting wheat, barley, rice, turnips, peas, bananas, and so forth in their colonies wherever they would grow and as soon as was practical after arrival. These crops were often particularly important in enabling the imperialists to live in numbers in areas where indigenous crops did not grow well. A good example of a successful European crop is wheat, which prospers where Native American cereals do not and provided the nutritional and economic foundation for large populations in the temperate-zone grasslands of North and South America and Australia.

Animals

European imperialists were most successful where there were few domesticated animals prior to their

Roundup on the Sherman Ranch, Geneseo, Kansas. The horses and cattle were brought to North America from Europe. New York Public Library.

arrival. In America imported pigs fed on a great variety of locally available substances propagated wildly, and pigs generously provided proteins and fats for the imperialists. Imported cattle turned what humans cannot eat—grasses and forbs (nongrass herbs)—into what they can eat—meat and milk—and were running in vast feral herds in northern Mexico and Argentina within a century or so of their arrival. Old World sheep also thrived in many of the colonies, and their numbers exploded in Australia and New Zealand. Where these and like quadrupeds—goats, for instance—did well, so did the Europeans.

Horses were slower than most imported quadrupeds to have population explosions, but they did so in time. They made supermen of the invaders in battle with native foot soldiers, most of whom had never seen such large animals before and none of whom had ever seen an animal carry a human and obey human will.

The biological revolutions underlying these successes were much more complicated than simply bringing crops and animals ashore. Whole ecosystems or at least several of their components had to be imported, too. For example, in the thirteen colonies and then the early states of the United States one of the problems of establishing large herds of domesticated animals from Europe was the fact that native grasses and forbs, products of millennia free from the tread and teeth of domesticated herds, did not tolerate heavy grazing pressure well. The importation and then often-rapid expansion of European forage plants—for instance, white clover and what Americans inaccurately call Kentucky bluegrass—unrolled a carpet of food for immigrant quadrupeds. Much the same thing happened in the humid zones of Argentina, Australia, and Argentina.

Diseases

In the first stage of European imperialism in the Americas and Oceania the triumph of the invaders over the natives seemed unlikely. The newcomers were always outnumbered. They were isolated by whole oceans from their home bases and were inexperienced in even how to survive in the new and alien environments. They were in need of powerful allies, such as the animals cited earlier and the germs they and their animals brought in their blood and breath. The Old World invaders' advantage was that their microorganic evolution and human history were different than those of the natives of the New World.

Heavy populations dependent on agriculture appeared earlier in the Old World than elsewhere, most significantly in crowded and filthy cities, providing the pathogens with food, habitat, and opportunity for transmission. Heavy populations of domesticated animals first appeared there likewise, providing more habitats for pathogens and opportunities for jumping from one species to another, including humans. The possibilities for epidemiological disasters were multiplied by the penchant of Old World peoples for long-range commerce.

When European imperialists crossed the oceans they brought with them infections unknown to American and Oceanic peoples, whose general density of population was low or relatively new, as were their cities. Large herds of domesticated animals were rare or nonexistent, and the tempo of long-range commerce was relatively low. Thus native peoples were unfamiliar with such infections as smallpox, measles, typhus, influenza, yellow fever, and malaria.

The most important or at least most spectacular of these infections in ecological imperialism was smallpox. It first arrived in the West Indies at the end of 1518, spread rapidly through the Greater Antilles and then on to Mexico, where Hernán Cortes and his conquistadors had just been driven out of the Aztec capital. All or nearly all of the Spaniards had already had the disease on the other side of the Atlantic and were immune. The peoples of Mexico were universally susceptible and died in droves.

Similar sequences of events occurred elsewhere in the Americas and Oceania. For example, the way was cleared for the Pilgrims who arrived in Plymouth, Massachusetts, in 1620 by some sort of devastating epidemic in 1616. For another example, smallpox raced through the aborigines of New South Wales in 1789 soon after the arrival of the Botany Bay colonists.

Failure of Ecological Imperialism

Where the Europeans' attendant organisms, macro and micro, triumphed, as in temperate zone regions of America and the southwest Pacific, the Europeans took over demographically. Where the triumph was mixed, as in tropical America and South Africa, the Europeans conquered militarily but not demographically. Where the attendant organisms had only minor effect, as in tropical Africa and Asia, the Europeans failed to found colonies of settlement and were ejected in the twentieth century.

Alfred W. CROSBY

University of Texas, Austin

See also Biological Exchanges; Diseases—Overview; Green Revolution

Further Reading

Campbell, Judy. (2002). *Invisible invaders: Smallpox and other diseases in aboriginal Australia, 1780–1880.* Victoria, Australia: Melbourne University Press.

Cook, N. D. (1998). *Born to die: Disease and New World conquest, 1493–1650.* Cambridge, U.K.: Cambridge University Press.

Cronon, W. (1994). *Changes in the land: Indians, colonists, and the ecology of New England.* New York: Hill and Wang.

Crosby, A. W. (1972). *The Columbian exchange: Biological and cultural consequences of 1492.* Westport, CT: Greenwood Press.

Crosby, A. W. (1986). *Ecological imperialism: The biological expansion of Europe, 900–1900.* Cambridge, U.K.: Cambridge University Press.

Diamond, J. (1996). *Guns, germs, and steel.* New York: W. W. Norton & Company.

Melville, E. G. K. (1994). *A plague of sheep: Environmental consequences of the conquest of Mexico.* Cambridge, U.K.: Cambridge University Press.

Merchant, C. (1989). *Ecological revolutions: Nature, gender, and science in New England.* Chapel Hill: University of Carolina Press.

Thornton, R. (1987). *American Indian holocaust and survival: A population history since 1492.* Norman: University of Oklahoma Press.

Todd, K. (2001). *Tinkering with Eden: A natural history of exotics in America.* New York: W. W. Norton & Company.

Energy

From simple mechanical muscle energy to the energy derived from radioactive materials, energy use has ebbed and flowed throughout history. The economic, social, and political consequences of these changes are great, correlating with the rise and fall of empires and eras. Energy use continues to evolve in tandem with humanity and will dictate which choices are available for future development.

When seen from the most fundamental physical point of view, all processes—natural or social, geological or historical, gradual or sudden—are just conversions of energy that must conform to the laws of thermodynamics as such conversions increase the overall entropy (the degree of disorder or uncertainty) of the universe. This perspective would make the possession and mastery of energy resources and their ingenious use the critical factor shaping human affairs. Also, given the progressively higher use of energy in major civilizations, this perspective would lead logically to a notion of linear advances with history reduced to a quest for increased complexity that is made possible by higher energy flows. People who could command—and societies and civilizations who could use large or high-quality energy resources with superior intensities or efficiencies—would be obvious thermodynamic winners; those converting less with lower efficiencies would be fundamentally disadvantaged.

Such a deterministic interpretation of energy's role in world history may be a flawless proposition in terms of fundamental physics, but it amounts to a historically untenable reductionism (explanation of complex life-science processes and phenomena in terms of the laws of physics and chemistry) of vastly more complex realities. Energy sources and their conversions do not determine a society's aspirations, its ethos (distinguishing character, sentiment, moral nature, or guiding beliefs) and cohesion, its fundamental cultural accomplishments, its long-term resilience or fragility.

Nicholas Georgescu-Roegen, a pioneer of thermodynamic studies of economy and the environment, made a similar point in 1980 by emphasizing that such physical fundamentals are akin to geometric constraints on the size of the diagonals in a square—but they do not determine its color and tell us nothing whatsoever about how that color came about. Analogically, all societies have their overall scope of action, their technical and economic capacities, and their social achievements constrained by the kinds of energy sources and by varieties and efficiencies of prime movers that they rely on—but these constraints cannot explain such critical cultural factors as creative brilliance or religious fervor, and they offer little predictive guidance regarding a society's form and efficiency of governance or its dedication to the welfare of its citizens. The best explanation of energy's role in history thus calls for a difficult task of balancing these two realities, of striving for explanations that take account of these opposites.

Periodization based on the dominant uses of primary energy cleaves world history into just two highly asymmetrical spans: the renewable fuel era and the nonrenewable fuel era. All premodern societies relied overwhelmingly on solar, that is, perpetually (when measured on civilizational time scales) renewable energies. They derived their heat and light from biomass (the amount of living matter) that is produced by

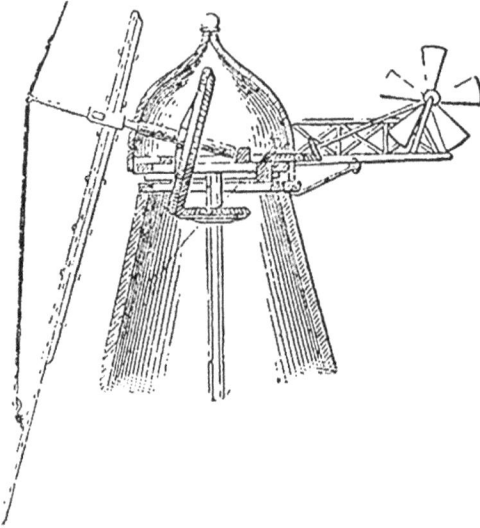

This diagram shows the primary mechanical parts of the upper portion of a windmill.

photosynthetic conversion of sunlight and harvested mostly as wood and crop residues, above all straws and stalks; plant and animal fats were also used in lighting. Their kinetic energy came from human and animal metabolism (energized, obviously, by eating the biomass) and, to a much lesser extent, from wind and flowing water, the two forms of converted solar radiation (after it is absorbed by the Earth's biosphere) that power the global water cycle and atmospheric circulation.

Fossil fuels, too, had their origin in photosynthesis, but the constituent biomass was subsequently transformed into qualitatively new materials over a period of 1 million to 100 million years by high temperatures and pressures in the uppermost layers of the Earth's crust. Consequently, fossil fuels—ranging, in the ascending order of quality, from peats through various coals (lignites to anthracites) to hydrocarbons (crude oils and natural gases)—are not renewable on historic time scales. This means that premodern, solar societies had an energy basis whose potential longevity coincided with the remaining duration of the biosphere (the part of the world in which life can exist) itself (i.e., still hundreds of millions of years to go). On the other hand, modern societies will have to change their energy base if they are to survive for more than a few hundred years.

Biomass Fuels

Biomass fuels had two inherent disadvantages: low power density (expressed in watts per square meter—W/m2) and low energy density (expressed in joules per kilogram—J/kg). Even in rich forests biomass was harvested with densities not surpassing 1 W/m2, but most people did not have tools to cut mature tree trunks and had to rely on smaller trees, branches, and leaves gathered with much lower density. Similarly, the collection of crop residues, needed also as feed and as a raw material, rarely yielded more than 0.1 W/m2. Consequently, extensive forested areas were needed in order to supply the energy needs of larger settlements. A large preindustrial city in a temperate climate would have required at least 20 to 30 watts (W) per square meter of its built-up area for heating, cooking, and manufacturing, and, depending on the kind fuel it used, it would have needed a nearby area of up to three hundred times its size to supply its fuel. The constraint is clear: no temperate-climate megacities of 10 million people or more could have existed during the era when wood was the main source of energy.

These power density limitations became even more acute after charcoal became used on a relatively large scale. Conversion from wood to charcoal was done to increase wood's low energy density: in its air-dried

Table 1.
Energy Densities of Common Fuels

Fuel	Density (MJ/kg)
Dried dung	10–12
Air-dried straw	14–16
Air-dried wood	15–17
Charcoal	28–29
Lignites	10–20
Bituminous coals	20–26
Anthracites	27–30
Crude oil	41–42
Gasoline	44–45
Natural gas (cubic meters)	33–37

Source: Smil (1991).

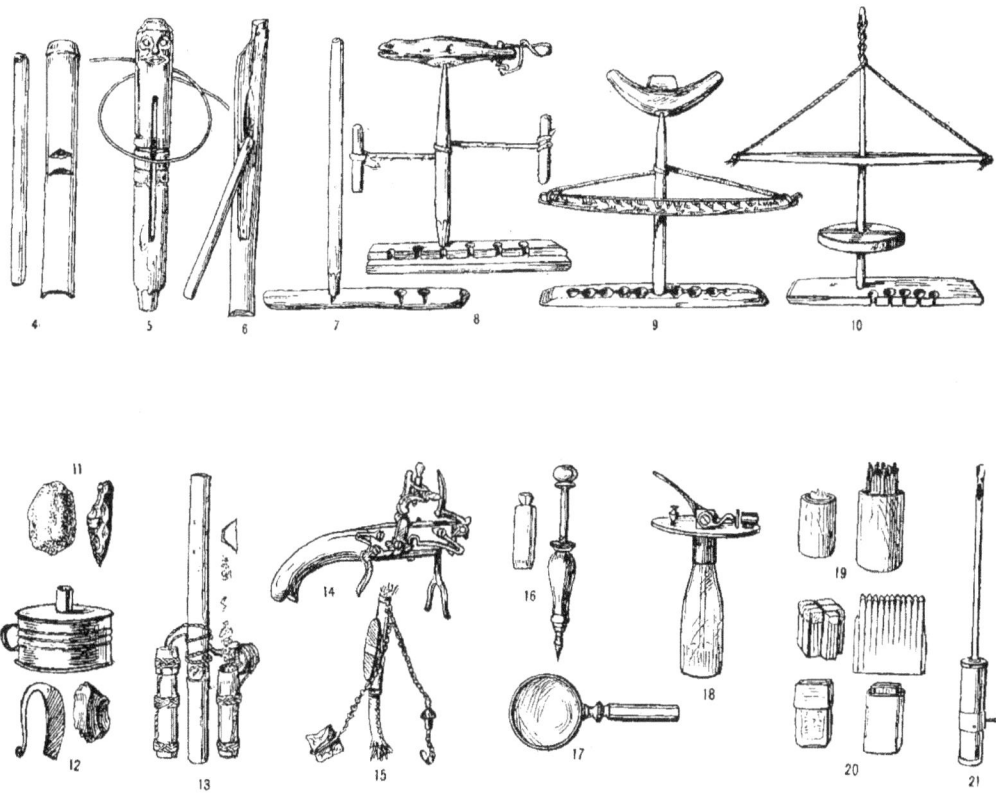

This series of drawings shows the variety of means used to make fire over time and across cultures: (4) fire saw from Borneo; (5) fire thong from Borneo; (6) fire plow from Polynesia; (7) fire drill from Native America; (8) fire drill from Inuit of Alaska; (9) fire drill from Inuit of Alaska; (10) fire drill from Iroquois of Canada; (11) strike-a-light from Inuit of Alaska; (12) strike-a-light from England; (13) strike-a-light from Malaysia; (14) tinder pistol from England; (15) strike-a-light from Spain; (16) fire syringe from Thailand and Malaysia; (17) lens from ancient Greece; (18) hydrogen lamp from Germany; (19) match light box from Austria; (20) matches; (21) electric gas lighter from the United States.

form (about 20 percent moisture) the fuel had about 18 MJ/kg, whereas charcoal rates about 60 percent higher at 29 MJ/kg. The obvious advantages of the better fuel include smaller mass to be transported and stored, smaller furnaces (or braziers), less frequent stoking, and less air pollution. But traditional charcoaling was inefficient, wasting about 80 percent of the initially used wood in the process. This waste would put a great strain on wood resources even if charcoal's use was limited to space heating and cooking, but its expanded use in various manufactures and in metallurgy made it an acutely limiting factor. For example, in 1810 the metallurgical charcoal needs of

the United States prorated annually to a forested area of roughly 50 by 50 kilometers (2,500 square kilometers), and a century later they would have amounted to an area of 170,000 square kilometers, equal to a square whose side is the distance between Philadelphia and Boston. The constraint is clear: no global steel-dominated civilization based on charcoal could exist, and coal-derived coke took over.

Human and Animal Muscles

Similarly, the limited power of human and animal muscles constrained productive capacities as well as

Russell Lee, *Filling Station and Garage at Pie Town, New Mexico* (1940). Color slide. This photo is part of an iconic series commissioned by the Farm Security Administration to document life in the United States after the Depression. Library of Congress.

aggressive forays of all traditional societies. Healthy adults can sustain work at 40–50 percent of their maximum aerobic capacity, and for men (assuming muscle efficiencies of 20 percent) this translates to 70–100 W of useful work. Small bovines (cattle and water buffalo) can sustain about 300 W, lighter horses around 500 W, and heavier animals 800–900 W (one horsepower is equal to 745 W). These rates give common equivalences of at least four men for an ox and eight to ten men for a horse. No less importantly, heavier draft animals can develop briefly maximum power well in excess of 3 kilowatts (kW) and can thus perform tasks unattainable by men (plowing heavy soils, pulling out tree stumps). Larger numbers of stronger draft animals thus greatly improved the productivity of traditional farming: even slow plowing was three to five times faster than hoeing.

These gains, however, had to be paid for by devoting more time to caring for these animals and devoting increasing amounts of land to their feeding. For example, feeding the peak number of U.S. farm horses and mules in 1919 (approximately 25 million) required about 20 percent of the country's farmland. Obviously, only countries endowed with extensive farmland could afford this burden: the option was foreclosed for Japan, China, or India. Heavier draft animals and better implements eventually cut the time that was spent in producing staple crops. For example, all fieldwork on a hectare of wheat required

180 hours in medieval England, 120 hours in early nineteenth-century Holland, and 60 hours on the U.S. Great Plains in 1900. But in any society where food production was energized solely by human and animal muscles, most of the labor force had to be employed in agriculture. The rates ranged from more than 90 percent in imperial China to more than 66 percent in the post–Civil War United States, and in all traditional agricultures children commonly helped adults.

Limits were also obvious in warfare because even trained muscles could impart relatively restrained destructive force to the tools of war, a reality made clear by comparing kinetic energies of common pre-industrial weapons. The kinetic energy of a single stone ball shot from a medieval cannon equaled that of five hundred arrows discharged from heavy crossbows or one thousand thrusts delivered with heavy swords. Pregunpowder battles thus consisted of limited expenditures of muscular energy, a reality that explains frequent preference for either sieges or stealthy maneuvers. Wars became much more destructive only with the introduction of gunpowder—in China during the tenth century and in Europe at the beginning of the fourteenth century.

Speed of travel was another obvious constraint imposed by animate metabolism and by inefficient conversion of wind. Speedy running and horse

The water mill at *Tranquille Mills, Kamloops Lake,* **British Columbia, 1871.** Photo by Benjamin F. Baltzly. McCord Museum.

riding were used only for urgent messaging, and impressive distances could be covered in a single day: the maximum on Roman roads was up to 380 kilometers. Speeds of normal travel, however, were restricted to 10–15 kilometers a day for men with wheelbarrows (a common means of transport in imperial China), not much more for wagons drawn by oxen, 30–40 kilometers for wagons pulled by heavy horses, and 50–70 kilometers for passenger horse carts on relatively good roads. The prohibitive costs of animate land transport are perfectly illustrated by prices noted in the Roman emperor Diocletian's famous *edictum de pretiis* (price edict): in 301 CE moving grain just 120 kilometers by road cost more than shipping it from Egypt to Ostia, Rome's harbor.

Preindustrial Inanimate Prime Movers

Most preindustrial Old World societies eventually introduced simple mechanical devices to convert two indirect solar energy flows—flowing water and wind—to rotary power, and they also used sails to propel their ships. The evolution of sails shows slow progress from inefficient square sails of ancient Egypt and classical Mediterranean cultures to triangular sails of the Muslim world, batten sails of medieval China, and finally complex rigging (flying jibs, fore, main, mizzen, topgallant, and spanker sails) of large ships that early modern Europe sent on its global conquests during the eighteenth and nineteenth centuries. Although seaborne transport was by far the cheapest alternative, it was both unpredictable and unreliable.

The best sailing ships—British and U.S. China clippers of the second half of the nineteenth century—could average more than 30 kilometers per hour for hours and came close to 20 kilometers per hour for entire intercontinental journeys, whereas the best Roman cargo vessels could not surpass 10 kilometers per hour. But all sailing ships had to resort to extensive tacking when sailing into the wind or could be becalmed by lack of winds. Consequently, grain ships sailing between Ostia and Egypt could take as little as a week or as long as three months or more, and two thousand years later homeward-bound English ships had to wait sometimes up to three months for the right wind to take them into Plymouth Sound.

The origins of waterwheels remain uncertain, but, notwithstanding such impressive examples as a cascade of Roman watermills in Barbegal in southern France, they were of limited importance in all classical societies where slave labor provided cheap energy for grain milling and manufacturing tasks. Waterwheels did become particularly important in some medieval societies where their power was used above all for food processing, wood sawing, and metallurgical processing. However, eight hundred years passed before the capacities of the largest wheels increased tenfold, and by the beginning of the eighteenth century, when they were the largest available prime movers, their European ratings averaged less than 4 kW, an equivalent of just five heavy horses. Windmills appeared only toward the end of the first millennium CE and, much as waterwheels, became eventually important in some Middle Eastern and Mediterranean countries and in parts of the coastal Atlantic Europe.

Table 2.
Sustained Power of Mobile Prime Movers

Prime Mover	Sustained Power (W)
Working child	30
Small woman	60
Strong man	100
Donkey	150
Small ox	300
Typical horse	600
Heavy horse	800
Early small tractor (1920)	10,000
Ford's Model T (1908)	15,000
Typical tractor (1950)	30,000
Honda Civic (2000)	79,000
Large tractor (2000)	225,000
Large diesel engine (1917)	400,000
Large marine diesel engine (1960)	30,000,000
Four gas turbines of Boeing 747 (1970)	60,000,000

Source: Assembled from data in Smil (1994 and 2003).

Again, however, even the relatively advanced Dutch machines averaged less than 5 kW during the eighteenth century.

As a result, societies that derived their kinetic energy almost exclusively or overwhelmingly from animate power that was supplemented locally and regionally by small waterwheels and windmills could not guarantee either an adequate food supply or a modicum of material comforts for most of their inhabitants. Nutrition remained barely sufficient even after good harvests (yields remained static for centuries), famines were recurrent, small-scale artisanal manufactures (except for a limited luxury trade) were inefficient and limited to a narrow range of crude products, typical personal possessions were meager, illiteracy was the norm, and leisure and travel were uncommon.

Fossil Fuels, Prime Movers, Electricity

All of those circumstances changed with the introduction of fossil fuels. Although people had used coal in parts of Europe and Asia in limited ways for centuries, the Western transition from biomass to coal took place (obviously with the exception of England) only during the nineteenth century (for example, in the United States wood supplied more than half of all primary energy until the early 1880s), and in the most populous Asian countries the transition was accomplished only during the second half of the twentieth century. The oldest fossil fuels (anthracites) go back 100 million years, the youngest ones (peats) go back just 1,000 years. Both solid fuels (different kinds of coal) and hydrocarbons (crude oils and natural gases) are found in often highly concentrated deposits from which they can be extracted with extraordinarily high-power densities: coal mines with multiple seams and rich oil and gas fields can produce between 1,000 and 10,000 W/m2, densities 10,000–100,000 higher than those for biomass fuels.

Moreover, fossil fuels, with the exception of marginal kinds such as low-quality lignites and peat, also have much higher energy densities: steam coal, now used largely for electricity generation, rates 22–26 MJ/kg, and crude oil and refined products rate 42–44 MJ/kg. Extraction and distribution of fossil fuels thus create energy systems that are the opposite of biomass-based societies: high-energy-density fuels are produced from a limited number of highly concentrated deposits and then distributed not just regionally or nationally but increasingly also globally. The distribution task is particularly easy with liquid hydrocarbons that are shipped by large tankers or sent through large-diameter pipelines. Not surprisingly, liquid fuels became the world's leading energy sources during the latter half of the twentieth century.

Desirable qualities of fossil fuels were greatly augmented by two fundamental technical revolutions: the invention and rapid commercial adoption of new mechanical prime movers, and by the creation of an entirely new energy system that produced and distributed electricity. Chronologically, the new inanimate prime movers were steam engines, internal combustion engines, steam turbines, and gas turbines, and their evolution has brought increased overall capacities and higher conversion efficiencies. The English inventor Thomas Newcomen's steam engines (after 1700) were extraordinarily wasteful, converting no more than 0.5 percent of energy in coal into reciprocating motion; the Scottish inventor James Watt's radical redesign

Table 3.
Sustained Power of Stationary Prime Movers

Prime Mover	Sustained Power (W)
Large Roman waterwheel (200 CE)	2,000
Typical European waterwheel (1700)	4,000
Large Dutch windmill (1720)	5,000
Newcomen's steam engine (1730)	10,000
Watt's largest steam engine (1800)	100,000
Large steam engine (1850)	250,000
Parsons's steam turbine (1900)	1,000,000
Largest steam engine (1900)	3,500,000
Typical steam turbine (1950)	100,000,000
Largest steam turbine (2000)	1,500,000,000

Source: Assembled from data in Smil (1994 and 2003).

(separate condenser) raised the performance to 5 percent by 1800, and his machines averaged about 20 kW, equivalent to two dozen good horses. Before the end of the nineteenth century gradual improvements increased the power of the largest steam engines to the equivalent of four thousand horses and their efficiency to more than 10 percent.

These machines powered the main phase of nineteenth-century industrialization by mechanizing many industrial processes, expanding productive capacities, and putting the cost of an increasing range of basic consumer products within the reach of average families. Their impact was particularly critical in coal mining, the iron and steel industry, and machine construction. They also offered unprecedented power for both landborne and waterborne transportation. By 1900 railways offered scheduled services at speeds an order of magnitude faster than those of horse-drawn carriages, and large steamships cut the transatlantic crossing to less than six days, compared to the pre-1830s mean of nearly four weeks.

Their peak was short-lived however: during the last two decades of the nineteenth century small steam engines began to be replaced by internal combustion machines and the large ones by steam turbines. Internal combustion engines of the German engineer Nicolaus Otto's motorcycle (commercialized as stationary machines after 1866 and as wheeled transport by the German engineers Gottlieb Daimler, Karl Benz, and Wilhelm Maybach starting in the 1880s) eventually reached efficiencies in excess of 20 percent. Inherently more efficient engines of the German engineer Rudolf Diesel (introduced after 1900) reached more than 30 percent. Inventions of the 1880s, the most innovation-packed decade in history, also laid lasting foundations for the development of the electric industry with the U.S. inventor Thomas Edison's development of an entirely new energy system (a contribution more important than his tenacious work on incandescent light), the U.S. inventor Nikola Tesla's electric motor, and the Irish engineer Charles Parsons's steam turbine.

Electricity provided the superlative form of energy: clean at the point of use, convenient, flexible to use (as light, heat, motion), and amenable to precise control. The latter fact revolutionized industrial production as electric motors (eventually more than 90 percent efficient) replaced unwieldy and wasteful steam-driven shafts and belts. The last of the modern prime movers, the gas turbine, was introduced for aircraft jet propulsion during the 1930s, and later it also became a common choice for generation of electricity. All of these machines were much lighter per unit of installed power than were steam engines—and hence more compact and (with the exception of large steam turbogenerators) suitable for mobile applications.

On the destructive side the Swedish manufacturer Alfred Nobel's invention of dynamite introduced an explosive whose detonation velocity was nearly four times that of gunpowder, and even more powerful compounds followed soon. By 1945 destructiveness was raised to an entirely new level by the development of nuclear-fission weapons, with fusion bombs following just a few years later. By the time the Cold War ended in 1990 with the demise of the USSR, the two superpowers had diverted significant shares of their total energy consumption to the assembly of an incredibly destructive arsenal that amounted to nearly twenty-five thousand strategic nuclear warheads whose aggregate capacity was equivalent to nearly half a million Hiroshima bombs.

Modern Energy Systems

Every component of fossil-fueled energy systems experienced impressive gains in capacity and efficiency,

A milk seller in Brussels, Belgium, circa the 1890s. The power of wind has been harnessed for centuries to mill grain.

the combination that resulted in large increases in per capita consumption of energy. Although the world's population nearly quadrupled between 1900 and 2000 (from 1.6 billion to 6.1 billion), the average annual per capita supply of commercial energy more than quadrupled, and higher efficiencies meant that in the year 2000 the world had at its disposal about twenty-five times more useful commercial energy than it did in 1900. As a result, today's affluent economies have experienced eightfold to tenfold increases in the per capita supply of useful energy services (heat, light, motion), and the corresponding multiples have exceeded twenty-, or even thirtyfold, in such industrializing countries as China or Brazil: never before in history had an even remotely comparable gain translated into enormous improvements in the quality of life.

Gains in energy flows that are controlled directly, and casually, by individuals were equally stunning. In 1900 even a well-off U.S. farmer holding the reins of six large horses controlled sustained delivery of no

more than 5 kW of animate power; a century later his great-grandson driving a large tractor controlled more than 250 kW from the air-conditioned comfort of his cabin. In 1900 a stoker on a transcontinental train traveling at 100 kilometers per hour worked hard to sustain about 1 megawatt (MW) of steam power; in 2000 a pilot of a Boeing 747 retracing the same route 11 kilometers above the Earth's surface merely supervised computerized discharge of up to 60 MW at a cruising speed of 900 kilometers per hour.

In 2000, however, the benefits of those spectacular energy flows remained unevenly divided. When measured in metric tons of oil equivalent (toe), annual per capita energy consumption in the year 2000 ranged from about 8 in the United States and Canada to 4 in Germany and Japan, less than 3 in South Africa, 1 in Brazil, about 0.75 in China, and less than 0.25 in many countries of sub-Saharan Africa. Yet a closer look at the rewards of high energy consumption shows that all of the quality-of-life variables (life expectancy, food supply, personal income, literacy, political freedom) relate to average per capita energy use in a distinctly nonlinear manner: clear diminishing returns set in for all of these variables as the energy use increases beyond 1–2 toe/capita, and there are hardly any additional gains attached to levels above roughly 2.5 toe. This reality becomes obvious when one asks a simple question: have the lives of U.S. citizens of the last two generations been twice as good (twice as long, healthy, productive, literate, informed, or free) as those of people in western Europe or Japan?

What does a rich energy endowment do for a country? In the United States it has obviously contributed to the country's emergence as an economic, military, and technical superpower—but it could not prevent the collapse of the USSR, which was in 1989 the world's largest producer of fossil fuels. Other prominent examples of the failure to use rich energy resources to build modern, prosperous societies include such different societies as Iran, Nigeria, Sudan, and Indonesia: none of them secured vibrant economies and prosperous lives for its citizens. In contrast, three energy-poor

Power windmills along the ancient Silk Roads route, near Korla, Xinjiang Uygur Autonomous Region, 1993. Photo by Joan Lebold Cohen.

countries of eastern Asia (Japan, South Korea, Taiwan) became the paragons of rapid economic growth and impressive improvements in average quality of life.

Finally, energy use cannot explain the rise and fall of major civilizations and powerful societies. Such notable consolidations and expansions as the rise of Egypt's Old Kingdom, maturation of the Roman republic, unification of Han China (206 BCE–220 CE), the spread of Islam, the Mongolian conquests in Eurasia, and the enormous eastward extension of the Russian Empire cannot be linked to any new prime movers or to new, or more efficient, fuel uses. As for the declines, no drastic change of fuel base and delivery (wood, charcoal) or prime movers (slaves, oxen, horses, sailing ships, waterwheels) took place during the long decline of the western Roman Empire (the eastern part managed to survive with the identical infrastructure for another millennium), and none of the great breaks of the early modern and modern world—the French Revolution, the collapse of the czarist Russian Empire, the fall of Nationalist China, the collapse of the USSR—could be given convincing (or indeed any) energy explanations.

Energy resources and uses are, undeniably, among the critical variables whose specific and unpredictable combinations determine the fortunes of societies. They promote, restrict, or complicate many economic and individual options, and once in place they are critical for setting the tempo of life and the levels of general welfare. Immutable dictates of thermodynamics also mean that higher socioeconomic complexity requires higher energy flows. This undeniable relationship is not a matter of continuous linear progress, however, but rather one of a relatively early saturation. Moreover, possession of abundant energy sources or their high consumption cannot guarantee well-functioning economies, decent quality of life, personal happiness, or a nation's security. Energy sources and uses constrain our actions but do not dictate our choices, do not assure economic success, and do not condemn civilizations to failure. In the modern world the only inescapable consequences of

The release of atom power has changed everything except our way of thinking . . . the
solution to this problem lies in the heart of mankind. If only I had known,
I should have become a watchmaker. • **Albert Einstein (1879–1955)**

Table 4.

Energy of Weapons

Projectile	Kinetic Energy of Projectile (J)
Arrow from a bow	20
Arrow from a heavy crossbow	100
Bullet from a Civil War musket	1×10^3
Bullet from an assault rifle (M16)	2×10^3
Stone ball from a medieval cannon	50×10^3
Iron ball from an eighteenth-century cannon	300×10^3
Shrapnel shell from World War I artillery gun	1×10^6
High-explosive shell from a heavy World War II antiaircraft gun	6×10^6
Depleted uranium shell from M1A1 Abrams tank	6×10^6
Hijacked Boeing 767 (11 September 2001)	4×10^9
Explosives	**Energy Discharged (J)**
Hand grenade	2×10^6
Suicide bomber	100×10^6
World War II gun shrapnel	600×10^6
Ammonium nitrate-fuel oil (ANO) truck bomb (500 kilograms)	2×10^9
Hiroshima bomb (1945)	52×10^{12}
U.S. ICBM warhead	1×10^{15}
Tested Novaya Zemlya fusion bomb (1961)	240×10^{15}

Source: Author's calculations using primary data from a variety of sources.

higher energy use are greater impacts on the Earth's biosphere: the fate of modern civilization may be ultimately decided by our capacity to deal with this challenge.

Vaclav SMIL

University of Manitoba

See also Natural Gas; Water Energy; Water Management; Wind Energy

Further Reading

Adams, R. N. (1982). *Paradoxical harvest.* Cambridge, U.K.: Cambridge University Press.

Basalla, G. (1988). *The evolution of technology.* Cambridge, U.K.: Cambridge University Press.

Chaisson, E. (2001). *Cosmic Evolution: The Rise of Complexity in Nature.* Cambridge, MA: Harvard University Press.

Cleveland, C. (Ed.). (2004). *Encyclopedia of energy.* Amsterdam: Elsevier.

Finniston, M., Williams, T., & Biseell, C. (Eds.). (1992). *Oxford illustrated encyclopedia: Vol. 6. Invention and technology.* Oxford, U.K.: Oxford University Press.

Jones, H. M. (1970). *The age of energy.* New York: Viking.

MacKay, D. J. C. (2009.) *Sustainable energy—without the hot air.* Cambridge, U.K.: Cambridge University Press.

Smil, V. (1991). *General energetics.* Cambridge, MA: MIT Press.

Smil, V. (1994). *Energy in world history.* Boulder, CO: Westview.

Environmental Movements

Although the term *environmentalism* was not used until much later, the roots of environmental movements date back to the 1800s, when demands for cleaner water and air and the protection of wilderness became common. Industrialization and colonialism sparked the first environmentalist voices. Though goals and intentions of the countless organizations vary, environmental movements as a whole remain an important aspect of modern society.

Environmental, or green, movements appeared around the globe during the second half of the twentieth century as people agitated in reaction to local problems, affected the policies and organization of national governments (including the origin of environmental departments in almost every nation), and helped to create national and international laws, international bodies, and important treaties. Few other popular movements spread so far, had such complex ramifications, and lasted so long with the promise of continuing influence.

To present green or environmental movements as a recent phenomenon, arising during the years after World War II, however, would be misleading. They had their roots in the conservation movement that began a century earlier. Many voices had demanded clean water and air, parks and open space, the humane treatment of animals and the protection of bird species, the preservation of wilderness, and the provision of outdoor recreation. Communities in many places began to see their welfare as being connected with the health of their land, their forests, their waters, and their clean air. Although people did not yet use the term *environmentalism*, the actions of people

to protect their valued habitats, to protest against developments that threatened to destroy them, and to search for ways to live in harmony with nature constituted an effort that has come to be known by that term.

People voiced those concerns during the late eighteenth and the nineteenth centuries when the Industrial Revolution was polluting and otherwise harming the landscape of the Western world, and colonialism was making depredations on the natural resources of the rest of the world. For example, deforestation altered small islands in the Atlantic and Indian Oceans so rapidly that European scientists who were sent out by the colonial powers noted exhaustion of timber and desiccation of climates and called for restorative action. Pierre Poivre, a French botanist, warned in 1763 that the removal of forests would cause loss of rainfall and recommended the reforestation of island colonies. Both France and Britain soon established forest reserves in their colonies, including British India. Unfortunately reserves often meant that local people were excluded from their own forests, and this exclusion produced outbreaks of resistance during the 1800s. Some European environmentalists raised their voices loudly against mistreatment of indigenous peoples. A few of these environmentalists were feminists, and some, such as the surgeon Edward Green Balfour, were willing to alarm their superiors with advocacy of not only conservation, but also anticolonialism.

The rapid sweep of resource exploitation across the North American continent aroused a few opposing voices. The artist George Catlin in 1832 advocated that a section of the Great Plains be set aside as a national park to preserve bison herds and their native

American Indian hunters. Writers William Wordsworth in England and Henry David Thoreau in the United States maintained that the authentic human self can best be realized in contact with wild nature. The Scottish-American writer John Muir became an advocate for wilderness and found many people agreeing with him. The first national park, Yellowstone, was designated in the United States in 1872, starting a movement to reserve natural areas that spread around the world. Australia declared a national park outside Sydney in 1879; Canada established Banff National Park in 1885; and South Africa in 1898 set aside an area that later became Kruger National Park. Eventually more than 110 countries established 1,200 national parks.

Through the public relations provided by many writers, including Muir, the conservation movement grew rapidly and produced many organizations. Muir's group, the Sierra Club, backed nature preservation of many kinds, successfully urging the creation of national parks and providing opportunities for its members to hike and camp in them. The Audubon Society followed in 1905, gaining protection for birds and including women leaders who convinced their peers that it was better fashion not to wear feathers in their hats. Stephen Tyng Mather, first director of the U.S. National Park Service, organized the National Parks Association in 1919 to provide support for the work of his agency. Groups appeared internationally; the World Wildlife Fund supported projects to preserve wildlife and wildlife habitats in many nations.

Voices for Sustainable Use

Not all conservationists argued for keeping natural areas in a pristine state. Some, often connected with governments, pointed out the importance of keeping reserves, especially forests, as a continuing source for needed resources such as timber. France established the Administration of Water and Forests as early as 1801, and Prussia established the Forest Service not long afterward. In 1864 the U.S. ambassador to Italy, George Perkins Marsh, published *Man and Nature*, a book warning that human-caused destruction

of forests, soils, and other resources threatened to impoverish societies everywhere. Marsh maintained that many of the changes that humans make in the natural environment, whether accompanied by good intentions or by disregard of the consequences, damage the environment's usefulness to humans. His influence was felt in the United States, Europe, and beyond, and helped to inform the movement for conservation of natural resources. In the United States that movement was exemplified by the founding of the American Forestry Association in 1875. Gifford Pinchot, who became the first chief of the U.S. Forest Service in 1905 under President Theodore Roosevelt (himself a conservationist), was a leading advocate of sustainable forest management. Pinchot had been informed by his study in French schools of forestry and by the work of Dietrich Brandis and the Forest Department in British India.

Conservationism during the early twentieth century was largely the work of committed individuals, energetic but relatively small organizations, and government land-management agencies in several countries. It was concerned with the preservation of forests, soils, water, wildlife, and outstanding natural places and the prevention of pollution in local areas, particularly in urban centers. During the years after World War II, however, more ominous and more widespread environmental problems forced themselves on the notice of people around the world to such an extent that the problems represented an environmental crisis. These problems could rarely be solved by local efforts alone: the spread of fallout from nuclear weapons testing and from accidents in nuclear power facilities, air pollution that crossed national frontiers and caused acid precipitation, persistent pesticides that lost their effectiveness even as they were applied ever more widely (and were detected in the fat of Antarctic penguins), supposedly inert chemicals that proved to attack the ozone layer, and greenhouse gases generated by countless human activities that apparently raise the temperature of the Earth. In the face of these problems, and the wider public awareness that they aroused, the conservation movement was transformed into environmental movements. The constitution of

Wildebeest graze in the Masai Mara, a wildlife refuge set aside in Kenya.

the first environmental organization under United Nations auspices, the International Union for the Protection of Nature, in 1949 defined its purpose as the preservation of the entire world biotic community. This organization became the International Union for the Conservation of Nature and Natural Resources (IUCN) in 1956.

The Emergence of Environmentalism

Environmentalism as a popular social movement emerged during the 1960s. It is often said to have begun in response to the American biologist Rachel Carson's 1962 book *Silent Spring*, which warned of the dangers of persistent pesticides such as DDT. That book dealt with only one environmental issue but found a wider international readership than any previous book on an environmental subject. Environmentalism was expressed in the first Earth Day (22 April 1970), an event primarily in the United States, although it later received international observance. By 2000 the membership of environmental organizations reached 14 million in the United States, 5 million in Britain and Germany, and 1 million in the Netherlands.

The first major international conference devoted to environmental issues was held in 1972: the United Nations Conference on the Human Environment in Stockholm, Sweden. This conference included representatives of 113 nations, 19 intergovernmental agencies, and 134 nongovernmental organizations. It marked a new awareness among nations that many environmental problems are worldwide in scope. Representatives of industrialized and developing countries attended and discussed the issues that divided those two groups. Unlike its successor conference in Rio de Janeiro in 1992, the conference in Stockholm in 1972 was not an "Earth summit." The only heads of state present were the host, Sweden's Prime Minister Olaf Palme, and Indira Gandhi of India, who served as an articulate spokesperson for views shared by developing countries. Some representatives of developing nations noted that environmentalist views were most vocal in the industrialized world—in the very nations that had reached their economic pinnacles by using natural resources from around the Earth and

A sign outside Invesco Field at Mile High in Denver (Democratic National Convention 2008), uses familiar slogans and logos to advocate recycling.

producing the major proportion of the planet's pollution. Would measures for conservation of resources and reduction of pollution limit the development of poorer countries while leaving the richer countries in relative affluence? Gandhi maintained that poverty and need are the greatest polluters and that the basic conflict is not between conservation and development but rather between environment and the reckless exploitation of humankind and nature in the name of economic expansion. She insisted that discussion of environmental problems be linked to issues posed by human needs. The Stockholm conference authorized the creation of the United Nations Environment Programme, headquartered in Nairobi, Kenya, which was given the responsibility of coordinating United Nations efforts on the environment worldwide. For example, the United Nations Environment Programme took a role in facilitating negotiation of

the 1987 Montreal Protocol for the protection of the Earth's ozone layer.

Environmental movements won legislative victories in a number of nations, creating laws to curb air and water pollution and to protect wilderness and endangered species. Most nations established governmental environmental agencies. In the United States the National Environmental Policy Act of 1969 required governmental agencies and businesses to subject development plans to environmental review.

Environmentalist political movements, which often emerged in the form of "Green" parties, appeared in Europe and elsewhere beginning during the 1970s. The German party, "Die Grünen" ("The Greens"), adopted a platform emphasizing environmental values, antinuclear activism, economic rights for workers, and participatory democracy, gaining support from groups other than environmentalists and winning

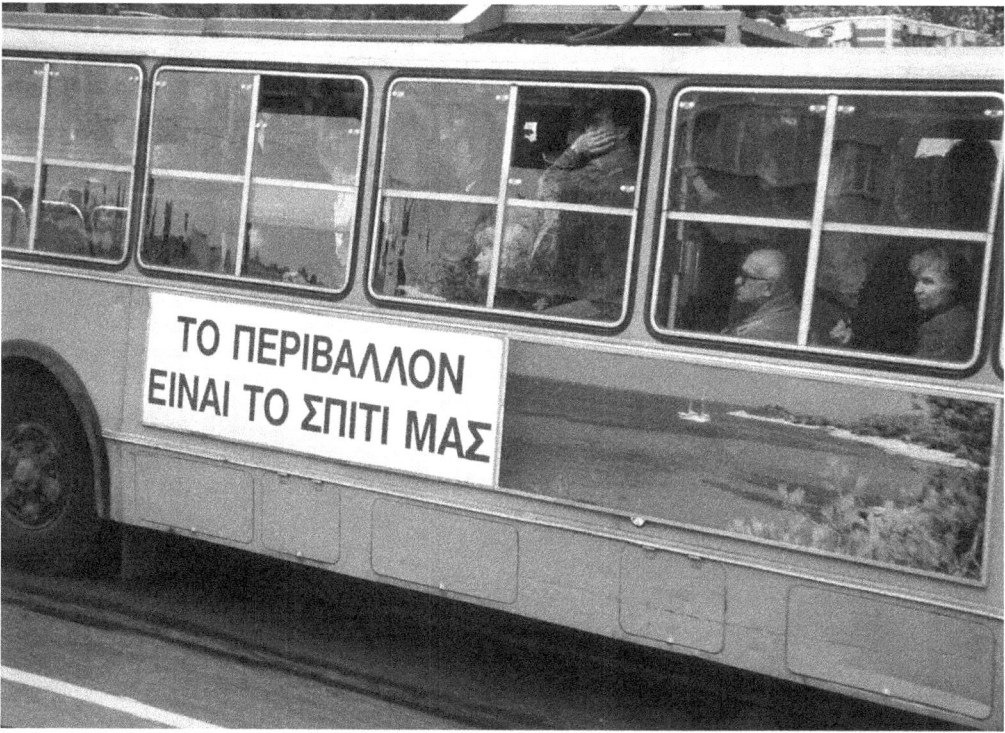

A bus in Athens carries a poster that exhorts, "The environment is our home."

enough representation in Parliament to wield a critical margin between left and right and to participate in coalition governments. Similar parties in other European countries generally polled under 10 percent of the vote. In the United States the Green Party received national attention during the presidential election of 2000 when its candidate, the consumer advocate Ralph Nader, may have garnered enough popular votes in some states to deprive Democratic candidate Al Gore, a moderate environmentalist and the author of the book, *Earth in the Balance*, of the electoral margin he needed for victory against George W. Bush.

Movements for environmental responsibility in business, investment, and commerce gained visibility, although the results were mixed. A movement for responsible business practices was urged by economists such as Herman Daly and Paul Hawken. Their "natural capitalism" advocated consideration of the total effect of businesses and industries in terms of social and environmental justice, and the

sustainability of the resources used, not just the financial "bottom line." Many corporations adopted green measures, although it was often hard to tell whether their efforts were genuine, or simply advertising ploys intended to appeal to buyers who wanted to make good environmental decisions.

Elements of environmental movements did not content themselves with seeking reform in governmental actions or international agreements, which seemed to them to be slow and inadequate. The Environmental Justice Movement organized protests reacting to the fact that many environmental hazards, such as toxic waste dumps and polluting industries, were located in neighborhoods inhabited by the poor and racial minorities. Protesters took direct action against environmentally damaging exploits such as the clear-cutting of ancient forests. In 1993, for example, Canadian citizens blocked roads being used by logging trucks of the MacMillan Bloedel Company to carry huge old-growth trees cut from the forests surrounding Clayoquot Sound on Vancouver Island. Police

The sign in this picture of a playground, painted in 1992 by a Russian school child living in Novozybkov (near the site of the 1986 Chernobyl accident), reads: "Closed: Radiation."

arrested 932 protesters, who were convicted and fined from $250 to $3,000 for defying a court injunction banning demonstrations. An eventual agreement, however, won protection for a large portion of the forests. Nonetheless, clear-cutting continued outside the protected areas by the Weyerhauser Company, MacMillan Blodel's successor, and was confronted by new environmental protests.

One of the most famous environmental protests was the Chipko movement, which began near Himalayan villages in north India in March 1973 when peasants stopped loggers from cutting down trees by threatening to hug (*chipko*) the trees and place their bodies in the path of the axes—civil disobedience inspired by the nonviolent methods of Indian nationalist Mohandas Gandhi. The trees were valuable to villagers for fuel, fodder, small timber, and protection against flooding. Many demonstrators were women, who are the wood gatherers there. Similar protests occurred elsewhere in India and met with some success. In Malaysia the Penan people of Sarawak carried out a series of direct actions, including blocking roads, to protest the destruction of their rainforest homeland by commercial loggers.

Those people who have demonstrated concern for the relationship of humans to nature have often suffered for that concern. Wangari Maathai, who began the Green Belt Movement in Kenya to enable the planting and caring for trees by women and children, was beaten and imprisoned. Subsequently, she received the

1994 Nobel Prize for her environmental work. The poet and playwright Ken Saro-Wiwa was executed by the dictatorship of Nigeria in 1995 for organizing a movement against oil drilling that produced air and water pollution in the lands of his Ogoni tribe without compensation. Judi Bari, a leader of the 1990 Redwood Summer protests against the logging of giant redwood trees in California, was maimed by a bomb placed under her car seat in an attempt to kill her. Chico Mendes, who organized the *seringueiros* (rubber tappers in the Amazon rainforest of Brazil) to defend the forest and their livelihood against illegal clearing, was murdered in 1988 by the agents of rich landowners whose financial interests in forest removal he threatened. The American Catholic nun, Sister Dorothy Mae Stang, a naturalized Brazilian citizen who had worked for thirty years on behalf of the rural poor and the environment of the Amazon basin, was shot to death at the order of landowners in 2005. Appropriately, she often wore a T-shirt with the motto: "The death of the forest is the end of our life."

One of the most striking developments in the early twenty-first century is the emergence of climate change, and specifically global warming, as the most prominent issue among those on the agenda of the environmental movement. This is the result of a growing consensus among climate scientists that the average temperature of the Earth's atmosphere and oceans has risen to a level unprecedented in recent history, to a large extent due to the release of carbon dioxide and other greenhouse gases as a result of human activities, which shows every sign of a continued increase. The consensus has been confirmed in a series of reports by the Intergovernmental Panel on Climate Change (IPCC), a large evaluative group of scientists under the auspices of the United Nations. The possible results of this increase include losses of polar and glacial ice, rising sea level and loss of coastal land, droughts and floods in some areas, increasing energy in storms including hurricanes, impacts on agriculture, and changes in range and abundance of animals and plants. The 2007 Nobel Peace Prize was awarded jointly to the IPCC and Al Gore, former vice president of the United States, for their work in disseminating knowledge about human-caused climate change and laying foundations for actions necessary to counteract it. Among the measures urged by environmental groups are restrictions on releases of carbon dioxide from sources in industry and transportation, and support for international agreements to accomplish that purpose.

Environmental movements in recent history have proved to be extraordinarily complex, including myriads of organizations, formal and informal. Their goals have been disparate, but they share the overall goal of making the Earth a better, safer, and cleaner place for its living inhabitants, human and nonhuman. Such movements have met with many successes and many failures, and their ultimate effects are still uncertain. But they are certainly among the most far-reaching and intrinsically important movements of the modern world.

J. Donald HUGHES
University of Denver

See also Climate Change; Deforestation; Desertification; Erosion; Nature; Rivers; Salinization; Timber; Water; Water Energy; Wind Energy

Further Reading

Bolin, B. (2007). *A history of the science and politics of climate change: The role of the Intergovernmental Panel on Climate Change.* Cambridge, U.K.: Cambridge University Press.

Brenton, T. (1994). *The greening of Machiavelli: The evolution of international environmental politics.* London: Earthscan Publications.

Carson, R. (1962). *Silent spring.* Boston: Houghton Mifflin.

Finger, M. (Ed.). (1992). *Research in social movements, conflicts and change, supplement 2: The Green movement worldwide.* Greenwich, CT: Jai Press.

Gore, A. (1992). *Earth in the balance: Ecology and the human spirit.* Boston: Houghton Mifflin.

Gore, A. (2006). *An inconvenient truth: The planetary emergence of global warming and what we can do about it.* Emmaus, PA: Rodale.

Grove, R. H. (1995). *Green imperialism: Colonial expansion, tropical island Edens, and the origins of environmentalism, 1600–1860.* Cambridge, U.K.: Cambridge University Press.

Guha, R. (1999). *The unquiet woods: Ecological change and peasant resistance in the Himalaya.* New Delhi, India: Oxford University Press.

Guha, R. (2000). *Environmentalism: A global history.* New York: Longman.

Hawken, P. (2007). *Blessed unrest: How the largest movement in the world came into being and why no one saw it coming.* New York: Viking.

Hays, S. P. (1982). From conservation to environment: Environmental politics in the United States since World War II. *Environmental Review, 6*(2), 14–41.

Hughes, J. D. (Ed.). (2000). *The face of the Earth: Environment and world history.* Armonk, NY: M. E. Sharpe.

Hughes, J. D. (2001). *An environmental history of the world: Humankind's changing role in the community of life.* London: Routledge.

Hughes, J. D. (2006). *What is environmental history?* Cambridge, U.K.: Polity.

Jamison, A., Eyerman, R., Cramer, J., & Lessoe, J. (1990). *The making of the new environmental consciousness: A comparative study of environmental movements in Sweden, Denmark, and the Netherlands.* Edinburgh, U.K.: Edinburgh University Press.

McCormick, J. (1989). *Reclaiming paradise: The global environmental movement.* Bloomington: Indiana University Press.

McNeill, J. R. (2000). *Something new under the sun: An environmental history of the twentieth-century world.* New York: W. W. Norton.

Merchant, C. (1992). *Radical ecology: The search for a livable world*. New York: Routledge.

Pepper, D. (1984). *The roots of modern environmentalism*. London: Croom Helm.

Prugh, T.; Costanza, R.; Cumberland, J. H.; Daly, H. E.; Goodland, R.; & Norgaard, R. B. (1999). *Natural capital and human economic survival*. Boca Raton, FL: Lewis Publishers.

Rothman, H. K. (1998). *The greening of a nation? Environmentalism in the United States since 1945*. Fort Worth, TX: Harcourt Brace.

Shabecoff, P. (1996). *A new name for peace: International environmentalism, sustainable development, and democracy*. Hanover, NH: University Press of New England.

Shabecoff, P. (2003) *A fierce green fire: The American environmental movement*. Washington, DC: Island Press.

Szasz, A. (1994). *Ecopopulism: Toxic waste and the movement for environmental justice*. Minneapolis: University of Minnesota Press.

Weiner, D. (1988). *Models of nature: Ecology, conservation, and cultural revolution in Soviet Russia*. Bloomington: Indiana University Press.

Young, J. (1990). *Sustaining the Earth*. Cambridge, MA: Harvard University Press.

Erosion

Erosion affects crop productivity and remains the largest cause of water pollution on Earth, depositing nutrients, sediments, pesticides, and fertilizers into water supplies. There are two types of erosion: natural and human-induced. Erosion prediction and the need for soil conservation became a focus in the twentieth century under President Roosevelt's New Deal, which helped spread the word about the threats of erosion.

One of the less-appreciated constants of world history has been soil erosion, because its effects may be unnoticed before crop productivity wanes. Soil erosion causes damage in two main places: where the removal occurs and where the sediment deposits. Where the erosion occurs, it removes particles, organic matter, and important nutrients since many dissolve into water. Thus the problems of on-site soil erosion are the physical loss of the medium of plant growth, nutrient depletion, and either land abandonment or the cost of conservation and reclamation. Severe erosion has removed as much as 50 meters of soil and sediment (or more) from surfaces, creating canyons where cornfields existed a few decades before. The off-site problems of erosion are at least as severe and include water pollution, sedimentation, and property burial. Indeed, soil erosion creates the largest water pollution problem on Earth by carrying nutrients and fertilizers, sediments, and pesticides into stream channels. Sedimentation fills up channels that must be dredged, or the channel capacity decreases, which cuts down on its holding capacity and increases flooding. Sedimentation has also buried whole towns and covered many valleys with several meters of often much less fertile sediment.

History

We can view the history of soil erosion as spanning several periods. It started long before human history as geological or "natural" erosion, which is generally a slow process, but given enough time it carved mile-deep and spectacular canyons. This soil erosion occurred in several temporal modes, but it was generally slow and steady over millions of years, though it could be episodically rapid and discontinuous. A second wave started with human-induced or human-accelerated erosion, when humans became technologically advanced enough to disrupt the surface vegetation through fire and the girdling of trees. Evidence suggests that cooking fires go back over 1 million years, but evidence indicates that the use of fire to control vegetation, and thus causing erosion, clearly started as a hunter-gatherer phenomenon in the Pleistocene era (about 60,000 BCE) in what is now Tanzania.

Significant soil erosion started when humans domesticated animals and plants, removed vegetation from larger areas, and thus intensified land use. This erosion presumably began with domestication and concentrated settlement around ten thousand years ago in the Near East and later elsewhere. A third period of erosion probably started with more active trail formation, continued active removal of vegetation for settlements, and soil manipulation for seedbeds. The first actual evidence for erosion seems to lag behind the earliest evidence for agriculture. This lag is about one thousand years in Greece, where the first erosion occurred in some regions about 5000 BCE. The lag also occurred in Mesoamerica, where evidence for agricultural-induced land-use change occurred around 3600 BCE, but the first wave of sedimentation from erosion occurred by 1400 BCE. Generally, this early erosion accelerated with the Bronze Age civilizations of Eurasia and the Early Pre-classic (before the first millennium CE) Americas as pioneer farmers ascended from the river valleys and lowlands and deforested steeper slopes in Mesopotamia, Mesoamerica, the Mediterranean, China, and the Indus Valley. Soil erosion waxed and waned in ancient cultures after this period, depending on soil conservation, climate change, and land-use intensity. In some parts of the Classic Americas (about the first millennium CE) in Mesoamerica and the Andes, soil conservation features sustained heavy soil use with high populations, though some studies argue that high soil demands and insufficient conservation figured in declines and collapses. The evidence for the Mediterranean is variable; there is some evidence for soil stability and some for erosion and sedimentation during the highly populated and intensely managed Hellenistic and Roman periods.

A fourth period of world soil erosion occurred with the vast breaking up of new lands around the world that resulted from colonial settlement during the sixteenth to the twentieth centuries. For the first time in history, large areas of previously uncultivated land fell under the plow in the Americas, Oceania, Siberia, Asia, and Africa. Moreover, farmers used to the relatively mild climates and low slopes of western Europe began to farm areas on steeper slopes with much more intensive precipitation or drier and more wind-erosion-prone conditions. These farmers were pioneers who came with little knowledge about their environments and ignored what conservation indigenous people had practiced. This ignorance led to devastating rates of soil erosion and lost land productivity.

The final period of world soil erosion came after World War II, with the expansion of mechanization and population growth fueled by better food and medicine. What once had been remote or marginal lands, such as steppes and tropical forests, became farmable due to the imperatives of high populations and the growing markets for tropical crops like coffee and bananas. Expanding populations and a variety of displacement processes drove farmers into lands extremely susceptible to erosion, such as that in the mountains of Central and South America, Africa, and south and east Asia. The mechanics of soil erosion alone explain why recent agricultural and wood-cutting expansion upslope into hills of Haiti, Rwanda, Madagascar, and Nepal have made human-induced soil erosion the largest agent of geomorphic change on the Earth today.

Unfortunately, even recently in the United States, with its large conservation efforts and scientific capability, almost one-third of its agricultural lands are eroding significantly faster than soil is forming. Despite this, American land continues to maintain its productivity, but at the cost of several immediate and long-term problems: sedimentation (the largest water pollutant) and its ecological impact; cost of fertilizer; and more fuel use.

Soil Erosion Processes

We cannot understand the history of soil erosion without recognizing the processes of soil erosion. Soil erosion is the movement of soil particles by wind and water moving in flows, streams, and waves. Geomorphology is the science that studies the processes and forms of the Earth's surface. Other geomorphic agents also sculpt the Earth's surface over time, including glaciers, chemical dissolution, mass movements or landslides, and of course tectonic and volcanic activities. For the most part, humans speed up Earth surface dissection in some places and sedimentation in others, playing their part in such processes as landslides, sinkhole formation, and soil, stream, and beach erosion. Soil erosion can start with raindrops that fall up to about 32 kilometers per hour and impact a soil surface, dislodging and splashing particles of mineral and organic matter upward. These particles will land slightly downwind, but this will only lead to slow creep if the vegetation cover is substantial or water does not run over the surface.

This runoff or overland flow is the second important step in erosion, and it only happens when rainfall or water delivery to a point occurs faster than soil

Rocinha favela, like many favelas in Rio and other Brazilian cities, is located on a steep hillside. A gutter running along the base of the mountain diverts runoff away from the neighborhood during the rainy season.

pores can take in water (infiltration). Runoff may also occur with snowmelt or ice melt and cause accelerated erosion on surfaces from which humans have cleared vegetation or which has been plowed. Initially with runoff, water flows over the surface and removes thin layers of soil, by raindrops dislodging particles and by the force applied by water flow. This occurs first as sheet erosion as planar flows remove particles evenly from the surface, except for the more resistant soil pedestals that are often left behind as testament to former soil surfaces. This interrill erosion occurs in the belt of no channels on the upper slopes, and can be insidious because it leaves only subtle clues but may cause high soil particle and nutrient losses.

Rills (small streams) start to form downhill from interrills where flow converges and start to dissect soil channels in three directions: headcut, downcut, and laterally cut. Rills can remove large quantities of soil, including whole sections of topsoil, but farmers can plow these out, though the plowing itself may loosen and make soils prone to erosion again. With more flow and greater turbulence, channels enlarge and tend to form in the same slopes where flows concentrate. Since plowing can expunge these larger rills, but they return in the same slope position, they are called ephemeral rills. These areas can be tilled out or left vegetated.

Gullies on the other hand are mature channels that have back, down, and laterally eroded over so large a space that normal tractors cannot plow them out. They can also be formed by waterfall erosion (runoff falls from one surface to another and undercuts the headwall surface), or by piping (water flowing underground intersects the surface, forming a surface outlet channel that erodes a larger area and undercuts surface soils that collapse along the subsurface channel). Gullies often start out being narrow and widen by channel flows undercutting their sides. Water flowing in these channels carries water in suspension and as bed load, rolling, creeping, and saltating (bouncing) downstream.

Human landscape alteration also increases the size and frequency of mass movements on slopes, stream bank erosion, coastal erosion, and wind erosion. Wind soil erosion occurs at natural and accelerated rates as well and over a large part of the Earth, especially on flat, drier, sandier, and less-vegetated areas. The key factors in wind erosion are surface cover, soil coherence, and wind intensity and duration. In many areas where all of these conditions prevail, such as in Loess Plateau of China, which has had among the highest rates of erosion for millennia, water erosion is also very high. The processes of wind erosion starts with sediment load in a channel being carried in suspension by winds fast enough to hold up particles or those particles being rolled or saltated along the ground. Over 90 percent of the sediment is carried less than 1 meter above the surface, and all soil textures (clay, silt, and sand and even gravel) can be carried by wind, depending on aggregation, shape, and density. Winds tend to carry the larger particles like sands over shorter distances as creep or saltation. They can and do carry clays over thousands of kilometers, but clays also cohere into large enough clods that they resist deflation. Thus under normal winds, silt and fine sand is often the texture size that deflates, suspends, travels, and drops out into deposits at predictable distances from the point of erosion. These deposition areas build up and become the world's extensive loess (wind-deposited, loamy soil) deposits, like those in China, central Europe, the Mississippi Valley, and the Palouse region of Washington State, often fertile but highly erosive landscapes.

Measuring and Predicting Erosion

Humans have recognized the on-site and off-site problems due to soil erosion for millennia. Terracing started at least five thousand years ago, and structures to divert runoff were common in many ancient societies. Yet it was not until the early twentieth century that policy makers and scientists recognized the need to predict

soil erosion. In 1908, President Theodore Roosevelt recognized that soil erosion was among the most dangerous environmental challenges. But the affective response to soil erosion in the United States only came during the mid-1930s in the form of the Soil Conservation Service (SCS)—formerly the Soil Erosion Service of 1933 and now the Natural Resources Conservation Service. The SCS was the largest factor in the spread of soil conservation in the United States, made possible by President Franklin D. Roosevelt's New Deal and enthusiastically championed by H. H. Bennett, the first and most prominent director of the service. The New Deal spread the word about erosion and conservation through funding rural development, art, and science. For example, it organized conservation demonstrations and the Civilian Conservation Corps projects that built check dams and terracing around the United States. The New Deal also used science and scientific management, building predictive models by collecting more than eleven thousand so-called plot years of erosion data from around the United States under different land uses and constant slope lengths and distances. (Scientists can measure erosion using many techniques that have helped them understand both natural and accelerated rates of soil erosion. Measurement has focused on pin studies on natural slopes that have recorded truncation of soils under a variety of land uses and rain intensities and under physically and mathematically simulated conditions.)

Scientists led by Walter Wischmeier at Purdue University forged the plot data into the Universal Soil Loss Equation (USLE), a predictive equation that could be used by farmers and scientists to estimate and compare soil erosion under different crop types and conservation practices. The equation applies well to the regions in the United States from which it was empirically derived, and many studies have adapted it to many other parts of the world with variable success. The equation predicts sheet and rill erosion based on six variables: rainfall intensity, soil erodibility, slope length, slope gradient, crop types, and conservation practices (RKLSCP). Scientists further adapted the USLE into the Revised USLE (RUSLE), which is based on the same set of factors. These

Gold miners gather on site in South Africa, circa early twentieth century. Mining has been a major cause of erosion for hundreds of years.

equations have become codified as tools for policy and as important foundations of conservation planning for many land uses and are now available for use around the world from the U.S. Department of Agriculture's Agricultural Research Service (2006). Many scientists have also worked on a variety of physically based or process-oriented models that attempt to simulate the natural, physical processes of soil erosion, such as detachment. This next generation of models, such as the Water Erosion Prediction Process (WEPP) model, should more accurately predict more types of erosion and deposition across a landscape from sheet, rill, and channel erosion.

Soil Erosion in Perspective

Soil erosion has ramped up and waxed and waned through five major periods in world history. Despite twentieth-century advances in understanding soil erosion and conservation in the United States and other developed nations, the rates of soil erosion have not really waned in much of the developing world in the last half-century. Indeed, humans today, through soil erosion, are the leading geomorphic agents on the Earth. The periods when soil erosion ramped up came as the result of technological breakthroughs and population expansions that allowed humans to alter the landscape: applying fire, domesticating animals, centralizing habitation and intensifying farming, expanding onto steeper slopes, and creating a greater demand for tropical crops. In many cases of severe soil erosion, pioneer farmers broke new lands with little understanding of them. History also shows that soil conservation arose at different times, curtailing soil losses and developing stable soil use during periods of increased population growth. The problem has always been how to sustain and preserve soil while speeding up the conservation learning curve of pioneer settlers.

Timothy BEACH
Georgetown University

See also Climate Change; Deforestation; Water

Further Reading

Beach, T. (1994). The fate of eroded soil: Sediment sinks and sediment budgets of agrarian landscapes in southern Minnesota, 1851–1988. *Annals of the Association of American Geographers, 84*, 5–28.

Beach, T., & Gersmehl, P. (1993). Soil erosion, T values, and sustainability: A review and exercise. *Journal of Geography, 92*, 16–22.

Beach, T., Dunning, N., Luzzadder-Beach, S., & Scarborough, V. (2003). Depression soils in the lowland tropics of northwestern Belize: Anthropogenic and natural origins. In A. Gomez-Pompa, M. Allen, S. Fedick, & J. Jiménez-Osornio (Eds.), *Lowland Maya area: Three millennia at the human-wildland interface* (pp. 139–174). Binghamton, NY: Haworth Press.

Brenner, M., Hodell, D., Curtis, J. H., Rosenmeier, M., Anselmetti, F., & Ariztegui, D. (2003). Paleolimnological approaches for inferring past climate in the Maya region: Recent advances and methodological limitations. In A. Gomez-Pompa, M. Allen, S. Fedick, & J. Jiménez-Osornio (Eds.), *Lowland Maya area: Three millennia at the human-wildland interface* (pp. 45–76). Binghamton, NY: Haworth Press.

Grove, R. H. (1995). *Green imperialism: Colonial expansion, tropical island Edens and the origins of environmentalism, 1600–-1860.* Cambridge, U.K.: Cambridge University Press.

Harbough, W. (1993). Twentieth-century tenancy and soil conservation: Some comparisons and questions. In D. Helms & D. Bowers (Eds.), *The history of agriculture and the environment* (pp. 95–119). The Agriculture History Society. Berkeley: University of California Press.

Hooke, R. (2000). On the history of humans as geomorphic agents. *Geology, 28*, 843–846.

McNeill, J. (2001). *Something new under the sun: An environmental history of the twentieth-century world.* New York: W. W. Norton.

Olson, G. W. (1981). Archaeology: Lessons on future soil use. *Journal of Soil and Water Conservation, 36*(5), 261–64.

Sims, D. H. (1970). *The soil conservation service.* New York: Praeger.

U.S. Department of Agriculture / Agricultural Research Service (n.d.). Revised Universal Soil Loss Equation. Retrieved April 21, 2010 from http://www.ars.usda.gov/Research/docs. htm?docid=5971

U.S. Department of Agriculture / Agricultural Research Service. (n.d.) Water Erosion Prediction Project (WEPP). Retrieved April 21, 2010 from http://www.ars.usda.gov/Research/docs. htm?docid=10621

Van Andel, T. H. (1998). Paleosols, red sediments, and the old stone age in Greece. *Geoarchaeology, 13*, 361–390.

Yaalon, D. H. (2000). Why soil—and soil science—matters? *Nature, 407*, 301.

Ethnobotany

Ethnobotany examines the cultural and biological relationships between plants and people, usually human populations organized into communities or linguistic groups. Ethnobotanists study how people use plants, modify habitats to benefit plant species, alter entire landscapes, and create new plants through genetic selection (domestication) and unnatural places to grow them (gardens and fields).

People without metal or advanced technology have been regarded as incapable of transforming the environment from its "pristine," pre-European contact condition. Ethnobotanists have demonstrated through extensive fieldwork that indigenous people worldwide had the means and knowledge to modify the landscape and to create anthropogenic plant communities. In North America their interactions were extensive enough to make a "domesticated" plant environment where the actual presence of plants, their distribution, associations, quantity, and physical condition were determined by indigenous people's behavior, utilitarian needs, and worldview.

Plant Species Management

Many techniques are used to target individual plant species to increase their productivity, ease of harvest, or spatial proximity to benefit people. Nonsedentary foragers, small-scale farmers, and agriculturists employ them. Burning clumps of a species will encourage sprouting for basketry or wooden tools. Redbud, hazel, and oak are manipulated by this means in Native California. Some plants are burned

seasonally to encourage edible seed production or greens for humans and grazing animals.

Weeding seasonally "useless" plants to reduce competition and raise visibility, shaking propagules to increase seedlings, and creating monotypic plots encourages other plants. These are forms of selective harvesting and tending. Another form of plant lifecycle intervention is harvesting plants' subterranean roots, tubers, or bulbs with a digging stick. This technique incidentally replants root cuttings (e.g., Jerusalem artichokes and sweet flag) and bulblets (e.g., onions and camas). Through cultivation, the soil seeds are sowed, the soil is aerated, allelopaths are oxidized, and nutrients are recycled. Sedge and bulrush rhizomes for baskets grow longer from these tilling practices. Another method to assure the availability of important plants, especially rare medicines found some distance from a community, is transplanting them in a garden or protected track. A final procedure commonly used is pruning or coppicing perennial trees or shrubs for basket canes, cordage, and firewood. Breaking fruit-laden branches of serviceberry and huckleberry reinvigorated them to stimulate vegetative growth, flowering, and fruits. The Pueblo Indians in the Southwest pruned dead limbs from piñon pines for firewood and knocked the branches to stimulate growth of more nuts from a healthier tree.

Anthropogenic Ecosystems

Humans create heterogeneous environments through their broadscale management practices. Plant manipulation and harvest methods follow a multiyear cycle of plant management according to species and their

From earliest history to the present day, humans have encouraged the growth of beneficial plants and discouraged the growth weeds.

locality. The result is an ecosystem composed of a mosaic of communities maintained by human cultural practices. Wildernesses only came to be when the indigenous managers lost their land, were killed in wars or by disease, or were replaced by foreign colonists.

Fire is a common tool throughout the world to alter plant communities. Fires set locally around acorn, hickory, and other nut trees clear brush, aid collecting or, indirectly, establish shade-intolerant seedlings. By burning grasslands and berry patches, new growth is stimulated and plant competitors are eliminated. By using fire, nutrients are recycled simultaneously, pests killed, and lower stages of plant succession maintained. The overall result is a patchwork of communities characterized by species diversity and vigorous growth.

The entire landscape is not managed the same annually. Patches are burned in different years and harvests varied according to biological factors but aided by human practices of settlement, social dispersion, and even ritual regulation for determining which plants can be harvested at different times and places.

Special anthropogenic spaces are gardens. These are not a duplication of other plant communities but instead are associations of plants, which exist nowhere else, brought together and maintained by humans, often women. They are convenient for procuring plant products, for their high productivity, and for their great diversity of utilitarian species. Gardens may consist of native species alone, domesticated plants, or a mixture of both categories.

Wild versus Domesticated Plants

Wild or domesticated is a difficult distinction. Most plants have been selected for by many cultivation techniques. Few have avoided these human-induced life-cycle alterations to be called truly "wild." Agricultural plants, on the other hand, have been selected for features useful to people. Their new genetic expressions are plant "artifacts" that do not exist in nature and probably would not reproduce without the assistance and habitat maintenance by people. Domesticated plants are found in all temperate and tropical continents except Australia. They include annual plant seed foods (wheat, barley, rice, millet, maize), vegetables (tomatoes, potatoes, onions, squash, spinach, cabbage), herbal spices (chilies, coriander, parsley), perennial tree fruits (apples, peaches, mangos) and nuts (walnuts, coconuts), and beverages (coffee and tea). People also domesticated utilitarian plants (bottle gourds, cotton, hemp). Each requires a beneficial habitat for growth, and people determine these. In arid lands, irrigation canals and lithic mulch fields are necessary to conserve water for plants. Examples are found in Arizona, Israel, India, and China. The soil is improved with the addition of animal manure and kitchen waste. Heat and the impact of direct sunlight are mitigated by intercropping shade plants with tea, coffee, and fruits. Stone terracing to create more arable land surface alters topography in Peru, Mexico, and China. Women often maintain gardens for culinary variation, dietary supplements, or the aesthetics of flowers. Small fields are maintained for subsistence and are weeded according to local cultural rules of plant use. Large fields are cleared for staple crops or for surplus to sell in markets.

Ethnobotany of Environmental History

Ethnobotany tracks the actions of people, guided by their belief systems, to learn about alternative

A man harvests herbs used in traditional Chinese medicine from Mount Emei.
Photo by Joan Lebold Cohen.

management techniques, and to understand how plant worlds are manipulated by different cultures. People use many techniques to secure a harvest of utilitarian plants. They have many management principles that regulate exploitation through scheduling their harvest activities, rotating collection areas, and limiting access by applying social and religious sanctions. These practices may benefit individual species and, simultaneously, increase habitat diversity through communities at different stages of plant succession and diverse landscapes of more productive plant associations.

The domestication of maize (*Zea mays*) and it methods of production present an example of the ethnobotany of environmental change. Maize is an artifact, created throughout human selection of phenotypic traits, which cannot reproduce without human assistance. To grow it humans must eliminate plant competition by clearing the land and providing the environmental qualities required for growth, mainly control over water and temperature. By clearing the land a habitat is created for ruderals, like pigweed (*Amaranthus*) or lamb's quarters (*Chenopodium*), which can be eaten as leaves and seeds by farmers or weeded according to cultural practices. After the field is abandoned, new plants volunteer that might be useful as well and create successional patches of diverse plants and animals. None would occur in nature without human manipulation of the environment for cultural purposes.

Richard FORD
University of Michigan

Further Reading

Anderson, E. N. (1996). *Ecologies of the heart: Emotion, belief, and the environment.* New York: Oxford University Press.

Blackburn, T. C., & Anderson, K. (Eds.). (1993). *Before the wilderness: Environmental management by native Californians.* Menlo Park, CA: Ballena Press.

Boyd, R. (1999). *Indians, fire and the land in the Pacific Northwest.* Corvallis: Oregon State University Press.

Day, G. M. (1953). The Indian as an ecological factor in the northeastern forest. *Ecology, 34(2),* 329–346.

Doolittle, W. E. (2000). *Cultivated landscapes of native North America.* Oxford, U.K.: Oxford University Press.

Ford, R. I. (Ed.). (1985). *Prehistoric food production in North America* (Museum of Anthropology, Anthropological Papers No. 75). Ann Arbor: University of Michigan.

Harris, D. R., & Hillman, G. C. (Eds.). (1989). *Foraging and farming: The evolution of plant exploitation.* London: Unwin, Hyman.

Minnis, P. E. (Ed.). (2000). *Ethnobotany, a reader.* Norman: University of Oklahoma Press.

Minnis, P. E., & Elisens, W. J. (Eds.). (2000). *Biodiversity and Native America.* Norman: University of Oklahoma Press.

Peacock, S. L. (1998). *Putting down roots: The emergence of wild plant food production on the Canadian Plateau.* Unpublished doctoral dissertation, University of Victoria.

Soule, M. E., & Lease, G. (Eds.). (1995). *Reinventing nature: Responses to postmodern deconstruction.* Washington, DC: Island Press.

Extinctions

Extinctions have occurred throughout the history of the Earth; extinction is in fact a critical component in the theory of evolution and is attributed to natural selection, random factors, or catastrophic events. The Earth has survived five mass extinctions—including one that destroyed the dinosaurs—all of which have shaped the world as we know it today.

The fossil record reveals that the history of life has been a process of speciation, or the diversification of organisms into new species, accompanied by extinction, or the disappearance of existing species. Speciation and extinction are equal partners in evolution. In neo-Darwinian theory, genetic variation and natural selection are the primary agents in evolution. Natural selection favors genetic variation that improves an organism's chances of surviving to reproduce within its environment. Successful variation is passed on to the next generation. Its frequency in the population increases from generation to generation until it eventually replaces the earlier, less advantageous trait. Acquisition of new traits sometimes enables organisms to invade new habitats. In neo-Darwinism, the environment is the prime source of selection. Therefore, environmental change—or change of environment, in the case of habitat invasion—is considered the chief cause of species evolution. New environmental conditions change selective pressures operating on populations of organisms. Populations must adapt to new circumstances or perish without descendants. In addition to natural selection, random factors and rare, catastrophic events also appear to play a role in extinctions.

Earth is some 4.6 billion years old. Geologists divide this time into eras, periods, epochs, and ages. (See table 1.) Life first appeared on Earth late in the Precambrian era some 3.5 billion years ago. The majority of species that evolved since that first appearance are now extinct. Through time, species generally disappear individually in "background extinctions." But during at least five mass extinction events, huge numbers of species perished together over (geologically) short spans. (See table 2.) By eliminating some previously successful species and allowing other, formerly minor, groups to expand and diversify, each mass extinction restructured the biosphere.

End-Cretaceous Extinctions

The Cretaceous (114 to 65 million years ago [mya]) was the final period in the age of dinosaurs. At its

Table 1.
Geological Time Scale

Eras	Periods	Epochs
Cenozoic (65 million years ago [mya] to present)	Quaternary	Holocene
Pleistocene	Tertiary	Miocene
Oligocene		Eocene
Paleocene	Mesozoic (248 to 65 mya)	Cretaceous
Jurassic		Triassic
Paleozoic (540 to 248 mya)	Permian	
Carboniferous		Devonian
Silurian		Ordovician
Cambrian		Precambrian (4.6 billion to 540 million years ago)

Table 2.
The "Big Five" Mass Extinction Events in Geological Time

End-Cretaceous period	c.	65 million years ago (mya)
Late Triassic period	c.	210 to 206 mya
Late Permian–Early Triassic period	c.	252 to 245 mya
Late Devonian period	c.	364 to 354 mya
Late Ordovician period	c.	449 to 443 mya

close, virtually all of these great beasts—together with more than 50 percent of Earth's species—disappeared suddenly and entirely. Many scholars attribute their extinction to climate change, but the disappearances were not gradual, and the dinosaurs appear to have been diversifying up to the end. The physicist Luis Alvarez and his colleagues (1980) note that rock layers dating to the Cretaceous boundary commonly contain a thin clay layer of iridium, a rare metal resembling platinum, and spherules or tektites, spherical bits of glassy rock formed from molten silicate droplets. They interpret this as evidence that one or more mighty asteroids or comets struck Earth around 65 million years ago. They hypothesize that the impact generated a giant vapor cloud (out of which the spherules condensed), sent shock debris across the globe, created an immense fireball, and cast a huge plume of dust into the atmosphere. As this dust plume ascended, atmospheric winds spread it into a globe-embracing cloud that blocked sunlight from the Earth's surface for a year or more. In this scenario, mass extinctions resulted from both the initial impact and the disruption of the food chain that followed. Perhaps the collision also ignited vast global fires that added huge smoke plumes to the sun-blocking haze of the windblown impact debris. A crater between 200 and 300 kilometers in diameter of the proper age and aspect that has been identified in the subsurface of the Yucatán Peninsula of Mexico may be the impact point. Asteroid collisions may have caused the earlier mass extinctions of the Late Devonian, the Permio-Triassic, and the Late Triassic as well. Whatever its cause, the Cretaceous extinctions ended the dinosaurs' domination and provided empty ecological space that was ultimately filled by the mammals, a hitherto insignificant class of vertebrates.

Pleistocene/Holocene Extinctions

The Pleistocene epoch (1.8 mya to 8000 BCE) was preceded by the Pliocene and followed by the Holocene epoch (8000 BCE to present). It is called the Ice Age because continental-scale glacial ice sheets cyclically advanced and retreated during this time. Near its close, anatomically modern people (*Homo sapiens sapiens*) evolved, probably in Africa, and spread throughout most of the Earth. Although background extinctions occurred throughout the epoch, Pleistocene animal life remained rich. Then, between 10,000 BCE and 6000 BCE, extinctions occurred on a massive scale. "Megafauna," species with large adult body sizes and body weights over 45 kilograms (100 pounds), were most severely affected.

Although extinctions occurred on all continents, they did not occur on them uniformly. The number of megafaunal species that disappeared in the New World was much higher than elsewhere. During the 4,000 years after 10,000 BCE, North and South America lost the Colombian mammoth, mastodon, horse, camelops, Shasta ground sloth, saber-toothed cat, and seventy other genera. Extinction rates in Europe and Eurasia were lower. Nonetheless, the woolly mammoth, woolly rhinoceros, Irish elk, and other cold-adapted creatures disappeared after 14,000 BCE. Musk oxen, steppe lions, and hyenas disappeared there but survived elsewhere. The distribution of horses and steppe bison became greatly restricted. Late Pleistocene extinction rates were lowest in Africa. Megafaunal extinctions that occurred there, frequently at the beginning of the epoch, were modest in number at its close.

What Was the Cause?

Rapid climate change at the Pleistocene's close is a possible cause. During the last 128,000 years of the epoch, the Northern Hemisphere experienced long continental glacial advances punctuated by short-term ice contractions or interstadials. Glaciation terminated abruptly about 10,000 BCE and was followed by rapid deglaciation and a warmer, moister climate. During this interstadial, European, Eurasian,

F. John, *Dodo oder Dronte* (1890). Color illustration. The dodo bird (*Raphus cucullatus*) is considered by scientists to be the "poster bird" for extinction.

and North American forests expanded northward, severely curtailing the range and population sizes of plains megafauna like the horse, mammoth, bison, and woolly rhinoceros. This interstadial ended about 9000 BCE, and glacial conditions returned for another thousand years. Extinctions were not entirely coeval with this deglaciation, however. Further, rapid climatic changes had occurred often during the Pleistocene without triggering similar waves of extinction. Presumably, most Pleistocene species had evolved physiological tolerance for climatic change or could migrate in the face of it. Further, some species, most notably the horse, became extinct in North America but survived in Eurasia to be reintroduced to the New World in historic times. If the environment of North America had been fatal to the horse at the end of the Pleistocene, would the wild descendants of Spanish mustangs be able to roam the western United States with such success today?

While climatic change cannot explain the Pleistocene extinctions, perhaps "anthropogenic overkill," human hunting on a limitless scale, does. Two kinds of evidence suggest this: (1) the asymmetry of worldwide extinctions and (2) the stratigraphic association between human stone tools and the bones of extinct species. Variation in the pace of extinction in Africa, Eurasia, and the New World may reflect the different arrival times of fully modern humans on each continent. Megafauna and the hominids evolved together in Africa over the last four to six million years and anatomically fully modern *Homo sapiens*

sapiens probably evolved there some 150,000 years ago. Some suggest that the extinction rate of African megafauna was low by the terminal Pleistocene because the species had evolved behavioral means of coping with human predation by that time. Anatomically fully modern *Homo sapiens sapiens* did not appear in Europe until around 35,000 years ago. The shorter period of association between European game animals and these new human predators may account for the greater rate of megafaunal extinctions in Europe compared to Africa.

The stratigraphic association between the stone tools and the bones of extinct megafauna found in the terminal Pleistocene age archaeological sites is also taken as evidence of human "overkill." The vast quantities of mammoth bones recovered from the celebrated kill sites in the Ukraine indicate Eurasian hunters slaughtered prodigious numbers of these beasts there. Such evidence is strongest in North America where direct and primary association between the distinctive lanceolate-shaped Paleo-Indian stone projectile points and megafauna is well documented. In North America, the extinction of key elements of Pleistocene megafauna, including ground sloths, camelopses, tapirs, mastodons, various species of bison, mammoths, and horses between 10,000 and 8000 BCE is clearly correlated with the abrupt appearance of the Paleo-Indians between 9500 and 9000 BCE. If the specialized Paleo-Indian hunters were the first people to arrive in the New World, they would have found a hunter's paradise filled with game but empty of

There is little doubt left in the minds of professional biologists that Earth is currently faced with a mounting loss of species that threatens to rival the five great mass extinctions of the geological past. • **Niles Eldredge (b. 1943)**

human competitors. That paradise would have been unlike anything in the Old World as the animals in it had not evolved the behaviors they needed for dealing with cunning, two-legged human predators. As Paleo-Indian peoples grew in number, they would have expanded southward and across the continent in an advancing wave. By employing game drives and other wasteful hunting strategies that indiscriminately killed large numbers of game, these early hunters may have extinguished megafauna on an ever-widening front. It seems plausible that anatomically modern humankind—practicing predation on the large and profligate scale reflected at kill sites like Solutré, Dolni Vestonice, and Olson-Chubbuck—tipped the balance against megafauna already stressed by changing climate. If these sites do indeed reflect human connivance in "megacide," they provide a cautionary tale: once destroyed, species do not come back.

The extinction of the megafauna must have forced big-game-hunting peoples to realign their subsistence. The archaeologist Mark Cohen (1977) asserts that, by reducing available game, the extinctions initiated a "food crisis" after around 8000 BCE that forced people in Eurasia, Europe, Africa, and the Americas to expand their subsistence bases and exploit a greater range of species and habitats. Hitherto neglected species like fish, crabs, turtles, mollusks, land snails, migratory waterfowl, and rabbits became a routine part of the diet, and plants were exploited systematically for fruit, tubers, nuts, and seeds. Ultimately this food crisis may have stimulated the development of agriculture.

Late Prehistoric and Historic Period

Extinctions at the hands of humans continued in the late Prehistoric and Historic periods through (1) habitat fragmentation and destruction, (2) the introduction of predators or foreign competitors (particularly on islands), (3) overhunting, and, more recently, (4) hunting or gathering wild organisms for market sale. By late prehistory, few of the world's habitats had not felt the impact of humankind. Nonetheless, all impact was not the same. While that of the hunter-gatherers was modest, agricultural

systems transformed the landscape. Extinction of species through habitat loss has chiefly been due to the spread of agriculture and the competition between indigenous fauna and domestic animals. Yet domesticants are not the only new arrivals that generate extinctions. On islands, numerous bird species have vanished following the human introduction of rats, mongooses, or snakes. The brown tree snake, brought to Guam around 1950, extirpated nine of the thirteen native forest birds on the island. Species extinction has also resulted from intentional human persecution. A dramatic example is found in the archaeological record of New Zealand. Long isolated from mainland Asia, New Zealand supported a unique array of large, ground-dwelling, flightless birds called moa. Moa species ranged from the size of turkeys to giant, ostrich-like creatures ten feet or more in height. Having evolved in the absence of predators, they probably had little fear of the Polynesian colonists who probably arrived on the island sometime in the thirteenth century. Within one hundred years, the eleven species of moa had been hunted to extinction.

Human persecution is especially likely to result in extinction when species are exploited for the market. The passenger pigeon inhabited eastern North America in uncounted numbers; their migrations darkened the skies for days. In the nineteenth century these birds were systematically harvested for market, and the species was extinct by 1914. Similar fates befell the great auk, the dodo, and numerous other bird species. An equally grim fate faces chimpanzees and gorillas, currently sold as "bush meat" in parts of Africa. Rhinoceroses are nearly extinct because ground rhino horn is regarded as an aphrodisiac in Asia. Marine fisheries worldwide are threatened by systematic market and sport fishing. Future extinctions may include cod, tuna, blue marlin, swordfish, and some species of whale. The dismal list goes on and on.

Extinction Matters

Extinctions have affected world history profoundly. First, the mass extinction of the dinosaurs at the end of the Cretaceous period allowed the diversification of

Thylacinus in the Washington D.C. National Zoo circa 1906. Scientists believe the thylacine became extinct during the 1900s. Photo by E. J. Keller, Smithsonian Institution Archives.

the mammalian order and, ultimately, the evolution of humans. That distant extinction event marks the nascent beginning of human history. Second, by forcing great changes in subsistence, the great extinctions in the Late Pleistocene may have triggered a "food crisis" that led to agriculture. Third, Late Pleistocene extinctions greatly impoverished the fauna of the New World. In the absence of key domesticable animal species, New World agriculture came to be based on plants. Old World peoples, living in an environment less impoverished by extinctions, domesticated many animal species and, as a result, were plagued by zoonoses, infectious diseases like smallpox and flu derived from them. As long as they remained isolated from the Old World, Native Americans remained free of such diseases. Following the arrival of Europeans and Africans, however, their lack of exposure and immunity laid them open to massive "virgin land infections" that contributed directly to their defeat and large-scale genetic replacement by peoples from the Old World. Late Pleistocene animal extinctions patterns thus helped to determine the human population makeup of the Americas.

A Sixth Mass Extinction?

Present rates of extinction appear to be between 1,000 and 10,000 times the rates seen through most of geological time. The possibility of global warming darkens the picture further as changing climatic patterns may cause extinctions by disrupting species distribution and abundance. Is the world on the brink of a *sixth* mass extinction event? And, if so, can anything be done to avert it? In the near term, international efforts at saving such critical habitats as the world's forests and ocean fisheries must be intensified. Introduction of foreign species into new environments must be curtailed and the protection of endangered species increased. Such protection is never cheap or easy, but experience with the California condor, the sea otter, the American bison, the whooping crane, and other species indicates that it can be done. Simultaneously, zoos and aquariums must act decisively to breed endangered species in their charge. Reproductive and developmental biology can help. Genome banking of sperm from endangered species is promising as are more experimental approaches like somatic cell cloning. Chinese biologists are seeking to increase giant panda populations using nuclear transfer techniques involving bears as egg donors and surrogate mothers. Attempts at genetically restoring vanished species like the Tasmanian tiger and the mammoth are in the offing.

Whatever we do, we must recognize that extinctions in the present age are caused by the inordinate success of our own species. Therefore, controlling our populations and bridling our destructive impulses are essential. Global economic underdevelopment intensifies both of these problems. Poor people do not kill rhinoceroses or hunt endangered apes out of malice.

They do so to relieve their poverty. Stopping these practices demands eliminating the economic inequalities that necessitate them. No small task this, but, if we fail in it, the final impact of extinction on world history may be the elimination of our own species.

D. Bruce DICKSON

Texas A&M University

See also Anthropocene; Biological Exchanges; Climate Change; Columbian Exchange; Deforestation; Diseases—Animal; Diseases—Overview; Diseases—Plant; Ices Ages

Further Reading

Alvarez, L. W., Alvarez, W., Asaro, F., & Michel, H. V. (1980). Extraterrestrial cause for the Cretaceous-Tertiary extinction. *Science, 208*, 1095–1108.

Anderson, P. K. (2001). Marine mammals in the next one hundred years: Twilight for a Pleistocene megafauna? *Journal of Mammalogy, 82*(3), 623–629.

Brook, B. W., & Bowman, D. M. J. S. (2002). Explaining the Pleistocene megafaunal extinctions: Models, chronologies, and assumptions. *Proceeding of the National Academy of Sciences, 99*(23), 14624–14627.

Cohen, M. N. (1977). *The food crises in prehistory*. New Haven, CT: Yale University Press.

Corley-Smith, G. E., & Brandhorst, B. P. (1999). Preservation of endangered species and populations: A role for genome banking, somatic cell cloning, and androgenesis? *Molecular Reproduction and Development, 53,* 363–367.

Fritts, T. H., & Rodda, G. H. (1998). The role of introduced species in the degradation of island ecosystems: A case history of Guam. *Annual Review of Ecology and Systematics, 29,* 113–140.

Grieve, R., & Therriault, A. (2000). Vredefort, Sudbury, Chicxulub: Three of a kind? *Annual Review of Earth and Planetary Sciences, 28,* 305–338.

Kerr, R. A. (2002). No "darkness at noon" to do in the dinosaurs? *Science, 295,* 1445–1447.

Myers, R. A., & Worm, B. (2003). Rapid worldwide depletion of predatory fish communities. *Nature, 423,* 280–283.

Olsen, P. E., Shubin, N. H., & Anders, M. H. (1987). New early Jurassic tetrapod assemblages constrain Triassic-Jurassic extinction event. *Science, 237,* 1025–1029.

Purvis, A., Jones, K. E., & Mace, G. A. (2000). Extinction. *Bioessays, 22,* 1123–1133.

Saegusa, A. (1998). Mother bears could help save giant panda. *Nature, 394,* 409.

Serjeantson, D. (2001). The great auk and the gannet: A prehistoric perspective on the extinction of the great auk. *International Journal of Osteoarchaeology, 11,* 43–55.

Vangelova, L. (2003). True or false? Extinction is forever. *Smithsonian, 34*(3), 22–24.

Walsh, P. D., Abernethy, K. A., Bermejos, M., Beyers, R., de Wachter, P., et al. (2003). Catastrophic ape decline in western equatorial Africa. *Nature, 422,* 611–614.

Famine

Throughout history people have experienced food shortages and famines. Only in relatively recent times has agricultural development progressed to the extent that sufficient accumulated food stocks could allow for the possibility of eradicating world famine. The fact that famines do still occur is not a consequence of insufficient food, but of political and social problems, including those associated with local distribution.

Famine is a complex social phenomenon and is distinguished from starvation by its social aspect. Individuals starve to death as a result of reductions in food supply, but societies experience a more complex response. Not all members of society suffer equally from food shortages. As Amartya Sen has pointed out, the poorer and less privileged sections of society, whose entitlements to food are least secure, suffer more than the richer, more privileged sections. The history of famine is not simply a history of factors that cause a reduction in food supply, or of the imbalance of food production against population growth. It includes the history of social and political responses to these problems, the history of social formations, and the history of social differentiation concerning food entitlement. While there has traditionally been a classification between natural and politically induced famines, the distinction does not really hold. Every famine that develops to take on significant mortality consequences indicates a failure of famine avoidance and relief measures. Most famines have had multiple causes.

All previous social formations have experienced food shortages and famines. It is only in relatively recent times that agricultural development has progressed to such an extent as to enable sufficient food stocks to be accumulated to pose the possibility of the eradication of world famines. The fact that famines do still occur is no longer a consequence of there being insufficient food, but of political and social problems including those associated with local distribution.

Famine in Early Social Formations

At earlier times there had not been a progressive move toward the eradication of hunger. The shift from hunter-gatherer to settled farmer societies was not associated with improved nutrition. The anthropologist Mark Nathan Cohen has assembled anthropometric data that indicates that early settled society was more vulnerable to food shortages, and he argues that starvation from this time may have been associated with political and economic issues more than with agricultural events. There is evidence in the earliest civilizations in Egypt, China, India, the Middle East, and classical Europe of considerable concern over food supplies and the establishment of large state granaries and famine relief and transportation systems.

In China the granary system dates back to antiquity and the tribute system was well developed before the Grand Canal was opened in 611 CE linking the Huang (Yellow) River in the north with the Yangzi (Chang) in the south. Part of this supply system was destroyed by the Mongol invasion of the thirteenth century, and imperial food supply problems were complicated when first Khubilai Khan and then the Ming emperors established the capital at Beijing in the north rather than in the Huang River basin at Xi'an (Chang'an) or Luoyang, or at Nanjing on the Yangzi. In 1325 there was a massive famine that is claimed to have killed between 4 and 8 million people. Faced with

A group of children deserted by their parents line up with caregivers in the Volga district of Russia, blighted by famine circa 1921. Library of Congress.

this challenge, the rulers revived the tribute system, granaries, and famine relief work and developed them to a new level. In the great drought of 1740–1743, at a time when the European subsistence crises were still causing a substantial number of deaths, the scale of Chinese famine relief was enormous and mass mortality was largely avoided. By the early part of the nineteenth century about 400,000 tons of grain a year were transported through the tribute system to feed the northern garrisons and a Beijing population of 800,000. Although the granary system began to decline from the time of the White Lotus Rebellion at the end of the eighteenth century, transport on the Grand Canal probably peaked in the first half of the nineteenth century, on the eve of the First Opium War (1839–1842), before the British cut this vital supply link and plunged the country into turmoil and a period of famine and rebellion.

There is some dispute as to how efficient the Chinese Empire was in the period before the troubles of the nineteenth century. Modern scholars argue that living standards were much higher than in Europe until the time of modern imperial troubles.

India under the Mughals had also developed successful ways of dealing with famines before the British advance into India following Clive's victory at the Battle of Plassey in 1757. It was under British rule that economic growth slowed below the rate of population growth and per capita living standards fell to dangerous levels. There were few signs of major famine in India before the Great Bengal Famine of 1770 under the administration of the East India Company.

As the classical urban population of the south of Europe grew in size, more grain had to be imported into these regions and the authorities became increasingly concerned about establishing granaries and other food support systems. Governments provided support to assist the transportation of grain into the major cities. Famines would occur when there was a breakdown in these supplies.

The European population then spread to the colder less hospitable areas to the north, where, given the technology of the time, the population was more vulnerable to the influence of the weather. The greatest recorded European famine was experienced in northern Europe from 1315 to 1322. Modern scholarship tends to question the Postan thesis, which presumed the existence of overcropping and soil exhaustion throughout a very large area of northern Europe. The exceptional damp weather for a number of years appears to have been the main factor. The result was massive social disturbance, food deprivation, and high mortality levels. The weakening of this generation may have contributed to the continued massive population losses from the Black Death a few decades later. Together the sharp population losses of these years appear to have caused a change in the relative values of land and labor, which probably contributed to the weakening of feudal relations and the growth of more commercial ones.

In this drawing from the late nineteenth century, Chinese farmers affected by famine take their house apart to rebuild it in a more auspicious location.

Subsequently European famines have never been so severe, although periodic subsistence crises would produce smaller-scale famines periodically down to the eighteenth century in many areas. The last of these great peacetime subsistence crises in the northern and central regions of Europe occurred in the early 1740s. The situation was worse in the extremities of Europe with major famines in Finland in 1696–1697, in Ireland in the 1840s, and in Russia in 1871, 1891, and into the twentieth century. The rest of the world experienced similar problems, but with the period of subsistence crises lasting much later, and with larger amounts of disruption to the traditional supply systems as a result of wars and colonial expansion.

Western colonialism is no longer seen as a benign process of modernizing the uncivilized world. There is a growing realization of the costs of the destruction of the local domestic economy and of the traditional coping practices, which made it difficult for these societies to respond adequately to the serious natural and political challenges that they faced at this time. The serious famines of the 1880s and 1890s in India, China, South America, and Egypt are presented rather provocatively as "Victorian Holocausts" (Davis 2001) in which colonial administrators hindered the local government from responding to the challenges in the El Niño Southern Oscillation.

Twentieth-Century Famines

During the two major world wars of the twentieth century, both sides attempted to disrupt their enemies' food supply channels and to cause famine and social disruption. The rationing and food securing operations of the main developed countries largely succeeded in avoiding this outcome. In several of the poorer countries in central and Eastern Europe and Asia, however, there were very serious consequences. Americans provided large amounts of food and famine relief to Belgium throughout World War I and to large areas in central and Eastern Europe and Russia after both of these wars. This did largely contain the crisis in these areas. There was, however, a major famine in Russia in 1921–1922, which was partly related to the continuation of civil war following World War I and the revolution. During World War II there was a famine in the occupied Greek islands, in the Netherlands after the Battle of the Bulge in 1944, and throughout the war in occupied and besieged parts of Eastern Europe and Russia. The famine in blockaded Leningrad is perhaps the best-known case.

In Asia World War II contributed to serious famines in China (1937–1945), India (Bengal, 1943), and Vietnam (1942–1944). In subsequent years famines have often accompanied minor military engagements between poorer countries.

There has been much controversy over the relationship between famine and Communism. While it is true that the three major famines of the twentieth century (USSR 1921–1922 with 3 million deaths, USSR 1930–1933 with 6 million deaths, and China

1958–1961 with 15–20 million deaths) all occurred in Communist countries, it is somewhat superficial to blame these famines on Communism per se. Both Russia and China had frequently suffered from famines before they became Communist, and in both countries the Communist revolution had taken place during and following a period of major economic collapse that had been associated with major famines. In China this was the extended period of troubles from the 1850s to 1948; in Russia it was a shorter period, from 1917 to 1922. During these troubled periods the major cities experienced extensive famines as the state structure weakened and the traditional supply system broke down. The successor revolutionary states that were born out of these troubled times were anxious to develop the economy and rebuild supply structures.

In the railway and industrial age there appeared to be great prospects for these states, which both experienced remarkable growth in the first decades of their revolution. In both cases the second decade brought about excessively ambitious plans to escape from the poverty trap, which in combination with unexpected poor weather led to the onset of a series of factors that resulted in the largest famines of the twentieth century. Attempts were made by both regimes to conceal these "Great Leap" famines and to deny their existence. It was only years later that the true scale of these disasters became apparent.

Despite these early Communist disasters, the USSR and China did develop their economies and industrialized to a certain extent. They have proved to be no match for the advanced Western economies, but their experience in central planning was for a while highly popular in the newly independent former colonies, which were also looking for a way of industrializing in a hurry. It is the underdeveloped world that has failed to industrialize that continues to experience famine, especially in sub-Sahelian Africa.

There are some scholars who claim that the Great Irish Famine of 1841–1845 and the Russian famine of 1931–1933 were both cases of genocide in which a major colonial power, Britain or Russia, attempted to weaken and control a troublesome region. Although in both cases the colonial power can be accused of acting insufficiently vigorously to reduce the famine, there is little evidence to support the case that these famines were caused on purpose.

Famine and Disease

Before the late nineteenth and early twentieth centuries famine had always been associated with major epidemic diseases, often typhus. Relatively few people had died from starvation, because other epidemic diseases killed them first. This applied to the Great Irish Famine of 1847, the Russian Famine of 1921–1922, and the Bengal Famine of 1943. But epidemic diseases have played a less important role in subsequent famines and especially in the Soviet Famine of 1931–1933 and the Chinese Famine of the Great Leap Forward, 1958–1961. We are now in a new age of famine demography in which simple medical and sanitary intervention can greatly reduce the likelihood of death from disease. Unfortunately, this has not resulted in an absence of great mortality in famines. It has, however, reduced the scale of mortality, which otherwise would have been considerably greater.

Outlook in the Twenty-First Century

The Malthusian threat of population growth outstripping growth in food supplies has failed to be realized in the twentieth century and is unlikely to emerge in the twenty-first century.

The threat of major world wars to cause famines by disturbing major supply channels also failed to emerge in the major countries in the twentieth century, although it has been an important factor in smaller poorer countries. It would be extremely rash to presume that any major conflict in the future would have a similar result. Disruptions in food supplies to the underdeveloped world are unfortunately continuing. Famine will remain a major challenge to the world in the twenty-first century, despite the ability of the world to produce food surpluses.

Stephen WHEATCROFT
University of Melbourne

Man can and must prevent the tragedy of famine in the future instead of merely trying with pious regret to salvage the human wreckage of the famine, as he has so often done in the past. • **Norman Borlaug (1914–2009)**

Further Reading

Arnold, D. (1988). *Famine: Social crisis and historical change.* Oxford, U.K.: Basil Blackwell.

Bhatia, B. M. (1967). *Famines in India, 1860–1965.* Bombay, India: Asia Publishing House.

Bin Wong, R. (1997). *China transformed: Historical change and the limits of European experience.* Ithaca, NY: Cornell University Press.

Cohen, M. N. (1990). Prehistoric patterns of hunger. In L. F. Newman (Ed.), *Hunger in history: Food shortage, poverty, and deprivation* (pp. 56–97). Cambridge, U.K.: Blackwell.

Conquest, R. (1986). *The harvest of sorrow: Soviet collectivization and the terror famine.* London: Arrow.

Davies, R. W., & Wheatcroft, S. G. (2004). *The years of hunger: Soviet agriculture, 1931–1933.* Basingstoke, U.K.: Palgrave Macmillan.

Davis, M. (2001). *Late Victorian holocausts: El Nino famines and the making of the Third World.* London: Verso.

De Waal, A. (1989). *Famine that kills: Darfur, Sudan, 1984–1985.* Oxford, U.K.: Oxford University Press.

Dreze, J., & Sen, A. (1991). *The political economy of hunger* (Vols. 1–3). Oxford, U.K.: Oxford University Press.

Dyason, T., and O'Grada, C. (Eds.). (2002). *Famine demography: Perspectives from the past and present.* New York: Oxford University Press.

Garnsey, P. (1998). *Cities, peasants, and food in classical antiquity: Essays in social and economic history.* Cambridge, U.K.: Cambridge University Press.

Jordan, W. C. (1996). *The great famine: Northern Europe in the early fourteenth century.* Princeton, NJ: Princeton University Press.

Jutikkala, E. (1955). The great Finnish famine in 1696–97. *Scandinavian Economic History Review, 111*(1), 48–63.

Maharatna, A. (1996). *The demography of famines: An Indian historical perspective.* Delhi, India: Oxford University Press.

Newman, L. F. (Ed.). (1990). *Hunger in history: Food shortage, poverty, and deprivation.* Cambridge, U.K.: Blackwell.

O'Grada, C. (1999). *Black '47 and beyond: The great Irish famine in history, economy, and memory.* Princeton, NJ: Princeton University Press.

Pomeranz, K. (2000). *The great divergence: China, Europe, and the making of the modern world economy.* Princeton, NJ: Princeton University Press.

Post, J. D. (1985). *Food shortages, climatic variability, and epidemic disease in preindustrial Europe: The mortality peak in the early 1740s.* Ithaca, NY: Cornell University Press.

Rotberg, R. I., & Rabb, T. K. (Eds.). (1985). *Hunger and history: The impact of changing food production and consumption patterns on society.* Cambridge, U.K.: Cambridge University Press.

Sen, A. K. (1981). *Poverty and famines: An essay on entitlement and deprivation.* Oxford, U.K.: Oxford University Press.

Will, P.-E. (1990). *Bureaucracy and famine in eighteenth century China.* Stanford, CA: Stanford University Press.

Yang, D. L. (1996). *Calamity and reform in China: State, rural society, and institutional change since the Great Leap Famine.* Stanford, CA: Stanford University Press.

Fire

Humans learned to control fire at least 400,000 years ago. Cooking over fire increased the variety of foods. Fire kept dangerous animals away from campgrounds and warmed living spaces so humans could leave tropical Africa and spread round the Earth; people burned dry vegetation as they migrated to improve hunting and thereby changed natural ecological balances. No single skill did so much to expand human power over nature.

The history of humankind is closely connected with the history of fire—so closely that the connection has become almost reciprocal. Of course, fire is much older than humankind; but ever since humans learned to exert some control over it, the frequency of fire and, even more, its manifold forms have increasingly been determined by human activities. Of all the fires burning on the planet Earth today, only a tiny portion have "natural" causes; in the great majority of cases the source of ignition has been human—intentionally or unintentionally.

These observations raise a whole range of intriguing problems concerning the history of the relationship between humankind and fire. How did this relationship begin? What were the conditions that made it possible? What were the feedback effects or functions that sustained it? How has the connection between humans and fire affected the course of history?

Our image of the first phases in the human domestication of fire was long dominated by mythology—as if the stories about Prometheus or other culture heroes who allegedly had stolen fire from the gods were the last word. Today we know better: with the aid of ecology and archaeology, of anthropology and

sociology, it is possible to reconstruct the general trajectory of the historical relationship between humans and fire.

Origins

Like all natural forces, fire has a history. Chemically, fire is a process of highly accelerated oxidation of matter (fuel) induced by heat (ignition). Three conditions are necessary for it to occur: oxygen, fuel, and heat. During the first eons in the history of the Earth, at least two of these—oxygen and fuel—were absent. Oxygen did not become available in the atmosphere until life emerged between three and four billion years ago. And it was less than half a billion years ago, during the Devonian geological age, when life assumed the form of plants, providing matter suitable for burning. From then on, most places on Earth with seasonally dry vegetation were regularly visited by fire, ignited on rare occasions by falling rocks, volcanic eruptions, or extraterrestrial impacts, but mostly by lightning.

Its domestication by humans opened an entirely new episode in the history of fire. Humans thoroughly altered the incidence and intensity of fires. They brought fire to regions of the planet where it seldom or never burned spontaneously, and they tried to banish it from places where without human interference it would have burned repeatedly. Thus, increasingly, "natural" fire receded and made way to "human," or, more precisely, *anthropogenic* fire.

Wherever humans migrated, they took their fire along. The presence of humans-with-fire deeply altered the landscape, including flora and fauna. The

Eanger Irving Couse (1866–1936), *Indian by Firelight*. When handled carefully fire can protect against the cold and keep predatory animals at bay.

human impact is amply documented (though still controversial) for Australia—a continent that was colonized by humans rather late. Everywhere on the planet, areas such as rain forests, deserts, and the polar regions that were not receptive to fire proved to be hard to penetrate for humans too.

A Human Monopoly

Humans are the only species which has learned to manipulate fire. Control over fire has become a "species monopoly," with an enormous impact on other species, both animals and plants, and on the civilizing process of humanity itself.

Evidence about the very first phase of the domestication of fire is insufficient and open to various interpretations. The most conservative estimates are from archaeologists who hold that the oldest undisputable evidence of human control of fire can be dated back at most 250,000 years. Other scholars, such as primatologist Richard Wrangham, argue that *Homo erectus* may already have been tending the remains of natural fires as long as 1.8 million years ago. According to the anthropologist Francis Burton, the turning point may be dated at even 5 to 6 million years.

While acknowledging these controversies over the actual chronology of the first domestication of fire,

we can still draw up some defendable propositions about its "phaseology"—the succession of phases. Three phases can be distinguished. During the first phase, there were no human (or hominid) groups possessing fire; there were only groups without fire. Then, there must have been a second phase, when there were both groups with fire and groups without fire. We do not yet know how long this phase lasted, but we do know that it was a transitional stage, leading up to the phase in which humankind has now been living for thousands of generations: the phase when there are no longer any groups without fire. For many thousands of generations, all human groups have been groups *with* fire.

The three phases are connected by two transitions. The first transition was marked by the initial domestication of fire by some human or hominid groups. Apparently they found it worthwhile not just to forage at the smoldering remains of a natural fire, but to see to it that the fire kept burning. They tended it, they protected it against rain, and they "fed" it with fuel. None of these activities were programmed in their genes; they had to be learned, and then transmitted, as traits of culture. But the *capacity* to learn all this had to be there, as a set of traits acquired in biological evolution. Those traits included physical features such as a bipedal gait, flexible hands, and a complex

A little fire is quickly trodden out; Which, being suffer'd, rivers cannot quench. • **William Shakespeare**, from *Henry IV*

brain, as well as concomitant mental and social features such as an ability to cooperate and to defer immediate gratification for the sake of consciously conceived goals.

Considering this combination of requisite traits we may find it almost self-evident that the control of fire became a monopoly, uniquely held by humans. The full significance of the monopoly can only be appreciated, however, if we regard it also in connection with the second transition, in which the monopoly became universally human. Whereas earlier hominid, and possibly human, groups had been able to survive without fire for many thousands of generations, a time came when apparently that was no longer possible.

If this sketch of phases and transitions is realistic (and it is hard to imagine why it should not be), it leaves us with an unavoidable conclusion: human societies with fire were in the long run more "fit to survive" than societies without fire. If we then ask why all societies without fire eventually disappeared, there seems to be only one plausible answer: because they had to coexist with societies *with* fire—and in the long run that proved impossible.

Implied in this line of reasoning is the idea that a change in some human groups led to changes in other human groups. If Group A had fire, and the neighboring Group B did not, Group B had a problem. It could either try to minimize contact with Group A, or do as Group A had done and adopt a fire regime—which should not pose insurmountable difficulties as long as the potential to learn from the other group was sufficient.

In terms of its formation and spread, the fire regime may be regarded as a paradigm for other regimes developed at later stages in human history—a paradigm in more than one sense. First of all, the regime by which humans learned to extend their care of and control over fire could subsequently serve as a model for taking care of and controlling other nonhuman natural resources such as plants and animals. Secondly, we may regard the domestication of fire as a model case in a "heuristic" or methodological sense, since it shows us some basic principles which are at work in social evolution and human history.

Hearths and Torches

The establishment of the species monopoly of control over fire amounted to a big step in the differentiation of behavior and power between humans and related animals, ranging from other primates to wolves or mammoths. As a new item in the behavioral repertoire, tending fire tilted the interspecies balance of power greatly toward human dominance. The original breakthrough may have been precarious and fraught with risks; but it had far-reaching consequences—which were, of course, unforeseeable at the time. The history of the domestication of fire clearly illustrates the intertwining of intentional actions and unintended effects.

Fire became the focus of human group life in the form of the hearth. Here fire was tended and thus kept regularly available so that group members no longer had to go searching for it. Around the hearth they could create small enclaves in the wilderness where the nights were less cold and dark and which offered some protection against predators. On the fire itself they could cook their food—again a form of behavior which, like the domestication of fire upon which it is based, is both uniquely and universally human. Through the destructive force of fire, substances that otherwise would be too tough to eat, or even poisonous, could be made edible and palatable—a good example of "production through destruction" (or, to use the economist Joseph Schumpeter's term, "creative destruction").

A second way in which fire was used from early on was by lighting the end of a stick in the hearth and turning it into a torch. Torches could be applied to burn down dry vegetation, thus clearing land and making it safer and more hospitable for human habitation. Many prairies and similar secondary grasslands in various parts of the world were created by such burning practices. On a smaller scale, but no less effectively, humans could apply their torches to scare away big predators. Caves long inhabited by bears or hyenas were taken over by humans armed with fire.

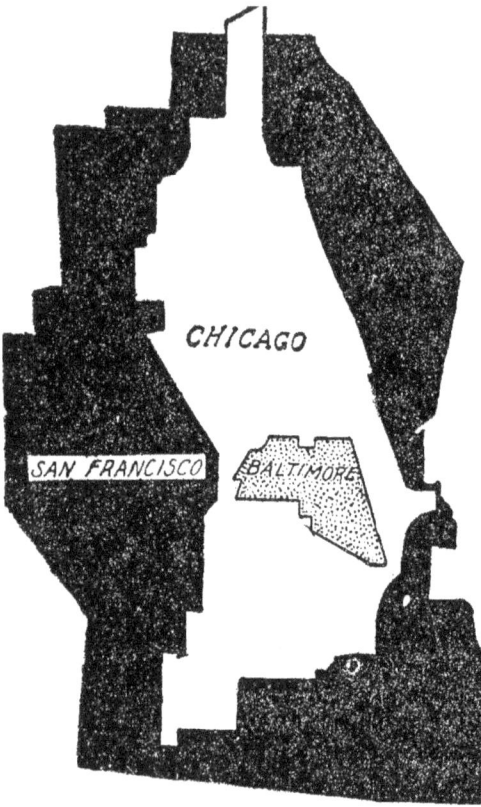

This map shows the comparative areas of three major urban fires in U.S. history. Wherever buildings were constructed from wood, fire was a constant hazard and often spread quickly from building to building.

Fire and Socioecological Transformations

If fire was the first great socioecological transformation in human history, it was a precondition for two more that followed: agrarianization and industrialization. Both were far more momentous in scope, but neither would have been possible without fire.

The rise of agriculture and animal husbandry, or "agrarianization," in many respects resembled the domestication of fire. Humans added new sources of energy to their own as they had done before by taming fire, this time by incorporating specific plants and animals into their societies. Certain wild plants were cultivated, certain wild animals were tamed, and all these species were made part of the human domain, the anthroposphere.

In most parts of the world, the conversion of savannahs and forests into fields and meadows was accomplished by means of fire. Flames and smoke marked the frontiers of agrarianization—as they still do today in Amazonia and elsewhere. Often agriculture remained closely associated with burning, as in the widespread practice of swidden farming, or shifting cultivation, in which tracts of land would be periodically burned and cultivated and left fallow again for a number of years, in a cyclical sequence.

Many agrarian societies passed through a phase of shifting cultivation, but then adopted more intensive techniques of working the land with higher average yields. As these societies gave rise to villages and towns, new uses of fire and new attitudes toward fire developed. During the long first phase of human fire use, the main concern always had been to keep the communal fire burning. In the agrarian towns, however, fire was no longer scarce. Its uses became increasingly more varied. Specialized pyrotechnic crafts emerged, such as blacksmithing and pottery. Public concern now turned mainly to keeping the many fires within their containers. Fire was regarded with greater anxiety, for with the proliferation of fires the risks of conflagrations increased, and with the accumulation of property, people had more to lose. Not surprisingly, blazes figure prominently in the local histories of towns and villages.

Of course, the eventual cause of destruction always lay in the very nature of the combustion process. But with the progressive domestication of fire, this natural force manifested itself more and more through manmade fires. With all the lamps and furnaces burning in a city, one moment of carelessness might spark a conflagration. People had to rely on other people's caution. Arson ranked second only to murder as a capital crime deserving the severest punishment. Among the worst fears of both farmers and city dwellers was to become the victims of organized murder and arson known as war.

In the cities of medieval Europe it was mandatory to "cover" all fires before nightfall: an institution known as *couvre feu*, or curfew. The directive to cover fire almost symbolizes a general tendency in urban environments toward reducing the omnipresence of fire, and certainly toward making it less conspicuous. That tendency was interrupted for a while, however, by the onset of industrialization.

The Industrial Age

A highly significant, but rarely noticed, aspect of the original domestication of fire was the invention of fuel—the discovery that dead wood, seemingly worthless material lying around to rot, could be most valuable if it was used for burning. No other animal ever made this discovery. Nor did any other animal ever learn the great potential of fossil fuels.

During the ten thousands years of agrarianization, wood remained by far the most important fuel. This was to change dramatically in the course of the two hundred and fifty years of industrialization, starting in the early eighteenth century, when ways were discovered of exploiting other sources of fuel as well: coal, oil, gas.

Industrialization began, like agrarianization, with great displays of fire. Its frontiers were marked by the fire and smoke of steam engines driven by burning coal. Humankind was entering, to use the image of Rolf Peter Sieferle, a newly discovered "subterranean forest," containing the fossil remains of hundreds of millions of years of organic growth, stocked in the mantle of the Earth as unburned fuel.

Industrialization was the third great ecological transformation brought about by humans. It involved, once again, the tapping of newly exploited natural resources—first coal, later also oil and natural gas—and incorporating these into human society, as had been done before with fire and with certain selected plants and animals.

Just like the transition to agriculture, when forests were burned down to create fields and meadows, the rise of modern industry was heralded by a huge and conspicuous use of fire. The familiar pictures of the early industrial landscape in Lancashire readily evoke the manifest ubiquity of fire, with smoke rising from the factory stacks at day, and a red glow illuminating the sky at night.

As industrialization advanced, fire continued to be important in practically every variety of industrial production; but its presence has become less prominent. The vital combustion processes tend to be hidden away, in the furnaces of power stations or under the hoods of motorcars. Partly as a result of this general tendency, cities in the advanced industrial world today are far better protected against the risks of fire than were preindustrial cities. The incidence of conflagrations in peacetime is much smaller now than it used to be until a few centuries ago. In times of war, however, the twentieth century has seen urban blazes of unprecedented size and intensity.

Current Developments

Ancient Greek cosmologists used to distinguish four elements out of which the world was composed: earth, water, air, and fire. While earth, water, and air are indispensable for all land animals, only humans have also come to rely upon fire. Furthermore, all known human groups have done so. The use of fire is not just an exclusively human attribute; it continues to be universally human as well.

In retrospect, we can detect a clear sequence in the history of humans and fire. First, there were no groups with fire. Then there were some with fire, but still none with fields cultivated for agriculture and animal husbandry. Then, there were some with fire and fields, but none with factories for large-scale industrial production. Today, all human groups take part in a socioecological regime extending over the entire planet, involving fire, fields, and factories.

For thousands of generations, the control of fire has deeply affected the human condition. It has made human groups, on the one hand, more productive and robust, but at the same time also more destructive and more vulnerable. Seen in this light, the control over fire appears to be a double-edged sword, eliciting the same ambivalence that is typical of the present human self-image in general.

Nowadays fire is continuously present in all human societies. It is used in many different forms, some mainly ceremonial and highly visible, most others primarily technical and largely hidden from public view and consciousness. The moment we consider the part played by combustion processes in transport and production, it becomes clear how thoroughly our lives are enmeshed in structures which are kept going by fire and fuel. We live in highly fuel-intensive economies, and most fires burning today are generated by those economies. Fire has become overwhelmingly anthropogenic, or manmade. Where there is smoke, there is fire; where there is fire, there are people.

We may safely assume that every single step in the long-term process of increasing use of, and control over, fire has been the result of planned human action—of the deliberate and consciously steered efforts of individuals who knew what they were doing. It is more difficult to imagine that the increases in dependency were also deliberately planned. And it is extremely unlikely that our early ancestors in the foraging era ever drew up a comprehensive plan covering hundreds of millennia and leading all the way to our present plethora of gas furnaces and internal combustion engines; the very idea is absurd. Clearly the succession and interaction of short-term planned activities has produced long-term processes that were neither planned nor foreseen. Here is one more way in which the control over fire can be seen as paradigmatic. It shows something of the stuff of which human history is made.

Johan GOUDSBLOM

University of Amsterdam

See also Anthroposphere; Deforestation; Energy

Further Reading

Burton, F. D. (2009). *Fire: The spark that ignited human evolution.* Albuquerque: University of New Mexico Press.

Elias, N. (2000). *The civilizing process: Sociogenetic and psychogenetic investigations* (Rev. ed.). Oxford, U.K.: Blackwell.

Goudsblom, J. (1992). *Fire and civilization.* London: Allen Lane.

Kingdon, J. (2003). *Lowly origin: Where, when, and why our ancestors first stood up.* Princeton, NJ: Princeton University Press.

McNeill, J. R. (2001) *Something new under the sun: An environmental history of the world in the twentieth century.* New York: Penguin Books Ltd.

Pyne, S. J. (1991). *Burning bush: A fire history of Australia.* New York: Henry Holt.

Pyne, S. J. (2001). *Fire: A brief history.* Seattle: University of Washington Press.

U.K.Sieferle, R. P. (2001). *The subterranean forest: Energy systems and the industrial revolution.* Cambridge, U.K.: White Horse Press.

Simmons, I. G. (1996). *Changing the face of the Earth: Culture, environment, history* (2nd ed.). Oxford, U.K.: Blackwell.

Wrangham, R. (2009). *Catching fire: How cooking made us human.* New York: Basic Books.

Yergin, D. (1991). *The prize: The epic quest for oil, money and power.* New York: Simon and Schuster.

Gaia Theory

The Gaia theory holds that Earth's physical and biological processes are inextricably linked to form a self-regulating system that maintains its own habitability. The theory asserts that living organisms and their inorganic surroundings have evolved together as a single living system that greatly affects the conditions of Earth's surface. The theory is often described in terms of Earth acting as a single organism.

In 1969 the British scientist James Lovelock postulated that life on Earth regulates the composition of the atmosphere to keep the planet habitable. The novelist William Golding, Lovelock's friend and neighbor, suggested Lovelock call the hypothesis Gaia, after the Greek Earth goddess. Although in its early exposition and in the popular press the Gaia hypothesis was understood as saying Earth itself was a living organism, the theory as Lovelock came to articulate it said rather that Earth acts like a living organism, with its living and nonliving components acting in concert to create an environment that continues to be suitable for life.

Development of the Gaia Hypothesis

The idea that life is more than a passenger on Earth dates back to the work of scholars and researchers in a number of disciplines: the Scottish geologist James Hutton (1726–1797) and was held by the British biologist T. H. Huxley, the animal physiologist Alfred Redfield, the aquatic ecologist G. Evelyn Hutchinson, and the geologist Vladimir Vernadsky. In 1924 Alfred Lotka—a U.S. chemist, ecologist, mathematician, and demographer—first proposed the radical notion that

life and the material environment evolved together as a system, but few took him seriously.

In the late 1960s, as part of its search for life on Mars, the National Aeronautics and Space Administration (NASA) gathered information on the composition of planetary atmospheres. Lovelock, then a NASA consultant, noted that Venus and Mars both had atmospheres dominated by carbon dioxide and close to chemical equilibrium. In contrast, gases made by living organisms dominate the atmosphere, which, despite being far from chemical equilibrium, is stable in the long term. Lovelock realized that such stability required a regulator and, since the atmosphere was mainly a biological product, proposed that Earth's collective life forms played this role.

In 1971 he began collaboration with the eminent biologist Lynn Margulis, who brought her extensive knowledge of Earth's microorganisms and added flesh to what was otherwise a chemical hypothesis based on atmospheric evidence.

Criticism and Refinement of the Gaia Hypothesis

Lovelock and Margulis's joint work brought strong criticism, mainly from other biologists. W. Ford Doolittle and Richard Dawkins, two vocal critics, stated that there was no way for living organisms to regulate anything beyond their individual selves. Some scientists in particular were critical of the hypothesis for being teleological, or assuming that all things have a predetermined purpose. Lovelock responded: "Neither Lynn Margulis nor I have ever proposed a teleological hypothesis" (1990, 100). Doolittle argued that there was nothing in the genome

131

of individual organisms to provide the feedback mechanisms Gaia Theory proposed. Dawkins has argued that organisms cannot act in concert, as this would require foresight and planning. Stephen Jay Gould, the renowned U.S. paleontologist and evolutionary biologist, wanted to know the mechanisms by which self-regulating homeostasis is possible. This criticism was in the best traditions of science and required a proper response.

In 1981 Lovelock answered the critics by creating the numerical model Daisyworld, an imaginary planet on which there were two species of plant, one light colored and the other dark colored. The planet was warmed by a star that, like Earth's sun, grew hotter as time passed. When the star was cooler, each dark-colored daisy warmed itself by absorbing sunlight, until dark daisies predominated and warmed the planet; as the star grew hotter, each pale-colored daisy, by reflecting sunlight, kept itself and the planet cooler. The competition for space by the two daisy species kept the planet's temperature constant, thus sustaining a habitable condition despite changes in the heat output of the star. The model showed that even without regulating anything other than themselves, organisms and their environment evolve together as a powerful self-regulating system. This demonstration, along with successful predictions of mechanisms for the regulation of the Earth's climate and chemistry, put Gaia on a firm theoretical basis, which was strengthened by a further suite of models from the ecologists Tim Lenton (in 1998) and Stephan Harding (in 1999).

The Heart of Gaia

Gaia views Earth's surface environment as a self-regulating system composed of all organisms, the atmosphere, oceans, and crustal rocks, which sustains conditions favorable for life. It sees the evolution of life and the evolution of Earth's surface and atmosphere as a single process, not separate processes, as taught in biology and geology. Organisms evolve by a process of natural selection, but in Gaia, they do not merely adapt to the environment, they change it. Humans, clearly, are changing the atmosphere, the climate, and the land surfaces, but other organisms, mostly microscopic, have in the past made changes that were even more drastic. The appearance of oxygen in the air two billion years ago is but one of them. Gaia stands to Darwinism somewhat as relativity theory stands to Newtonian physics. It is no contradiction of Darwin's great vision but an extension of it.

What use is Gaia? It has been a fruitful source of new research and an inspiration for environmentalists. It led to the discovery of the natural compounds dimethyl sulfide and methyl iodide, which transfer the essential elements sulfur and iodine from the oceans to the land. It showed how life in the soil and on the rocks increases the rate of removal of carbon dioxide from the air and so regulates both the levels of carbon dioxide and, consequently, climate. Its most daring prediction stated in 1987 by Robert Charlson, Lovelock, Meinrat Andreae, and Stephen Warren, was that the microscopic algae of the oceans are linked by their emission of a gas, dimethyl sulfide, with the clouds and with the climate. As Earth gets hotter, the theory says, these algae release more dimethyl sulfide into the atmosphere, which increases Earth's cloud cover, which in turn cools the Earth: without clouds, the earth would be hotter by 10–20°C. This idea is crucial to the proper understanding of climate change. The authors received the Norbert Gerbier Prize and medal from The World Meteorological Office for this theory in 1988. Ten years later hundreds of scientists worldwide were studying the links between ocean algae, atmospheric chemistry, clouds, and climate. Climatologists and even physiologists have used Daisyworld in their research. Over the years, Gaia has changed the way scientists think. There is no better example of this change than the Amsterdam Declaration of 2001. A conference of environmental scientists in 2001 issued the declaration, which had as its first bullet point: "The Earth System behaves as a single, self-regulating system comprised of physical, chemical, biological and human components" (Open Science Conference 2001). Although not yet a full statement of Gaia theory, it a substantial advance on the separated view of earth and life sciences that went before.

In recent years, the Gaia theory has become part of general discussion and popular journalism, especially in relation to global climate change. Its subject, the complex interdependencies of planetary life, is part of the academic curriculum under the name "Earth Systems Science."

The Revenge of Gaia

In a 2006 book, Lovelock made the argument that environmental degradation and climate change are testing Gaia's capacity to self-regulate and maintain Earth's habitability. He believes that it is already too late to avoid significant climate change, thus rendering large portions of our planet much less hospitable for humans. Sustainable development and renewable energy are two hundred years too late to be of much help; it is now time to direct greater efforts towards adaptation. Lovelock is an advocate of nuclear power as a short-term solution for maintaining energy demands, but other clean alternative energy sources are thought to be too little too late. Given the range of environmental stresses, he claims that human civilization will find it difficult to survive as is, with the human population experiencing significant decline during the next hundred years. Lovelock claims that Gaia's self-regulation is likely to prevent any catastrophic wipeout of life on Earth, but the present course of action is unsustainable, and there will be changes to life on Earth one way or the other.

James LOVELOCK
European Communities Information Office

See also Anthroposphere; Biological Exchanges; Climate Change; Environmental Movements

Further Reading

Charlson, R. J., Lovelock, J. E., Andreae, M. O., & Warren, S. G. (1987). Oceanic phytoplankton, atmospheric sulphur, cloud albedo and climate. *Nature, 326*(6114), 655–661.

Crist, E., & Rinker. H. B. (Eds.) (2009). *Gaia in turmoil: Climate change, biodepletion, and Earth ethics in an age of crisis.* Cambridge, MA: MIT Press.

Harding, S. P. (1999). Food web complexity enhances community stability and climate regulation in a geophysiological model. *Tellus, 51*(B), 815–829.

Lenton, T. (1998). Gaia and natural selection. *Nature, 394,* 439–447.

Lotka, A. (1956). *Elements of mathematical biology.* New York: Dover. (Original work published 1924)

Lovelock, J. E. (1969). Planetary atmospheres: Compositional and other changes associated with the presence of life. In O. L. Tiffany & E. Zaitzeff (Eds.). *Advances in the astronautical sciences* (Vol. 25, pp. 179–193). Tarzana, CA: American Astronautical Society.

Lovelock, J. E. (1979). *Gaia: A new look at life on earth.* Oxford, U.K.: Oxford University Press.

Lovelock, J. E. (1988). *The ages of Gaia: A biography of our living earth.* New York: W.W. Norton.

Lovelock J. E. (1990). Hands up for the Gaia hypothesis. *Nature, 344,* 100–102.

Lovelock, J. E. (1991). *The practical science of planetary medicine.* London: Gaia Books.

Lovelock, J. E. (2006). *The revenge of Gaia: Earth climate crisis & the fate of humanity.* New York: Basic Book.

Lovelock, J. E. (2008). *The vanishing face of Gaia: A final warning.* New York: Basic Books.

Lovelock, J. E., & Margulis, M. (1973). Atmospheric homeostasis by and for the biosphere: The Gaia hypothesis. *Tellus, 26,* 2–10.

Lovelock, J. E., & Watson, A. J. (1982). The regulation of carbon dioxide and climate: Gaia or geochemistry. *Planet. Space Science, 30*(8), 795–802.

Open Science Conference (2001, July 10–13).The Amsterdam declaration on global change. Retrieved September 5, 2002, from http://www.sciconf.igbp.kva.se/Amsterdam_Declaration.html

Watson, A. J., & Lovelock, J. E. (1983). Biological homeostasis of the global environment: The parable of Daisyworld. *Tellus, 35*(B), 284–289.

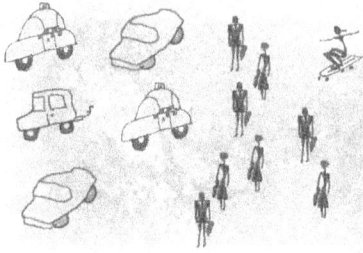

Green Revolution

The successful development of higher-yielding hybrid strains of corn and wheat ("miracle seeds") in the early 1960s led to the controversial Green Revolution: big businesses and governments see it as a breakthrough in agriculture and food safety, while small farmers and ecologists see it as ruining the environment, destroying agricultural productivity, obliterating indigenous cultural and agricultural practices, and creating even greater global inequalities.

William Gaud, director of the U.S. Agency for International Development (USAID), coined the term *Green Revolution* in March 1968, and its origins help explain its contested meaning in contemporary history: government development agencies as well as transnational chemical and biotechnology corporations and multilateral organizations such as the World Bank see the Green Revolution (GR) as a miraculous breakthrough in agricultural productivity and food security, whereas small farmers, ecologists, social scientists, indigenous peoples, and community activists see it as ruining the environment, destroying agricultural productivity, obliterating indigenous cultural and agricultural practices, and creating even greater global inequalities through excessive debt burdens for the developing world that further enrich the developed world. How did the Green Revolution give rise to such polarized reactions and assessments? Part of the answer lies in the fact that the Green Revolution, as an application of modern science and technology to agriculture, has never been about just the superiority of one agricultural technology or practice over others—it has been a political, economic, and social event from the start, and so one cannot

be surprised that it has attracted controversy. Part of the answer also lies in how one assesses where and to whom the major benefits of this agricultural revolution went, that is, did they reach the intended recipients?

Definition

The basic elements of the Green Revolution are highly mechanized and energy-intensive production methods (e.g., the use of tractors and mechanical harvesters); a dependence on the intensive use of chemical or synthetic fertilizers, pesticides, and fungicides; a reliance on petroleum-powered machinery and petroleum by-products; the utilization of high-yielding hybrid seeds; uniform planting of one crop species over a large acreage (monoculture); double cropping (two crop seasons per year); large-scale irrigation; and a continuous supply of patented technology and inputs (seeds, fertilizers, pesticides, etc.). The goal was to increase the capacity of plants to use sunlight, water, and soil nutrients more efficiently, and the heart of this revolution in agriculture was the development of certain varieties of patented seeds that fit the requirements of Green Revolution technologies.

Origins

Although its antecedents date to earlier genetic research, the Green Revolution as we know it today began with research conducted in Mexico by U.S. scientists in a wheat and maize research center sponsored by the Rockefeller Foundation during the 1940s and 1950s. Their goal was to develop higher-yielding hybrid strains of corn and wheat.

The remains of the Union Carbide pesticide plant after the 1984 disaster in the city of Bhopal, Madhya Pradesh, India. Photo by Luca Frediani.

The most important person in initiating the Green Revolution in northwestern Mexico was the plant pathologist and geneticist Norman Borlaug. His wheat strains responded well to heavy doses of nitrogen fertilizer and water; the International Center for Wheat and Maize Improvement, established in 1966 by the Rockefeller Foundation in cooperation with the Mexican government, continued his work. With the help of money from the Ford and Rockefeller Foundations, the United Nations Food and Agricultural Organization, and USAID, "miracle seed" spread outside Mexico after 1963 and had its greatest success in an area from Turkey to northern India. The Rockefeller Foundation also sponsored a rice research center, the International Rice Research Institute, in the Philippines in 1960. The institute created high-yield dwarf rice varieties of "miracle rice" that spread to the rice-growing areas of east and southeastern Asia. Researchers at these and private corporate research centers selectively bred high-yielding strains of staple crops, mainly wheat, maize, and rice with sturdy stalks, which were responsive to chemical fertilizers and irrigation water, resistant to pests, and compatible with mechanical harvesting.

Chemical and seed corporations and government officials in developed and developing countries championed the Green Revolution as the solution to problems of famine and malnutrition around the world. More was involved, however: Excluding Mexico, the U.S.-sponsored enterprise encircled the Communist world from Turkey to Korea. Although fears of the spread of Communism motivated U.S. politicians and businesspeople, the idea of scientifically designed crops to improve living standards was also promoted within socialist societies from the Soviet Union to China to Cuba. In many ways the Green Revolution started as an economic wing of Cold War politics.

Positive Results

The incubation of the Green Revolution occurred during the 1950s and 1960s, and it dramatically altered food production during the 1970s and 1980s. In 1970 around 15 percent of the Third World's wheat- and rice-growing areas were cultivated with the new hybrid seeds. By 1983 the figure was more than 50 percent, and by 1991 it was 75 percent. Proponents argue that more than half of all economic benefits generated by GR technologies have gone to farmers and that plentiful harvests became commonplace in much of the world during the thirty-five years after 1960: Crop yields of wheat nearly tripled, those of rice nearly doubled, and those of corn more than doubled in ninety-three countries. Because of high-yield rice and wheat, scores of countries kept food production ahead of population growth.

The Green Revolution promised agricultural plenty and prosperity. Photo by Joan Lebold Cohen.

Learning from the mistakes of its first applications, newer GR technologies promised increased net returns and reduced chemical loads for farmers. The Green Revolution was most successful in India in increasing aggregate food production: During 1978 and 1979 India established a record grain output of 118 million metric tons and increased its grain yield per unit of farmland by 30 percent since 1947. India has not had a famine since 1965–1966. However, no other country that attempted the Green Revolution matched India's success or the number of jobs in auxiliary facilities such as chemical factories and hydroelectric power stations.

Proponents such as Martina McGloughlin point out that GR technologies create more food for sale, increase foreign exchange and national income, and generate a steady income source for successful growers as well as new nonagricultural jobs. Proponents do not believe that the adoption of biotechnology crops is creating genetic uniformity or inducing vulnerability to new strains of pathogens. They assert that GR technologies are size neutral and can promote sustainable agriculture centered on small farmers in developing countries. Despite such claims, the Green Revolution has promoted monoculture worldwide because each hybrid seed crop has specific fertilizer and pesticide requirements for maximum growth: Farmers save money by buying seed, fertilizer, and pesticide in bulk and by planting and tending the same crop uniformly on their land.

Negative Outcomes

The picture is not all rosy, however. Despite claims by proponents, monoculture did make crops more susceptible to infestations and damage by a single pest. When farmers turned to heavier doses of petroleum-based pesticides, the more-resistant pests survived, and their offspring returned the next year to cause even greater losses. Famous cases of such resistance are the southern corn leaf blight in 1970 and 1971 in the United States; the brown planthopper, which attacked the various strains of "miracle rice" during the 1970s and 1980s in the Philippines, Sri Lanka, Solomon Islands, Thailand, India, Indonesia, and Malaysia and in Thailand, Malaysia, and Bangladesh again in 1990; and the recent potato blight in the Andes. Millions of people, mostly agricultural workers, suffer from acute pesticide poisoning, and tens of thousands die every year from it. The horrific explosion at Union Carbide's Bhopal, India, plant on 2 December 1984 killed an estimated 3,000 people and injured 200,000 more. The chemical Sevin manufactured at Bhopal was essential for India's Green Revolution. In addition, ever-rising doses of pesticides have meant that they ended up in water supplies, animal and human tissues, and soil with often unforeseen consequences. Along the Costa Rican coast 90 percent of the coral reefs are dead due to pesticide run off from plantations that monocrop bananas for export and that have ruined 80,000 hectares of former banana plantation land with copper residues from pesticides so that the land can no longer be used to grow food for either domestic consumption or export. Costa Rica now imports basic staple grains: beans, corn, and rice.

The irrigation required by the Green Revolution has led to massive dam-building projects in China, India, Mexico and elsewhere, displaced tens of thousands of indigenous peoples, and submerged their farmland. The frequent result of massive irrigation has been the creation of soil with a high salt content that even large does of fertilizer cannot repair. Critics have documented the reduction in species diversity that followed the Green Revolution. Rice, wheat, and maize have come to dominate global agriculture: They supply 66 percent of the world's entire seed crop. They have edged out leafy vegetables and other food crops that do not respond to nitrogen- and water-rich farming regimes. Critics note that human beings cultivated more than three thousand plant species as food sources before the Green Revolution, whereas today fifteen species (among them rice, corn, wheat, potato, cassava, the common bean, soybean, peanut, coconut, and banana) provide more than 85 percent of all human nutrition.

The energy requirements for this agriculture are high: In what Southern Illinois University professor of anthropology Ernest Schusky has dubbed the "neo-caloric revolution" GR agriculture is one-half as energy efficient as ox-and-plow agriculture and one-quarter as energy efficient as hoe agriculture. The model of GR agriculture, U.S. grain farming, is remarkably energy inefficient: It consumes eight calories of energy for every one calorie it produces. For critics thirty years of the Green Revolution have left a legacy of environmental degradation, unsustainable agricultural practices, social disruption, homeless farmers, ruined farmland, crushing international debt burdens for developing countries, and the export of needed food to meet loan payments.

A Mixed Legacy

Opponents and proponents alike admit that the benefits of the Green Revolution are unevenly spread. Wealthier farmers with dependable access to water and credit prospered, whereas those farmers who skimped on fertilizer and irrigation because of the extra costs did not do well, and their yields were no greater than before. Agrochemical industries, banks, large petrochemical companies, manufacturers of agricultural machinery, dam builders and large landowners have been major beneficiaries. The social results in the United States and elsewhere have been a reduction in the number of small family farms, the concentration of agricultural wealth in fewer hands, growing social inequality, and migration to cities. In the case of Taiwan, South Korea, and Indonesia, producing more food with fewer people and the exodus of people to cities helped fuel industrialization. In other countries it merely increased the urban slum-dwelling poor. Internationally, South Korea, China, India, and Mexico reduced or eliminated food dependence, and India became a net food exporter. Other nations did not fare so well: Until 1981 the developing world was a net exporter of food; after 1981 it was a net importer.

Although India is the Green Revolution success story, its Punjab region has experienced all of the revolution's negative ecological and social consequences, and Indian children are suffering from a vitamin A deficiency that is causing blindness in forty thousand children a year. Enthusiasts of the new "Gene Revolution" report that scientists are genetically altering rice so that it contains beta-carotene, which enzymes in the intestine convert to vitamin A when needed. Critics argue that vitamin A deficiency is best seen as a symptom of broader dietary deficiencies caused by a change from diverse cropping systems to rice monoculture: Indian children have vitamin A deficiency because their diet has been reduced to rice and little else. Under a mixed agricultural regime, Indian farmers grew *brathua*, a traditional plant rich in vitamin A, along with their wheat, but in GR monocultures *brathua* is regarded as a pest and is destroyed with herbicides.

In reaction to the myriad problems caused by the Green Revolution, an alternative agriculture called "LISA" (low-input sustainable agriculture) emerged in the United States, Cuba, western Europe, and elsewhere in the late 1980s (in 1990, in the United States, it was renamed Sustainable Agriculture Research and Education Program [SARE]). It sought to promote ecological sustainability in farm production by replacing dependence on heavy farm machinery and chemical inputs with animal traction, crop and pasture rotations, soil conservation, organic soil amendments, biological pest control, and microbial biofertilizers and biopesticides that are not toxic to humans. A carefully watched experiment with LISA occurred in Cuba, where the end of Soviet pesticide and petroleum subsidies in 1991 led to the collapse of GR-based food production 'and near famine from 1991 to 1995. In 1993 the Cuban government began breaking up large state farms, changed land tenure toward cooperatives, and replaced the Soviet Green Revolution model with the LISA model on a national scale. Food production rose slowly from its low in 1995 to approach its old levels by 2005, and continues to rise. A contributing factor is the cooperative system (as of the 2008, the state owns about 65 percent of all tilled land; the cooperatives comprise 35 percent but produce 60 percent of all Cuba's agricultural crops).

Implications and Directions

The Green Revolution has fervent admirers and detractors. Admirers who wish to mitigate its worst effects are promoting the Gene Revolution, which combines specific genes (and their desirable traits) among unrelated species to yield plants with novel traits that cannot be produced by farmers practicing traditional breeding. The result is the engineering of "transgenic" crops such as rice with beta-carotene or plants that produce pesticides to protect themselves or vaccines against malaria and cholera. Those people who promote LISA endorse agroecology, which entails grassroots efforts by small farmers and scientists to meld traditional and modern farming methods, to reduce pesticide and chemical fertilizer use, to select natural seed varieties suited to different soils and climates, to end monoculture and export orientation,

and to use science to enhance natural ecological systems of agricultural production and protection. The choices that people make in the first decades of the twenty-first century will shape not only the kinds and amounts of foods that people will have available to eat but also the ecological health of the planet itself.

Alexander M. ZUKAS
National University

See also Environmental Movements

Further Reading

Altieri, M. A., & Rosset, P. (1996). Comment and reply: Strengthening the case for why biotechnology will not help the developing world: A response to McGloughlin. *AgBioForum: The Journal of Agrobiotechnology Management & Economics*, 2(3–4), 14. Retrieved January 22, 2004, from http://www.agbioforum.org/v2n34/v2n34a14-altieri.htm

Environmental Health Fund and Strategic Counsel on Corporate Accountability. (1999). *Beyond the chemical century: Restoring human rights and preserving the fabric of life: A report to commemorate the 15th anniversary of the Bhopal disaster December 3, 1999.* Retrieved January 22, 2004, from http://home.earthlink.net/~gnproject/chemcentury.htm

Evenson, R. E., Santaniello, V., & Zilberman, D. (2002). *Economic and social issues in agricultural biotechnology.* New York: CABI Publishing.

Foster, J. B. (2001). *The vulnerable planet: A short economic history of the environment.* New York: Monthly Review Press.

Foster, J. B. (2002). *Ecology against capitalism.* New York: Monthly Review Press.

Foster, J. B. (2009). *The ecological revolution: Making peace with the planet.* New York: Monthly Review Press.

Funes, F., Garcia, L., Bourque, M., Perez, N., & Rosset, P. (2002). *Sustainable agriculture and resistance: Transforming food production in Cuba.* Oakland, CA: Food First Books.

Ganguly, S. (1998). *From the Bengal famine to the Green Revolution.* Retrieved January 22, 2004, from http://www.indiaonestop.com/Greenrevolution.htm

Greenpeace. (2002). *The real Green Revolution—Organic and agroecological farming in the South.* Retrieved January 22, 2004, from http://archive.greenpeace.org/geneng/highlights/hunger/greenrev.htm

The destiny of world civilization depends on providing a decent standard of living for all mankind. • **Norman Borlaug (1914–2009)**

Hughes, J. D. (2001). *An environmental history of the world: Humankind's changing role in the community of life.* London: Routledge.

Lappe, F. M., Collins, J., & Rosset, P. (1998) *World hunger: Twelve myths* (2nd ed.). New York: Grove Press and Earthscan.

Leff, E. (1995). *Green production: Toward an environmental rationality.* New York: Guilford.

McGloughlin, M. (1999). Ten reasons why biotechnology will be important to the developing world. *AgBioForum: The Journal of Agrobiotechnology Management & Economics, 2*(3–4), 4. Retrieved January 22, 2004, from http://www.agbioforum.org/v2n34/v2n34a04-mcgloughlin.htm

McNeill, J. R. (2000). *Something new under the sun: An environmental history of the twentieth century.* New York: W. W. Norton.

Perkins, J. H. (1997). *Geopolitics and the Green Revolution: Wheat, genes, and the Cold War.* New York: Oxford University Press.

Pimentel, D., & Pimentel, M. (1979). *Food, energy, and society.* New York: Wiley.

Pimentel, D., & Lehman, H. (Eds.). (1993). *The pesticide question: Environment, economics, and ethics.* New York: Chapman & Hall.

Poincelot, R. P., Horne, J., & McDermott, M. (2001). *The next Green Revolution: Essential steps to a healthy, sustainable agriculture.* Boca Raton, FL: CRC Press.

Raffensperger, L. (2008). Changes on the horizon for Cuba's Sustainable Agriculture. Retrieved April 26, 2010, from http://earthtrends.wri.org/updates/node/306

Rosset, P., & Benjamin, M. (Eds.). (1994) *The greening of the revolution: Cuba's experiment with organic agriculture.* Melbourne, Australia: Ocean Press.

Schusky, E. L. (1989). *Culture and agriculture: An ecological introduction to traditional and modern farming systems.* New York: Bergin & Garvey.

Sharma, M. L. (1990). *Green Revolution and social change.* Lahore, Pakistan: South Asia Books.

Shiva, V. (1992). *The violence of the Green Revolution: Third World agriculture, ecology and politics.* London: Zed Books.

Sinha, R. K. (2004). *Sustainable agriculture: Embarking on the second Green Revolution with the technological revival of traditional agriculture.* Jaipur, India: Surabhi Publications.

Tolba, M. K., & El-Kholy, O. A. (Eds.). (1992). *The world environment, 1972–1992.* London: Chapman & Hall.

World Resources Institute. (1996). *World resources, 1996–1997.* New York: Oxford University Press.

Ice Ages

At least five prolonged ice ages—epochs when glaciers cover entire continents—have occurred throughout the Earth's 4.6 billion–year history. These five ice ages represented unusual, relatively short episodes in the whole of Earth's climatic record (spanning a total of 50 to 200 million years, only 1 to 4 percent), and yet they destroyed entire ecosystems, leaving behind tremendous piles of glacial debris.

Ice ages are epochs of time when massive ice sheets and smaller ice masses called glaciers cover extensive areas of the Earth's surface. During an ice age the planet is cold, dry, and inhospitable. Whereas few forests can be supported, ice-covered areas and deserts are plentiful. Winters are longer and more severe, and ice sheets grow to enormous sizes, accumulating to thicknesses that measure thousands of feet in depth. These ice sheets move slowly from higher elevations to lower regions, driven by gravity and their tremendous weight. During that process, they alter river courses, destroy entire regional ecosystems, flatten landscapes, and, along their margins, deposit great piles of glacial debris.

Evidence of Ice Ages

Proof of ice ages—glaciation over continent-sized regions—comes from several sources. There is the widespread deposition of unique sediments of dirt (called "till") found under melting glaciers. These sediments contain a wide variety of rock forms that have been accumulated from disparate areas. In addition, glaciation leaves telltale marks in the form of grooved, striated, polished bedrock pavements, faceted stones

in the till, and interspersed layers of gravel containing different rock types. Ice ages also are substantiated by erosional forms believed to have been produced by advancing ice sheets, among them sculptured landscapes, such as glacial uplands or U-shaped valleys.

Such evidence suggests at least five prolonged ice ages: (1) during Precambrian era, 1.7–2.3 billion years ago; (2) during the end of the Proterozoic eon, about 670 million years ago; (3) during the middle of the Paleozoic era, about 420 million years ago; (4) during the Carboniferous period, in the late Paleozoic era, beginning 290 million years ago; and (5) during the Pleistocene epoch of the Quaternary period, beginning 1.7 million years ago. In this most recent era, ice sheets developed in the highlands of North America and Europe and dominated the Northern Hemisphere. Massive ice sheets covered all of present Canada, south of the Great Lakes region, as well as Greenland, Scandinavia, and Russia. Each ice age lasted at least a million years, during which great ice sheets migrated back and forth across a huge paleocontinent (ancient or prehistoric continent). The span of these ice ages totaled 50 to 200 million years, which accounts for only 1 to 4 percent of the Earth's 4.6 billion-year history. Ice ages thus represent unusual, albeit relatively short, episodes in the Earth's climatic record.

Theories about Causes of Ice Ages

Although scientists have extensively studied glaciation, no single theory is widely accepted as explaining the causes of ice ages. However, several theories converge into two categories. First are terrestrial theories. Among these, in 1941 the Canadian geologist

Illustration of a mammoth from *The Natural History of Man* by A. de Quatrefages, published in 1875. The mammoth's woolly coat allowed it to survive the harsh temperatures of the great ice ages.

and explorer A. P. Coleman suggested that change in the elevations of continents provided a natural explanation for an ice age. That is, the uplifting of continental blocks creates increases in the height of land areas by mountains rising or sea levels falling, which cooled the land and produced glacial conditions. A second theory is linked to the changing continental positions associated with plate tectonics. The notion of continental drift, set out by the German geophysicist Alfred Wegener in 1922, proposes that continents sliding around on the globe's surface could be brought into colder climatic conditions, thereby allowing ice sheets to develop, especially because a continent's climate is mainly determined by its latitude and size. A third theory suggests that extensive volcanic activity, which spews out dust and ash into the atmosphere, reflects radiant solar heat back into space, thereby producing cooler temperatures on the Earth's surface. Closely related is the ocean-atmospheric hypothesis. The assumption here is that the only adequate supply of water for massive ice accumulations is the ocean. Because creation of ice sheets on land depends on wind and weather patterns, logic suggests that profound changes between the ocean and the atmosphere could contribute to the onset of ice ages. Another hypothesis was put

forward in 1998 by the American climatologist, Maureen Raymo. She proposed the idea that Earth's cooling climate over the last 40 million years was caused by a reduction in atmospheric carbon dioxide due to enhanced chemical weathering in the mountainous regions of the world, particularly the Himalayas, and that the growth of the Himalayas may, in fact, have triggered the start of the ice ages.

The second category of theories to explain ice ages is extraterrestrial. As early as 1875 the Scottish scientist James Croll proposed that astronomical variations in the Earth's orbit around the sun produced conditions for the onset of ice ages. He believed that disturbances by the moon and sun cause periodic shifts in the Earth's orbit, thereby affecting the distribution of solar heat received by the Earth and climatic patterns on the surface. Less heat produces colder climates.

Croll's theory was modified in 1938 by a Yugoslav scientist, Milutin Milankovitch, in what is today the most popularly accepted theory for climate changes during the Pleistocene epoch. Milankovitch believed that the amount of solar radiation is the most important factor in controlling the Earth's climate and in producing ice ages. The amount of radiation varies, he argued, according to three key factors. (1) The

Earth doesn't rotate perfectly like a wheel about an axis; it spins like a wobbling top. Every twenty-two thousand years, Milankovitch calculated, there is a slight change in its wobble (called "precession of the equinoxes"). (2) Every 100,000 years there is a change in the Earth's orbit about the sun (which he labeled "eccentricity"). The Earth's almost-circular orbit becomes more elliptical, taking the Earth farther from the sun. (3) Finally, Milankovitch discovered that every forty-one thousand years there is a change in the tilt of the Earth's axis, moving either the Northern or Southern Hemisphere farther from the sun (a process known as "obliquity"). These cycles mean that at certain times less sunshine hits the Earth, so there is less melting of snow and ice. Instead of melting, these cold expanses of frozen water grow. The snow and ice last longer and, over many seasons, begin to accumulate. Snow reflects some sunlight back into space, which also contributes to cooling. Temperatures drop, and glaciers begin to advance. These effects are sufficiently substantial to cause cyclical expansion and contraction of the massive ice sheets. By taking climatic effects and solar insulation of these variations and applying them to computer models of ice sheet behavior, scientists have demonstrated that a correlation exists between these cycles and the cyclic growth and decay of Pleistocene ice sheets over the past 600,000 years. The combination of orbital cycles results in lower summer insulation (exposure to the sun's rays) at fifty-five degrees north latitude. Such cooler summers in high latitudes tend to preserve each winter's snowfall, which over thousands of years leads to snow from successive winters inducing growth in the northern ice sheets, evidentially causing the onset of a new ice age.

The Earth may be currently in an ice age because within each major glaciation ice caps and mountain glaciers are oscillating between extension and retreat. The last retreat concluded approximately ten thousand years ago and probably represents only an oscillation, not a final ending. The recent trend toward global warming, however, has reduced fears of any imminent return of an ice age.

Christopher C. JOYNER
Georgetown University

See also Climate Change

Further Reading

Andersen, B. G., & Borns, H. W. (1994). *The ice age world*. New York: Scandinavian University Press.

Erickson, J. (1990). *Ice ages: Past and future*. Blue Ridge Summit, PA: TAB Books.

Fagan, B. (2009). *The great warming: Climate change and the rise and fall of civilizations*. London: Bloomsbury Press

Macdougall, D. (2006) *Frozen earth: The once and future story of ice ages*. Berkeley: University of California Press

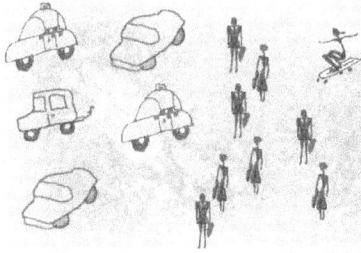

Islands

Islands are almost as diverse as they are numerous: large or small, rich or poor, inhabited or populated. From the earliest times, as populations settled ever farther around the globe, humans have coveted islands as stepping stones and colonies. Islands have served as trading posts, warehouses, naval bases, and refueling stations. They are still valued today for their often exotic environments and remote locales.

Geographers tell us there are 5,675 islands on the Earth measuring from 10 square kilometers (3.86 square miles) to 1 million square kilometers (3.86 million square miles), plus almost another eight million smaller islets. Islands cover only 7 percent of the planet's surface but hold 10 percent of its population and constitute 22 percent of its sovereign states, whose claims to territorial waters extend to a quarter of the oceans.

Islands are almost as various as they are numerous. A "continental" island is part of a continental shelf (Great Britain and Ireland, for instance, are continental islands attached to the European continental shelf); "oceanic" islands are the product of deep sea volcanic eruptions. Some islands stand alone; others belong to archipelagoes. Islands host a vast range of flora and fauna. There are islands that have never been inhabited and those that have seen a sequence of occupations. There are tropical and arctic islands whose temperatures remain about the same year round and temperate islands that experience changing seasons. There are islands linked to the mainland by bridges and tunnels and islands that can only be reached by water or air. Economically, there are poor and rich islands, islands that are sovereign and those that are dependent on other nations. Islands come in all kinds of political persuasions, from democracies to dictatorships. Britain and Japan can be considered the two most prominent island nations in world history, but many islands have attained levels of development that are the envy of mainlands.

Defining Islands

Despite their variation, we tend to stereotype islands. Their history and geography have been defined by mainlanders, who are in the habit of thinking of them as uniformly small, peripheral, remote, isolated, and timeless. Islands and islanders have suffered the enormous condescension of continents. Up to the fifteenth century, Western geographers considered the world to consist only of islands—one large one, Orbis Terrarum, and many smaller ones. Early European explorers assumed that every land they encountered was an island, and it was not until the sixteenth century that continents and islands were finally distinguished from one another, islands being defined as any land completely surrounded by water.

Even now it is hard to separate islands from continents, as the latter are also seagirt (surrounded by the sea), and there has been a systematic questioning of the metageography of both islands and continents. It is now clear that islands have never been wholly peripheral or remote—nor have they been isolated or static. Considering them in the context of history reveals what a huge role islands have played in every stage in the mental as well as physical development of humanity. The species we know as *Homo sapiens* originated at the edge of the sea.

The South Island of Cies, in Galicia, as seen from the island of Faro. Fascination with islands (*islomania*) is a cornerstone of the modern tourist industry.

Once humans left east Africa behind, they began a process of island hopping that did not end until the whole Earth was occupied. Water has been the greatest facilitator of human movement and contact, an advantage that explains why islands have often been at the forefront of development. Prehistoric foragers used islands as fishing camps and trading posts. The fruits of the inland agriculture revolution in the Levant (eastern Mediterranean region) were transferred to Europe by way of the island of Cyprus about 6000 BCE.

Island Importance

Islands were vital to the ancients' mastery of the Indian Ocean and the Mediterranean Sea, where Phoenicians and then Greeks established colonies on islands. The first conquest of the Pacific, which began in remote Oceania about 4000 BCE, and was completed on the shores of New Zealand in 700 CE, was accomplished by island hopping. Pacific islanders think of themselves as occupying a great sea of islands they consider not at all remote or peripheral. Atlantic voyaging came much later but was accomplished in a similar manner. The Vikings island-hopped, and, had Columbus not imagined the sea to be filled with islands (most of them legendary), he would never have set out westward. He was

so convinced he had reached the offshore islands of India, that he misnamed the Caribbean Islands the West Indies. Until the early nineteenth century, searches for a sea route to India were inspired by the idea that North America was archipelagic and therefore passable by water.

From the earliest times, islands have been coveted as colonies. The Phoenicians and Greeks used them as access points to hinterlands. The European seaborne empires of the sixteenth and seventeenth centuries all used islands extensively. They served as fishing stations and fur trading posts. Sugar planting was transferred from the isles of the Mediterranean to the Madeiras and Canaries, and then to the Caribbean. Trading for slaves from the islands off the west coast of Africa made it unnecessary for Europeans to risk their health in the tropical interior. As European empires spread to the Indian and Pacific oceans, islands were vital as entrepots (intermediary centers of trade and transshipment), victualing stops, and naval bases. For the next years, they were the most fought over properties in the world, at the very center of commercial, capitalist development. By the eighteenth century, the Atlantic had become its own sea of islands, brought close together by advances in navigation and a shared cosmopolitan culture. Until the nineteenth century, continents—not islands—were truly insular.

A self does not amount to much, but no self is an island; each exists in a fabric of relations that is now more complex and mobile than ever before. • **Jean-Francois Lyotard (1924–1998)**

Cultural Significance

Islands have played an exceptionally large role in Western minds. They have long been the object of spiritual quests, both pagan and Christian. They have frequently been identified with paradise, but also with hell (as in the case of the Galapagos Islands as described by Herman Melville). Thomas More used a fictional island to envision the first great utopia. William Shakespeare chose an island as the setting for his play, *The Tempest*, while Daniel Defoe's famous novel, *Robinson Crusoe*, is about a sailor shipwrecked on an island. Anthropology got its start on islands that served as laboratories for the naturalists Charles Darwin and Alfred Russel Wallace, founders of the science of evolution. Fascination with islands, sometimes referred to as *islomania*, continues to be a major theme in Western culture, and is a cornerstone of the modern tourist industry.

But even as the cultural significance of islands increased, their economic and political centrality declined. In the nineteenth century, the shift from commercial to industrial capitalism coincided with the rise of continents at the expense of islands. The new industrial cities were located on mainlands. The end of slavery in the nineteenth century produced a labor crisis in many island plantation systems. With the rise of steam power and the spread of railroads, the age-old advantage of water transport was much diminished. The value of islands as entrepots, victualing stops, and fishing stations declined. In the twentieth century, islands all around the world lost population. Politics as well as economies of scale put islands at a disadvantage. In the wave of decolonization that followed World War II, many islands became politically independent only to find that they were still economically tied to their old imperial masters. In the postwar era, islands came to be seen as peripheral, isolated, and backward.

Island Challenges

Islands today find themselves challenged in a number of ways. Of all Earth's land forms, they are most affected by rising sea levels and the frequency of storms caused by global warming. They continue to lose population to mainlands. Islanders constitute one of the world's largest diaspora populations, and many islanders left behind by relatives striking out for new lands are dependent on private remittances for survival. (Cuba's economy, for instance, has long depended on remittances, many of which are sent from Cuban Americans; the U.S. government placed further caps, in 2004 and again in 2009, on the amount allowed, and tightened standards so that remittances can be sent only to immediate family members.) On the other hand, islands have seen an in-migration of tourists and mainlanders looking for holiday homes. Assisted by bridge and tunnel building, this influx has led to the gentrification of islands nearest to mainland population centers. While the new arrivals come seeking the "island way of life," older residents fear the disappearance of *their* way of life.

Connectivity

In earlier phases of globalization, islands were often the facilitators of international trade and economic development. Today, they continue to play this role, though in a different manner. The world's largest single industry—tourism—is heavily dependent on them. Their offshore locations make them ideal headquarters not only for legitimate multinational businesses but also for drug smugglers, pirates, and spy operations. As so much of the world's commerce is carried by ship, their importance as naval and air bases is again growing. Because of their small size, many islands have proved exceptionally nimble in adopting new technologies. But, as the experience of Iceland has shown, when islands become models of interconnectivity they can become vulnerable to world economic crises. Iceland's economic boom, low unemployment, and relatively equal distribution of wealth—a result of the rapid global expansion of its financial sector in the early 2000s—proved unsustainable; exposure to the world market resulted in the sharp depreciation of the krona and the subsequent failure of Iceland's three largest banks in 2008.

Today, few islands are truly remote, peripheral, or insular. Islands certainly do not exist in stasis. It no longer makes sense to distinguish islands and continents or to stereotype them or their inhabitants. The Earth is itself can be seen as an island in a larger universe. Its inhabitants occupy a sea of islands, some large, some small, but all intensely interconnected and interdependent. The future of both mainlands and islands depends on how well that fact can be reconciled. Only by viewing islands in the proper context of world history can their agency and significance be appreciated.

John GILLIS
Rutgers University

Further Reading

Baldacchino, G. (Ed.). (2007). *A world of islands: An island studies reader.* Charlottetown, Prince Edward Island: Institute of Island Studies.

Cosgrove, D. (2001). *Apollo's eye: A cartographic genealogy of the Earth in the Western imagination.* Baltimore: Johns Hopkins University Press.

D'Arcy, P. (2006). *The people of the sea: Environment, identity, and history in Oceania.* Honolulu: University of Hawaii Press.

Gillis, J. R. (2004). *Islands of the mind: How the human imagination created the Atlantic world.* New York: Palgrave Macmillan.

Wigen, K. E., & Lewis, M. W. (1997). *The myth of continents: A critique of metageography.* Berkeley: University of California Press.

Mountains

Mountains evolved as havens of bio- and cultural diversity and have long been associated with indestructibility, ruggedness, and characteristics hostile to human endeavors. Until the U.N. designated 2002 the International Year of the Mountain, environmentalists ignored the fragility of mountain regions. Poor, indigenous mountain peoples, victimized by central governments, often have little choice but to overexploit their environment, and are threatened by warfare ubiquitous in many mountainous lands.

T he word *mountains* may conjure up an image of gigantic rock precipices, sharp peaks, glaciers and snow—and a team of grim-faced mountaineers, roped together, risking avalanches, rock falls, and blizzards in their arduous upward progress—the sort of scene one might see in the upper sections of the Alps or the Himalayas, or in the many other dramatic high landscapes of the planet. But that scene represents only a small fraction of our mountain environment. While there has been much debate among academics over how to define *mountain*, no simple statement has evolved. The people of Wales and northwestern England would insist that they live among mountains, yet their highest summits barely exceed 1,000 meters (about 3,280 feet) above sea level. Nomads of Tibet or agricultural peasants of southern Peru who live 4,000 meters (more than 13,120 feet) above sea level would be classified as mountain folk, yet their local landscapes may be as flat as the North American prairies.

Nevertheless, a varying combination of high altitude and steepness of slope make for short growing seasons and slow soil formation processes. The variation in average annual temperature with altitude and latitude has combined to give the Lofoten Islands of North Norway, close to sea level and 70° north, and the upper reaches of the Swiss Alps, above 2,000 meters and 46° north, similar landscapes, referred to as "alpine." Both are above the limits of tree growth (timberline) and have been molded by glaciers. In contrast, locations at high altitudes (above 3,500–4,000 meters, or roughly 11,500–13,120 feet) that are close to the equator, such as in Ethiopia, Kenya, or Ecuador, with rather rounded landforms, may support flourishing agriculture. Carl Troll (1900–1975), the famous German mountain geographer of the twentieth century, remarked that above 3,000 meters (about 9,850 feet) in Indonesia, for instance, there are high mountains without a high mountain (alpine) landscape.

In its efforts to ensure a critical assessment of the importance of mountains to sustainable human progress, the United Nations adopted a pragmatic approach in its declaration of 2002 as the International Year of Mountains (IYM), claiming that mountains occupy about 20 percent of the world's terrestrial surface and provide the direct life-support base for about 10 percent of humankind. Indirectly, in terms of their resources, such as provision of more than half of all fresh water, forest products, minerals, grazing lands, and hydropower, mountains are vital to the survival of over 50 percent of the total population. Furthermore, mountains have provided the spiritual essence of all major and many minor religions. Second only to coastal areas, they are the major focus of tourism, the largest and most rapidly expanding industry in the world. Mountains shelter some of the world's most important centers of biodiversity

People living near the Pamir Mountains in Tajikistan call them both "the roof the world" and "the feet of the sun." Photo by Jack D. Ives.

and a large share of its cultural diversity. Finally, climate change, especially the currently anticipated global warming, would have some of its earliest and most noticeable effects in mountain regions. It follows that mountains are becoming a serious object of concern.

Geographical Distribution of Mountains

Mountains are found on every continent, from the equator to the poles as far as land exists. Taken together as a single great landscape category or ecosystem, they encompass the most extensive known array of landforms, climates, flora, and fauna, as well as human cultural diversity. From a geological and tectonic point of view they comprise the most complex of the Earth's underlying structures.

Mountains and uplands incorporate the inhuman and extremely cold and sterile high ice carapaces of Antarctica and Greenland as well as the high, dry, hypoxic, and almost uninhabitable ranges of Central Asia and the south central Andes. They also include richly varied and even luxuriant ridge and valley systems of the humid tropics and subtropics, such as the eastern Himalayas, the Hengduan Mountains (Yunnan, China), Mount Cameroon, sections of the northern Andes, and parts of New Guinea. In east Africa and Ethiopia, the flanks and valleys of the high mountains have long been the preferred human habitat compared with the arid lowlands that surround them. An enormous array of other mountains must be included—for instance, the high volcanoes of the Caribbean and Central America, Indonesia, Japan, and Hawaii, where humans have long benefited from access to rich soils regardless of exposure to extreme fiery hazards. So-called middle mountains (German: *mittelgebirge*) range from Tasmania to South Africa and from central and northern Europe to the Urals and Siberia. While the Urals contrast with the Alps

Multiple hand-built terraces and rice paddies in the Nepal Middle Mountains east of Kathmandu are a remarkable feat of engineering; the irrigation system demonstrates how indigenous peoples prove to be outstanding soil conservationists. Photo by Jack D. Ives.

(the epitome of "high mountains," German: *hochgebirge*) because of their more subdued relief, their other mountain attributes warrant special policies to ensure sustainable resource use and preservation of their traditional landscapes.

The high mountains of the world are associated with the most recent, or Tertiary to present, geological period of mountain building resulting from movement of the Earth's tectonic plates. This has established two great systems of mountain ranges: the circum-Pacific and the transverse Atlas-Pyrenees-Alps-Caucasus-Hindu Kush-Himalaya-Indonesian arc. Collectively they form the loci of most of the world's active volcanoes and the majority of seismic epicenters (earthquakes). Mountains are dangerous places to live, given the combination of gravity, steep slopes, often very high levels of precipitation, tectonic disturbance, and volcanic activity. Many mountain regions are also dangerous because of the actions of people.

Changing Attitudes Toward Mountains

Try to picture the classical image of a mountainous landscape: the physical characteristics, together with relative inaccessibility and remoteness from the mainstreams of world society, provide images of indestructibility, ruggedness, and hostility to most human endeavor. Yet these same characteristics over a long timeframe have led to unparalleled biodiversity and cultural diversity. Mountain communities evolved in semi-isolation, developing and preserving local languages, costumes, customs, and intricately adapted farming and grazing practices. They frequently retained high levels of independence. The independence of mountain communities, however, was bought at a price: hard physical labor for survival, the risk of natural hazards, and periodic forced out-migration as population growth depleted local resources.

A young Lisu woman, a member of a hill tribe living in northern Thailand. Photo by Jack D. Ives.

Many mountain communities became famous as providers of fiercely effective mercenaries for the national armies of lowland powers. For example, the Swiss mountain contingents contributed to many premodern European armies, a surviving remnant being the Vatican's Swiss Guard. More recently, during two world wars and the Falkland Islands campaign, the Gurkhas of Nepal won international fame. They continue to supply contingents to the Indian and British armies.

Prior to the early twentieth century, remoteness, lack of "modern" communication links, and low population densities led to mountain regions being established as buffer zones with only roughly surveyed frontiers between powerful lowland-based empires. Those imperial conflicts and compromises left many present-day states with irrational frontiers, such as those possessed by Afghanistan—a nineteenth-century product of the rivalry between the British Empire and imperial Russia. This has frequently led to major political and military problems and insurgencies for

which the world as a whole is paying a disastrous price today.

As far as the affluent West was concerned, until the last decades of the twentieth century, mountains were virtually the preserve of mountaineers and tourists, especially winter-sport enthusiasts and warmer-season trekkers, and a relatively small number of scientists. The people who lived and made their livelihood in the mountains were largely ignored.

In Europe, as nations industrialized and modernized during the nineteenth century, roads and railways were built, and the first waves of affluent tourists and mountaineers began to penetrate the Alps, bringing with them money. In the twenty-first century we think of Switzerland and Austria as regions of great wealth, but national government policy recognizes that mountain agriculture, essential to the conservation of the beauty that makes the mountains a tourist attraction, depends upon heavy subsidy. In this sense a broad division can be made between the development of mountain regions in the

Climb the mountains and get their good tidings. • **John Muir (1838–1914)**

industrialized countries and those of the developing world—the difference being that industrialized countries have money to help preserve the scenic nature of the mountains whereas developing countries focus on exploitation. A further subdivision must be made between mountain regions of the Old World (Europe) and those of the New World (the North American West, New Zealand, and Australia). In contrast to the European Alps, for example, that have a very long history (pre-Roman) of settlement and environmental adaptation, mountain regions of the New World have experienced colonization and development only very recently (from about the mid-nineteenth century).

Globalization has spread mass tourism from industrial countries into selected areas of the mountain regions of developing countries. Where tourism, especially mountaineering and trekking, has selectively penetrated parts of the developing world's mountain regions, it has brought about significant change. Tourism does bring increased wealth, but very selectively, and most of the commercial profits go back to the industrialized countries as investment profits. The recent, similar "moneyed" approach of nouveau riche Chinese entrepreneurs is having a parallel impact on "within-country" regions, such as northern Yunnan Province in China's scenic southwest

Tourism can and has caused serious disruption to local cultures. (The outstanding example is the Mount Everest region of Nepal, whose inhabitants, the Sherpas, have become relatively affluent.) The 1970s and 1980s recognized the growing need to preserve the Alps and to avert (perceived) imminent environmental catastrophe in the Himalayas. In the Alps, uncontrolled growth of two-season tourism threatened the traditional mountain landscape, although staunch Swiss and Austrian democratic processes have tempered that threat. In the Himalayas massive deforestation was blamed on "ignorant" mountain subsistence farmers; their rapid population growth (Nepal, for instance, at 2.7 percent per year) and their dependency on the forests for construction materials, firewood, and fodder, led to the assumption that the (perceived) impending environmental collapse was due entirely to imprudent indigenous land use on the

mountain slopes. Furthermore, increased numbers of landslides and acceleration of soil erosion, influenced by gravity and torrential monsoon downpours, was widely believed to cause downstream siltation and an increase in severe flooding in Gangetic India (the region formed by alluvial deposits of three great river systems, including the Ganges), and in Bangladesh. Thus the potential for international dispute was added to the threat of environmental disaster. Regardless, prior to 1992 concern remained limited.

Why, as recently as the 1970s or even the 1980s, were mountains not afforded a more prominent place on the world's political agenda, when environmental movements had been in full swing for some time? A partial answer is that mountains had not yet attracted an effective constituency. During the 1972 U.N. Stockholm Conference on the Environment, great strides were made in recognizing the growing gap between the have and have-not regions of the world and by the establishment of ministries of the environment in numerous member countries. Yet mountains did not even merit a footnote. It was not until the 1992 United Nations Conference on Environment and Development (UNCED; the Rio de Janeiro Earth Summit) that a real breakthrough appeared possible with the inclusion of a special chapter for mountains in Agenda for the 21st Century (Agenda 21), the summit's plan for fostering governmental and individual sustainable action. Chapter 13 (which deals with managing fragile ecosystems and sustainable mountain development) of Agenda 21 led ten years later to the U.N. General Assembly's designation of 2002 as the "International Year of Mountains."

Problems Facing the World's Mountains

Undoubtedly, mountains are threatened by general overuse of natural resources—water, forests, grasslands, and minerals—that can lead to soil erosion, water and air pollution, and downstream damage. This is particularly severe on steep slopes (as compared with regions of gentle relief). Indiscriminate road construction on unstable slopes and erection of

A Tibetan lady holds a bunch of radishes (1979). Tibetans who live 4,000 meters above sea level would be classified as mountain folk, yet their local landscapes may be as flat as the North American prairie. Photo by Jack D. Ives.

high dams, usually for the sole benefit of downslope communities, are aggravating factors. Unregulated mass tourism can also lead to environmental degradation, loss of biodiversity, disruption of mountain cultures, and an augmented sense of deprivation as well as actual deprivation on the part of many poor mountain people. These are the topics that hit the news headlines. But they are frequently over-dramatized. Too often the causes, as outlined in the case of the Himalayas, are misunderstood, oversimplified, or even falsified for political advantage. In any case, mountain communities, whether they are in the Alps or in the Himalayas, are in economically marginal positions compared with their lowland counterparts. A large proportion of the world's poverty, especially in Asia and South America, is located in mountain regions. It is difficult to make a precise statement because demographic and related data are usually aggregated by their inclusion into larger political survey units, so that specific information is unobtainable.

The entire complex of mountain problems has been further exacerbated by an apparent unwillingness, until very recently (principally after the terrorist attacks of September 11, 2001), to publicize the single most devastating process that is occurring within mountains: warfare in all its forms. This includes conventional armed conflict, guerrilla insurgencies, drug wars, and terrorism. Moreover, mistreatment of mountain peoples has caused a great increase in the number of internal and international refugees. The U.N. Food and Agriculture Organization (FAO) claimed during the launch of the IYM on 11 December 2001 that of the twenty-seven wars affecting the world at that time, twenty-three were located in mountains regions. This disproportionate burden that the mountains and their people carry signals real disaster—human, economic, environmental, political—on an unprecedented scale.

In terms of overall conflict, mountain peoples are frequently victimized by the central governments. In northern Thailand, western China, and the

Himalayan countries, they are unfairly and wrongly blamed for catastrophic environmental degradation. The real culprits are frequently large commercial interests intent on resource exploitation and central governments seeking access to resources at the expense of the local people who are often marginalized minorities with little political clout. Nevertheless, poverty often leaves the local mountain people with little alternative but to overexploit their own environment. Regulations, such as logging bans, are imposed by the bureaucracies in the lowlands, and they often lead to unsatisfactory solutions that may further exacerbate mountain poverty, thus generating further unrest. This acute dissatisfaction has erupted over the last decade into widespread insurrections in many of the world's mountain regions, from Pakistan, Nepal, and northeast India to Colombia and Bolivia.

Future Directions

The vast extent of the world's mountainous territory, together with its extreme complexity, both in terms of the inherent natural phenomena and the innumerable ways in which human communities have adapted to them, are a challenge indeed to sustainable development. Mountains as a whole are among the least known and least understood areas of the world. The International Year of Mountains has provided an unprecedented opportunity for expanding research and for rapid growth in communication. This has combined with the growing awareness that many of the forecasted negative aspects of global warming will have early major and accelerating impacts in mountain regions. Such concern has resulted in an enormous upsurge in interdisciplinary and international research collaboration, the expected results of which await future application. The first task, however, is to reduce the burden of conflict and, related to this, to facilitate involvement of mountain people in management of their local resources and in development of relations with society at large.

Jack D. IVES
Carleton University

See also Climate Change; Environmental Movements; Erosion

Further Reading

Bowman, W. D., & Seastedt, T. R. (Eds.). (2001). *Structure and function of an Alpine ecosystem.* Oxford & New York: Oxford University Press.

Funnell, D., & Parish, R. (2001). *Mountain environments and communities.* London & New York: Routledge.

Gerrard, A. J. (1990). *Mountain environments.* Cambridge, MA & London: MIT Press.

Hofer, T., & Messerli, B. (2006): *Floods in Bangladesh: History, dynamics and rethinking the role of the Himalaya.* Tokyo: United Nations University Press.

Ives, J. D. (2004). *Himalayan Perceptions: Environmental change and the well-being of mountain peoples.* London & New York: Routledge

Ives, J. D. (2007). *Skaftafell in Iceland: A thousand years of change.* Reykjavik, Iceland: Ormstunga.

Ives, J. D., & Messerli, B. (1989). *The Himalayan dilemma: Reconciling development and conservation.* London and New York: Routledge and United Nations University Press.

Messerli, B., & Ives, J. D. (Eds.). (1997). *Mountains of the world: A global priority.* London and New York: Parthenon.

Zurick, D. & Karan, P. P. (1999). *Himalaya: Life on the edge of the world.* Baltimore: Johns Hopkins University Press.

Natural Gas

Natural gas consists primarily of methane. It is often located alongside other fossil fuels. Cleaner than other fossil fuels, gas is an important source of energy, both as a gas and in a liquified state, used in heating, cooking, and powering automobiles. Before it can be used as a fuel, gas must be processed to make it near pure methane.

Natural gas is a flammable mixture of hydrocarbon gases, formed primarily of methane (CH_4) and produced by the anaerobic decay of organic material over the course of millions of years. The history of natural gas usage goes back in time at least three thousand years, to the ancient civilizations of India, Greece, Persia, and China. But extensive use of natural gas only occurred following the 1960s.

At the beginning of the third millennium, natural gas fulfils a vital role in the global supply of energy. As with other important sources of energy, such as oil, the forces of demand and supply dictate that the location of known natural gas reserves brings with it a certain degree of political and economic power. As of 2009, Russia is the both the world's largest producer of natural gas and home to the world's largest proven natural gas reserves. The Middle East—including Iran, Qatar (home to the world's largest natural gas field), Saudi Arabia, and the United Arab Emirates—is also known to have significant proven reserves of natural gas.

When early civilizations first came across natural gas seeping out from under the earth's surface through fissures in rock and in the form of mysterious flames, they believed it to emanate from supernatural powers. Such experiences with natural gas flames were especially common in ancient India, Greece,

Natural gas spurts from an underground well.
New York Public Library.

and Persia. However, around 600 BCE the Chinese learned to use natural gas flames to boil brine, separating out the salt and providing drinkable water. Indeed, Confucius wrote of wells 100 feet deep along the Tibetan border.

154

In 1785 Britain was the first country to commercialize the use of natural gas, using it to light up houses, streets, and the like. Some four decades later, in 1816, natural gas started to be used for street–lighting in the United States. Natural gas was first discovered in North America as early as 1626, when explorers observed that Native Americans in the area of Lake Erie were igniting gases that seeped out from the earth's surface. The first natural gas well, however, was only dug in the United States in 1821, in Fredonia, New York, by William Hart. On 27 August 1859, Edwin Drake found both natural gas and oil at some sixty-nine feet below earth's surface. Drake's findings marked a new age for natural gas production in North America. Prior to his work, natural gas was primarily produced from coal. In order to commercialize his well's capacity, a pipeline was built from the well to a nearby village, Titusville, Pennsylvania.

Generally speaking, in the nineteenth century it seemed that natural gas was about to gain a vital role in Europe and North America as a lighting fuel for homes and public streets. But its role was limited due to the difficulty in transporting it from the well to its end-users, as the existing pipeline infrastructure was not capable of doing the job. Moreover, with the advent of electric power in the 1880s, natural gas lights were replaced by electric lights.

As natural gas had lost its role as a lighting source, the natural gas industry searched for new uses for its product. In 1885 the inventor Robert Bunsen invented a device that used natural gas for cooking and heating, allowing its flame to be regulated. The Bunsen burner diversified the potential benefits of natural gas and encouraged the global demand for it. However, the difficulty in transporting gas to its potential users continued to restrict its actual usability.

Improvements in pipe-making, metals, and welding technologies during World War II made pipeline construction more economically attractive. Thus, after the war the world began building an extensive network of gas pipelines. Today, this network consists of over 1 million miles in the United States alone (enough to stretch to the moon and back twice). The location and control of these pipelines, particularly across international borders, is a potential source of political and diplomatic tensions; as occasionally experienced between Russia and some of its former satellites, such as Belarus and Ukraine, during the early 2000s. Moreover, the utilization of natural gas was diversified to include water heating, space heating and cooling, and as a fuel for generating electricity. The transportability of natural gas opened the possibility of using it for a variety of home appliances—for oven ranges and clothes dryers, for example.

The oil shortages of the 1970s turned the world's attention toward ways of conserving energy, while a search for cheaper, more available energy sources also began. The rise of environmental awareness in the 1960s and 1970s further impacted the energy industry, encouraging the development of energy generation sources that would be less polluting. As a result of these developments, natural gas became the preferred fuel for energy generation. But while natural gas is cleaner than other fossil fuels, it nevertheless does contribute to carbon emissions, and given that it consists primarily of methane, natural gas is a greenhouse gas.

Continued oil shortages and concerns about environmental quality are expected to further increase the demand for natural gas. Compressed or liquefied natural gas is considered a cleaner and economically competitive alternative to automobile fuels such as petroleum and diesel. As of 2009 there are approximately 10 million natural gas powered vehicles in use around the world, many of them as public transport such as buses. Changes in the generation segment of the power industry, such as turning to fuel cells, which are combustion-free, and the quest for pollution-free power generators capable of being sited at the end-user's place of consumption, also are expected to increase our reliance on natural gas.

Eli GOLDSTEIN
Bar-Ilan University, Israel

See also Energy

Further Reading

Castaneda, C. J., & Smith, C. M. (1996). *Gas pipelines and the emergence of America's regulatory state: A history of Panhandle Eastern Corporation: 1928–1993.* Cambridge, U.K.: Cambridge University Press.

Clark, J. A. (1963). *The chronological history of the petroleum and natural gas industries.* Houston, TX: Clark Books.

Herbert, J. H. (1992). *Clean cheap heat: The development of residential markets for natural gas in the United States.* New York: Praeger.

MacAvoy, P. W. (2000). *The natural gas market: Sixty years of regulation and deregulation.* New Haven, CT: Yale University Press.

Peebles, M. W. H. (1980). *Evolution of the gas industry.* New York: New York University Press.

Nature

All cultures depend on the natural world—plants and animals, the weather, the sun and the sea—for their sustenance. Likewise, each culture has creation stories that classify and provide ethical concepts about its place in the natural world. But not all cultures embody the multitude of universal laws, physical matter, and forms of life on Earth as Western culture does, and attempt to express it all as a single concept called *nature*.

The cultural historian Raymond Williams, in his book *Keywords,* traces the changes in usage of the word *nature* in the English language from the thirteenth to the eighteenth century. He concludes that *nature* "is perhaps the most complex word in the language" (Williams 1976, 184).

Scholars who study the history of concepts of nature often point to Asian cultures such as China and Japan to make the distinction between Eastern and Western concepts of nature. In their essay collection, *Asian Perceptions of Nature*, Ole Bruun and Arne Kalland find that no Asian culture has a single term that encapsulates all of nature. Kalland and S. N. Eisenstadt say that among the Japanese, "reality is structured in shifting contexts and even in discrete ontological [relating to existence] entities, as opposed to the absolutist Western approach" (Bruun and Kalland 1995, 11). Likewise, when a researcher asked villagers in Sri Lanka if they had one word "which means things such as forests, wild animals, trees, birds, grass and flowers," responses varied, including "thick jungle," "sanctuary," and "all sentient beings" (Bruun and Kalland 1995, 153).

The literature on the etymology of the word *nature* is complicated. *A Documentary History of Primitivism*, Arthur O. Lovejoy's study of nature in Greek and Roman history, outlines the birth of the concept. The word *natura* meant "genesis, birth, origin." The Greek poet Homer (c. 700 BCE), in providing a physical description of an herb, also provided its character, its "nature." To the Greek dramatist Aeschylus (524–456 BCE), "nature" referred to visible characteristics that are assumed to be innate. The contrast between reality (nature) and appearance occurred as well. For example, the pre-Socratic philosophers distinguished between the appearance of a couch and the true nature of a couch—the wood from which it is constructed. During this period people also came to think of nature as the entire cosmic system and its laws.

The English writer C. S. Lewis in his *Studies in Words* writes: "A comparatively small number of speculative Greeks invented *Nature*—Nature with a capital." This invention required "taking all things they knew or believed in—gods, men, animals, plants, minerals, what you will—and impounding them under a single name; in fact, of regarding Everything as a thing, turning this amorphous and heterogeneous collection into an object or pseudo-object" (Lewis 1967, 35, 37). Clarence Glacken, in his *Traces on the Rhodian Shore*, reviews the force of the design argument in the history of nature from its emergence as early as the Greek historian Herodotus (484–425 BCE) through the seventeenth century CE. Conceptions of the "purposefulness in the creation—that it was the result of intelligent, planned, and well-thought-out acts of a creator," including a sense of the fitness of nature to human needs, have been important in Western constructions of nature (Glacken 1967, 39).

From its beginning then the word *nature* referred to the whole material world and to intrinsic form and creative forces. One meaning of the word

nature was enfolded within another. During the fourteenth century *nature* as "the essential quality or character *of* something" took on the additional sense of "inherent force." By the seventeenth century *nature* as the material world overlapped with *nature* as intrinsic form and creative forces. Thus, *nature*, which refers to a "multiplicity of things and creatures, may carry an assumption of something common to all of them" (Williams 1976, 185).

People also personify and abstract nature. The ancient Greek philosophers, taking a stance that was common in paganism at the time, believed that the natural world is alive, an all-encompassing animal with both mind and soul, binding animals (including humans) and plants in intellectual, psychic, and physical kinship. Plato (428/7–348/7 BCE) in his *Timaeus* conceived of the soul as female. Lovejoy suggests that the Roman orator Cicero (106–43 BCE) propelled the concept of nature as goddess from the Greeks into the eighteenth century. On the other hand, Carolyn Merchant, in *The Death of Nature*, traces the tradition from the Neoplatonism (Platonism modified in later antiquity to accord with Aristotelian, post-Aristotelian, and Eastern conceptions) of the Roman philosopher Plotinus (204–270 CE) to twelfth-century Christianity, which placed a female nature "as more powerful than humans, but...subordinate to God" (Merchant 1980, 10). Nature personified as female contains a good deal of ambiguity, being seen as chaotic and destructive, as innocent and tainted, and as an expression of the divine order. C. S. Lewis argued that this personification of nature as female has been the most difficult to overcome, but many environmental historians say the seventeenth and eighteenth centuries were the time when nature was most rigidly confined and its long history of vitalism (a doctrine that the functions of an organism are caused by a vital principle distinct from physicochemical forces) reduced.

Modern Times

Carolyn Merchant locates "the death of nature" in the rise of mechanical philosophy. Such thinking is associated with the philosophers Francis Bacon (1561–1626) in England and René Descartes (1597–1650) in France. These men, critical of organic worldviews in which the world is personified as a forceful, living body, viewed nature as passive, inert matter that is acted upon by physical laws that are set in motion by a clockmaker deity. One result of the Scientific Revolution was that female nature was transformed "from an active teacher and parent...[to] a mindless, submissive body." That body was submissive first to God and then through God to humankind (Merchant 1980, 190).

Natural historians, strongly influenced by the explanatory power of mathematics and physics, continued to search for stable order in the rapidly increasing numbers of animals and plants that resulted from the voyages of discovery from the fifteenth to the nineteenth century. The Swedish botanist Carolus Linnaeus (1707–1778) created the first universally accepted system for organizing the members of living nature in an arrangement that apparently revealed God's design. Continuing a Greek tradition, however, Linnaeus viewed change in nature as fundamentally cyclical, always returning to the same starting point.

Mechanical philosophy located nature in mathematically based laws that play out in the physical world, in which the Earth can be understood through "a series of deductions from abstract premises" with little consideration for final causes and less interest in the abundance of life (Glacken 1967, 406). Although Linnaeus participated in the urge to render a nature ordered by abstract laws, he also inspired the rise of natural history by giving naturalists tools to organize their botanical discoveries. The obsession with documenting and organizing the abundance of life derives as well from a group of writers, many of them influenced by Linnaeus, who returned to classical ideas of

Many cultures attempt to control nature through ritual. This drawing shows Tohono O'odham (Papago) in the desert of southern Arizona participating in a rain dance.

organic nature, argued for final causes and design in nature, and sought them in observations of the sensory world. The Englishman John Ray (1627–1705), the leading natural theologian, in his *The Wisdom of God in the Works of Creation* (1691), emphasized the interrelatedness of animals, plants, and habitats as evidence of a wise creator. Naturalists who came later continued to investigate the intricacies of relationships in nature even as they moved away from the argument from design.

One of the most persistent characteristics of nature throughout the sixteenth to eighteenth centuries was the law of subordination. Lovejoy, in his *The Great Chain of Being*, outlines the belief that the deity appointed each species a fixed place in an eternal chain of being from the lowliest maggot through humans to God. The task of natural history was to fit new discoveries into the appropriate link in the chain. The environmental historian Donald Worster, in his *Nature's Economy*, traces the history of nature as both a sacred and an economic system from the Greek word for "house" (*oikos*) through its amplification to refer to household management, the political "oeconomy" of human societies, and nature's economy. Thus, Linnaeus, in his essay, "The Oeconomy of Nature"

(1749), describes nature as the "earth household" in which God is the "Supreme Economist" who rationally ordered the cosmos and "the housekeeper who kept it functioning productively" (Worster 1985, 37).

By the beginning of the nineteenth century two scientists—the English geologist Charles Lyell (1797–1875) and the German geographer Alexander von Humboldt (1769–1859)—began a discovery process that swept away the singular chain and the stable taxonomy (scientific classification) and led to questions about the role of a designing deity. In their footsteps walked the English naturalist Charles Darwin (1809–1882), who discovered a basic key to understanding the history of nature. Benefiting from Lyell's understanding of the age of the Earth's crust and its history of sometimes-violent change and from Humboldt's discoveries of geographical diversity and mutual dependency in plant groupings, Darwin sailed to the New World, arriving in 1835 at the Galapagos Islands, an isolated archipelago off the coast of Ecuador in South America. The creatures that he saw there were very like and yet very different from South American species. His observations led him to develop the theory that isolation, chance migration, and fit with a specific environment lead to the evolution of new species.

The English economist Thomas Malthus's (1766–1834) *An Essay on the Principle of Population* gave Darwin the mechanism for evolution: the elimination of the weak and the survival of the fit. Darwin called this mechanism "natural selection." When he published *On the Origin of Species* in 1859, the objectified view of material life of the mechanical philosophers, as well as the eternally fixed singular chain of being of the natural theologians, was challenged by a world that Darwin called "an entangled bank, clothed with many plants of many kinds, with birds singing on the bushes, with various insects flitting about, and with worms crawling through the damp earth." The result was nature that, although partaking of universal, unchanging physical laws, had a distinctive history: "whilst this planet has gone cycling on according to the fixed law of gravity, from so simple a beginning endless forms most beautiful and most wonderful have been, and are being, evolved" (Darwin 1964, 489–490).

The Age of Ecology

Nature, in gaining history, regained some of the vitality that it had lost under the reign of mechanical philosophy. Darwin took the Linnaean conception of a stable chain of being and put it in motion through competition and co-adaptation. The historian Donald Worster emphasizes the shift during the late nineteenth and early twentieth centuries to an imperfect nature—communities of competing lives that are contingent along axes of space and time. The ecologist Paul Sears situates Darwin's centrality to ecology in his observation that "environment had from the beginning built itself into the very form and organization of all forms of life" (Sears 1950, 56). Scholars generally credit the German zoologist and comparative anatomist Ernst Haeckel (1834–1919) with coining the term *oecologie* (by 1893, *ecology*) in 1866. Worster agrees with Sears that Haeckel grounded the web of life in Darwin's theory that the economy of nature is governed by relationships that derive from the struggle for existence.

The lack of a designer did not imply that no order exists in a nature that is conceived of as ecological. During the early twentieth century botanists and plant geographers in the United States and Europe gradually discovered in plant communities a changeful, active nature. By the 1930s this nature was defined most forcefully in the work of the U.S. botanist Frederic Clements (1874–1945). He argued that nature is dynamic but that change occurs in patterns of "successional development" over time. Innovation through competition is progressive in the sense that a specific habitat "begins with a primitive, inherently unbalanced plant assemblage and ends with a complex formation in relatively permanent equilibrium with the surrounding conditions" (Worster 1985, 210).

Both ecology and the earlier natural history understated the roles of inorganic forces in the creation and maintenance of life. Under the ecosystem concept that was developed by the British botanist Arthur George Tansley (1871–1955) in 1935, mechanical philosophy returned through twentieth-century thermodynamic physics as a powerful approach to constraining nature. Uniting living and nonliving aspects of the world under the processes of energy flow emphasized nature's processes as historical while repudiating the organic community posited in Clements's version of nature. Nature as ecosystem is as linear as nature as climax community, but time moves toward entropy (gradual decline into disorder) rather than toward progress. As Donald Worster describes it, "the ecosystem of the earth, considered from the perspective of energetics, is a way-station on a river of no return. Energy flows through it and disappears eventually into the vast sea of space; there is no way to get back upstream" (Worster 1985, 303). Both Clements and Tansley, however, assume a predictable trajectory in natural history.

Historical nature by the end of the twentieth century had acquired randomness, chaos, and chance. The ecologist Daniel Botkin's *Discordant Harmonies* posits an organic nature, a "living system, global in scale, produced and in some ways controlled by life" (Botkin 1990, 189), which may be modeled through computer programs, uniting Clements and Tansley, but with a critical twist. Nature abstracted is essentially ambiguous, variable, and complex; time is not singular but rather a sheaf whose arcs and marks are defined by probability, "always in flux, changing over many scales of time and space, changing with individual births and deaths, local disruptions

and recoveries, larger scale responses to climate from one glacial age to another" (Botkin 1990, 62). In the twenty-first century nature has a radically contingent history that is particularly troublesome in light of the role of nature in human history.

Nature and Humans

Exploring the other side of the equation—how to place nature in history—requires considering the place of humans in nature. Glacken's *Traces on the Rhodian Shore* covers the preindustrial history of humans and nature. He posits that throughout time the West has regarded the natural world with several questions, all arising from the sense that the Earth is an inherently habitable place for humankind. Is this Earth apparently so fitting an environment for organic life, "a purposely made creation"? What is the influence of the Earth's climates, physical terrain, and continental configuration, that is, the environment in which life is embedded, on the shape of human culture and on individual health and morality? Finally—and coming increasingly into play from the eighteenth century to the present—in what manner have humans through their artifice acted as "geographic agents" changing nature "from its hypothetical pristine condition" (Glacken 1967, vii)?

Much of people's attempt to describe the history of nature has centered on the first issue—on teleological aspects of nature. Although the idea of nature as a product of design arose independently of the concept of environmental influence, each reinforced the other. Organic life (including humans and their cultures) was seen as adapting to "purposefully created harmonious conditions" (Glacken 1967, vii). Human artifice, distinct from "first" nature and exemplifying the human place in the chain of being just below the Creator, constituted a "second" nature cultivating and adding improvements to the design. From the Greeks until the eighteenth century Western conceptions of nature in human history portrayed it as the world out there to which humans adapt—but part of that adaptation is to order nature. Human creations of second nature, through domesticating animals and hunting, through cultivating crops and digging canals, settled

wild lands. However, until the seventeenth and eighteenth centuries such activity assumed an inviolate stability in first nature.

As nature itself began to develop a contingent history during the modern era, humans began to recognize their role as agents of geographic change. Human history—emerging during the Renaissance out of a growing self-consciousness about the power of human control over nature and pushed by the belief that such power distinguishes humans from the rest of nature—became a narrative about harnessing the elements (through arts such as alchemy, which was a medieval chemical science and speculative philosophy aiming to achieve the transmutation of base metals into gold) and transforming the landscape for aesthetic and economic purposes. Just as the Age of Exploration contributed to an emerging sense of nature's history, it also offered comparative evidence of the interactions between human history and natural history. In addition to new animals and plants, the discovery and exploration of the New World offered an aspect of nature seemingly untouched by human artifice. Glacken says that by the eighteenth century the French naturalist George Louis Leclerc, Comte de Buffon (1707–1788), relied on the contrasts between Europe and the Americas to construct his history of the Earth as ultimately "seconded" by the history of human striving. Buffon, who little appreciated the wild, uninhabited places on Earth, saw second nature as both an improvement of first nature and an improvement of human civilization.

Agents of Geographic Change

In the New World the importance of modern humans as agents of geographic change was more obvious. Early commentators such as the Swedish botanist Peter Kalm (1716–1779) noted that settlers were replacing old environments with new and raised questions about their impact on first nature and whether second nature improved the prospects for human habitation. Industrialization in the United States and Britain accelerated the transformations of nature, sharpened the distinctions between city, country, and wild places, and dislocated increasing

The flesh grows weary. And books, I've read them all. / Off, then, to where I glimpse the spray and squall / Strange birds delighting in their unknown skies! • **From "Sea Breeze" by Stéphane Mallarmé (1842–1898), translated by Richard Wilbur (b. 1921)**

populations from labor on the land to labor inside factories.

Romanticism, a transcontinental philosophy that granted privilege to first nature as an organic force in human history, made the most influential critique of people's attempts to second nature. Where Buffon argued that Earth history is improved by the shift from first nature to second nature, the U.S. Romantic transcendentalist and nature writer Henry David Thoreau (1817–1862) countered that Earth has its own history, which humans destroy by seconding nature. For the Romantics people who embedded themselves in first nature—returning at least to the countryside and at best to more untrammeled spaces—countered what the Romantics viewed as the growing dominance of mechanical philosophy and its attendant materialism and repression of the innate spirit in life.

Another key figure in the effort to place nature in history was a contemporary of Thoreau—the U.S. scholar George Perkins Marsh (1801–1882). Environmental historians widely credit Marsh's *Man and Nature: or, Physical Geography as Modified by Human Action* (1864) as the first comprehensive analysis of the harmful effects of human modifications on nature. Marsh compared soil erosion and forest destruction in Vermont with degraded environments in the Mediterranean basin and histories of land and resource use in Europe and Asia and concluded that "man [sic] is everywhere a disturbing agent. Wherever he plants his foot, the harmonies of nature are turned to discord" (Marsh 1965, 36). Marsh urged his contemporaries to be cautious in seconding nature, always to consider what must be learned from the priorities of first nature.

However, Marsh's image of people as disturbers of a pristine nature raises one of the most controversial meanings of nature for contemporary environmental history. Marsh and Thoreau, like many people of the nineteenth and twentieth centuries, make sharp contrasts between a world of nature "out there" and people. The question of people's place in nature has been answered ambiguously for the past two thousand years. One of the dangerous ambiguities about nature is that it may both contain and exclude people. During the nineteenth century critics of industrialism often

argued, as Marsh and Thoreau do, that the artifices of people had shifted from improvement to destruction and were not seconding but rather were disturbing nature's history. People and their artifices then become unnatural, alien to nature. Similarly, during the early twentieth century two key figures in the age of ecology, Clements and Tansley, disagreed on the role of people in nature, with Clements making a sharp distinction between the disturbance brought by the plow and presettlement prairie biota (the flora and fauna of a region) and Tansley arguing that people can make ecologically sound changes by their artifices.

The U.S. environmentalist Aldo Leopold said that the twentieth century would require an ecology-based "land ethic" that "changes the role of *Homo sapiens* from conqueror of the land-community to plain member and citizen of it. It implies respect for his fellow-members, and also respect for the community as such" (Leopold 1949, 204). Marsh, Clements, and Thoreau shared Leopold's view.

This controversy over the role of nature in human history continues into the twenty-first century. Most fundamental is the question of whether one may speak of a nature as existing free from human modification. Raymond Williams says that "we have mixed our labor with the earth, our forces with its forces too deeply to be able to draw back or separate either out" (Williams 1980, 83). Drawing on Williams, the historian William Cronon suggests that the trouble with wilderness is its erasure of the history of human striving from natural history, and the historian Richard White poses nature in contemporary times as an "organic machine"—a symbiotic meld of natural processes and human artifices (White 1995, ix). But for Williams the second nature that people have created is socially repressive, materialist, and polluted— toxic for humans and the rest of the organic world. The historian J. R. McNeill's *Something New under the Sun* reinforces the troubling reciprocity between recent understanding of the history of nature as not only changeful but also unpredictable and the disruptive forces of human history. McNeill says that during the twentieth century people took a planet whose future was uncertain and made change even more volatile, primarily through technological and economic imperatives, thus creating a "total system of global society and environment…more uncertain, more chaotic than ever" (McNeill 2000, 359). Indeed, the most pressing global issue for the twenty-first century is the environmental future.

Vera NORWOOD
University of New Mexico

See also Desertification; Erosion

Further Reading

Botkin, D. (1990). *Discordant harmonies: A new ecology for the twenty-first century.* New York: Oxford University Press.

Bruun, O., & Kalland, A. (Eds.). (1995). *Asian perceptions of nature: A critical approach.* Surrey, U.K.: Curzon Press.

Collingwood, R. G. (1945). *The idea of nature.* London: Oxford University Press.

Cronon, W. (1983). *Changes in the land: Indians, colonists and the ecology of New England.* New York: Hill and Wang.

Cronon, W. (Ed.). (1995). *Uncommon ground: Rethinking the human place in nature.* New York: Norton.

Darwin, C. (1964). *On the origin of species.* Cambridge, MA: Harvard University Press. (Original work published 1859)

Eisenstadt, S. M. (1995). The Japanese attitude to nature: A framework of basic ontological conceptions. In O. Bruun & A. Kalland (Eds.), *Asian perceptions of nature: A critical approach* (pp. 189–214). Surrey, U.K.: Curzon Press.

Evernden, N. (1992). *The social creation of nature.* Baltimore: Johns Hopkins University Press.

Flader, S. (1974). *Thinking like a mountain: Aldo Leopold and the evolution of an ecological attitude toward deer, wolves, and forests.* Madison: University of Wisconsin Press.

Glacken, C. J. (1967). *Traces on the Rhodian shore: Nature and culture in Western thought from ancient times to the end of the eighteenth century.* Berkeley and Los Angeles: University of California Press.

Krech, S. (1999). *The ecological Indian: Myth and history.* New York: Norton.

Leopold, A. (1949). *A Sand County almanac and sketches here and there.* London: Oxford University Press.

Lewis, C. S. (1967). *Studies in words.* Cambridge, U.K.: Cambridge University Press.

Lovejoy, A. O. (1936). *The great chain of being: A study of the history of an idea.* Cambridge, MA: Harvard University Press.

Lovejoy, A. O., Chinard, G., Boas, G., & Crane, R. S. (1935). *A documentary history of primitivism and related ideas.* Baltimore: Johns Hopkins University Press.

Malthus, T. (1890). *An essay on the principle of population.* London: Ward. (Original work published 1798)

Marsh, G. P. (1965). *Man and nature.* Cambridge, MA: Harvard University Press. (Original work published 1864)

McNeill, J. R. (2000). *Something new under the sun: An environmental history of the twentieth century world.* New York: Norton.

Merchant, C. (1980). *The death of nature: Women, ecology and the Scientific Revolution.* San Francisco: Harper & Row.

Merchant, C. (1989). *Ecological revolutions: Nature, gender, and science in New England.* San Francisco: Harper & Row.

Plato. (1952). *Timaeus, Critias, Cleitophon, Menexenus: Epistles.* Cambridge, MA: Harvard University Press.

Ray, J. (1759). *The wisdom of God manifested in the works of creation.* London: John Rivington, John Ward, Joseph Richardson. (Original work published 1691)

Sandell, K. (1995). Nature as the virgin forest: Farmers' perspectives on nature and sustainability in low-resource agriculture in the dry zone of Sri Lanka. In O. Bruun & A. Kalland (Eds.), *Asian perceptions of nature: A critical approach* (pp. 148–173). Surrey, U.K.: Curzon Press.

Sears, P. (1950). *Charles Darwin: The naturalist as a cultural force.* New York: Scribner's.

Soule, M., & Lease, G. (Eds.). (1995). *Reinventing nature? Responses to post-modern deconstruction.* Washington, DC: Island Press.

Thoreau, H. D. (1906). *The writings of Henry David Thoreau: Journal VIII.* Boston: Houghton Mifflin.

White, R. (1995). *The organic machine: The remaking of the Columbia River.* New York: Hill and Wang.

Williams, R. (1976). *Keywords: A vocabulary of culture and society.* London: Fontana/Croom Helm.

Williams, R. (1980). *Problems in materialism and culture.* London: Verso.

Worster, D. (1985). *Nature's economy: A history of ecological ideas.* Cambridge, U.K.: Cambridge University Press.

Worster, D. (1993). *The wealth of nature: Environmental history and the ecological imagination.* London: Oxford University Press.

Oceans and Seas

Oceans and seas comprise 98 percent of the biosphere and cover about 70 percent of the Earth's surface. Water is circulated between the oceans and seas, the atmosphere, and the land by evaporation and precipitation, thus transporting chemicals and heat, determining the Earth's climate, and fertilizing and eroding the land. Humans depend on ocean resources, harvesting marine life, for instance, and drilling the ocean beds for oil.

The oceans of the Earth consist of four confluent (flowing together) bodies of saltwater that are contained in enormous basins on the Earth's surface. Seas are lesser bodies of saltwater. Oceans and seas cover 361 million square kilometers (70.8 percent of the Earth's surface) and 98 percent of the volume of the biosphere (the part of the world in which life can exist). Saltwater comprises about 97.2 percent of the water on the planet, the remainder being freshwater. By evaporation and precipitation water is circulated between the oceans and seas, the atmosphere, and the land. The hydrological cycle (the sequence of conditions through which water passes from vapor in the atmosphere through precipitation upon land or water surfaces and ultimately back into the atmosphere as a result of evaporation and transpiration) transports and stores chemicals and heat, determines the Earth's climate, and fertilizes and erodes the land. The average salinity of the oceans and seas is 3.5 percent, deviations being determined by evaporation and inflow of freshwater. Ocean surface temperatures around the equator may be 30°C or more, decreasing toward the poles, where seawater freezes at –2°C. Below-surface temperature is fairly constant, decreasing to around 0°C in the deep ocean.

The largest ocean is the Pacific, which has a surface area of 166 million square kilometers, almost the size of the three other oceans together: the Atlantic (84 million square kilometers), the Indian (73 million square kilometers), and the Arctic (12 million square kilometers). The Antarctic, or Southern, Ocean is sometimes counted as the fifth ocean, consisting of the waters of the southern parts of the Pacific, Indian, and Atlantic. Sections of the oceans may be described as enclosed and marginal seas. Enclosed seas—such as the Mediterranean Sea, Hudson Bay, the White Sea, the Baltic, the Red Sea, and the Mexican Gulf—cut into continental landmasses. Marginal seas—such as the Caribbean and Bering Seas, the Sea of Okhotsk, the East China Sea, the Sea of Japan, and the North Sea—are separated from the oceans by archipelagos.

The depth of the oceans increases to about 200 meters on the continental shelves, increasing further to 3,000–4,000 meters on the ocean basin floor and to 6,000–11,000 meters in the deepest areas. The ocean bed is covered by sediments of dead marine organisms, eroded soil from the continents, and red clay.

The waters of the oceans are circulated by changing winds, air pressures, and tides. The gulf current brings warm water to the North Atlantic and thus makes it possible to sustain human life at more northerly degrees in Europe than anywhere else on the globe. The upwelling areas on the margins of the Pacific and Atlantic oceans off the coasts of Chile and Peru, California, and Namibia in Africa bring cold, nutrient-rich waters to the surface of the sea, and the combination of sunlight and nutrient richness makes the relatively narrow continental shelves rich in marine life. But El Niño (an irregularly occurring flow of unusually warm surface water along the western coast of South America) may reverse ocean currents in the Pacific and cause abnormal climate effects both on land and sea.

Life began in the oceans, but science has incomplete knowledge of marine life-forms. About fifteen thousand species of marine fish are known, but it is estimated that five thousand species remain to be identified. The estimate of 200,000 ocean floor species of the North Atlantic alone may be low by a factor of three or four. Whereas the open oceans are blue deserts due to the lack of nutrients, the continental shelves are home to abundant marine life, and tropical coral reefs are habitats of large biodiversity (biological diversity as indicated by numbers of species of animals and plants).

Marine Resources

Humans utilize the oceans for transportation and trade, benefit from harvesting marine life, and drill the ocean bottoms for oil, thus creating the potential for exploitation and pollution.

Oceanic transportation is the cheapest and most important way to move goods between the continents, but it imposes severe environmental stress on marine habitats and biodiversity. Prior to the fifteenth century the oceans presented a formidable obstacle to contact between continents. Foraging (Paleolithic) era (2 million–10,000 BCE) migrants did spread from Africa and Eurasia to Australia and the Americas by crossing the straits of Torres and Bering; the Polynesian migrations into the Pacific islands around 2000 BCE and the Viking migration across the North Atlantic also testify to early maritime skills. However, the first contact between a major civilization and another continent was aborted in 1435 when the Chinese emperor decided to discontinue the explorations of the Chinese fleet to Africa across the Indian Ocean. The subsequent voyages of Columbus across the Atlantic from Spain to the Caribbean Sea, however, opened the way

for a sustained exchange—causing great environmental impact—with the New World. With the development of the three-masted sailing vessel and nautical instruments, global seafaring allowed an exchange of terrestrial plants and animals that had substantial consequences for the recipient countries. Marine habitat changes followed as ports and bunker areas for loading coal were extended along shorelines and estuaries and as mud-dredgers changed tidal currents and coastal erosion. In the twentieth century tanker ships impacted marine ecosystems substantially when they discharged ballast water transported over thousands of kilometers. Ballast water is one of the most serious threats to marine biodiversity and has caused irreparable changes to ecosystems. Introduced species, which have no natural enemies in new environments, can multiply and eradicate original life-forms.

Humans have harvested inshore marine environments since earliest historical times. Whales, seals, fish, crustaceans, and algae have been fished for human consumption, and seaweeds, salt, sponges, corals, and pearls have been brought to consumers for diverse uses. Today important medicines, from anticoagulants to muscle relaxants, are derived from marine snails.

Beginning in the sixteenth century, thanks to the shipping revolution, whaling and fishing operations were taken to distant islands and continents. As marine life in these distant waters was depleted, the operations became oceanic, first in the Northern Hemisphere and later in the Southern Hemisphere. These operations extinguished some life-forms, such as the Stellar's sea cow in the Bering Sea, the gray whale in the European and later the American Atlantic, and the Caribbean monk seal. The early human impacts on pristine ecosystems are believed to have been important not only to a few signal species but also to the whole ecosystem, which may have experienced regime shifts when top predators that controlled ecosystem dynamics were fished out. Today most of the commercially important fish species are exploited to the full or beyond sustainable levels. Because of such heavy fishing pressure, many of the most valuable fish stocks of the world are in decline,

A biologist from the Florida Keys National Marine Sanctuary photographs the damage done to a coral reef from a boat grounded on the reef. National Oceanic and Atmospheric Administration.

and some have become locally extinct. The most dramatic case is the Newfoundland cod fishery, which collapsed in 1991, causing not only enormous and possibly irreparable harm to the ecosystem but also the disappearance of the very means of existence for many people in Atlantic Canada.

Commercial exploitation of minerals in the ocean bed is only beginning and is expected to increase dramatically in the twenty-first century. The ocean bed contains energy in the form of oil and natural gas, and minerals such as sodium chloride (salt), manganese, titanium, phosphate, and gold are found in the oceans. People also have begun to utilize tidal power from the oceans. The development of industrialized societies has increased the discharge of sewage and other waste into the oceans and also has created the phenomenon of oil spills.

About two-thirds of the world's population live within 60 kilometers of a coast, and almost one-half of the world's cities with more than 1 million people are located near estuaries. This settlement pattern is a result of people choosing the oceans instead of agriculture as a source of food and employment; the oceans also have provided access to communication, transportation, and trade. However, people have had a prejudice against coastal settlement in some historical periods. The most marked instance of this prejudice occurred in many Neolithic (8000–5500 BCE) cultures with the introduction of agriculture, which increased the incentive to settle virgin inland territories. The nineteenth-century frontier movement of North America was also decidedly terrestrial, although migrants had to cross the Atlantic to pursue opportunities. In contrast, other colonizing experiences, such as the ancient Phoenician and Greek city-states, were decidedly maritime.

The French historian Fernand Braudel (1949) was the first to attempt a history of an enclosed sea—in this case, the Mediterranean—as a natural environment and a highroad for communication and cultural exchange. He argued that the common environmental conditions prevailing on the coasts of the Mediterranean provided the basis for a common culture. He showed how life in the mountains, plains, and coastal lowlands related with the sea across European and Arabic civilizations, and he stressed that the seaways were a key to the growth of the European economy. Braudel perceived of Europe as three regions: the Mediterranean, the Continent, and the Second Mediterranean of Europe; that is, the North Sea and the Baltic, or collectively the Northern Seas. Many other historians have since recognized that if the Mediterranean shores had a common culture, the same would hold true for other seas, with differences due to natural circumstances (such as enclosed or marginal character of the sea and accessibility of its shores) and historical experiences. The problem with the arguments of such historians is that they tend to list those aspects that the shores of a sea have in common but do not compare contacts inside and outside of the regional system.

It isn't the oceans which cut us off from the world—it's the American
way of looking at things. • **Henry Miller (1891–1980)**

Other approaches to the question of the role of oceans in human history have stressed the problems of overcoming distance. This is the dominant theme, of course, in the study of the Age of Exploration (c. 1491–1750), but it also resonates in the study of the more recent history of U.S. and European relations and most forcefully in the study of the history of Australia, which until the age of global airlines lived under the "tyranny of distance"—the fact that any visit abroad required weeks if not months of sea travel.

In the age before modern transport systems, sea transport was generally cheaper than land transport but not faster. Ship movements had many natural and unpredictable constraints. Delays of weeks occurred frequently because of unfavorable winds, and although some skippers would travel day and night because of a good knowledge of local waters, most dared sail only in daytime. Calculations of actual distances traveled by ships indicate that in spite of good winds sometimes bringing a ship's speed to 10 knots per hour (18 kilometers per hour), the distance covered during full trips, including the time spent waiting at anchor, seldom averaged more than 1 or 2 nautical miles (1.85–3.7 kilometers) per hour spent at sea. The distance covered per day thus works out to 45–90 kilometers. This calculation corresponds with actual travel distances on land. Whereas one cartload normally contained only twelve to eighteen barrels of grain or fish, even a small shipload might contain many times more. A typical ship of two hundred tonnes required a maximum crew of only ten men. The person-to-ton ratio would thus be 1:10 for the ship as against 1:1 for the cart, whereas distance traveled per day would be the same. Thus coastal urban markets received supplies by sea at a rate competitive with supplies from inland. A recent study of medieval England showed a ratio 1:4:8 for transport costs by sea, river, and road. Because the efficiency of land transport did not develop to the same pace as productivity increased in other trades such as agriculture, land transport costs grew relative to other costs until the eighteenth century.

The sea did not necessarily facilitate cultural impulses, such as aesthetic, dietary, or religious preferences, in the same way. The transportation of information and cultural impulses was not related to bulk freight rates but rather relied as much on individual travel patterns, most often by foot or horseback. Although enclosed and marginal seas may often have contained a well-developed trade and transport infrastructure, cultural relations do not necessarily mirror this and indeed may show quite different patterns of communication. Nevertheless, during the age of sail, roughly from 1500 to 1850, maritime regions played a decisive role in many parts of the world. Coastal stretches of enclosed or marginal seas had an unusual concentration of maritime capital and labor that made possible the development of a distinctively maritime culture. This concentration was often based on the availability of timber for shipbuilding, although lack of forests did not preclude some regions rising to maritime preeminence.

The industrial transport revolution of the nineteenth century greatly enhanced long-distance and even global travel, but it lessened the importance of regional transport economics. Improved roads, railways, and steam shipping created a world market for many more goods than before, and regional markets gave way to the global market. Most small maritime communities were not able to raise the capital needed to participate in the global transport market, and as a result the coastal landscape changed from a string of human settlements to a few port towns with a concentration of maritime capital. In the industrial age, therefore, the age of regional seascapes came to an end.

Port towns are the nodes of the maritime transport system. The first port towns were well developed in the Mediterranean three thousand years ago. A port town may have its own home fleet, the crucial characteristic being that the town is a hub of inland and seaborne trade. Port towns tend therefore to utilize natural assets such as ease of multimodal transportation (land, river, and sea transport), access to a productive hinterland and a market, and strategic advantages such as control of waterways. Port towns provide access to the economic arteries of a country

Sea levels have been rising since 1900 with the rate of change accelerating in the last half century. Researchers from NOAA's National Geodetic Survey conduct a shoreline survey. National Oceanic and Atmospheric Administration.

and therefore have historically been keenly regulated both for fiscal and military purposes. Occasionally they have gained full or partial sovereignty, as did the Italian city-states and the towns of the Hanseatic League, or have dominated a territorial state, such as the Netherlands in the sixteenth to eighteenth centuries, but most often they have been controlled by larger territorial powers. With the increased demands of shipping in the nineteenth century came the need for a larger workforce, and port towns became densely populated with laborers. The towns themselves sprawled along wharves and quays to become unwieldy entities, congested and heavily polluted. As a result of the spread of coal-fired steamer traffic in the second half of the nineteenth century, however, adhering to strict time schedules became possible and of utmost importance. Thus new infrastructures of bunker ports and dedicated quays sprang up along the coasts to facilitate the steamers. Wind-powered ships continued to defeat the steam ships as long as a line of bunker ports did not dot the margins of the seas, but eventually the steam ships took possession of more and more sea routes so that by the early twentieth century the slow windjammers to Australia were the last to give in.

By that time diesel engines were being introduced, and by the 1950s coal was all but given up. At that point, passenger ships lost their edge in the oceanic transportation of people to the airlines, but a new era for the shipping of goods more than compensated for the loss to ship owners. In the first half of the twentieth century ships were designed to provide optimum cargo facilities and quicker turn-around times in ports. The Argentine meat industry and the Canary Island banana trade demanded refrigerated ships, and the oil industry gave rise to tanker ships. By the 1960s a design revolution took place, introducing the all-purpose shipping container, a metal box that could be refrigerated or otherwise modified and that conformed to standard measures and therefore allowed for convenient storage on board. The container ship became the vehicle for the globalization of trade, which severed the links between origin of resource, modification and packaging, and consumption.

To achieve optimum handling the once-prolific system of ocean ports has been minimized to a system of a few world ports that are the nodes of a few big container lines. Servicing the system are a number of feeder lines from lesser ports and a prolific number of trucking services that ensure that the individual container is brought to its final destination.

The environmental impact of the globalized container system is enormous. Although the system undoubtedly brings rationalization of the economic system, it is dependent on the availability of abundant and cheap energy, which will marginalize, for example, the costs of moving east Asian tiger prawns to Morocco to be peeled by cheap labor before they are moved to Germany to be packaged before they are eventually consumed in, for example, a restaurant in Paris.

Sea Law and Sea Powers

The oceans and seas have long been governed by law. Hugo Grotius, a Dutch lawyer, historian, and theologian laid down the first principles for an international law of the seas his 1609 treatise *Mare Liberum* (The Free Sea). He observed that the sea is an inexhaustible, common property and that all should have open access to it. These principles were adhered to in theory by all major European naval states and eventually were introduced as the guiding principles for access to all oceans and seas. Most states claimed dominion over territorial or coastal waters, but commercial ships were allowed free passage. The most important exception to this principle was the Danish Sound, providing access between the North Sea and the Baltic. The Danish government in 1857 lifted its toll on the sound and the right of inspection only after international treaty and compensation. The shooting range of a cannon originally defined the width of territorial waters, but during the nineteenth century a 3-nautical-mile (5.5 kilometers) limit was increasingly accepted and laid down in international treaties. After World War II, U.S. President Harry Truman claimed wider rights to economic interests on the North American continental shelf against Japan, and Chile and Peru claimed a 200-nautical-mile (370 kilometers) exclusive fishing zone off the coasts against U.S. tuna fishers. Iceland followed soon after with claims to exclude British fishers from Icelandic waters. Oil and fisheries were the main economic motives for these claims. In 1958 the United Nations called the first International Conference on the Law of the Sea to establish a new consensus on sea law. The conference extended territorial limits to 12 nautical miles (22 kilometers) but failed to settle the issue. A second conference in 1960 made little progress. During the 1960s and 1970s positions changed dramatically. It became much more evident that the supplies of fish stocks were limited and that depletion was becoming more prevalent. Attempts to manage resources through international bodies were proving to be largely ineffective. Many coastal states, both developed and developing, felt increasingly threatened by the large fleets of distant-water states off their coasts. Simultaneously, the issue of control over the mineral resources in the deep ocean beds raised the demands of developing states for a more equitable distribution of ocean wealth. The third international conference, which lasted from 1974 to 1982, resulted in a convention that is internationally recognized. The main innovation was the declaration of the right of coastal states to a 200-nautical mile "extended economic zone" (EEZ), which may be claimed by a coastal state for all mineral and living resources. The convention was signed by 157 states, while the United States, United Kingdom, and Germany took exception to the stipulations on seabed mineral resources. The EEZs represent the largest redistribution of territorial jurisdiction sine nineteenth century colonialism.

The choice of 200 nautical miles as a limit for jurisdiction has no relevance to ecosystems or indeed to the distribution of mineral wealth but is simply a result of international negotiations. Whatever the imperfections of the convention, it has, however, provided coastal states with the authority to manage the resources within their zone. The short history of EEZs shows that they may be implemented to promote conservation interests in addition to the national economic interests for which they were designed.

Management and Protection

Whereas the law of the sea provides only a broad framework for international regulation of matters relating to oceans and seas, nation-states have developed intricate policies and institutions that impact the oceans. Two policies for the marine environment have been developed in recent years: integrated coastal zone management (ICZM) and marine protected areas (MPA). The specific policies that deal with issues such as watersheds and coastal development to seabed utilization by their very nature fail to take issue with the complete set of challenges that confronts people when they seek to manage, preserve, and develop the marine environment. This is the justification for the development of integrated coastal zone management. ICZM has developed as a cross-cutting policy for coastal and inshore management concerns since the 1980s, but it is implemented only to a limited degree in most countries. Marine protected areas have been designated throughout the world as areas where human access is restricted in order to conserve marine habitats. Coral reefs, fragile spawning areas, and hot spots of marine biodiversity have often been selected, but by 2000 only about 1 percent of the oceans were protected even by limited restrictions. The oceans and seas are still subject to open access and unrestricted human practices in most regions of the world, and the underwater world remains the last frontier, still to a large degree unexplored by humans.

Poul HOLM
Trinity College Dublin

See also Climate Change; Natural Gas; Oil Spills

Further Reading

Anand, R. P. (1982). *Origin and development of the law of the sea: History of international law revisited.* The Hague, The Netherlands: Nijhoff.

Borgese, E. M. (1998). *The oceanic circle: Governing the seas as a global resource.* New York: United Nations Publications.

Braudel, F. (1996). *The Mediterranean and the Mediterranean world in the age of Philip II.* Berkeley and Los Angeles: University of California Press.

Carlton, J. T., Geller, J.B., Reaka-Kudla, M.L., & Norse, E. (1999). Historical extinctions in the sea. *Annual Review of Ecology and Systematics, 30,* 515–538.

Chaudhuri, K. N. (1985). *Trade and civilisation in the Indian Ocean: An economic history from the rise of Islam to 1750.* Cambridge, U.K.: Cambridge University Press.

Chaudhuri, K. N. (1990). *Asia before Europe: Economy and civilisation of the Indian Ocean from the rise of Islam to 1750.* Cambridge, U.K.: Cambridge University Press.

Cicin-Sain, B., & Knecht, R. (1998). *Integrated coastal and ocean management: Concepts and practices.* Washington, DC: Island Press.

Day, T. (1999). *Oceans.* Chicago: Fitzroy Dearborn Publishers.

Garrison, T. (1995). *Oceanography: An invitation to marine science* (2nd ed.). Belmont, CA: Wadsworth Publishing.

Horden, P., & Purcell, N. (2000). *The corrupting sea: A study of Mediterranean history.* Oxford, U.K.: Oxford University Press.

Houde, E., & Brink, K. H. (2001). *Marine protected areas: Tools for sustaining ocean ecosystems.* Washington, DC: National Academy Press.

Masschaele, J. (1993). Transport costs in medieval England. *Economic History Review, 46,* 266–279.

McPherson, K. (1993). *The Indian Ocean: A history of people and the sea.* Mumbai (Bombay), India: Oxford University Press.

Mills, E. L. (1989). *Biological oceanography: An early history, 1870–1960.* Ithaca, NY: Cornell University Press.

Reid, A. (1993). *Southeast Asia in the age of commerce, 1450–1680.* New Haven, CT: Yale University Press.

Roding, J., & van Voss, L. H. (Eds.). (1996). *The North Sea and culture (1550–1800).* Hilversum, The Netherlands: Verloren Press.

Thorne-Miller, B., & Earle, S. A. (1998). *The living ocean: Understanding and protecting marine biodiversity* (2nd ed.). Washington, DC: Island Press.

Oil Spills

Oil in myriad forms has been used for hundreds of purposes for at least six thousand years. Oil spills occur naturally and as a result of oil exploration, transportation, and processing. Several disasters have led to more stringent environmental standards, such as double-hulled ships. The drilling-platform explosion and subsequent oil leak in the Gulf of Mexico in April 2010 has brought renewed global attention to the dangers of oil spills.

Oil is a main source of energy. Because it is unevenly distributed in the world, it must be transported on the seas and in pipelines to distant lands. Although the major oil transport and transfer activities occur on the seas, ports, and rivers, they are not limited to these areas. Accidental spills can occur wherever oil is drilled, stored, handled, refined, transported, and transferred. These spills can be either massive and catastrophic or chronic. Few other environmental problems are as common or ubiquitous or have the potential for immediate environmental damage and long-range effects. Recent or dramatic oil spills include those involving the ships *Amoco Cadiz*, *Exxon Valdez*, and *Sea Empress*, and the massive intentional oil spills during the Gulf War. As this encyclopedia goes to press, an oil spill resulting from the explosion of the British Petroleum drilling platform *Deepwater Horizon* is still flowing into the Gulf of Mexico from 64 kilometers (40 miles) off the coast of Louisiana; it is considered to be the worst environmental disaster in U.S. history.

Crude petroleum or oil is a liquid or semiliquid mixture of hydrocarbon compounds that contains sulfur, oxygen, nitrogen, other elements, and metals.

The hydrocarbons are the decayed remains of small marine animals and plants that flourished in the shallow inland seas that once covered large areas of the continents. Over hundreds of thousands of years, the dead remains of these tiny organisms drifted to the sea bottom. Covered by mud, this organic matter changed into the complicated hydrocarbons we call petroleum. For the past 600 million years, incompletely decayed plant and animal remains were buried under thick layers of rock, often accumulating one layer at a time. Because petroleum, natural gas, and coal formed from organisms that lived millions of years ago, they are called fossil fuels.

Since the Paleozoic era (from 570 to 245 million years ago), this organic matter has been slowly moving to more porous and permeable rocks, such as sandstone and siltstones, where it was trapped. The oil accumulates because of the presence of impermeable rock lying over these reservoirs. Some oil fields extend laterally in the rock over several kilometers and may be several hundred meters deep. Some oil enters the oceans through natural seeps, and these natural oil spills can have massive effects on the organisms living nearby.

Some of the hydrocarbon products of petroleum include dissolved natural gas, gasoline, benzene, naphtha, kerosene, diesel fuel and light heating oils, heavy heating oils, and tars of various weights. Petroleum yields these products through elaborate refining processes. They are then further refined and combined into other products such as solvents, paints, asphalt, plastics, synthetic rubber, fibers, soaps and cleansing agents, waxes and jellies, medicines, explosives, and fertilizers. Oil spills can occur during the refining process or during transport.

Sir Lawrence Alma-Tadema, *The Finding of Moses* (1904). Oil on canvas. Nile River boats were caulked with asphalt, and when the infant Moses was set adrift he was cradled in a raft of bulrushes "daubed with pitch." Despite the fanciful depiction, Alma-Tadema's painting was renowned for archeologically precise details.

History of Small Oil Spills

For over six thousand years people have used asphalt, pitch (bitumen), and liquid oil in numerous and ingenious ways. People living in river valleys of ancient Mesopotamia used local asphalt from hand-dug pits as building cement and caulking for boats. The legend of the flood described in the Book of Genesis records that the ark was well caulked. Nile River boats were caulked with asphalt, and the infant Moses was cradled in a raft of bulrushes "daubed with pitch" when he was set adrift. The Elamites, Chaldeans, Akkadians, and Sumerians mined shallow deposits of oil-derived pitch or asphalt to export to Egypt to preserve the mummies of great kings and queens and to make mosaics to adorn their coffins. (Ancient Egyptians used liquid oil as a purgative and wound dressing, since it aided the healing process and kept wounds clean.) Archeological remains in Khuzestan, Iran, show that asphalt was commonly used for

bonding and jewel setting during the Sumerian epoch (4000 BCE). Asphalt served as cement in the Tower of Babel and in the walls and columns of early Babylonian temples. As early as 600 BCE the Babylonians set clay cones and tiny semiprecious stones in bitumen to form elaborate mosaics.

Soon fossil fuels were recognized for their light-giving properties: according to the Greek biographer Plutarch, in about 331 BCE Alexander the Great was impressed by the sight of a continuous flame issuing from the Earth in Kirkuk, Iraq, probably a natural gas seep set ablaze. The Romans used oil lamps in the first century BCE. The Chinese first used oil as a fuel around 200 CE, employing pulleys and hand labor to suction the oil from the ground through pipes. Oil spills resulting from these uses were small and limited in scope.

Oil was quickly adopted for military purposes, especially naval skirmishes, which resulted in larger spills. Oil-filled trenches were set aflame to defend cities in ancient times. The Persians developed the first distilling processes to obtain flammable products for use in battle, catapulting arrows wrapped in oil-soaked cloths toward their Greek enemies during the siege of Athens in 480 BCE. At close range, what eventually became known as Greek fire was propelled through tubes onto Persian ships attacking Constantinople in 673 CE, resulting in the Greek's near destruction of the fleet. The Byzantines used liquid fire against the Muslims in the seventh and eighth centuries; thrown onto enemy ships from pots or tubes, liquid fire (probably some combination of oil, naptha, and chemical substances such as sulfur and quicklime), caused extensive damage and terror. (The exact "recipe" remains unknown, but historians believe it was passed down from emperor to emperor.) The Saracens used Greek fire against St. Louis at the crusades, and the Knights of St. John used it against the invading Turks at Malta. The Mongols also burned petroleum products in their siege of Central Asia. Bukhara in western Asia fell in 1220 because Chinggis (Genghis) Khan threw pots full of naphtha and fire at the gates of the castle, and it burst into flame. People were forced to flee the city or else die.

During the Renaissance, the transport of oil developed, leading to more significant oil spills in the wake of trade. In 1726 Peter the Great of Russia issued ordinances regulating the transport of

This sculpted goat, excavated from the royal cemetery in the Sumerian city of Ur, is made from gold, silver, lapis lazuli, copper, shell, red limestone, and bitumen (pitch). Ancient civilizations also used pitch and asphalt as mosaic "cement." The University Museum, Philadelphia, Pennsylvania.

oil from Baku on the Caspian Sea, by boat, up the Volga River. Oil became a valued commodity to barter, trade, or steal. In the New World, the natives of Venezuela caulked boats and hand-woven baskets with asphalt, and liquid oil was used for medicine and lighting. Native North Americans used oil in magic, medicines, and paints. The first barrel of Venezuelan oil was exported to Spain in 1539 to alleviate the gout of Emperor Charles V.

The modern era of oil transportation began in 1820 when a small-bore lead pipe was used to transport natural gas from a seep near Fredonia, New York, to nearby consumers, including the local hotel. From this time on, the possibility of oil spills due directly to transport and transfer increased with the decades.

The Modern Oil Spill Era

The majority of known oil reserves are in the Middle East, followed by North America. The Organization of Petroleum Exporting Countries (OPEC) has the greatest reserves, with Saudi Arabia leading the member nations. The global distribution of oil deposits influences production and transport patterns and thereby determines the potential distribution of oil spills. World oil production rose from 450 million metric tons in 1950 to 2.7 billion metric tons by 1996 and continues to rise slowly. Oil spills rise along with production.

The primary method of transportation of oil is by oil tanker, and traditional shipping lanes have developed between the oil-producing countries and the oil-importing countries. At present, major oil routes go from the Middle East to Japan, Europe, and the United

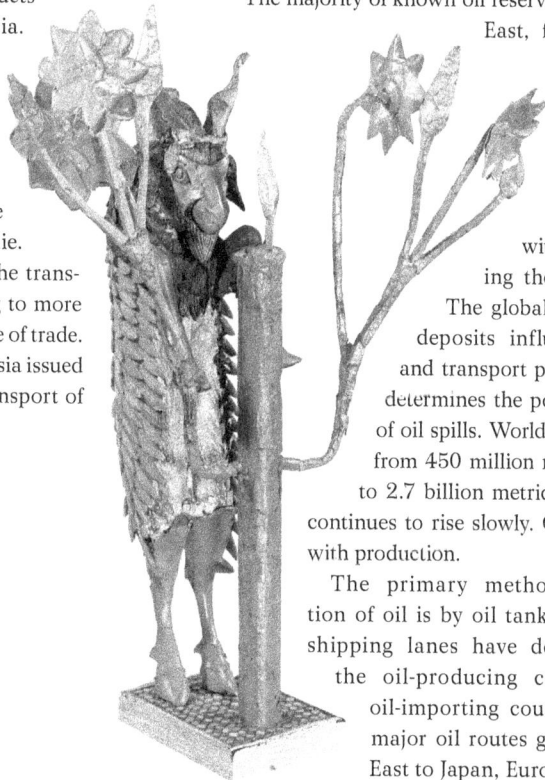

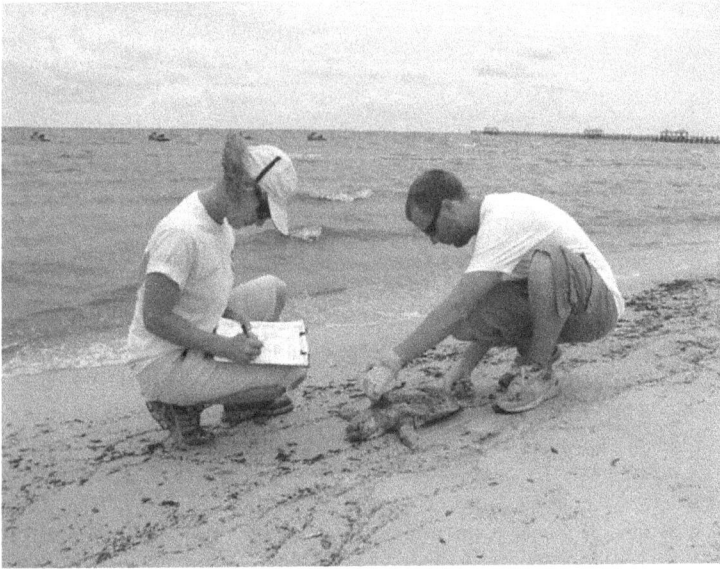

Scientists measure a dead Kemp's ridley sea turtle on the Gulf Coast of Mississippi. This endangered species is especially at risk in an oil spill because it feeds indiscriminately and has no behavioral mechanism for avoiding oiled waters. National Oceanic and Atmospheric Administration.

States. Oil is also transported through pipes over vast distances to refineries. Oil spills occur mainly along these oceanic and land routes and along the shores where oil transfers take place. Small spills occur during the transfer of oil from tanker to tanker, from tanker to refinery, from damaged, underground pipes, and around oil refineries and storage facilities. About 7.56 billion liters of oil enter the oceans from spills and other accidents each year.

Large spills usually occur during tanker accidents. With the increase in the size of oil tankers, the potential for accidents has increased. The tankers of the 1880s had a capacity of 3,000 metric tons, compared to 16,500 in 1945, 115,000 in 1962, and 517,000 in 1977. In the modern era of tankers, considered to be post-1989 and the *Exxon Valdez* disaster, tankers are commonly classified by size and the sea lanes they travel: Panamax and Suezmax tankers, for instance, are the largest crude carriers that will "fit" through the Panama and Suez canals, respectively. Recent requirements and conventions, such as the International Maritime Organization's International Convention for the Prevention of Pollution from Ships, dictate that only double-hulled ships can ply international waters; this should decrease the number of tanker spills in the future, although not all regulations and conventions are legally binding. Oil spill–susceptible single-hulled

ships are due to be taken out of service worldwide by 2010, although it remains to be seen whether this will happen or not.

Although the large oil spills receive media attention, only about 4 percent of oil entering the oceans comes from tanker accidents. Another 25 percent enters from tanker operations, 14 percent from other transport accidents, and 34 percent from rivers and estuaries. About 11 percent of the oil entering the oceans comes from natural seeps.

Major Spills

Since 1978 there has been a steady increase in the number of small spills, whereas the number of large spills has remained relatively constant. One to three spills of over 38 million liters happen each year. One or two catastrophic accidents in any given year can substantially increase the amount of oil spilled onto the land and into the oceans. The small spills of less than 378,000 liters apiece add up to about 38 million liters a year worldwide. Even without major disasters, large quantities of oil spill into marine and inland habitats.

The largest spill on record dumped 907 million liters into the Persian Gulf in 1991 as Iraqi forces sabotaged hundreds of wells, oil terminals, and tankers when they withdrew from their position in Kuwait during the Gulf War, but most spills are

After the *Exxon Valdez* spill in Prince William Sound, workers attempted to clean the shoreline using high-pressure, hot-water washes in which oil is hosed from the beaches, collected within floating boom, and then skimmed from the surface of the water. National Oceanic and Atmospheric Administration.

smaller. The 1970s were the worst decade on record in terms of both numbers of oil spills and quantities of oil spilled, according to the International Tanker Owners Pollution Federation (ITOPF). Other large spills have included the oil well Ixtoc-1 in Mexico (529 million liters, 1979), Norwruz Field in Arabia (302 million liters, 1980), Fergana Valley in Uzbekistan (302 million liters, 1992), *Castillo de Bellver* off South Africa (294 million liters, 1983), and the *Amoco Cadiz* off France (257 million liters, 1978). All other spills were less than 189 million liters each. The *Exxon Valdez* spill of 1989 in Alaska was twenty-eighth on the list, with 41 million liters, although the spill was particularly devastating because of the fragile nature of the affected sub-Arctic ecosystem. Because the 2010 Gulf of Mexico spill is not yet fully contained at this writing, nearly three months after the explosion of the *Deepwater Horizon* platform—and because the estimates of how much oil spilled per day varied so dramatically, depending on the source—determining its place in this world hierarchy is premature. According to Kayvan Farzaneh, writing in the 30 April 2010 issue of *Foreign Policy*, the Gulf spill would clearly dwarf the *Exxon Valdez* disaster, however, based on average estimates of 5,000 barrels spilled a day for 90 days, or about 75 million liters.

Effects of Oil Spills

Animals and plants and the nonliving parts of ecosystems are not equally vulnerable to oil spills. Some plants are fragile and have narrow habitat ranges, and they grow only in isolated sites. Some animals are very specialized, living in only a few places or eating only a few kinds of foods. Such species are particularly vulnerable to even small oil spills. Plants and animals in Arctic environments are fragile because of the limited growing season, limited diversity, and slow decay of the oil itself.

Other species are generalists, with wide tolerances for different environmental conditions, broad food requirements, and large geographical distributions. Such animals and plants are very adaptable and often can recover quickly from an oil spill, although the initial death toll may be high. Still other animals, such as some birds, fish, and mammals, can move away from a spill if its spread is slow.

Factors that determine whether an oil spill has devastating effects on plants and animals include size of the spill, type of oil, time of the spill (particularly in relation to the lifecycle of the organisms), vulnerability of particular plants and animals, and the vulnerability of particular ecosystems. Location of a spill can determine effects. In spills in intertidal marshes or estuaries where there is little tidal flow, there is a reduced opportunity for the oil to be carried out to sea, where dilution can blunt the effects. Oil often concentrates at the edge of marshes where there is also a high concentration of invertebrates, young fish, and foraging birds. Many invertebrates do not have the ability to move or move only very

Oil is like a wild animal. Whoever captures it has it. • **J. Paul Getty (1892–1976)**

short distances, making them particularly vulnerable to oil.

The timing of a spill is critical. A spill that occurs during the migratory season of birds, fish, or mammals may result in unusually high exposure of vast numbers of animals. A spill during the spawning season of invertebrates or fish can eliminate reproduction for a season, and a spill during the migration season of marine mammals can kill or weaken a significant portion of the local populations of seals, sea lions, sea otters, whales, and other mammals. Seabirds are particularly at risk because they spend most of their time in the oceans or in estuaries, where massive oil spills usually occur. Seabirds also nest in large colonies of hundreds or thousands, where an oil spill can "oil" or kill hundreds at a time. Oiled parents bring oil back to the nests, killing eggs or young chicks. Because they are so visible, birds often serve as bioindicators of the severity of oil spills, although only a fraction of the birds that die in oceanic or coastal oil spills are ever recovered. Spills that occur during hurricane or cyclone seasons can be particularly hard to clean up.

People can be injured or become ill during oil spills or during the cleanup and can become ill by consuming oil-tainted fish or shellfish. Oil spill accidents can result in the death of workers on the tanker, refinery, or pipeline or the people employed in cleanup. Oil spills often occur during bad weather and stormy seas, making the hazards for the tanker crew more severe.

The effect of oil spills on fishing communities can be devastating. Fishing communities are affected both in the short term and the long term. For many weeks or months the fish are tainted or contaminated, grounding the fisheries completely. The effects of oil on the fish may result in lower harvests for years after the oil has disappeared. Fishing losses were documented for at least six years after the *Exxon Valdez* spill. Fishers lost income because of the low yields and restricted fishing areas, and guides and hotels lost money because recreational fishers did not come back for many years. Fishers and guides lost their jobs and their lifestyle. Native American communities also lost their ability to harvest traditional resources, including fish and shellfish, resulting in a permanent change in their lives. The effects cascaded because much of the local economy depended upon fishing and tourism. The effects of oil spills on aesthetics and existence values, as well as on fishing and tourism, are massive and extensive. The full effects of the ongoing British Petroleum *Deepwater Horizon* spill on the fragile ecosystems of the Gulf of Mexico cannot yet be calculated as of this writing, but the long- and short-term consequences on the wildlife and fishing and tourism industries will be catastrophic indeed. A synchronous oil spill on the other side of the planet, at Dalian, an important coastal resort city in China, made it clear that disasters resulting from the continued search for concentrated forms of ancient biological life—fossil fuels—affect ecosystems, human health, and regional economies. If there is a silver lining, it is to be hoped that the disaster will lead to more robust, legally binding international laws regarding the exploration, transportation, and processing of the world's oil, and a renewed sense of urgency of finding alternative sources of energy.

Joanna BURGER
Rutgers University

Further Reading

Burger, J. (1997). *Oil spills.* New Brunswick, NJ: Rutgers University Press.

Cahill, R. A. (1990). *Disasters at sea:* Titanic *to* Exxon Valdez. San Antonio, TX: Nautical Books.

DeCola, E. (1999). *International oil spill statistics.* Arlington, MA: Cutter Information Corp.

U.S. Department of Energy. (1980–1998). International energy annual reports. Washington, DC: Author.

Gin, K. Y. H., Huda, K., Lim, W. K., & Tkalich, P. (2001). An oil spill-food chain interaction model for coastal waters. *Marine Pollution Bulletin, 42*(7), 590–597.

Gottinger, H. W. (2001). Economic modeling, estimation and policy analysis of oil spill processes. *International Journal of Environment & Pollution, 15*(3), 333–363.

Griglunas, T. A., Oplauch, J. J., Diamatides, J., & Mazzotta, M. (1998). Liability for oil spill damages: Issues, methods, and examples. *Coastal Management 26*(2), 67–77.

International Tanker Owners Pollution Federation (ITOPF). (2010). Statistics: Numbers and amount spilt. Retrieved July 13, 2010, from http://www.itopf.com/information-services/data-and-statistics/statistics/#no

Louma, J. R. (1999). Spilling the truth. Ten years after the worst oil spill in American history, Alaska is still feeling the effects of the *Exxon Valdez* disaster and cleanup. *Audubon, 101*(2), 52–62.

Rice, S. D., et al. (2001). Impacts to pink salmon following *Exxon Valdez* oil spill: Persistence, toxicity, sensitivity, and controversy. *Reviews in Fisheries Science, 9*(3), 165–211.

Peterson, C. H. (2002). The *Exxon Valdez* oil spill in Alaska: Acute, indirect, and chronic effects on the ecosystem. *Advances in Marine Biology, 39*, 3–84.

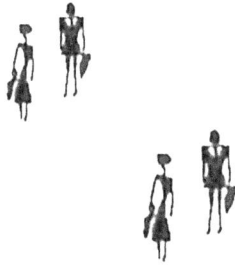

Population and the Environment

Examples throughout history reveal that the simple formula—more people equals more environmental disruption—does not always apply. Nonetheless, in most circumstances, population growth has brought accelerated environmental change and continues to do so. Since the mid-twentieth century, as human population growth approached its maximum rate, the relationship between population growth and the environment has been the subject of popular and scholarly debate.

The relationship between human population and environment, contrary to popular belief, is anything but simple. In the past half-century, as concern over environmental degradation mounted, popular discussion more often than not emphasized the simple, appealing equation: more population equals more environmental degradation. Although this is true in many circumstances, it is by no means invariably so. Scholars have expended great energy trying to tease out the relationship, but with limited success. The question, in both popular and scholarly debate, has been for fifty years and remains to this day a highly political one, with deeply felt principles involved.

History of Human Population

Efforts to count the number of people in a given territory began in ancient times. The first effort to take a census for an entire polity (Tuscany) was made in 1427. Reasonably reliable censuses date from about 1800 and for most of the world from about 1950. So, reconstructing the history of the entire human population inevitably involves a hefty amount of inference and educated guesswork. Opinions vary, although there is remarkable consensus on the general trajectory. (See table 1.)

Although it is unclear exactly when humans became humans, when they did there were few of them. Living as hunter-gatherers they were constantly on the move. Carrying multiple small children was a great burden, so early humans checked their fertility by prolonged breast-feeding (which reduces a woman's fertility) and probably checked population growth via infanticide and abandonment. In any case, population growth was extremely slow by today's standards, although it should be understood that today's standards are a bizarre anomaly: for most of human

Table 1.
Estimated Global Populations

Date	Population (in millions)
300,000 BCE	1
10,000 BCE	4
1000 BCE	50
1 CE	200
500 CE	200
1000 CE	270
1200 CE	380
1400 CE	370
1600 CE	550
1800 CE	920
1900 CE	1,625
2000 CE	6,000

Source: (Cohen 1995, appendix 2)

178

Various aspects of farming in ancient Egypt are depicted in the Tomb of Nakht, on the West Bank of Luxor.

history population growth in net terms was close to zero, and that population declined almost as often as it grew.

With the shift to food production and more sedentary ways of life, the chief constraint on population growth, the difficulty of carrying around small children, eased. The origins of agriculture date to about ten thousand years ago, at which time there were 4 million (more cautiously, 2 to 20 million) people on the Earth. Where agriculture first took root, in southwestern Asia and the tropical lowlands of the Americas, population growth accelerated somewhat. Birthrates climbed, and although death rates eventually did as well, they did not keep pace. Death rates eventually climbed because agricultural societies acquired new diseases, most of them transfers from herd animals such as pigs, cattle, and camels, that quickly killed people, especially young children. Crowding helped spread such diseases rapidly and promoted others that flourished where human beings lived amid their own wastes.

Gradually agriculture spread throughout much of the suitable terrain on Earth, and most of the human population lived in agrarian societies in which villages formed the social nucleus. Irrigation, especially in Egypt, southern Asia, and East Asia, allowed more productive farming and still denser populations. By 3500 BCE cities began to emerge, first in Mesopotamia. The efficiency of agriculture is extremely variable, depending on soils, crops, tools, and other factors, but as a general rule it can support ten times the population density that hunting and gathering can. For this and other reasons agricultural societies spread fairly rapidly at the expense of the less populous communities of hunter-gatherers.

In agrarian societies, children from the age of about five could perform useful labor, such as tending chickens or weeding gardens. Without the requirement of constant migration, children were more an economic asset than a liability, and so, except in conditions of land scarcity (and even sometimes in such conditions), people tended to marry young and reproduce prolifically. Fertility (here presented in the form of the crude birthrate) reached levels of perhaps 50 per 1,000 per year (about four times as high as the current birthrate in the United States), although rates of 35–40 per 1,000 were probably more typical. Even so, reproductive exuberance barely kept up with the toll from disease and famine, which every now and then reached catastrophic levels, pruning back the population growth of happier years. This, in broad strokes, was the demographic regime of agrarian society, the majority experience of humankind from at least 3000 BCE until 1800 CE.

During that time population grew much faster than it had during pre-agricultural times, although still slowly in comparison to today's growth rates. And there were times when population declined. On local and regional scales, epidemics and famines produced such catastrophes fairly regularly, normally at least once or twice within every generation. On the global scale there were at least two great catastrophes, each of which probably brought global population decline (although the figures are not reliable enough to say with assurance). The first

Aerial view of Mexico City. Urban sprawl is one direct result of population growth. Photo by ardelfin (www.morguefile.com).

of these was the great pandemic of the fourteenth century known as the Black Death, probably a result of the spread of bubonic plague throughout most of Asia, Europe, northern Africa, and perhaps parts of sub-Saharan Africa. It reduced the population of Europe, Egypt, and southwestern Asia by perhaps one-quarter or one-third and on a global level by perhaps one-seventh or one-tenth. In Europe the population took 150 years to recover from the plague's ravages. The second great catastrophe came when the population of the Americas was exposed to Eurasian and African diseases in the wake of voyages made by Christopher Columbus and other explorers. Estimates of the population loss for the period from 1500 to 1650 range from 50 to 90 percent. Because there are no good data on the size of the pre-Columbian population in the Americas, it is impossible to know how large the global effect of this disaster may have been. It might have lowered total global population, although more likely, because there were far more people in Eurasia and Africa

than in the Americas, the total effect repressed world population growth without forcing it below zero.

Accelerating Growth

During the eighteenth century human population embarked on its current spectacular expansion. In several parts of the world epidemics and famines started to recede, and death rates fell. The reasons behind this remain uncertain, although ecological adjustment among pathogens (agents of disease) and their human hosts was surely part of it, as were improvements in food supply and famine management. In some places birthrates also rose slightly. During the nineteenth century world population almost doubled, and then in the twentieth century it almost quadrupled as death rates tumbled. Better sanitation, vaccines, and antibiotics lowered the toll from disease, and much more productive agriculture increased the food supply sharply. In Europe by the 1890s families responded by consciously limiting the number of births, a reaction that occurred later but more quickly in most other parts of the world. When and where birthrates shrank, population growth slowed; when and where birthrates remained robust, as in much of Africa, Central America, and parts of southern and southwestern Asia, population growth spurted after 1950. Globally, the growth rate peaked around 1970 at about 2.1 percent per year, and population increased by another billion every 12 to 15 years. By 2009 annual growth had declined to 1.1 percent per year, or about 73 million additional people annually. Demographers now expect the world's population to reach 9 or 10 billion around 2050.

For most of history roughly three-fourths of humanity lived in Eurasia. That remains the case today, but the proportion living in the Americas grew sharply after 1750, and the proportion living in Africa leapt upward after 1950. (See table 2.)

Population Policy

People have voiced concern that humanity is too thick on the ground since at least 1600 BCE. Such concern, however, has been rare until recently. Political authorities, when they gave any consideration at all to population, generally took the view that the more people there were within their borders, the better. All the major religions favored population growth, too. This is not surprising: until the last 250 years survival was so precarious that maximizing births

was usually a sensible insurance policy against disaster. But in the mid- and late-twentieth century a few governments began to see matters differently. India and China, by far the two most populous countries, committed themselves to birth control, and in China's case to stern restrictions that between 1978 and 2009 kept the population 300 million lower than it would otherwise have been (it was 1.33 billion in 2009). Other countries in the twentieth century, especially in Europe, sought to increase their birthrates but to very little effect.

Population and Environment

At all times and places the relationship between population and environment is one of mutual interaction. Environmental conditions affect population's trajectory and population growth (or decline) affects the environment.

Historically, the environmental conditions that most influenced population were climate, disease, and agriculture. Major climate shifts, such as the waxing and waning of ice ages, strongly affected human population by changing the proportion of the Earth that was habitable and by changing the biological productivity of the parts not covered with ice. The onset of the last ice age presumably reduced human population, and its end encouraged population growth. Since the end of the last ice age ten thousand years ago, climate change has played only a small

Table 1.
Regional Populations from 1750 to 2000

		1750	1800	1850	1900	1950	2000
	(in millions)						
	Asia	480	602	749	937	1386	3766
	Europe	140	187	266	401	576	728
	Africa	95	90	95	120	206	840
	N. America	1	6	26	81	167	319
	South and Central America	11	19	33	63	162	531
	Australia and Oceania	2	2	2	6	13	32

Source: McNeill (2000, 271).

The transformation of habitats resulting from logging, deforestation, and land development has put heightened pressure on many species.

role in determining human population size on the global level.

As noted, the human burden of disease became markedly heavier when and where people took up cultivation, especially settled cultivation, especially when domesticated animals were involved. In tropical lands, except at high altitudes, sustaining dense settled populations was difficult because so many more disease organisms flourished in the warmth. The emergence of cities also created lethal disease environments, mainly because people lived cheek by jowl, communicating infections daily, and because few cities adequately disposed of wastes. So, cities generally, perhaps invariably, were black holes for humanity, sustained only by recurrent migration from healthier, rural landscapes. This situation remained in force until the end of the nineteenth century and in many countries until the middle of the twentieth century. Eventually, mainly through scientific sanitation after 1880, cities became even healthier than rural areas, and one of the great historic constraints on population growth, the lethality of city life, was lifted.

Changes in agricultural conditions also helped to regulate human population by affecting the food supply. Irrigation agriculture, as noted, could support more people than could rainfall agriculture. But irrigation often generated salinization (the accumulation of salts, harmful to plant growth), which over centuries could spoil farmland, as in Mesopotamia, where environmental degradation probably played a role in

episodes of depopulation around 1900 BCE, around 1375 BCE, and before 1250 CE. Over centuries, even over decades, soil erosion could also significantly lower the productivity of agricultural land, which, if not otherwise compensated for, could reduce population. Salinization and erosion could easily affect local and regional populations severely, although at the global level their impacts have always been negligible.

A more recent change in agricultural conditions, the Green Revolution, has had impacts at every scale. Since the 1950s agronomists (agricultural scientists dealing with field-crop production and soil management) have bred new strains of most of the major food crops of the world, making them responsive to heavy doses of fertilizer and timely doses of irrigation water, more resistant to crop diseases and pests, and more suited to machine harvesting. As a result, modern chemicalized agriculture doubled and quadrupled crop yields. The global effect as of 2000 was to increase the world's food supply by about one-third, an essential component of the contemporary surge in world population.

Population growth, or decline, also affects the environment. Just how much it does depends on many factors, including rates of growth, existing densities of population, resilience and stability of ecosystems, the technologies available, and just which aspect of the catch-all phrase *the environment* one chooses to measure. The amount of nuclear wastes around the world, for example, has had little to do with population levels or growth rates but everything to do with technology and politics. Conversely, urban sprawl has resulted directly from population growth (although other factors have been involved).

The circumstances under which population growth proved maximally disruptive to environments were probably those in which initial levels of population were either zero or very low, the growth rate vigorous, and the transformative technologies at hand powerful. The history of New Zealand provides an apt illustration. New Zealand was long isolated from outside influence and had no human population for millions of years—a sanctuary for species from the Cretaceous era. People first arrived around 1300 CE (perhaps as early as 1000), at first probably only a few. But the Maori—New Zealand's original settlers—found ample resources in seals, mollusks, and large flightless birds (moas), which they hunted. They burned the forest to make better forage for creatures they hunted and to make room for crops. In the course of a few centuries, they drove the moa and a few other species to extinction and reduced the forest cover of New Zealand by about one-third or one-half. Similar dramatic changes followed upon initial human settlement of other isolated islands such as Madagascar (c. 400 CE) and Iceland (c. 870 CE). Presumably the impacts of initial human settlement in the pre-agricultural past were less pronounced, although the occupation of Australia (about sixty thousand years ago) and the Americas (about fifteen thousand years ago) may have brought on—this is the majority view but by no means a consensus view—numerous extinctions of large and midsized mammals. Even without much technology beyond spears and fire, humans, when entering landscapes in which species had no prior experience of human ways, proved highly disruptive.

With more powerful technologies at hand, population growth could be even more disruptive. After 1769, and especially after 1840, New Zealand acquired another settler population, primarily from Great Britain. These settlers had metal tools, which the Maori had not had, grazing animals, and eventually steam engines and the entire panoply of industrial machines. In the span of two centuries, New Zealand's population went from less than 100,000 to about 3 million, almost all of whom used modern technologies. New Zealand lost most of the rest of its forest cover and many more of its indigenous species (mostly birds), and most of the landscape (discounting inhospitable extremes) became pastureland. Population growth alone, of course, was not responsible for this transformation of New Zealand, although it was crucial. Also crucial was the existence of overseas markets for wool, mutton, and butter, on which New Zealand's pastoral economy rested.

Population growth has been least disruptive where heavy labor has been required to stabilize an environment. The best examples of this concern soil erosion. Farmers, when working on slopes, inevitably risk rapid soil erosion unless they can construct and maintain terraces. But that is extremely labor intensive. In the Machakos Hills district of Kenya, for example, early in the twentieth century farmers caused high erosion rates by tilling the soil. They did not have enough people to undertake the backbreaking labor of terrace construction. But by the 1960s population growth had changed that. Farmers built and maintained terraces, stabilizing their soils. A reduction in population density in terraced mountain environments can bring accelerated soil erosion because too few people remain to keep the terracing in place. This happened in the twentieth century in the mountain regions of southern Europe when birthrates fell and young people emigrated. The endless terraces of Java or southern China would be difficult to maintain without dense population.

Population decline destabilized other landscapes as well. In eastern Africa, for example, by the nineteenth century people had learned that to keep sleeping sickness at bay they had to burn off the bush (which reduced the habitat for the tsetse fly that carries sleeping sickness). Sleeping sickness killed cattle more easily than people; it was an economic as well as a health problem. But bush control required labor, and when lethal epidemics broke out at the end of the nineteenth century and the beginning of the twentieth, one result was to make it difficult for people to control the vegetation surrounding their villages. Thus a costly ecological change proceeded: more bush, more tsetse fly, more sleeping sickness. This example, like the terraces of southern Europe, is a case in which an environment, already modified by human action and in a more or less stable state, was disrupted by population decline.

Population, when unchecked, increases
in a geometrical ratio. • Thomas Malthus (1766–1834)

These examples show that a simple formula (more people equals more environmental disruption) does not necessarily apply. Nonetheless, in most circumstances, population growth has brought accelerated environmental change and continues to do so. In the context of the last half-century, when human population growth reached its maximum rate, the role of population has probably been greater than in previous times (with the exception of local- and regional-scale examples such as New Zealand's initial settlement). Cropland has increased by one-third since 1950, a process mainly driven by population growth. The proportion of land occupied by roads and buildings has grown roughly in step with population and chiefly because of population. The transformation of habitats, including deforestation, the extension of cropland, pastureland, and developed land, has put heightened pressure on many species lately, especially in tropical forests. This pressure, one of the signal environmental changes of modern history, has been driven in part by population growth, although it is difficult to specify how large that part might be.

Population growth also has been a factor in the increased pollution loads of modern history. In cases such as water pollution derived from human wastes, it has been a large factor indeed. But in other cases, such as the pollution of the stratospheric ozone layer by chlorofluorocarbons, population growth played only a little role, and technological change (the invention of chlorofluorocarbons) a much larger one. Thus, among types of pollution, as among environmental changes in general, the degree to which population growth can logically be held responsible varies tremendously from case to case.

In the future it is likely that population will decline in importance as a variable in shaping environmental change. This is partly because the extraordinary pulse of population growth of the past century, and especially the past half-century, will sooner or later come to an end. But this is also because technology looms ever larger as a mediator

between people and their environments, and the pace of technological change seems unlikely to slow any time soon. If global population stabilizes after 2050, as many demographers suppose it will, population shifts locally and regionally will still exert pressures of one sort or another. And it remains possible that because there are already so many people on Earth the addition of another 2 or 3 billion will have a much stronger impact than the addition of the last 2 or 3 billion. That is, there may be nonlinear effects with respect to the consequences of population growth, thresholds that, if surpassed, bring major changes. Observers have predicted catastrophic consequences from population growth for millennia but most consistently (and most plausibly) in the last forty years. It has not happened yet. If it does, it will happen within the next fifty years.

J. R. McNEILL

Georgetown University

See also Carrying Capacity; Deforestation; Diseases—Overview; Erosion; Green Revolution; Salinization

Further Reading

Bogin, B. (2001). *The growth of humanity.* New York: Wiley-Liss.

Caldwell, J., & Schindlmayer, T. (2002). Historical population estimates: Unraveling the consensus. *Population and Development Review, 28*(2), 183–204.

Cipolla, C. (1962). *The economic history of world population.* Harmondsworth, U.K.: Penguin.

Cohen, J. (1995). *How many people can the Earth support?* New York: Norton.

Demeny, P. (1990). Population. In B. L. Turner II, W.C. Clark, R.W. Kates. J.F. Richards, J.T. Matthews, & W.B. Meyer (Eds.), *The Earth as transformed by human action* (pp. 41–54). New York: Cambridge University Press.

Erickson, J. (1995). *The human volcano: Population growth as geologic force.* New York: Facts on File.

Livi-Bacci, M. (2001). *A concise history of world population.* Malden, MA: Blackwell.

Lutz, W.; Prskawetz, A.; & Sanderson, W. C. (Eds.). (2002). Population and environment: Methods of analysis. *Population and Development Review, 28*, 1–250.

Penna, A. (2009). *The human footprint: A global environmental history.* New York: Wiley-Blackwell.

Redman, C. (Ed.). (2004). *The archeology of global change: The impact of humans on their environments.* Washington, D.C.: Smithsonian Press.

Ts'ui-jung, L.; Lee, J.; Reher, D. S.; Saito, O.; & Feng, W. (Eds.). (2001). *Asian population history.* Oxford, U.K.: Oxford University Press.

Whitmore, T. M.; Turner, B. L.; Johnson, D. L.; Kates, R. W.; & Gottschang, T. R. (1990). Long-term population change. In B. L. Turner, W. C. Clark, R. W. Kates, J. F. Richards, J. T. Matthews, & W. B. Meyer (Eds.), *The Earth as transformed by human action* (pp. 25–40). New York: Cambridge University Press.

Rivers

The geographer Lewis Mumford's observation—that all great historic cultures thrived by traveling along the natural highway of a great river—is particularly resonant today, as the world's rivers bear the brunt of human manipulation. Pollution and habitat loss (two main side effects of hydraulic engineering), as well as climate change, pose unprecedented challenges to agriculture, manufacturing, urban water supplies, and wildlife conservation.

By common definition, a river refers to water flowing within the confines of a channel (as suggested by its Latin root, *ripa*, meaning "bank"). More precisely, a river forms the stem of a drainage system that transports water, soil, rocks, minerals, and nutrient-rich debris from higher to lower elevations. In a broader sense, rivers are part of the global water cycle: they collect precipitation (snow, sleet, hail, rain) and transport it back to lakes and oceans, where evaporation and cloud formation begin anew. Energized by gravity and sunlight, rivers sculpt the land around them, wearing down mountains, grinding rocks, and carving floodplains through the earth's crust. As carriers of water and nutrients, rivers also provide complex biological niches for fish, sponges, insects, birds, trees, and many other organisms.

Rivers can be compared by basin size, discharge rate, and channel length, although there are no universally recognized statistics for any of these dimensions. The Amazon forms the world's largest drainage basin at approximately 7 million square kilometers, followed distantly by the Congo (3.7 million square kilometers) and the Mississippi-Missouri (3.2 million square kilometers). As regards discharge rate, the Amazon once again stands supreme at around 180,000 cubic meters per second, followed by the Congo (41,000 cubic meters per second), the Ganges-Brahmaputra (38,000 cubic meters per second), and the Yangzi (Chang) (35,000 cubic meters per second). At around 6,650 kilometers, the Nile is the world's longest river, followed closely by the Amazon (6,300 kilometers) and the Mississippi-Missouri (6,100 kilometers). Other rivers with large area-discharge-length combinations include the Ob'-Irtysh, Paraná, Yenisey, Lena, Niger, Amur, Mackenzie, Volga, Zambezi, Indus, Tigris-Euphrates, Nelson, Huang He (Yellow River), Murray-Darling, and the Mekong. Two rivers—the Huang and Ganges-Brahmaputra—also stand out for their huge annual sediment load, which makes them especially prone to severe flooding. There is no agreed-upon minimum size, length, or volume for a river, but small rivers are usually called streams, brooks, creeks, or rivulets. Great or small, rivers that form part of a larger drainage system are known as tributaries, branches, or feeder streams.

Although rivers vary greatly in size, shape, and volume, most rivers share certain characteristics. A typical river has its headwaters in a mountainous or hilly region, where it is nurtured by glaciers, melting snow, lakes, springs, or rain. Near the headwaters, swift currents prevail and waterfalls are common, owing to the rapid drop in elevation or the narrowness of the valley though which the river flows. As a river leaves the high region, its velocity typically slackens and its channel begins to meander, bifurcate, or braid. Often its floodplain broadens as it picks up tributary waters. As the river reaches its mouth, it usually loses most of its gradient. It becomes sluggish, allowing some of its sediment load to settle to the bottom, clogging

Edwin Lord Weeks (1849–1903), *Water Carriers of The Ganges* (n.d.). Oil on canvas. The Ganges, long a sacred site for Hindu ritual, is threatened by sewage and fertilizer pollutants.

the channel. The river responds by fanning around the sediment deposits, classically forming the shape of a delta (the fourth letter in the Greek alphabet, Δ), before emptying in a lake, sea, or ocean.

Unique climatic and geographic conditions determine a river's annual discharge regime (its seasonal variations in water quantity), but as a rule rain-fed tropical rivers flow more steadily year-round than do snow-fed temperate rivers. A river is called perennial if it carries water all or almost all of the time, and intermittent or ephemeral if it does not. A water-carved channel in an arid region is often called an arroyo or dry gulch if it carries water only on rare occasions. For hydrologists, the term *flood* refers to a river's annual peak discharge period, whether it inundates the surrounding landscape or not. In common parlance, a flood is synonymous with the act of a river overflowing its banks. In 1887, a massive flood on the Huang caused the death of nearly a million Chinese people. In 1988, flooding on the Ganges-Brahmaputra temporarily displaced over 20 million in Bangladesh.

Human Manipulation of Rivers

Rivers contain only a minuscule portion of the total water on earth at any given time, but along with lakes, aquifers, and springs they are the principal sources of fresh water for humans as well as for many plants and animals. Rivers are therefore closely associated with the emergence of settled agriculture, irrigated crops, and early urban life. The great civilizations of Mesopotamia (literally "the land between the rivers") from Sumer to Babylonia emerged beginning around 4500 BCE along the Tigris and Euphrates floodplains of modern-day Iraq. Egypt, as the Greek historian Herodotus once famously noted, was "the gift of the Nile." The Huang spawned early Chinese civilization, just as the Indus produced the first cultures of southwest Asia, and the river valleys of coastal Peru shaped urban life in the Andes. "All the great historic cultures," the geographer Lewis Mumford noted with only slight exaggeration, "have thriven through the movement of men and institutions and inventions and goods along the natural highway of a great river" (McCully 1996, 9).

For most of human history, river manipulation was slight, consisting mostly of diverting or impounding a portion of a river's water for the purpose of irrigating crops. Even modest modifications of this type, however, can have severe environmental consequences. In arid regions, salinization is a common problem. Unless properly drained, irrigated fields slowly accumulate the minuscule amounts of dissolved salts naturally found in soil and water. Over time this salt buildup will eventually render the fields incapable of growing most crop species. Siltation is a common problem caused when farmers and pastoralists deforest or overgraze river valleys, inadvertently setting in motion excessive erosion downstream. As the silt settles to the channel bottom, it elevates the

Otto Johann Heinrich Heyden (1820–1897), *The River Nile with the Gizeh Pyramids* (n.d.). Oil on canvas.

river above the landscape, making it more prone to flooding.

Ancient Roman, Muslim, and Chinese engineers possessed a sophisticated understanding of the art of hydraulics, as the still-extant aqueducts, canals, and waterworks of Rome, Baghdad, Beijing, and other Eurasian cities amply demonstrate. But river engineering as a mathematical science first emerged in Europe between 1500 and 1800 CE. The crucial breakthrough came when Italian engineers calculated the formula for determining the amount of water flowing in a river at any given time by measuring width, depth, and flow rate. Thereafter, water experts knew how to "tame" a river—that is, manipulate its banks, bed, and velocity in order to contain floods, reclaim land, and promote navigation—with a greater degree of precision, and therefore a higher chance of success, than had previously been feasible.

Today's methods for controlling rivers are remarkably similar to those employed in the past—chiefly the construction of dams and weirs, the reinforcement of banks, and the straightening (and often widening) of channels—but materials and techniques have improved greatly over the past two centuries. Modern dams are designed to store water, regulate minimum channel depth (usually in connection with a lock), generate electricity, or perform all three tasks. Reinforced banks help keep the water in a designated channel, thereby reducing the frequency of flooding and opening up former floodplain for agricultural, urban, industrial, and other human uses. Channel straightening gives a river a steeper gradient and thus a faster discharge rate; by reducing the total length of a river, it also facilitates the transportation of goods between ports. Collectively, these engineering methods transform a mercurial and free-flowing stream (a "floodplain river") into a predictable deliverer of energy, goods, and water (a "reservoir river"). Nowadays, the Nile and Yangzi produce kilowatts for industries and cities, just as the Mississippi and Rhine transport freight for companies and consumers, and the Colorado and Rio Grande deliver water for farmers and homeowners.

Environmental Consequences of Hydraulic Engineering

River engineering fosters bank-side economic growth by opening up arable land, reducing floods, promoting trade, and generating electricity, but it also has a disruptive impact on riverine environments. The problems can be divided into two interrelated types: those that compromise the purity of the water in the channel (water pollution) and those that reduce the amount of living space in its channel and floodplain (habitat loss). Both typically result in a reduction in a river's biodiversity.

River Pollution

Water pollutants can be divided into three broad categories: nutrient-based, chemical, and thermal. The most common nutrient-based pollutants are fecal matter from untreated human sewage and agricultural runoff from phosphorus and nitrogen fertilizers. When introduced into a lake or river, these organic substances serve as food for phytoplankton (free-floating algae), which are huge consumers of the water's dissolved oxygen. If the river moves slowly, and if the "algal blooms" are large or frequent enough, the river will gradually become eutrophified (oxygen-depleted), with negative consequences for other organisms that require dissolved oxygen for respiration. The Po and Ganges are examples of sewage-fertilizer rivers.

The most pernicious chemical pollutants include heavy metals (zinc, copper, chromium, lead, cadmium, mercury, and arsenic), and chlorinated hydrocarbons such as polychlorinated biphenyls (PCBs) and dichlorodiphenyltrichloroethane (DDT). These substances bioaccumulate; that is, they pass unmetabolized from simple organisms to more complex organisms, magnifying in concentration as they move up the food chain. The Mersey, Rhine, Hudson, Ohio, and Donets are all examples of industrial-chemical rivers.

Thermal pollution is a problem on rivers that have numerous nuclear-, coal-, or oil-generated power plants on their banks. The heated wastewater from the plant-cooling facilities artificially raises the water temperature, and the higher temperature in turn affects the type of species capable of living in the streambed. The Rhône and Rhine are examples of thermal rivers.

Most of the world's manipulated rivers can loosely be labeled "agricultural" since the majority of engineering projects are geared toward land reclamation

Rafts on the Yangzi River, China. Photo by Joan Lebold Cohen.

*No man ever steps in the same river twice, for it's not the same river
and he's not the same man.* • **Heraclitus (544–483 BCE)**

(flood control) and the lion's share of dam water is still utilized for the purpose of irrigating crops. As industrialization spreads globally, however, chemical pollutants are increasingly becoming the single greatest threat to river systems; indeed, few rivers remain completely free of any trace of industrial contaminants. Today, the cleanliness or filth of a river is often more determined by the average income of the humans who live on its banks than by the number of farms and factories in its watershed. Wealthy nations have invested in urban and industrial sanitation plants over the past fifty years, and water quality has correspondingly improved. Poorer countries, unable to afford these techno-fixes, have seen their rivers continue to deteriorate.

Habitat Loss

Water pollution compromises a river's biological robustness by killing off organisms and by creating an unfavorable environment for nourishment and reproduction. But it is the engineering projects themselves that account for most of the habitat loss on rivers and are thus primarily responsible for the drop in biodiversity. Natural ("untamed") rivers contain an abundance of diverse biological niches: headwaters and tributaries, main and secondary channels, deep pools and islands, banks and bed, and marshes and backwaters. Channels provide longitudinal passageways along which organisms travel, while river edges provide access routes to the adjacent marshes and floodplains where many organisms find their nourishment and reproduction sites. Floodplains nurture trees, shrubs, and reeds, which help stabilize the channel bank while providing shade and protection to other organisms. A river basin hosts a complex web of life, ranging from simple organisms such as fungi, bacteria, algae, and protozoa, to more complex organisms such as flatworms, roundworms, and wheel animals, and on up to mollusks, sponges, insects, fish, birds, and mammals.

Engineering alters a basin's natural structure in ways that are detrimental to many species. Dams and weirs block a river's longitudinal passageways,

making it difficult for organisms to take full advantage of the channel's living space. Migratory fish are particularly hard hit because their life cycles require them to move from headwaters to delta and back again. Most famously, salmon disappeared from the Columbia, Rhine, and many other rivers when dams were built on their banks. Reinforced banks have a similar impact: they sever the links between a river's channel and its floodplain, depriving many organisms of their feeding and breeding sites. As a river loses all or part of its natural channel, bed, banks, islands, backwaters, marshes, and floodplain, it is transformed into a narrow and uniform rather than a broad and diverse biological site. Typically this results in a precipitous drop in both the number and type of species that it supports.

Aside from reducing the total amount of living space on a river, engineering can also trigger dramatic population upsurges in certain species, creating an ecological imbalance. The zebra mussel—a hearty algae eater and rapid reproducer—has migrated from its home in the Caspian Sea to the industrial rivers of America and Europe, displacing local mollusk species along the way. Similarly, after the completion of the Aswan Dam in the mid-1930s, snails infected with deadly schistosomes (parasitic worms) began to colonize the Nile's new irrigation canals, debilitating and killing Egyptian farmers and fishermen.

Responding to environmentalists and to reformers from within their own ranks (such as Gilbert F. White), engineers have developed new and more sophisticated methods of river manipulation over the past thirty years. More attention is now paid to preserving the original river corridor as channel beds and banks are fortified and dredged. Dams and weirs are fitted (or retrofitted) with fish ladders to ease fish migration. More floodplain is left intact. In some cases, rivers have even been re-meandered and rebraided so that they better replicate the natural conditions that once prevailed on their banks. Nevertheless, the recent Three Gorges Dam project on the Yangzi—the largest dam-building project of all time—serves as a reminder that the environmentally unfriendly practices of the past are still in widespread use today.

Most climate scientists predict that global warming will have far-reaching impacts on river systems worldwide. High mountains such as the Alps and Himalayas may begin to shed their snowpack earlier each spring. Higher evaporation rates may cause some regions to experience significant alterations in their annual precipitation patterns. Warmer water temperatures may make some rivers inhospitable to salmon and other cold-water fish. Rising sea levels may partially or wholly inundate the Netherlands, Bangladesh, and other delta regions. Although the effects on rivers will vary from region to region, collectively these changes will pose unprecedented challenges to agriculture, manufacturing, urban water supplies, and wildlife conservation.

Mark CIOC
University of California, Santa Cruz

See also Biological Exchanges; Climate Change; Erosion; Nature; Water; Water Energy; Water Management

Further Reading

Cowx, I. G., &. Welcomme, R. L. (Eds.). (1998). *Rehabilitation of rivers for fish: A study undertaken by the European Inland Fisheries Advisory Commission of FAO.* Oxford, U.K.: Fishing News Books.

Czaya, E. (1983). *Rivers of the world.* Cambridge, U.K.: Cambridge University Press.

Giller, P. S., & Malmqvist, B. (1998). *The biology of streams and rivers.* Oxford, U.K.: Oxford University Press.

Goubert, J.-P. (1986). *The conquest of water: The advent of health in the industrial age.* Princeton, NJ: Princeton University Press.

Harper, D. M., & Ferguson, A. J. D. (Eds.). (1995). *The ecological basis for river management.* Chichester, U.K.: John Wiley & Sons.

Hillel, D. (1994). *Rivers of Eden.* New York: Oxford University Press.

McCully, P. (1996). *Silenced rivers: The ecology and politics of large dams.* London: Zed Books.

Moss, B. (1988). *Ecology of freshwaters: Man and medium.* Oxford, U.K.: Blackwell Scientific Publications.

Nienhuis, P. H., Leuven, S. S. E. W., & Ragas, A. M. J. (Eds.). (1998). *New concepts for sustainable management of river basins.* Leiden, The Netherlands: Backhuys.

Przedwojski, B., Blazejewski, R., & Pilarczyk, K. W. (1995). *River training techniques: Fundamentals, design and applications.* Rotterdam, Netherlands: A. A. Balkema.

Rand McNally and Company (1980). *Rand McNally encyclopedia of world rivers.* Chicago: Rand McNally.

Roads

The first roads were built to facilitate the movement of armies over uneven landscapes. Paved road systems reached new levels of sophistication during Roman times but fell into disrepair with the fall of the empire. The dawn of modern road building began with the invention of the automobile, evolving into today's intricate networks of street and highway systems.

Roads that allow marching men and wheeled vehicles to move easily across indefinite distances have existed for thousands of years. The earliest roads were built for military use, since rulers were eager to move armies as fast as possible to meet hostile forces wherever they might appear. But merchants and other travelers immediately benefited from roads as well, and over time everyday use for peaceful purposes matched and eventually outweighed their military significance.

Road construction is not easy, for roads must often cross flowing water and/or dry streambeds and usually need specially constructed bridges to do so safely. On dry ground, rain erodes soft earth and forms puddles that quickly turn into impassable mud holes unless builders construct a pavement of flat stones, compacted gravel, concrete, or asphalt. Drains are often needed to keep the road surface intact for any length of time. In addition, since the invention of automobiles and trucks, curves and slopes must be designed to accommodate vehicles moving at high speed. This sometimes requires building tunnels, leveling hill crests, and moving millions of tons of rock.

Jan Asselyn (1610–1652), *Italian Landscape with the Ruins of a Roman Bridge and Aqueduct*. Oil on canvas. Many feats of Roman engineering—such as bridges and aqueducts—still exist as majestic ruins; with the fall of the empire Roman roads fell into disrepair.

Early Roads

Babylonian and Assyrian kings built the first road systems historians know of in modern Iraq. They did so for military purposes, beginning when horse-drawn chariots became supreme on battlefields after about 1400 BCE. The Persians later built a so-called royal road that ran all the way from their capital at Susa to the shores of the Aegean Sea, a distance of about 2,857 kilometers (1,775 miles). Xerxes's army used that road when invading Greece in 480 BCE, and the Greek historian Herodotus wrote that it took ninety-three days to travel its length, an average of about 31 kilometers (19 miles) a day.

Other early empires in China and India also created lengthy road systems, but canal boats in China later became the main means of long distance transport, being cheaper and far more capacious than overland carriage. Roads assumed local, short-range significance in China thereafter, and when camel caravans became normal for long distance trade and raid (c. 200 CE), road building in the arid zones of central and western Asia lost its earlier importance. Wheeled vehicles became marginal wherever camels prevailed, so even the famous Silk Roads that connected China with western Asia after about 100 BCE were no more than a network of unimproved caravan tracks.

Roman Roads

Around the Mediterranean, however, the Roman Empire relied on a system of elaborately constructed roads designed primarily for military use but important for trade as well. Roads were a standard 8-meters (twenty-six-feet) wide, topped with multiple layers of flat stones and gravel to produce a surface on which relays of horses could pull light, two-wheeled chariots as much as 120 kilometers (75 miles a day), while heavy carts were content to travel 24 kilometers (15 miles) a day. At its apex the Roman state maintained about 85,295 kilometers (53,000 miles) of such roads in Europe, western Asia, and North Africa, using them primarily to deliver supplies for army garrisons stationed along the frontiers.

In sub-Saharan Africa, Australia, and the Americas, where human portage was the prevailing form of transport, roads were not needed since human feet could traverse uneven ground just as well as camel hoofs. But, in Peru, Incan rulers constructed a road system rivaling that of the Roman Empire, presumably for military reasons. Two main roads ran from Ecuador southward for about 3,219 kilometers (2,000 miles), one along the coastal plain and a second inland through the high Andes. They were linked by side roads built along suitable river valleys. Incan roads were as much as 7.62 meters (25 feet wide); suspension bridges crossed wide ravines; and flat stone surfaces smoothed the way for human traffic and llama caravans.

Canaletto, *Grand Canal: The Rialto Bridge from the South* (1727). Oil on copper. Roads that need to cross flowing water require specially constructed bridges.

The road was new to me, as roads always are going back.
• **Sarah Orne Jewett (1849–1909),** *The Country of the Pointed Firs*

In Eurasia, the collapse of the Roman Empire (430 CE) disrupted road maintenance, and traffic soon decayed. The East Roman, or Byzantine, Empire—centered in Constantinople (later called Istanbul)—relied mainly on ships and navigable rivers for transport and gave up the effort to station troops on distant land frontiers, so eastern Europe, too, saw Roman roads deteriorate. Economic revival and population growth after about 900 increased trade, but for a long time no public authority existed that was capable of restoring a road system in any of the separate kingdoms and principalities into which Europe divided. Local cities did something to pave streets and public spaces, but overland hauling remained short range, slow, and expensive. Inland communities were almost self-sufficient for food and other essentials. Seafaring and boats moving along the slow-flowing rivers of the north European plain provided the principal means of transport.

Modern Systems

After 1650 or so the situation began to change when privately constructed, stone-surfaced toll roads, carrying swift passenger coaches and heavy freight wagons, proved profitable in a few unusually busy locations. But Roman-style construction of multi-layered stone roads was expensive, so large-scale road building depended on the invention of cheaper methods of construction. After 1750, experiments began in both France and England using relatively thin layers of loose rock and gravel—as little as 224 millimeters (10 inches)—laid on top of ordinary soil raised above the level of adjacent ground and drained by ditches on either side. In England, John Louden McAdam (1756–1836), appointed surveyor general of metropolitan roads in Great Britain in 1827, attached his name to this cheaper way of building roads, and a boom in "macadamized" road construction ensued. But the advent of railroads, beginning in the 1830s, soon eclipsed toll roads for most long-distance traffic.

Other European countries and European settlements overseas imitated the cheaper form of French and English road building very quickly but still saw railroads eclipse toll roads. Only when trucks and cars became numerous in the 1920s did a new era of road building emerge. Concrete slabs and/or smooth asphalt topping quickly replaced gravel roads, reducing dust and speeding driving. In the 1930s, Italy and Germany pioneered the construction of limited-access superhighways with a median

Henry Alken (1785-1851), *A Coach and Four on an Autumn Road* (n.d.). Oil on panel.

strip to separate opposite traffic flows. This set a new standard for speed and safety and in Germany was also designed for military use. The United States, after 1956, caught up by building an interstate system of limited-access highways that links all major cities in the country; wherever cars and trucks abound similar throughways have speeded traffic. But as vehicles multiplied they often increased traffic congestion. How long our present road system will retain its importance depends on the cost and availability of gasoline and diesel fuel or on the development of alternative technologies.

William H. McNEILL
University of Chicago, Emeritus

Further Reading

Bulliet, R. W. (1990 [1975]). *The camel and the wheel.* New York: Columbia University Press.

Forbes, R. J. (1934). *Notes on the history of ancient roads and their construction.* Amsterdam: Noord-Hollandsche Uitgevers-Mij.Hindley, G. (1972). *A history of roads.* New York: Citadel Press.

Moran, J. (2009). *On Roads: A hidden history.* London: Profile Books Ltd.

Rose, A. C. (1952). *Public roads of the past,* 2 vols. Washington, DC: American Association of State Highway Officials.

Rose, A. C. (1976). *Historic American roads: From frontier trails to superhighways.* New York: Crown Publishers.

Schreiber, H. (1961). *History of roads from the amber route to motorway.* London: Barrie & Rockliff.

Salinization

Salinization, the process by which salts accumulate in soil, has long been (and continues to be) one of the world's major challenges for sustaining agricultural production. In natural and managed ecosystems, salinization regulates plant and animal communities, and it determines the way in which water is circulated and distributed on and below the Earth's surface and in the atmosphere.

Salinization is a natural and human-induced process by which soluble salts accumulate in soil. Salts enter soil systems mainly when they are dissolved in groundwater or irrigation water, when they are deposited from the atmosphere, and when minerals are weathered. Salts are further concentrated as water is removed from the soil via evaporation and transpiration (the uptake of water by plants). Slow-draining clayey soils are much more susceptible to salinization than are rapid-draining sands. Salt concentrations in soils tend to increase in the direction of surface or groundwater flow, that is, from uplands to low-lying depressions or bottoms. Salinization thus affects many of the Earth's major biogeochemical cycles of chemical elements and compounds between the living and nonliving parts of the biosphere.

The predominant soil salts are chlorides and sulfates salts, which are generally balanced by sodium, calcium, magnesium, and potassium. Soils with elevated salts are known as "saline," and those with sodium-dominating salt composition are known as "sodic" or "natric." Sodium salts are particularly problematic in soils for physical, chemical, and biological reasons. Excess sodium can stress many plants, especially if calcium concentrations are low, is associated with very high pH (above 9) and causes conditions directly injurious to plants by worsening deficiencies in nutrients such as phosphorus, copper, iron, boron, manganese, and zinc.

High sodium also adversely affects soil's physical and chemical properties, causing soil clays and organic matter to disperse into individual particles instead of remaining flocculated (i.e., attracted together in packages or aggregates of multiple particles of clay and soil organic matter). Sodium-enriched soils that are dispersed can be a near-complete barrier to water entry as dispersed clay particles block soil pores. Sodium-caused dispersion also reduces the rate of gas movement in soils. Soils that are sodium enriched readily become waterlogged and stress oxygen-demanding processes such as root and microbial activity. Only well adapted salt-tolerant plants and microbes are able to grow in salinized soils.

Plants range widely in their ability to tolerate salts in their root zone. Plants that readily accumulate or tolerate salts are called "halophytes" and include salt-tolerant grasses, herbs, and shrubs, species that are native to deserts, shorelines, and salt marshes. Most food crops are not halophytic and exhibit high sensitivity to salt, including many legumes, corn, rice, oats, and wheat. Crop plants that tolerate or benefit from halophytic properties include beets, date palms, spinach, jojoba, and barley.

Geographical Distribution of Salt-Affected Soil

Salinization occurs chiefly in arid, semiarid, and subhumid regions. Salt-affected soils are not a widespread problem in humid regions because precipitation is

196

Table 1.
Distribution of Saline and Sodic Soils on Five Continents

	Saline Soils	Sodic Soils	Ratio of Sodic/Saline
	(in thousands of km²)		
Africa	535	270	0.5
Asia	1,949	1,219	0.6
Australia	386	1,997	5.2
North America	82	96	1.2
South America	694	596	0.9

Source: Naidu, R., Sumner, M. E., & Rengasamy, P. (1995). *Australian sodic soils*. East Melbourne, Australia: CSIRO.

sufficient to dissolve and leach excess salts out of the soil into groundwater and eventually the ocean. Some saline soils occur along humid seacoasts where seawater inundates the soil.

The importance of salinization can be illustrated by the large areas soils that are enriched in salts throughout the world. (See table 1.) Fully one-quarter to one-third of the world's 1.5 billion hectares currently under cultivation are saline or sodic, a statistic that demonstrates the impact of salinization on world food production. Salinity is most problematic in cultivated soils that are irrigated. Irrigated lands with large areas of saline and sodic soils include Australia, India, Pakistan, Russia, China, the United States, the Middle East, and Europe. In some nations, salts seriously affect more than 50 percent of irrigated lands. Salinization will be a major problem for successfully doubling to tripling food production in the coming decades.

Reclamation of Saline and Sodic Soils

Salinization is an insidious problem, and early soil symptoms are often ignored. To control salinization and maintain irrigation-based agriculture over the long term requires soil analysis and careful monitoring of water and salt budgets (amounts) of local fields to river-basin scales. Such monitoring provides the technical basis for remedial action.

To diagnose soil salinity problems, soil samples are rinsed with water, and the water's electrical conductivity is measured. The soil water's conductance is linearly related to the concentration of soluble salts. The conductance at which the growth of many plant species is diminished by salts is well established. Sodium problems are also diagnosed from the ratio of the soil sodium to calcium.

Leaching with high-quality (dilute) water can potentially rid a soil of its salinity problems, but the reclamation of sodic soils is not straightforward. Because elevated sodium tends to disperse soil clays and greatly reduce the rate at which water moves through soil, the ratio of soil sodium to calcium needs to be decreased if sodium leaching is to be effective. Calcium, especially in the form of gypsum, tends to aggregate or flocculate clays, allowing sodium to be dissolved and to leach through the soil-rooting zone. Reclamation of sodic soils may, however, require large amounts of gypsum, sometimes several thousand kilograms per hectare. Gypsum additions can be costly, especially if the only sources of irrigation water have high sodium and salinity.

Reclamation of salt-affected soils requires a suitable system of disposal. In many cases the drainage is too brackish (salty) to be directly recycled. Moreover, in contemporary agricultural systems, drainage effluents also contain other constituents such as fertilizer nutrients, sediments, and pesticides, all of which may influence disposal. Nonetheless, irrigation effluents are often simply exported to streams or rivers, a practice that salinizes and pollutes the local water supplies. Receiving streams will become progressively saltier, and lower reaches may become unfit as a water supply for humans, animals, or crops. Adverse effects on aquifers and estuaries are direct and potentially serious. Improving the efficiency of water and salt budgets of irrigated lands is one of the highest priorities for contemporary agronomy (the branch of agriculture dealing with field-crop production and soil management).

Salinization Historically

Salinization affected the first great agricultural societies such as the Sumerian and Akkadian cultures,

Salt-affected soils on rangeland in Colorado. Salts dissolved from the soil accumulate on the ground and at the base of the fence post. National Resources Conservation Service (NRCS).

societies that developed on the alluvial soils of the Tigris and Euphrates Rivers. The region was initially developed into extensive agricultural fields with irrigated grain, forage, and palm production in the southern reaches of these rivers. Complex canal systems served both for transportation and irrigation, cities were built, and civilization flourished. Over time the irrigated lands shifted significantly northward along these rivers, a pattern frequently explained by a salinity-affected decline in agriculture in the south. Archeological records of the Sumerian civilization suggest that grain production also shifted over the centuries from the -preferred but salt-sensitive wheat to salt-tolerant barley.

The history of salinization in ancient Egypt contrasts greatly with that in Mesopotamia. Salt budgets and timing of annual floods along the Egyptian terraces of the Nile are much more conducive to long-term management than terrace soils of the Tigris and Euphrates. Alluvial soils along the Nile are relatively narrow and well drained, except in the Nile's delta. The Nile's river channel tends to be deeply incised along much of its course, ensuring that the rise and fall of the river affects relatively large fluctuations of the groundwater under river terraces. The Nile's agricultural resources are generally considered to be nearly ideal, given the particular combination of high-quality water, relatively predictable flooding, soil fertility, nutrients, and organic matter. Salinization

has not developed into an acute problem along the Nile, and irrigation-based cropping has continued for about five millennia.

Salinization has stressed other agricultural civilizations in the past. One of the largest of these developed in the Indus River valley of Asia, approximately coincident in time with ancient Sumeria. The area of Indus irrigation systems apparently exceeded those in ancient Egypt and Sumer. Relatively few records exist for these Indus civilizations, although several excavations partly tell their tale (at Harappa, for example). Although archeologists suggest that catastrophic floods, earthquakes, and soil erosion wore down these ancient civilizations, salinization was also probably a major problem. In the twentieth century, salinization greatly stresses irrigation-based agriculture which has spread across nearly 15 million hectares of the Indus River valley.

Historical patterns of salinization in Australia's enormous Murray-Darling River basin are also instructive, given the ample documentation of the effects of land-use history on contemporary soils and agro-ecosystems. Although the basin covers about 15 percent of Australia's total area, it provides far more than this percentage of the nation's agricultural production, much of which is supported by irrigation. Since European settlement began in earnest by the mid-nineteenth century, extensive areas of deeply rooted *Eucalyptus* forests have been cut over and converted to relatively shallow-rooted annual crop systems, an ecosystem transformation that has reduced plant transpiration (the use of water by plants) and allowed a larger fraction of annual precipitation to percolate through soil and elevate local groundwater systems. Because the underlying groundwater is saline, substantial quantities of soluble salt have been mobilized into the upper soil and root zone. Evapotranspiration (loss of water from the soil both by evaporation and transpiration from plants) concentrates salts, and about 500,000 hectares of the Murray-Darling River basin are estimated to have saline groundwater within 2 meters of the soil surface. Australians refer to these circumstances as "secondary" salinization (i.e., human affected), reserving the term *natural salinization* to describe naturally occurring saline soils that occur in association with salt lakes in drier regions of the continent or adjacent to estuaries.

Salinization in the Future

Irrigated land today totals approximately 0.3 billion hectares of the 1.5 billion hectares of total cultivated land. About 35 percent of total crop output is currently derived from irrigated systems, a percentage that is expected to increase. Between the 1960s and the late 1990s irrigated land increased at the rate of about 3 percent per year. Five nations account for about two-thirds of the irrigated area: China, India, Pakistan, Russia, and the United States. Other nations dependent on irrigated systems include Egypt, Indonesia, Iraq, Jordan, and Israel. All indications are that in the future, irrigation management of water and salts will be increasingly important because global agricultural production is so dependent upon irrigation. The challenge, however, is that contemporary management of irrigated systems is far less than optimal and in fact presents serious concerns for the future. Several examples illustrate the challenges.

The extensive modern irrigation system along the Indus River, mainly in Pakistan, is one of the major agricultural regions of the modern world. Alluvium and associated native groundwater reservoirs are deep in this great basin, which drains the western Himalayas. Nearly 15 million hectares were under irrigation by the mid 1990s, with the length of irrigation watercourses, farm channels, and field ditches estimated to exceed 1.5 million kilometers. Early in the development of this massive system, saline groundwater tables were observed in the rooting zone of many fields, and by the 1960s a massive drainage project was launched that by the 1990s had benefited about one-third of the entire system. Currently, between 2 and 5 million hectares of irrigated fields are adversely affected by salts. Keeping this system operational will require an incredible continuity of effort, especially because the Indus drainage channels have such low elevation gradients (e.g., about a 0.02 percent gradient), which must transport water many hundreds of kilometers to the ocean outlet.

In modern Egypt the challenges of controlling salinization in irrigated agro-ecosystems have become similarly serious. From ancient times to the beginning of the nineteenth century, the human population of the Nile River valley totaled several million people, most of whom were supported by the river's irrigation-based agriculture. Through most of this past, Egypt was able to export enormous amounts of food, a situation that is no longer the case. Modern Egypt has now about 60 million inhabitants, a total that is expected to grow to 90 to 100 million by 2030. Along with rising agricultural imports, Egypt is placing enormous demands on its irrigated soils for domestic food production. The Aswan High Dam, constructed in the 1960s, established management control over the Nile's flood flows and thereby expanded opportunities for irrigation. On the other hand, with river flow controlled, the seasonality of river flow no longer regularly and flushes soils of salts. Particularly in the alluvial soils of the great Nile Delta, salts have grown to be an increasingly common problem. Future expansions of irrigation agriculture along with highly engineered drainage projects to control salts are widely contemplated.

Future problems with salinization are hardly confined to irrigated lands. Natural cycles of rainfall in arid and semiarid climates can be associated with expansion and contraction of saline and sodic soils.

The saline ecosystems of Amboseli National Park in Kenya at the foot of Mt. Kilimanjaro provide a celebrated and much debated example. From the 1950s on, the vegetation of much of the Park has markedly changed from forested savannahs with *Acacias* to a landscape more dominated by salt-tolerant grasses and shrubs with only occasional trees. A long-standing hypothesis for the ecosystem transformation has been that when regional rainfall increased through the 1960s, highly saline groundwaters rose into the root zone of *Acacia*-dominated savannas, causing widespread tree decline. Whether or not the transformation of the Amboseli is explained by salinization, the Amboseli serves as an outstanding example of how future climate change in the decades and centuries ahead may affect salt balances and salinization across wide areas and thereby the structure and function of natural ecosystems.

Daniel D. RICHTER Jr.
Duke University

See also Agricultural Societies; Harappan State and Indus Civilization; Water; Water Management

Further Reading

Allison, G. G., & Peck, A. J. (1987). Man-induced hydrologic change in the Australian environment. *Geoscience, 87,* 35–37.

Ayers, R. S., & Wescot, D. W. (1976). *Water quality for agriculture* (FAO Irrigation and Drainage Paper No. 29). Rome: United Nations.

Buol, S. W., & Walker, M. P. (Eds.). (2003). *Soil genesis and classification* (5th ed.). Ames: Iowa State Press.

Dales, G. F. (1966). The decline of the Harappans. *Scientific American, 214,* 92–100.

Hillel, D. J. (1991). *Out of the earth.* New York: Free Press.

Holmes, J. W., & Talsma, T. (Eds.). (1981). *Land and stream salinity.* Amsterdam: Elsevier.

Lal, R. (1998). *Soil quality and agricultural sustainability.* Chelsea, MI: Ann Arbor Press.

Naidu, R., Sumner, M. E., & Rengasamy, P. (1995). *Australian sodic soils.* East Melbourne, Australia: CSIRO.

Rengasamy, P., & Olsson, K. A. (1991). Sodicity and soil structure. *Australian Journal of Soil Research, 29,* 935–952.

Richards, L. A. (Ed.). (1954). *Diagnosis and improvement of saline and alkali soils* (Agricultural Handbook No. 60). Washington, DC: United States Department of Agriculture.

Singer, M. J., & Munns, D. N. (2002). *Soils: An introduction.* Upper Saddle River, NJ: Prentice Hall.

Soil Survey Staff. (2001). *Keys to soil taxonomy.* Washington, DC: United States Department of Agriculture.

Sparks, D. L. (1995). *Environmental soil chemistry.* San Diego, CA: Academic Press.

Western, D. (1997). *In the dust of Kilimanjaro.* Washington, D.C.: Island Press.

Wolman, M. G., & Fournier, F. G. A. (Eds.). (1987). *Land transformation in agriculture.* New York: John Wiley and Sons.

Yaalon, D. H. (1963). On the origin and accumulation of salts in groundwater and soils of Israel. *Bulletin Research Council Israel, 11G,* 105–113.

Timber

Timber, or lumber, is wood that is used in any of its stages—from felling through to processing—in the production of construction materials, or as pulp for paper. Timber has been a resource around the world for many centuries in the craft and construct of all manner of objects and utensils, from dwellings to ships to tables to toothpicks.

Since the Neolithic revolution, timber, with its many uses, has been an important commodity in the development of social life. Throughout human history from at least 3000 BCE onward, available forests have been used to meet the needs of an evolving world. Starting from the early urban communities, such as Egypt, Mesopotamia, and Harappa, timber has been a constant feature of economic life. Timber in its many forms has been used as a source of fuel and as a basic material for building construction, shipping, and for storage purposes, such as barrels). In addition to these uses, timber was important to other aspects of human activity, such as in manufacturing and for the extraction of other resources such as coal and ore (timber beams were used in shoring up mine shafts). The level of timber utilization grew in proportion to increases in urbanization, commerce, and population. The increasing size of urbanized communities and growth in population often led to the need to transport resources to feed the growing population centers of the ancient world. Shipping was the normal mode of transportation of these resources. With growing levels of trade, the increase in maritime shipping resulted in further timber consumption. Exuberant lifestyles also developed, leading to the construction of extravagant buildings, such as palaces

and temples, which often required timber for their construction.

These tendencies were pronounced as long as 4,500 years ago. In the riverine valleys of Mesopotamia and the Indus, the Mesopotamians and the Harappans deforested their own hills and mountains, and conducted military campaigns and trade relations with their neighbors to secure a regular wood supply in order to meet their economic needs. The Egyptians, for example, sought timber in neighboring areas of Lebanon and parts of the Syrian coast.

Timber utilization on a similar scale also was practiced in other parts of the world. About 2500 BCE in

Cutting timber in Washington State, 1898. New York Public Library.

201

northern China around the Hwang Ho river basin and in Southeast Asia timber was sought to meet socioeconomic needs. The use of wood intensified as the urbanization process progressed globally, with hinterland areas supplying the wood needs of the more economically transformed civilizations, empires, and nation-states. During different time periods, certain areas of the globe were effectively the wood yards of other regions. For example, the North American forests and those of the Baltic shores provided the timber supply for northwestern Europe in the mid-seventeenth century. By the late twentieth century, parts of Africa, Asia, Latin America, northern Europe, and Russia became the main timber sources.

With the advent of agriculture and the urban revolution, deforestation has been a constant feature for at least the last 5,000 to 6,000 years. It is literally as old as the hills. This level of deforestation reached epic proportions by the end of the twentieth century. The size of the world's forests has shrunk by nearly half from 6 billion hectares 8,000 years ago to 3.6 billion hectares presently. According to the World Commission on Forests and Sustainable Development, forests have virtually disappeared in twenty-five countries, eighteen others have lost more than 90 percent of their forests, and eleven countries have lost around 90 percent. In an attempt to slow deforestation and to help reduce the environmental impact of cutting trees for timber, some states and timber producers have planted special plantations of fast-growing trees specifically so they can be cut for timber. When the trees are felled, new saplings are planted in endeavor to make plantation timber environmentally sustainable. Selective logging of mature trees in a forest of mixed age is another method of combating deforestation.

There is common agreement that deforestation has consequences for human communities. Negative outcomes such as soil erosion and the climatic changes that we are witnessing also occurred in the past. The "modern" problems of soil erosion leading to flooding and silting of rivers and canals also occurred in early Mesopotamia and had a severe impact on economic production. The effects of soil erosion and its consequences also appeared in northwestern India, China, Mycenaean Greece, and Minoan Crete, engendering pressures on these societies and civilizations. Deforestation also has engendered climate changes and precipitation. The removal of the forests cools the lower atmosphere while warming the ground surface. The reduction of evapotranspiration

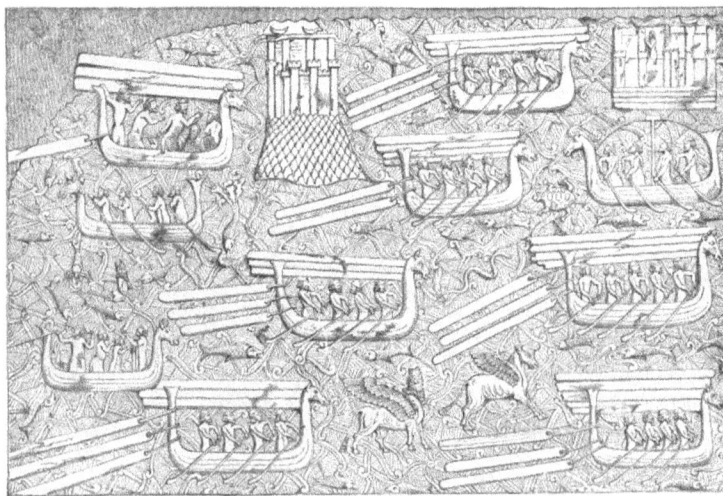

An illustration of Aramaic bas-relief sculpture from Assyria depicts ships transporting timber, both aboard and towed by rope. New York Public Library.

Out of timber so crooked as that from which man is made nothing entirely straight can be carved. • **Immanuel Kant (1724–1804)**

causes aridity. Forest loss also means that there is a reduction in carbon sequestration as the trees fix carbon and metabolize carbon compounds. This loss exacerbates the process of global warming. Recent studies have suggested that this process has been an ongoing for at least 6,000 years following the spread of agriculture that had facilitated the removal of the forests.

Sing C. CHEW
Humboldt State University

See also Climate Change; Deforestation; Trees

Further Reading

Chew, S. C. (2001). *World ecological degradation (accumulation, urbanization, and deforestation) 3000 bc–ad 2000.* Walnut, CA: Alta Mira Press.

Perlin, J. (1989). *A forest journey.* Cambridge, MA: Harvard University Press.

Marchak, P. (1995). *Logging the globe.* Kingston, Canada: McGill/Queen's University Press.

Williams, M. (2003). *Deforesting the earth.* Chicago: University of Chicago Press.

World Commission on Forests and Sustainable Development. (1999). *Our forests, our future.* New York: Cambridge University Press.

Trees

Trees are vastly older than the human species, and the study of trees is itself a vast subject. With its focus on human/tree interaction through the ages, this article considers trees as objects of human veneration, as sources of food or obstacles to agriculture, and as wildlife whose "behavior" is affected by human actions.

Trees evolved some 360 million years ago, long before the humans whose cultures venerated them throughout history for spiritual or aesthetic reasons. Human interactions, however, from the earliest hunter-gatherers in the forests of the Paleolithic, have posed threats to forests and woodlands. Today the most serious involves the "mixing up" of diseases and pests from one part of the world to another.

Trees before Humans

Trees are wildlife. They have existed for very much longer than people. Over 360 million years ago they evolved their own diverse agendas in life before they ever knew human contact. There are now tens of thousands of species of trees, each doing its own thing. All trees form partnerships with fungi, and many with ants and pollinating insects and birds. Different species grow from the tropics to the fringes of the arctic. Some grow in forests, some in savannas (grassland with scattered trees). Some are eaten by animals, some are distasteful or poisonous; animals evolved in turn to depend on trees in a multitude of ways, from the super-elephants that could break down and devour a big tree to the primates (forerunners of humanity) and birds that live on tree fruits and seeds. Some trees will burn and sustain forest fires (many trees depend on fire for their continued existence or propagation); others are incombustible. Some grow from seed, others from root sprouts.

In the last two million years, climatic changes of the ice ages, which rendered much of the world's land area incapable of growing trees, disrupted this story of gradual change and adaptation. Trees found themselves having to make do with environments into which accidents of history thrust them.

Trees before Farmers

Next appear the hominids (other species of mankind) followed by the human species itself. In Africa, their land of origin, people probably dwelt in savannas, but over tens of thousands of years they came to inhabit both forests and the treeless landscapes of cold or dry climates. Humanity at this stage—small numbers of hunter-gatherers—would have interacted with trees in four ways:

1. Tree fruits and other products presumably formed part of the human diet; thus Mesolithic people took advantage of the nuts in the vast extent of hazel woodland in Britain.
2. People developed tools for felling small trees, which provided firewood and the material for wooden artifacts. (The name Stone Age is misleading because the stone tools that have survived were probably far less numerous than the wooden objects that have not been preserved.) As yet, the quantities involved would have been insignificant in comparison with the growth-rate of trees.
3. Wherever savanna or forest happened to be flammable, people used fire in land management,

manipulating the vegetation in favor of those animals and plants that they preferred.

4. Early humanity was probably responsible for exterminating the super-elephants and other living bulldozers, which survive in an attenuated form in Africa. In turn this would favor the growth of trees.

Arguably, the last two examples represent the greatest effects that the human species has had (until now) on the world's vegetation. Whether Paleolithic and Mesolithic people interacted with trees in cultural and spiritual ways, and whether this made any difference to the trees themselves, it is impossible to say.

Trees before Metals

Further interactions came within the last 10,000 years. After the last ice age, trees returned to northern countries like Britain; traditionally they are thought to have generated a continuous "primeval forest," which in practice may have been more savanna-like, with areas of grassland. Then people acquired the Neolithic arts of farming, keeping livestock and growing crops, building permanent houses, and indulging in pottery, temples, graveyards, and all the trappings of settled civilization. These were invented separately in various parts of the world and spread slowly almost throughout the globe, except in Australia.

In temperate climates trees are the farmer's enemy, because arable crops will not grow in shade. Common domestic animals require open grassland. They live in forests only in small numbers: they eat the low vegetation and when that is gone they starve. Hence farming began in savanna or grassland, since cultivation of forested lands required a great investment of effort in digging up trees and making fields. This is documented with European settlement in America; presumably it happened also in northern Europe in Neolithic times, but without the metal tools and labor-saving devices available to settlers in historic times.

In the tropics, matters would have been somewhat different because some tropical crops grow in shade and some of the trees themselves have edible fruit. So forests were not necessarily destroyed but sometimes converted to orchards and cultural savanna.

At this stage if not earlier, people made the momentous discovery that some trees sprout from the stump or roots when cut down, and the resulting

Jean-Pierre Houël, *Castagno dei cento cavalli* [The Chestnut Tree of One Hundred Horses] (1782). Gouache. Located 8 kilometers from Mt. Etna's crater, this is the oldest known chestnut tree in the world. According to legend it sheltered a queen of Aragon and her company of a hundred knights when caught in a thunderstorm during a trip to the mountain.

If you reveal your secrets to the wind, you should not blame the wind for revealing them to the trees. • **Kahlil Gibran (1883–1931)**

poles are more useful than the original tree-trunk. Thus woodland management originated, of which the first certain evidence comes from the Neolithic of the Somerset Levels in England, some five thousand years ago. People could (with difficulty) fell forest giants, but big trees of most species have only one use before the invention of power tools—making dugout boats. The human population, although increased from hunter-gatherer times, was still too few to have more than a local effect merely by cutting down trees.

Thus began the characteristic ways in which settled people influence forests:

1. Digging up trees in order to use the land for farming.
2. Cutting down trees in order to use the timber or wood, either for carpentry or as firewood (including fuel for making pottery).
3. Managing the remaining woodland in order to produce a permanent supply of trees small enough for one or two men to handle.
4. Exterminating or reducing many of the wild herbivorous animals.
5. Replacing wild beasts with domestic livestock, often in large enough numbers to hold back the regrowth of felled trees.
6. Moving tree species around the world, for example the cultivated apple, brought to Britain by the Romans from its native Kazakhstan.

From small beginnings in the Neolithic these spread around the globe. It has been claimed that even in prehistory the reduction in forests was sufficient to have a significant effect on the carbon dioxide content of the atmosphere. However, the land area involved seems too small to account for the known carbon dioxide anomaly—unless, perchance, the equation needs to include the efforts of Australian Aborigines and American indigenous populations in preventing forests from overrunning the vast areas of savanna in those continents.

A less familiar use of trees is pollarding or shredding, that is, cropping the branches to provide leaves on which to feed livestock. This began in the Neolithic, as cattle and sheep were introduced into forested regions that lacked grassland. It still continues in parts of the world where the growing season for grass is brief. Trees so treated are often very long-lived and grow into characteristic shapes.

Trees before Intercontinental Travel

In later prehistory uses of trees multiplied, especially in those cultures that invented metals. Bronze and iron made it easier to cut down trees and also greatly increased the need for fuel to smelt and work metals. The Romans had an abundance of fuel-using activities—baths, brickmaking, glassmaking, as well as domestic heating and making throwaway pots. Increasing population as well as developing technology multiplied the demands on the woods. Only locally, however, was mere human labor yet sufficient to cut down trees faster than they could grow again. It was possible to transport and work great trees for exceptional purposes, such as the roof timbers of Solomon's Temple in Jerusalem, but this was a rare achievement: in most cultures trees small enough to handle were the stuff of everyday uses.

By late prehistory humanity had come to affect virtually all the world's mainland forests and savannas, at least by interfering with the relation between trees and herbivorous animals and (where applicable) by altering the frequency of fire. Islands such as those of the Mediterranean, which already had native mammals, were probably not much affected by human settlement; but particularly devastating was the later effect of introducing goats and pigs to oceanic islands like St. Helena, where the vegetation was not adapted to any sort of land animal. The last large areas without human contact were Madagascar and New Zealand, reached by humanity around 2,000 and 800 years ago. The world's very last "virgin forests," unaffected by humanity, were probably on some remote island in the eighteenth century.

Agriculture gradually spread from its homeland in the sparsely tree'd regions of southwestern Asia into the much more wooded and less congenial regions of Europe. Even now, little is known of how, still less why, forests were converted into farmland. Although arable farming in Italy was well developed from the Neolithic onward, even in imperial Roman times the great city of Rome transported most of its food supply from North Africa, leaving Italy to supply most of its timber and fuel.

England followed an apparently unusual pattern with its high density of population. By the Iron Age (the last few centuries BCE) most of the wildwood had given way to farmland or moorland, and the pattern of the modern countryside was already developing. Domesday Book, a survey of 13,418 English settlements commissioned by William the Conqueror in 1085), gives uniquely detailed statistics of a landscape in which only 15 percent of the area was woodland, less than France has now. This was reduced still further, to only about 6 percent by 1349, when the Black Death put an end to increasing population.

Woodland conservation probably originated from the need to maintain a continuous supply of smallish trees, but gained a further impetus as woods acquired scarcity value (i.e., the less of a commodity in existence, the more it is worth). In England many woods mentioned in medieval documents are still there today; they are recognizable by their distinctive names and shapes, by banks and ditches protecting the boundaries, the massive bases of coppice stools (trees that have been felled and have grown again and again), and special plants that do not spread into recent woodland.

Trees also grew in hedges and other non-woodland situations to supply timber and underwood. Orchard culture developed from Roman times onward in Europe and independently in other continents.

International trade in timber—both precious timbers like Cretan cypress and ordinary timber—became significant in the Middle Ages. England, the Netherlands, and Spain drew increasing quantities of pine and oak from the Baltic: not merely because they had insufficient woodland of their own, but because the exporting countries had developed equipment and skills for processing trees.

Destruction of forests to create farmland and pasture was not a one-way process. Trees grow very easily provided they are left alone. Whenever land was abandoned through pestilence or slave-trading or because people discovered an easier way to make a living, woods returned or savanna turned into forest. Thus in England many of the great wooded areas of the Middle Ages contain remains of farms, settlements, and monuments of prehistory or Roman times.

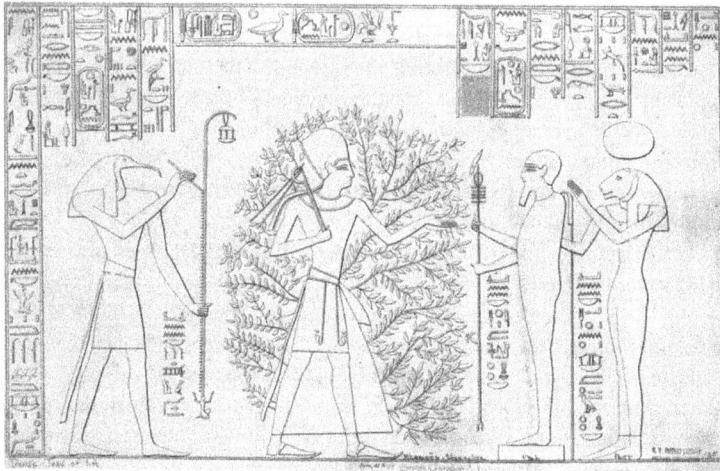

Ramses and the Tree of Life, a nineteenth-century illustration, depicts an Egyptian mural painted circa 1330 BCE. New York Public Library.

Cultural and Spiritual Qualities of Trees

Ethnographers have described a vast diversity of relations between people and trees other than the physically utilitarian, ranging from the overtly spiritual (a tree as the home of a god) to the purely aesthetic (a tree providing a "splash of color" in a formal garden).

Veneration and love of trees are characteristic of a very wide range of separate human cultures, but largely lack a time-dimension unless there are written records. The exact part played by the trees is often ill defined, since travelers who were half-informed about (or hostile to) another culture were often the ones to record information about it. Whether trees played any part in the ancient designs of Stonehenge or Angkor Wat is difficult to say unless remains of the trees themselves survive. Archaeologists are seldom perceptive in detecting and recording surviving trees among the ruins of ancient sites.

Individual trees have been widely venerated as the home of minor gods, as with the sacred trees in the ancient city of Rome, or the innumerable sacred trees (of many species) in the Shinto religion of ancient and modern Japan. Conversely, all the trees of a particular species, or big trees in general, may be venerated. Many religions have sacred groves surrounding temples and shrines, or in which rites and ceremonies are enacted. Particular species may play a part in celebrations, like laurel in the triumphs of ancient Rome, holly at Christmas, and palms (or some northern substitute for palms) on the Christian Palm Sunday.

Monotheistic religions celebrate specific sacred trees, at least unofficially. Jews, Muslims, and Christians venerated "Abraham's Oak," at Hebron in Palestine. England has its ancient churchyard yews, some dating from the early centuries of Christianity. In Wales, ancient yews are associated with the saintly hermits of the first millennium CE.

Trees in parks and gardens—other than fruit trees—are a feature of many cultures. The sacred groves of the ancient Greeks, like those of Buddhist temples and Shinto shrines in modern Japan, could range from natural woodland to formal gardens. The ancient Romans set up secular parks and planted trees in them, preserving as well the existing trees. How far this applies to other monumental cultures that have no written records is difficult to say.

Urban trees vary enormously. Most towns and cities of the Middle Ages were small and closely packed, seldom with room for many trees, apart from trees on sacred sites embedded in the city or on flood plains. With more diffuse fashions in town planning from the eighteenth century onward, urban trees became a normal feature, to the point that many European and American cities now have more trees than the surrounding countryside.

Appreciation of ancient and distinctive individual trees is widespread in human cultures, but is not universal. In England, ancient trees were preserved as giving an air of respectable antiquity to a new country-house park: this veneration ebbed in the mid-twentieth century but has since revived with renewed interest in "veteran trees." Notable ancient trees occur in the Mediterranean, especially olives and chestnuts. In Japan, ancient trees are venerated as memorials to past emperors, are preserved even when dead, and are imitated in miniature in the craft of bonsai. Most ancient trees are monuments to cultural activities such as pollarding or orchard culture.

Trees also have medicinal and magical uses in many cultures, although not to a greater extent than other plants. Well-known examples are quinine bark as a treatment for malaria, or the British naturalist Gilbert White's account of the "shrew-ash," a tree used for treating the ailment of cattle supposedly caused by shrews running over them.

Trees in the Age of Machinery

The seventeenth to twentieth centuries saw further technological development. Many inventions had begun in a small way in the Middle Ages, but now were employed on a much larger scale and taken to woods in distant parts of the globe.

Discovery and colonization let loose European-style agriculture on other continents. Destruction of forest and savanna to make farmland, which in

Europe had taken thousands of years, was compressed into decades in America and Australia. Even well into the twentieth century much of this was still done by multitudes of axe men and oxen, followed by special "stump-jump" machinery for cultivation.

Woods increased in other countries, especially where the ground was too infertile or too steep for mechanized farming. In eastern North America in the nineteenth century and in the Mediterranean in the twentieth, huge areas have reverted to forest.

Shipbuilding had previously had a local influence on woodland. But as ships got bigger and more numerous, went to distant continents and spent long periods rotting in tropical waters, and as European navies indulged in arms races, timber shipbuilding increased until for a short period (1800–1860) it was a major influence on European woodland and even affected tropical forests.

In the nineteenth century international trade turned intercontinental as North American pines and tropical hardwoods were widely used in Europe. People developed technologies for felling and converting big trees. Sawmills, another medieval invention, became more widespread and bigger until (with the help of railways) a use was at last found for rain-forest giants. In what was presented as a triumph of technology, the giant trees of the Pacific coast of the United States, of southwestern Australia, and of the more accessible parts of the tropics were converted into railway sleepers, fence posts, and paving blocks.

Forestry plantations—or areas of trees for timber—were invented in medieval Germany and independently in Japan. From then on it became possible (in theory) to grow trees for specific uses—assuming that those uses would still exist by the time the trees had grown. There have been several attempts at planting trees on a huge scale in dry countries, in the belief that this would restrict the spread of deserts. In the nineteenth century plantations became the staple of modern forestry; German or French forestry ideals and practices were imposed on countries like India and later Britain, marginalizing local practices and skills. By the late twentieth century native forests were being destroyed and replaced by plantations, in countries like Chile and Tasmania, on a scale that gives rise to great concern among conservationists. There is a risk that natural forests will become confined to steep slopes, nature reserves, and other areas beyond the reach of machinery.

Ancient management practices were neglected. In England competition from the increasing use of coal, transported by railways to rural areas, led to woods being abandoned as sources of fuel. Japan, like England, took to plundering other countries' wildwood for timber supplies while neglecting its own woods.

Forests and savannas are threatened by the effects of humanity on mixing up all the world's animals and plants. A famous example is the frivolous introduction of the grey squirrel from North America to Britain, where it has multiplied to an extent which threatens the very existence of some indigenous trees; it has also reduced the native red squirrel to near-extinction.

This applies to plants also. Why is it so easy to destroy tropical rainforest? Felling the marketable trees might not matter much: the redwood forests of Pacific America have grown again (although they have probably not recovered all the plant and animal life of the original forest). When trees are felled now, however, the site is often taken over by one of the giant "elephant-grasses" from another part of the tropics; these interfere directly with the regrowth of the trees, and also are very flammable, introducing fire to forests that previously did not have it and are not adapted to it.

Climate change has some effect. Tropical forest trees are growing faster than before, possibly in response to increased carbon dioxide in the air. Trees confined to mountaintops, as with some tropical cloud-forests and the "sky islands" of the southwestern United States, are threatened because they have nowhere to go in the face of warming climate. But the most significant effect of global warming is probably where trees have been introduced into places where they do not withstand increasingly hot summers, as with some beech and spruce plantations in England.

In the late twentieth century big game increased in many parts of the world to the point where plant and bird life, and even the existence of woods is threatened. England now has more deer than for over a thousand years, and more species of deer than ever before: deer eating woodland have become the top conservation problem. The same happens in much of North America, partly because hunters demand artificially huge numbers of deer to shoot, and even in Japan.

Probably the greatest threat to the world's trees and woods is the effect of twentieth-century humanity in mixing up all the world's pests and diseases. In the state of Ohio, in less than a hundred years, chestnut, most elms, many oaks, flowering dogwood, and fir have been removed, each by its accidentally introduced European or Asian fungus parasite. This leaves ash as the commonest remaining tree; the United States has spent millions of dollars in a vain attempt to keep out an Asian insect that destroys it. Such a story can be repeated in many other countries. At this rate, how much will be left in another hundred years?

Oliver RACKHAM

Corpus Christi College, Cambridge, United Kingdom

See also Biological Exchanges; Deforestation; Diseases—Plant; Nature; Timber

Further Reading

Cronon, W. (1983). Changes in the land: Indians, colonists, and the ecology of New England. New York: Hill & Wang.

Fairhead, J. & Leach, M. (1998). *Reframing deforestation*. London: Routledge.

Frazer, J. G. (2007[1890]) *The golden bough: A study in magic and religion*. Charleston, SC: Biblio Bazaar.

Grove A. T. & Rackham, O. (2001) *The nature of Mediterranean Europe: An ecological history*. New Haven, CT: Yale University Press.

Juniper, B. E. & Mabberley, D. J. (2006). *The story of the apple*. Portland, OR: Timber Press.

Kirby, K. J. & Watkins, C. (Eds.). (1998). *The ecological history of European forests*. Wallingford, U.K.: CAB International.

Pakenham, T. (2002). *Remarkable trees of the world*. London: Weidenfeld & Nicholson.

Rackham, O. (2006). *Woodlands*. London: Harper Collins.

Rackham, O. (2008). Ancient woodlands: Modern threats. *Tansley Review, New Phytologist, 180*, 571–586.

Ruddiman, W. F. (2005). *Plows, plagues and petroleum; How humans took control of climate*. Princeton, NJ: Princeton University Press.

Williams, M. (1989). *Americans and their forests*. Cambridge, U.K.: Cambridge University Press.

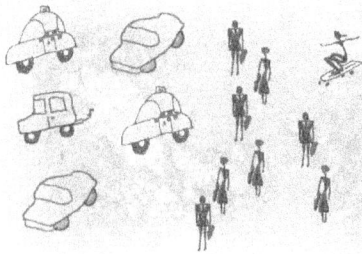

Water

Water is essential for life. In addition to consumption, water is used for travel, power generation, hygiene, recreation, agriculture, industry, ritual, and more. While water covers about three-quarters of the Earth's surface, less than 2 percent of it is fit to drink. Access to water continues to play a crucial role in the location and movement of peoples and communities.

Water covers nearly 75 percent of the Earth's surface and is an integral component of every living being. Fresh water is essential for human survival; while a person can live for weeks without food, one can only survive a few days without water. Throughout history, the location of available water has played an important role in human development and influenced settlement patterns and farming, social customs, religion, transportation, and power generation.

Settlement

The availability of fresh water for human and animal consumption and crop irrigation has influenced human settlement for many millennia. Even though water covers much of the Earth's surface, less than 2 percent of it is potable. While many different peoples have learned to adapt to harsh or unforgiving environments, water from natural springs, rivers, or rainfall is a necessity for survival. During the early history of humans, the availability of water played an important factor in their survival strategy.

During the Neolithic Age, hunters and gatherers stopped migrating, built permanent dwellings, and became farmers and herdsmen. When they chose a site to build their towns, it was usually near an available water source, such as a river or lake. One of the oldest towns, Catalhuyuk in Turkey, serves as a model for these early Neolithic sites. Catalhuyuk, which was established around 7500 BCE, was located very close to several standing bodies of water, and archaeologists believe water was available near the town all year round. Its farmlands appear to be several kilometers farther away from the town than the water supply, underscoring the importance of easy access to water. This model can also be seen at other Neolithic sites, like Choirokoitia in Cyprus, which dates to 7000 BCE.

As the population steadily increased during the period from the Neolithic Age to the Iron Age, settlements began appearing in areas where water was not readily available in large quantities or was not available throughout the year. To survive in these regions, humans had to find ways to adapt their survival strategy to provide enough water to sustain life. One of the most widely practiced solutions was to collect water during times when it was plentiful for use at a later time when it was scarce. Different cultures found various ways to accomplish this. In Greece, Italy, and Mesopotamia, the farmers relied on winter rains to provide enough rainfall to allow summer "drought farming." The winter rains provided enough water that farmers could successfully grow crops with minor modifications to their schedule. They would plant their crops in the early spring while the soil was still well watered from the winter rains and harvest them in the early summer before all the moisture was lost from the soil due to warm and arid summer weather patterns. Inhabitants in these regions relied on natural springs and rainwater collected in large cisterns

People socialize while drawing water from the community well in a village in India. Photo by Klaus Klostermaier.

to ensure an adequate drinking-water supply for the summer and fall months.

In Arabia, the Nabataeans used a system of rock-cut channels and pipes to collect rainwater for storage in underground cisterns, which were lined with waterproof cement. In Egypt, the Nile provided water for irrigating fields, and the annual flooding of the river deposited new soil on the fields and prevented soil depletion. In the Hellenistic Age, an elaborate system of irrigation ditches was implemented to expand the amount of cultivable land. This irrigation system continued to develop and expand through the Roman, Byzantine, and Islamic periods.

In ancient Persia farmers developed the underground irrigation systems known as *qanat*s as early as the first millennium BCE as a method for delivering water to their crops. A *qanat* was an underground enclosed canal that collected groundwater in the mountains and carried it to fields in low-lying areas using gravity. Along the length of the *qanat*, shafts would be placed at regular intervals to allow access to the water channel for cleaning and repair. *Qanat*s often involved extensive engineering, were up to 40 kilometers in length, and were buried up to 100 meters below the surface. This system of irrigation was adopted by the Arabs and Byzantines. There are more than forty thousand known *qanat*s in Iran with many still in use today.

Collecting and storing water for long periods often created a new problem when the water became impure or collected sediment. Many ancient civilizations developed techniques for purifying stored water in an attempt to produce better drinking water. Ancient Sanskrit writings dating to 2000 BCE describe different methods for purifying water by boiling or using sand or charcoal for filtering out impurities. Egyptian tomb paintings depict a device for filtering water that allowed sediment and other impurities to settle to the bottom of a collection device, allowing the clear water to be collected from the top.

While farmers needed to live near water sources for crop irrigation, as cities grew larger they also needed water for the sustenance of their citizens and for maintaining sanitary conditions in the city. Cities depended upon engineers to design systems for delivering water from its source across many miles to its final destinations in the city. Both Rome and Constantinople developed impressive aqueduct systems for bringing water to numerous baths, fountains, and private houses. During the third century CE, Rome had nine functioning aqueducts, which provided over 3 million gallons of water each day to the city. The longest of these aqueducts was more than 95 kilometers in length. The beginning of the aqueducts was simply a channel cut into the earth with a slight downward gradient that used gravity to move the water toward Rome. As the aqueduct left the hills and approached the city the water channel was carried on raised arches, often more than thirty meters above ground. These channels were 1 meter wide and 1.8 meters high so that workers could enter the channel for cleaning. Three of the aqueducts are still functioning today.

Social Aspects

Water has also played an important role in social customs. Bathing was an important ritual in ancient Greece and Rome. Public baths became common in Greece starting in the fifth century BCE. Adopted by the Romans, bathing became an important social aspect of everyday Roman life by the first century CE, and an important center for social interaction between citizens. Every town would have at least one public bathing structure, and houses of wealthier citizens would have private baths. These bathing complexes would have rooms with differing water temperatures: cold water, tepid, and hot water baths. Larger complexes even had large swimming pools. As the Roman Empire expanded in the second and third centuries CE, these complexes became more and more elaborate with vaulted ceilings, glass windows, exotic artwork, and intricate plumbing systems. The baths built by the Roman emperor Caracalla (Marcus Aurelius Antoninus) in 217 CE could accommodate over 1,600 bathers at

the same time. These bathing complexes were an important tool for the spread of Roman culture and ideas throughout the empire. Bathing is still an important aspect of some modern cultures like Japan and Finland.

Religion

In ancient Greece and Rome, water was an important element in religious rites. Natural springs were considered powerful locations and often became cult worship sites. Along with fire, water was used as a purification element in birth, marriage, death, and sacrificial ceremonies. The idea of water as a tool to purify or remove evil is reinforced by the numerous flood stories from around the globe that recount how god(s) cleansed the Earth of evildoers and made a fresh start with a chosen one, such as Noah in the Old Testament, Deucalion in Greek mythology, Utnapishtim in the *Epic of Gilgamesh,* or the East African story of Tumbainot.

In Greek philosophy and cosmology, water was considered to be one of the four basic elements of the universe in addition to fire, air, and earth. The pre-Socratic philosopher Thales of Miletus, writing in the late fifth century BCE, believed the principal element of all things was water, and everything else in the universe was a creation of water.

In Zoroastrianism, cultivation of the soil was praised and any action that promoted culti-

Paolo Uccello, *Flood and Waters Subsiding* (1447–1448). The fresco, in Santa Maria Novella in Florence, illustrates the Old Testament story of Noah and the ark.

Humans throughout history traveled waterways large and small as they explored and settled the Earth. In this early-twentieth-century photo, a traveler and his guide raft down the Amazon River in South America.

vation was encouraged. This motivated the Sasanian kings who ruled Persia (modern-day Iran) from the third to seventh centuries CE to build dams and extensive irrigation systems.

In early Christianity, water was seen as a symbol of purification and life. In Byzantine church liturgy, the blessing of the water was an important ritual and was believed by the church leaders to commemorate Jesus Christ's baptism by John the Baptist. Water remains an important purifying element in modern religions. In many modern Christian sects, baptism (either by sprinkling or immersion) in water to wash away earthly sin is an initiation rite of the faith. In Islam, believers wash their hands, arms, feet, and head to cleanse themselves before praying. Judaism also uses water to purify believers and to cleanse them after coming into contact with unclean items, such as a dead body.

Transportation and Empires

With so much of the Earth covered by water, boats have been a necessity for exploration and travel.

Travel via water transport, until modern times, has been faster and less expensive than travel overland. The edict issued by the Roman emperor Diocletian in 301 BCE, which was designed to control maximum prices, provides historians with enough information to formulate standard costs of transportation during this period. The document shows transporting goods overland cost between 30 and 50 percent more than sending them by boat. Travel time was also significantly less, provided the weather was favorable.

As commerce increased, merchants and nations tried to find ways to increase the speed and capacity of ships. This led to the development of the carrack and caravel, ship types that could carry larger cargoes and sail faster and required fewer sailors. Another method of shortening the time of sea travel was the creation of canals that linked major bodies of water, eliminating circumnavigation. This led to the building of the Grand Canal (486 BCE), Erie Canal (1825 CE), Suez Canal (1869), Corinthian Canal (1893), Panama Canal (1914), and Rhine-Danube Canal (1992).

Cities or nations whose citizens became skilled at seamanship or building boats were able to capitalize on this and create large empires, commercially or militarily. By the eighth century BCE, the Phoenicians were able to create a trading network that included the entire Mediterranean Sea and as a result spread Phoenician culture to many different regions. The success of the Phoenicians was repeated on a smaller scale by the Venetians in the Mediterranean and the Hanseatic League in the Baltic Sea in the thirteenth and fourteenth centuries CE.

Cultures that relied on overseas transportation for their commercial goods often developed a strong navy to protect their commercial interests. In the fifth century BCE, the city-state of Athens was able to use its strong maritime presence in the Aegean to create the Athenian Empire. In the fifteenth century CE, England was able to use the development of its mercantilist policies to create both a strong merchant marine and a strong navy. England was able to use its naval power to further its political policies abroad and build up an empire that spanned the globe.

Water Power

Water has also been used to drive machines and create energy. One of the earliest inventions was a waterwheel that used falling or flowing water to drive a shaft that would then turn the mill. Ancient Greeks and Romans were the first to use water-wheels to power mills for grinding grain into flour, and this practice continued through the medieval period.

With the development of a successful steam engine in the early eighteenth century, the use of water-wheels declined. In the United States during the eighteenth and nineteenth centuries, waterwheels were used to supply power to sawmills, grain mills, and textile factories. In 1882 the first power plant that derived its energy from water was constructed in Wisconsin. By the early 1940s hydroelectric power provided nearly 40 percent of U.S. energy consumption. Today, Canada, New Zealand, Norway, Switzerland, and Sweden depend heavily upon hydroelectric power.

Water in the Twenty-First Century

Since the mid-1980s many nations have come to realize that water is not a limitless commodity and that steps have to be taken in order to protect this valuable resource for future generations. In the twenty-first century several key water issues have emerged. First, as the world's population increases, more countries are unable to meet the increased demand for drinking water. Second, industrialization leads to increased pollution, which further decreases the amount of available drinking water. Third, continued urbanization and deforestation have led to increased flooding and soil erosion. Fourth, as countries look to augment their existing water supply, conflicts over water sharing, particularly of international rivers, have increased. Increased public awareness about these important environmental issues has resulted in the formation of international agencies that are attempting to solve these problems and implement water resource management plans.

While access to clean water is an increasing concern, it is thought that there is currently enough water for everyone. The problem is the inefficient and ineffective management of water resources. As such, every year millions of people die from waterborne diseases because of their lack of essential access to a clean water supply. Some of the possible remedies to water shortages and inequities include recycling and redistribution.

R. Scott MOORE
Indiana University of Pennsylvania

See also Desertification; Oceans and Seas; Rivers; Salinization; Water Energy; Water Management

Further Reading

Beaumont, P., Bonine, M. E., & McLachlan, K. (1989). *Qanat, kariz, and khattara: Traditional water systems in the Middle East and North Africa.* London: School of Oriental and African Studies.

Crouch, D. P. (1993). *Water management in ancient Greek cities.* Oxford, U.K.: Oxford University Press.

de Villiers, M. (2001). *Water: The fate of our most precious resource.* New York: Mariner Books.

Gischler, C. E. (1979). *Water resources in the Arab Middle East and North Africa.* Cambridge, U.K.: Middle East and North African Studies Press.

Goubert, J.-P. (1989). *The conquest of water: The advent of health in the Industrial Age* (A. Wilson, Trans.). Princeton, NJ: Princeton University Press.

Guillerme, A. E. (1988). *The age of water: The urban environment in the north of France, a.d. 300–1800.* College Station: Texas A&M University Press.

Hodge, A. T. (1992). *Roman aqueducts and water supply.* London: Gerald Duckworth.

Horden, P., & Purcell, N. (2000). *Corrupting sea: A study of Mediterranean history.* Oxford, U.K.: Blackwell.

Kandel, R. (2003). *Water from heaven: The story of water from the Big Bang to the rise of civilization, and beyond.* New York: Columbia University Press.

Oleson, J. P. (1984). *Greek and Roman mechanical water-lifting devices.* Dordrecht, The Netherlands: D. Reidel.

Outwater, A. (1997). *Water: A natural history.* New York: Basic Books.

Pearce, F. (2007). *When the rivers run dry: Water—the defining crisis of the twenty-first century.* Boston: Beacon Press.

Pisani, D. J. (1996). *Water, land, and law in the West: The limits of public policy, 1850–1920.* Lawrence: University of Kansas Press.

Potts, D. T. (1997). *Mesopotamian civilization: The material foundations.* Ithaca, NY: Cornell University Press.

Raikes, R. (1967). *Water, weather, and prehistory.* New York: Humanities Press.

Reynolds, T. S. (1983). *Stronger than a hundred men: The history of the vertical water wheel.* Baltimore: Johns Hopkins University Press.

Schoppa, R. K. (1989). *Lakes of empire: Man and water in Chinese history.* New Haven, CT: Yale University Press.

Shaw, R. E. (1990). *Canals for a nation: The canal era in the United States, 1790–1860.* Lexington: University Press of Kentucky.

Solomon. S. (2010). *Water: The epic struggle for wealth, power, and civilization.* New York: Harper.

Smith, N. (1977). *Men and water: A history of hydro-technology.* New York: Charles Scribner's Sons.

Squatriti, P. (1998). *Water and society in early medieval Italy, ad 400–1000.* Cambridge, U.K.: Cambridge University Press.

Ward, D. R. (2002). *Water wars: Drought, flood, folly, and the politics of thirst.* New York: Penguin Putnam.

Yegul, F. (1992). *Baths and bathing in classical antiquity.* New York: Architectural History Foundation.

Water Energy

Mechanical (kinetic) energy of flowing or falling water was traditionally converted to rotary motion by a variety of waterwheels, and, starting in the 1880s, by water turbines that have been used to turn generators. Unlike fossil fuels, this form of electricity generation does not produce air pollution directly, but its other environmental impacts have become a matter of considerable controversy.

I t is not known by how many generations or centuries the origins of waterwheels predate the first reference to their existence by Antipater of Thessalonica, who wrote during the first century BCE about their use in grain milling. A millennium later such simple devices were common in parts of Europe: in 1086 the *Domesday Book* listed 5,624 mills in southern and eastern England, one for every 350 people. The usual arrangement was to channel flowing water through a sloping wooden trough onto wooden paddles, often fitted to a sturdy shaft that was directly attached to a millstone above. Vertical waterwheels, first mentioned by Vitruvius in 27 BCE, were much more efficient. All of them turned the millstones by right-angle gears, but they were propelled in three distinct ways.

Wheels and Turbines

Undershot wheels were driven by kinetic energy of moving water. As doubling the speed boosts the capacity eightfold, they were preferably located on swift-flowing streams. The best designs could eventually convert 35–45 percent of water's kinetic energy into useful rotary motion. Breast wheels were powered by a combination of flowing and falling water and operated with heads between 2 and 5 meters. Overshot wheels were driven primarily by the weight of descending water and hence could be located on streams with placid water flows. With heads over 3 meters their conversion efficiencies were commonly in excess of 60 percent with peaks of up to 85 percent. Wheels, as well as shafts and gears, were almost completely wooden until the beginning of the eighteenth century; hubs and shafts were the first iron parts and the first all-iron wheel was built early in the nineteenth century.

Besides the wheels fixed in streams there were also floating wheels on barges and tidal mills and common uses of waterwheels eventually expanded far beyond grain milling to power machines ranging from wood saws and oil presses to furnace bellows and forge hammers, and to mechanize manufacturing processes ranging from wire pulling to tile glazing. Even as their uses widened, capacities of waterwheels remained limited, averaging less than 4 kilowatts in early eighteenth-century Europe. Post-1750 innovations led to a rapid increase of individual capacities as arrays of waterwheels, sometimes rating in excess of 1 megawatt (one megawatt equals one thousand kilowatts), became the leading prime movers of expanded mass manufacturing in Europe and North America. In 1832, Benoit Fourneyron's invention of the reaction turbine ushered in the era of much more powerful water-driven machines. James B. Francis designed an inward-flow turbine in 1847, Lester A. Pelton patented his jet-driven turbine in 1889, and Viktor Kaplan introduced his axial flow turbines in 1920.

Energy can be generated from hydroelectric dams. Here power lines carry electricity generated from a river.

Hydroelectricity

The first water turbines were used merely to replace waterwheels as the prime movers in many industries, but by the late 1880s the machine began to be coupled with generators to produce electricity. The first American hydroelectric plant was built in 1882 in Wisconsin. More than century later, water turns turbines that supply almost 20 percent of the world's electricity. In dozens of tropical countries, water power is the dominant means of electricity production.

Most of the world's hydro energy remains to be tapped. Worldwide total of economically feasible hydro generation is over 8 petawatt-hours (PWh, that is 1015—one quadrillion—watt-hours) or roughly three times the currently exploited total. Europe has the highest share of exploited capacity (more than 45 percent), Africa the lowest (below 4 percent). The greatest boom in construction of large dams took place during the 1960s and 1970s, with about five thousand new structures built per decade.

Advantages and Drawbacks

The air pollution advantage of hydropower is the most obvious one: if coal-fired power plants were to generate electricity that is currently produced worldwide by running water, the global emissions of carbon dioxide and sulfur dioxide would be, respectively, 15 percent and 35 percent higher. Hydrogeneration also has low operating costs, and its spinning reserve (zero load synchronized to the system) in particular is an excellent way to cover peak loads created by sudden increases in demand. Moreover, many reservoirs built primarily for hydrogeneration have multiple uses—serving as sources of irrigation and drinking water, as protection against flooding, and as resources for aquaculture and recreation. But during the closing years of the twentieth century, large dams were widely seen as economically dubious, socially disruptive, and environmentally harmful.

Displacement of a large number of usually poor people has been the most contentious matter. Construction of large dams dislocated at least 40 million people during the twentieth century (some estimates go as high as 80 million), and during the early 1990s, when the work began on three hundred new large dams began every year, the annual total reached 4 million people. China and India, the two countries that have built nearly 60 percent of the world's large dams, had to relocate most people: more than 10 million in China and at least 16 million in India. Large hydro projects also have a multitude of undesirable environmental impacts, and recent studies of these

A hydroelectric dam on the Connecticut River between Vermont and New Hampshire, seen through the mist of the rushing water.

previously ignored changes have helped to weaken the case for hydrogeneration as a clean source of renewable energy and a highly acceptable substitute for fossil fuels.

Perhaps the most surprising finding is that large reservoirs in warm climates are significant sources of greenhouse gases emitted by decaying vegetation. Water storage behind large dams has increased the average age of river runoff and lowered the temperature of downstream flows. Several of the world's largest rivers have reservoir-induced aging of runoff exceeding six months or even one year (Colorado, Rio Grande del Norte, Nile, Volta). Many tropical reservoirs create excellent breeding sites for malaria mosquitoes and for the schistosomiasis-carrying snails, and most dams present insurmountable obstacles to the movement of migratory fish. Multiple dams have caused river channel fragmentation that now affects more than three-quarters of the world's largest streams.

Other environmental impacts caused by large dams now include massive reduction of aquatic biodiversity both upstream and downstream, increased evaporative losses from large reservoirs in arid climates, invasion of tropical reservoirs by aquatic weeds, reduced dissolved oxygen and hydrogen sulfide toxicity in reservoir waters, and excessive silting. The last problem is particularly noticeable in tropical and monsoonal climates. China's Huang (Yellow) River, flowing through the world's most erodible area, and India's Himalayan rivers carry enormous silt loads. Silt deposition in reservoirs has effects far downstream as it cuts the global sediment flow in rivers by more than 25 percent, and reduces the amount of material, organic matter, and nutrients available for alluvial plains and coastal wetlands downstream, and hence increases coastal erosion.

The ultimate life span of large dams remains unknown. Many have already served well past their designed economic life of fifty years but silting and structural degradation will shorten the useful life of many others. As a significant share of the Western public sentiment has turned against new hydro projects, some governments took action. Sweden has banned further hydrostations on most of its rivers, and Norway has postponed all construction plans. Since 1998, the decommissioning rate for large U.S. dams has overtaken the construction rate. Major hydro projects of the twenty-first century will thus be built only in Asia, Latin America, and Africa.

Vaclav SMIL
University of Manitoba

See also Water; Water Management

Further Reading

Devine, R. S. (1995). The trouble with dams. *The Atlantic Monthly, 276*(2), 64–74.

In the world there is nothing more submissive and weak than water. Yet for attacking that which is hard and strong nothing can surpass it. • **Laozi (sixth century** BCE**)**

Gutman, P. S. (1994). Involuntary resettlement in hydropower projects. *Annual Review of Energy and the Environment, 19*, 189–210.

International Hydropower Association. (2000). *Hydropower and the world's energy future.* London: IHA.

Leyland, B. (1990). Large dams: Implications of immortality. *International Water Power & Dam Construction, 42*(2), 34–37.

Moxon, S. (2000). Fighting for recognition. *International Water Power & Dam Construction, 52*(6), 44–45.

Reynolds, J. (1970). *Windmills and watermills.* London: Hugh Evelyn.

Shiklomanov, I. A. (1999). *World water resources and water use.* St. Petersburg: State Hydrological Institute.

Smil, V. (1994). *Energy in world history.* Boulder, CO: Westview.

Smil, V. (2003). *Energy at the crossroads.* Cambridge, MA: The MIT Press.

World Commission on Dams. (2000). *Dams and development.* London: Earthscan Publisher.

Water Management

Water has many essential uses, including in agriculture, industry, recreation, and domestic consumption, most of which require fresh water (as opposed to saltwater). Only 3 percent of Earth's water supply is fresh, and most of that is frozen. While fresh water is a renewable resource, supply is limited while demand is increasing. This requires careful management of existing water resources.

Land-based life on Earth revolves around sweet (nonsalty) water. Domesticated plants require a regular and sufficient supply of sweet water. People must manage this water resource; they also must manage the supply of sweet water for humans, for domesticated animals, and for manufacturing.

Most of the surface of our planet is water, but most of it is too salty for use by organisms living on land. But the hydrological cycle (the sequence of conditions by which water passes from vapor in the atmosphere through precipitation onto land or water surfaces and back into the atmosphere) provides a continuous supply of sweet water in the form of rain and snow. After precipitation hits the ground it either runs off on the surface, as rivers and other streams, or soaks into the soil. From the point of view of a farmer cultivating fields in a fixed place, the water environment is sweet, with water running on the surface, water in the top layer of the soil (soil water), and water deeper underground (groundwater).

As is true for most life processes, an ideal amount of water exists for the farmer. The environmental supply of water is variable, however, fluctuating from place to place and from time to time on daily, monthly, and yearly schedules. Combining the need for an ideal amount of water with the unending fluctuation yields three kinds of conditions: about right, too much, and too little. "About right" rarely occurs.

Water has several physical characteristics that are relevant for managing a farm. First, water is liquid and flows easily. Thus all water responds to gravity and naturally flows downhill. It always takes the shortest possible route. Water is easy to move if a downhill path can be found. But because water is a liquid, a sealed container must be used if a person wants to lift it. Second, water is heavy. Lifting it requires not only a sealed container but also considerable energy. Third, water is an excellent solvent. One of the major functions of water in the life of the green plant is to dissolve nutrients (from the soil) and transport them into the plant, but water can also dissolve poisons (including salts). Fourth, water can carry many solid particles in suspension. Erosion of the landscape by running water transports such solid particles downstream.

The farmer wants sweet water for plants in the right amounts, at the right times, moving at the right speeds, and containing the right components (dissolved, suspended). Irrigation is the technology that increases the water supply to plants, and drainage is the technology that reduces the water supply to plants.

The major energy sources for moving water are gravity, human muscle, animal muscle, wind, and heat engines (mechanisms, such as internal combustion engines, that convert heat energy into mechanical or electrical energy). For irrigation we supply water at a high point, and for drainage we remove it at a low point.

221

The dam at Simatai in March 2004. This Great Wall tourist location to the far north of Beijing is an example of the Chinese commitment to dam building.

Irrigation

The elements of a canal irrigation system are an intake, where ditches tap into a water source; a main canal (sometimes many kilometers long); and a series of branch canals that deliver water to the farmer's fields. Movable gates may control water flow into the branch canals, or the system may be designed so that water flows in every channel simultaneously.

The ditches move the water from the source to the fields. The technology for digging these ditches is simple and has been invented virtually everywhere. People use digging sticks, shovels made of wood, and hoes made of stone to loosen the dirt. Such tools are old and widespread. People use baskets to move the loosened dirt. Because water responds so quickly to gravity, people can easily test whether a ditch has the right slope and change the slope if they have made errors.

Most irrigation systems are what we call "run of the river," meaning that the water available to them is what is in the river (the source) at the time. The construction problems are obvious (water must flow downhill, dirt must be moved), and the solutions have been invented many times. A significant problem with irrigation systems is variation in environmental moisture. For example, a drought can reduce a river's water supply to a trickle, posing a threat to crops.

One solution to such variation is to store water in a reservoir; however, water storage was quite rare in early world history. The city of Jawa in the Jordanian desert had a storage dam by about 4000 BCE. Tank irrigation systems that stored water behind a small dam were widespread in southern and southeastern Asia by the first millennium BCE. Roman engineers built many small storage dams of masonry, but these dams may have been meant for domestic use rather than for irrigation. An early dam in the Americas was the Purron Dam in Mexico, dated to about 800 BCE. That dam was made of earth and at its maximum was 19 meters tall. The dam was in operation for approximately one thousand years and could store more than 3 million cubic meters of water. Purron was one of only two storage dams known to have existed in the highland area of Mexico. Since the late nineteenth century people have built many massive storage dams in most parts of the world. Machinery and modern materials—and a plentiful supply of money—have been central to these efforts.

Early irrigation systems built with simple tools were probably widely distributed. Their existence is difficult to document because all subsequent irrigation systems in the same place used the same routes for the ditches. Thus researchers have difficulty finding and dating the earliest occurrence. Scholars, however, think they have evidence of irrigation early in all of the world's civilizations. Irrigation may have existed during Neolithic times as well. The tools to build such systems were already available, as was the social organization. Only so many effective designs of an irrigation system exist, and they have existed around the world during all time periods.

Drainage

Drainage systems are the reverse of irrigation systems. Irrigation systems move large amounts of water to the top of the fields, and then break it down into smaller and smaller packages for distribution to fields. Drainage systems collect small amounts of water at many places high up in the system, combine these small amounts into larger and larger channels, and collect the total at the bottom of the field system. The problem then is where to put the drainage water; if it accumulates it can flood the lower fields. The drainage water so collected is eventually put into a large body of water (a river, the ocean), and often people can use gravity to put it there. Gravity works well as an energy source, and ditches again are used to channel the water. Another technology for draining water is tile pipes. The pipes, with holes in them, are installed in ditches in the fields and then covered up. The lower end of the pipes must drain into something, usually a riverbed. Tile pipes are effective and virtually invisible to all but the most discerning eye.

Another way to drain water is to dig dirt out of a swamp and pile it up so that the top is above the water level, producing what are often called "raised fields." These fields can vary in size from a few square meters at the edge of a swamp to thousands of hectares. Among the earliest water management systems using raised fields were in highland New Guinea, dated to about 5000 BCE.

Lifting Water

Because of water's weight and liquid nature, people had difficulty lifting water for many millennia. People used human muscle to lift small amounts of water in pots to water individual plants in the Valley of Oaxaca, Mexico, about 2000 BCE. In Egypt they could lift larger amounts with the *shadoof* (a beam on top of a pole with a counterweight at one end and a container for the water on the other end). Human muscle powered the *shadoof*. Wells (vertical shafts from the surface down to the water table) have been dug for a long time, but extracting large amounts of water has been difficult. People have used large domesticated animals to power the raising of larger amounts of water, but the output has not been substantial.

In the dry mountain belt from Turkey to western China, horizontal wells (called *qanat*s or *foggara*) were widespread. A shaft was dug from the point of use (often an oasis) into a mountain, gently sloping upward, until the shaft met with water-bearing earth. Then a vertical shaft was dug down to the horizontal shaft to remove dirt and to gain access for repairs. Horizontal wells could exceed 60 kilometers in length. They could provide water for centuries if properly maintained.

The first major innovation that increased people's ability to lift water was the windmill, which became prominent in northwestern Europe during the thirteenth century. The Dutch reclaimed low land from the sea by building protective dikes, and they then drained the water out of the low land behind the dikes. They ganged together large windmills to lift the water out of the low land and dump it into the sea or a river outside the dikes. The height to which water could be raised was limited, however, and the windmills could operate only when the wind was the right speed.

With the advent of the heat engine during the Industrial Revolution the limits on lifting water were eliminated. One of the first tasks given to steam engines was to drive pumps that drained water from flooded coal mines. Later uses included pumping drainage water out of a basin and lifting water for irrigation. Water could be lifted from a surface source (such as a river or lake) or from a deep well. Today a great deal of irrigation water is acquired from deep underground; this could not be done without the heat engine to drive a pump.

With the introduction of the internal combustion engine, small pump and driver (an engine that powers the pump) sets became feasible, even to the point that farmers could own such sets and move them around the farm to where they were needed. Although such sets save labor, they are expensive in terms of energy.

A modern innovation in irrigation technology is the pressurized system. Two major forms are used: sprinkler systems and drip systems. In sprinkler systems a pump and driver pressurize water, which is then moved through a series of pipes that is above the level of the plants that are to be irrigated. These pipes have multiple nozzles, and the water distribution mimics light rain. There are two major advantages of this system: (1) water use is much more efficient (more than 90 percent of the water reaches the crop root zone; by contrast, ditches have efficiency as low as 50 percent), and (2) no need exists to sculpt the surface of the soil, thus saving labor and energy. A small computer can operate a number of these sprinkler systems, saving even more labor. These systems also can deliver chemicals (fertilizers, pesticides) in the water. The major disadvantage is that the technology is energy intensive. Sprinkler systems are used throughout much of the world; people flying at 10,000 meters in an airplane can see the green circles made by a rotary sprinkler system.

The other form of pressurized system is drip irrigation. Developed mainly in Israel (where the need to conserve water is great), drip irrigation uses long hoses with holes in them that are buried in the root zone. Water is forced through the hoses and exits the hoses through the holes. Fertilizer and pesticides can be added to the water, thus delivering them directly to the root zone. These systems are even more efficient than sprinkler systems, approaching zero-percent water loss, and they save on the labor to apply fertilizer and pesticide. A major disadvantage is the cost in energy to run the system. Another disadvantage is that the holes in the pipes can clog, which requires that the hoses be exposed; this means excavating them, with possible damage to the crops.

Water Management in History

People have used irrigation systems and drainage systems to manage water for thousands of years and have built and operated such systems without writing and without scientific laboratories. The relationship between water stress (too much, too little) and the health of a green plant is obvious to most observers. People can use simple tools, easily made, to loosen and move dirt to dig ditches. A modern scientific understanding of water, green plants, soil, solutions, the hydrological cycle, and photosynthesis began during the nineteenth century and is still generating knowledge. People needed instruments (microscope, thermometer, balance) and the disciplines of physics, chemistry, anatomy, and physiology to achieve the scientific knowledge that we now have.

The impact of irrigation and drainage on world history has been great. Irrigation and drainage permit people to grow crops where otherwise it would be difficult or impossible. The growing of crops in turn permits a larger, denser population. These technologies have been important in the birth of cities and have played a role in economic surplus, full-time division of labor, metal tools, astronomy, and eventually other sciences. But people also built and operated water management systems for millennia in areas that did not necessarily establish cities and acquire writing (such as New Guinea in the Malay Archipelago and the Hohokam people in Arizona).

Irrigation and drainage change the water balance of the landscape, and along with agriculture they change the plants and animals there. In order to safely grow domesticated plants and animals, people often have wanted to eliminate native plants and especially animals that are dangerous. Entire landscapes have been changed in ways that we could call domestication. At the same time, however, we have provided habitats for small, dangerous life forms that generate and carry diseases, such as malaria. The blessings are mixed.

The simple tools and knowledge needed to build and operate irrigation systems and drainage systems exist everywhere, and traditionally there was little variation in the forms of such systems. With the

Multiple hand-built terraces and rice paddies in the Nepal Middle Mountains east of Kathmandu are a remarkable feat of engineering; the irrigation system demonstrates how indigenous peoples prove to be outstanding soil conservationists. Photo by Jack D. Ives.

Industrial Revolution, however, European colonial powers built large storage dams during the nineteenth and twentieth centuries. Storage dams were not new, but the scale of them was. The practice of lifting water with heat engines diffused widely. Today people everywhere use heat engines linked to pumps, replacing traditional systems. Significantly, the technology is also manufactured just about everywhere.

The Future

The future of water management is unclear. World population is growing, and such growth will increase the demands for food and space for buildings. A substantial portion of the world's food is now grown with irrigation, and this portion will only increase in the near future. An easy way to gain space to build is to drain wetlands. With industrial technology and (cheap) energy, we have the technical capacity to build and operate large water management systems.

But the best places for storage dams have already been taken, and finding new sources of water will be increasingly difficult. The draining of wetlands has significant environmental consequences. Industrial populations are voracious users of water (for toilets, manufacturing, mining, irrigation, recreation, etc.), and thus pressure to limit the amount of water that farmers can use is growing. Multiple uses of sweet water (for navigation, recreation, biological diversity) grow in number and in intensity. No clear way exists to solve the water problems that occur in nearly every nation. One technical solution is to increase the efficiency of our water use, and science and technology will be crucial in that solution. The problems are not just technical ones—the beliefs and expectations of the consumers of water are also relevant and far less understood than are the properties of dirt, plants, and water.

Robert C. HUNT
Brandeis University

See also Desertification; Oceans and Seas; Rivers; Water Energy

Further Reading

Adams, R. M. (1966). *The evolution of urban society: Early Mesopotamia and prehispanic Mexico.* Chicago: Aldine.

Butzer, K. W. (1976). *Early hydraulic civilization in Egypt: A study in cultural ecology.* Chicago: University of Chicago Press.

Childe, V. G. (1951). *Man makes himself.* New York: New American Library.

Denham, T. P., Haberle, S. G., Lentfer, C., Fullagar, R., Field, J., Therin, M., Porch, N., & Winsborough, B. (2003). Origins of agriculture at Kuk swamp in the highlands of New Guinea. *Science, 301,* 189–193.

de Villiers, M. (2001). *Water: The fate of our most precious resource.* New York: Mariner Books.

Doolittle, W. E., Jr. (1990). *Canal irrigation in prehistoric Mexico: The sequence of technological change.* Austin: University of Texas Press.

Gumerman, G. (Ed.). (1991). *Exploring the Hohokam: Prehistoric desert peoples of the American Southwest.* Albuquerque: University of New Mexico Press.

Hall, A. R., & Smith, N. (Eds.). (1976). *History of technology: Vol. 1. From early times to fall of ancient empires.* London: Mansell.

Helms, S. W. (1981). *Jawa, lost city of the desert.* Ithaca, NY: Cornell University Press.

Hills, R. L. (1994). *Power from wind: A history of windmill technology.* Cambridge, U.K.: Cambridge University Press.

Hunt, R. C. (2002). Irrigated farming. In J. Mokyr (Ed.), *Oxford encyclopedia of economic history* (Vol. 3, pp. 165–168). Oxford, U.K.: Oxford University Press.

Scarborough, V. L. (2003). *The flow of power: Ancient water systems and landscapes.* Santa Fe, NM: School of American Research.

Service, E. R. (1975). *Origins of the state and civilization: The process of cultural evolution.* New York: W. W. Norton.

Wikander, O. (Ed.). (2000). *Handbook of ancient water technology.* Leiden, The Netherlands: Brill.

Wilkinson, T. J. (2003). *Archaeological landscapes of the Near East.* Tucson: University of Arizona Press.

Wittfogel, K. (1957). *Oriental despotism.* New Haven, CT: Yale University Press.

Wind Energy

Sails were one of the first inventions to convert wind energy into motion, and windmills have been used since the tenth century to harness the power of the wind for grain milling and water pumping. In the early twenty-first century, wind is the fastest growing renewable energy source, forecasted to provide 20 percent of the world's electricity by the year 2040.

O nly a small portion of incoming solar radiation (less than 2 percent) powers the atmospheric motion. The combination of diurnal and seasonal changes of insolation (exposure to sun's rays) and of differential heating of surfaces (vegetated vs. barren, land vs. water) mean that wind frequencies and velocities range from prolonged spells of calm to episodes of violent cyclonic (rainstorms, tornadoes, hurricanes) flows. Sail ships, used by the earliest civilizations of the Old World, were undoubtedly the first converters of wind energy into useful motion. And before the end of the twentieth century, one of the world's oldest energy sources has become one of the most promising modern providers of renewable energy as wind-generated electricity has been the fastest growing segment of modern renewable energetics.

The first written record of windmills comes a millennium after the first mention of water wheels: al-Masudi's report of 947 CE notes the use of simple vertical-shaft windmills in Seistan (in today's eastern Iran) to raise water for irrigating gardens. The first European record comes only from the closing decades of the twelfth century. Subsequent development of windmills was uneven in both time and space.

Windmills and Their Uses

The earliest vertical designs were used basically unchanged for many centuries in the Near East, as were the horizontal European machines. These mills pivoted on a massive central post that was supported usually by four diagonal quarterbars, and the whole engine house had to be turned to face the wind. Post mills were unstable in high winds and vulnerable to storm damage, and their low height limited their efficiency. Still, unlike China and India, where wind power made historically little difference, post mills became a major source of rotary motion in Atlantic Europe.

As with watermills, grain milling and water pumping (the Dutch drainage mills being the most prominent examples of this application) were the most common applications of wind power. Other common uses included grinding and crushing, papermaking, sawing, and metalworking. Post mills were gradually replaced by tower mills and smock mills. Only the top cap of these machines had to be turned into the wind, and after 1745 the English introduction of the fantail made it possible to turn the sails automatically. The fantail catches the wind bearing away from the sails and it turns the cog ring at the top of the tower until the sails are returned square on to the wind. More than a century before this innovation the Dutch millers introduced the first relatively efficient blade designs that provided more lift while reducing drag. But true airfoils, aerodynamically contoured blades with thick leading edges, were introduced in England only by the end of the nineteenth century.

America's westward expansion on the windy Great Plains created demand for smaller machines to pump

Windmill on Hay Ground Hill, Long Island, New York (1922). Windmills of this traditional design, unchanged for centuries, were most often used for grain milling and water pumping. Photo by Eugene L. Armbruster, New York Public Library.

water for steam locomotives, households, and cattle. These windmills were made of a large number of fairly narrow blades or slats that were fastened to solid or sectional wheels, and they were usually equipped with independent rudders and either the centrifugal or the side-vane governor.

Windmills reached the peak of their importance during the latter half of the nineteenth century: in 1900 about thirty thousand machines with a total capacity of some 100 megawatts worked in countries around the North Sea, and the U.S. sales of smaller brands of American windmills amounted to millions of units during the second half of the nineteenth century.

Wind Electricity

Many machines that continued operating in the twentieth century were connected to generators to produce electricity for immediate household use and for storage in lead-acid batteries. Gradual extension of electricity networks ended this brief era of wind-generated electricity and little research and even less field testing on converting wind into useful energy was done until the early 1970s, when the Organization of Petroleum Exporting Countries (OPEC) suddenly quintupled the price of crude oil, reigniting the interest in renewable energies.

Modern Wind-Driven Electricity Generation

The first modern boom in wind energy was launched by U.S. tax credits during the early 1980s. By 1985 the country's wind turbines had installed capacity of just over 1 gigawatt, and the world's largest wind facility (637 megawatts) was at Altamont Pass in California. Low load factors, poor turbine designs, and the expiration of tax credits in 1985 ended this first wind wave. Better turbine designs, with blades optimized for low speeds, and larger turbine sizes have led the expansion that began around 1990. The average size of new machines rose from a mere 40–50 kilowatts in the early 1980s to over 200 kilowatts a decade later, and today's typical sizes in new, large wind farms are 1–3 megawatts (one megawatt equals 1 million watts, or one thousand kilowatts). Germany, Denmark, and Spain have been the leaders of this expansion. New laws that guarantee a higher fixed price for wind-generated electricity have been essential, and the Danish government has been particularly active in promoting wind power: the country now has the highest per capita installed capacity, and it dominates the world export market in efficient wind turbines. Germany is the world leader in absolute terms, and by 2007 Europe had about 60 percent of the globally installed wind capacity.

Wind-generating capacity in the United States rose from 1 gigawatt (1 billion watts) in 1985 to 2.5 gigawatts by the end of 2000, and it reached 20 gigawatts by September 2008. Global capacity of wind turbines reached 1 gigawatt in 1985, 10 gigawatts in 1998 (equal to nuclear plants in 1968), and 17.4 gigawatts in 2000, and then it grew rapidly to 59.1 gigawatts

I was born on the prairies where the wind blew free and there was nothing to break the light of the sun. I was born where there were no enclosures. • **Geronimo (1829–1909)**

by 2005 and to nearly 94 gigawatts by 2008. As a result wind-driven electricity generation is seen as the most promising of all new renewable conversions, far ahead of other solar-based techniques both in terms of operational reliability and unit cost. Some experts argue that at the best windy sites, even unsubsidized wind electricity is already competitive with fossil-fueled generation, or even cheaper than coal or gas-fired production, and hence we should go for a more aggressive maximization of wind's potential. Some plans foresee 20 percent of the world's electricity demand generated by wind by the year 2040, and 20 percent of America's electricity coming from wind by 2030. That is not a modest goal considering that in the year 2000 wind generation produced just 1 percent of the country's electricity.

Available resource is no obstacle to even the boldest dreams. Only about 2 percent of all solar energy received by Earth is needed to drive the atmospheric motion, and if a mere 1 percent of this flux could be converted to electricity, the global capacity would be some 35 terawatts (one terawatt equals 1 trillion watts), or more than ten times the 2000 total installed in all fossil, nuclear, and hydro stations.

A much more restrictive estimate that considers only wind speeds above 5 meters per second up to 10 meters above ground puts the global wind power potential at about 6 terawatts, or about 350 times larger than the total installed in 2000. The main problems associated with tapping this potential result from the fact that wind is unevenly distributed in both space and time.

Many windy sites are far away from centers of electricity consumption, and many densely populated areas with high electricity demand experience long seasonal periods of calm or low wind speeds and hence are utterly unsuitable, or only marginally suited, for harnessing wind's energy. Virtually the entire southeastern United States, northern Italy, and Sichuan Province (China's most populous province) are in the latter category. Wind's intermittence means that it cannot be used for base-load generation. Its fluctuations are only imperfectly predictable, and peak wind flows only rarely coincide with the time of the highest demand. Inevitably, these realities complicate efficient commercial utilization. The visual aspect of siting large turbines and building connection and transmission lines is another concern. Offshore

A wind farm in California. These modern-day windmills are used to generate electricity. Photo by Kevin Connors (www.morguefile. com).

siting of wind turbines should help to minimize or eliminate these impacts.

Vaclav SMIL
University of Manitoba

See also Energy

Further Reading

Braun, G. W., & Smith, D. R. (1992). Commercial wind power: Recent experience in the United States. *Annual Review of Energy and the Environment, 17,* 97–121.

Danish Wind Industry Association. (2002). Read about wind energy. Retrieved December 3, 2002, from http://www.wind-power.dk/core.htm.

McGowan, J. G., & Connors, S. R. (2000). Windpower: A turn of the century review. *Annual Review of Energy and the Environment, 25,* 147–197.

Pasqualetti, M. J., Gipe, P., & Righter, R. W. (2002). *Wind power in view: Energy landscapes in a crowded world.* San Diego, CA: Academic Press.

Reynolds, J. (1970). *Windmills and watermills.* London: Hugh Evelyn.

Smil, V. (1994). *Energy in world history.* Boulder, CO: Westview.

Smil, V. (2003). *Energy at the crossroads.* Cambridge, MA: The MIT Press.

Sørensen, B. (1995). History of, and recent progress in, wind-energy utilization. *Annual Review of Energy and the Environment, 20,* 387–424.

Stockhuyzen, F. (1963). *The Dutch windmill.* New York: Universe Books.

Wolff, A. R. (1900). *The windmill as prime mover.* New York: John Wiley.

Index

Notes: 1) Names, terms, and page-number ranges in **bold** denote chapter entries.

Notes: 1) Names, terms, and page-number ranges in **bold** denote chapter entries.

Notes: 1) Names, terms, and page-number ranges in **bold** denote
chapter entries.

Editorial Board and Staff

Author Credits

Introduction: World Environmental History
by **Shepard KRECH III**
Brown University
J. R. McNeill
Georgetown University
Carolyn Merchant
University of California Berkeley

Anthropocene
by **David Christian**
Macquarie University, Sydney

Anthroposphere
by **Johan Goudsblom**
University of Amsterdam

Biological Exchanges
by **J. R. McNeill**
Georgetown University

Carrying Capacity
by **Mark Nathan Cohen**
State University of New York, Plattsburgh

Climate Change
by **Anthony N. Penna**
Northeastern University

Columbian Exchange
by **Alfred W. Crosby**
University of Texas, Austin

Deforestation
by **Michael Williams**
Deceased, formerly of Oriel College

Desertification
by **Andrew S. Goudie**
St. Cross College

Deserts
by **Juan García Latorre**
Association for Landscape Research in Arid Zones

Diseases—Animal
by **Raymond Pierotti**
University of Kansas

Diseases—Overview
by **William H. McNeill**
University of Chicago, Emeritus

Diseases—Plant
by **Christopher M. Cumo**
Independent scholar, Canton, Ohio

Earthquakes
by **Christa Hammerl**
Central Institute for Meteorology and Geodynamics

Ecological Imperialism
by **Alfred W. Crosby**
University of Texas, Austin

Energy
by **Vaclav Smil**
University of Manitoba

Environmental Movements
by **J. Donald Hughes**
University of Denver

Erosion
by **Timothy Beach**
Georgetown University

Ethnobotany
by **Richard Ford**
University of Michigan

Extinctions
by **D. Bruce Dickson**
Texas A&M University

Famine
by **Stephen Wheatcroft**
University of Melbourne

Fire
by **Johan Goudsblom**
University of Amsterdam

Gaia Theory
by **James Lovelock**
European Communities Information Office

Green Revolution
by **Alexander M. Zukas**
National University

Ice Ages
by **Christopher C. Joyner**
Georgetown University

Islands
by **John Gillis**
Rutgers University

Mountains
by **Jack D. Ives**
Carleton University

Natural Gas
by **Eli Goldstein**
Bar-Ilan University, Israel

Nature
by **Vera Norwood**
University of New Mexico

Oceans and Seas
by **Poul Holm**
Trinity College Dublin

Oil Spills
by **Joanna Burger**
Rutgers University

Population and the Environment
by **J. R. McNeill**
Georgetown University

Rivers
by **Mark Cioc**
University of California, Santa Cruz

Roads
by **William H. McNeill**
University of Chicago, Emeritus

Salinization
by **Daniel D. Richter Jr.**
Duke University

Timber
by **Sing C. Chew**
Humboldt State University

Trees
by **Oliver Rackham**
Corpus Christi College, Cambridge, United Kingdom

Water
by **R. Scott Moore**
Indiana University of Pennsylvania

Water Energy
by **Vaclav Smil**
University of Manitoba

Water Management
by **Robert C. Hunt**
Brandeis University

Wind Energy
by **Vaclav Smil**
University of Manitoba

This **BERKSHIRE** *Essentials* book was distilled from the

Berkshire Encyclopedia of World History 2ND EDITION

William H. McNeill

Jerry H. Bentley, David Christian,

Ralph C. Croizier, J. R. McNeill,

Heidi Roupp, and Judith P. Zinsser

Editors

Brett Bowden

Associate Editor

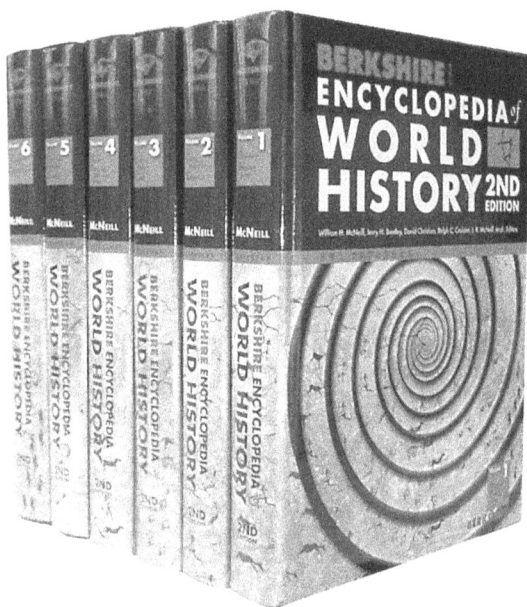

This landmark work has grown from 5 to 6 volumes and includes over 100 new articles on environmental history, world art, global communications, and information technology, as well as updates on events such as earthquakes and the global economic crisis. Hundreds of new illustrations enhance visual appeal, while updated Further Reading sections guide readers toward continued study.

6 VOLUMES · 978-1-933782-65-2
Price: US$875 · 3,152 pages · 8½ × 11"

CHOICE

"Challenging traditional encyclopedias that offer the standard who, what, when, and where, the second edition of the *Berkshire Encyclopedia of World History* continues to focus on cultural comparisons and interactions using broad themes. The second edition offers much more material on such distinctive and interdisciplinary entries. Groups of entries, such as the nine on trading patterns and the nine on revolutions, allow for easy comparisons between cultures. The big, traditional encyclopedias lack much of the unique content offered in this work, and do not focus on the historical significance of topics such as sweet potatoes and trees or discuss emerging trends such as "big history" and trade cycles. **Summing Up:** Highly recommended. Lower-division undergraduates and above; general readers."

Booklist

"One of the great strengths of this unique resource is that although it is accessible to novices and younger users, it is still useful to more advanced researchers and scholars. It succeeds in tying specific and local histories to larger patterns and movements. Overall, this magnificent set provides an interconnected and holistic perspective on human history and is recommended for most libraries."

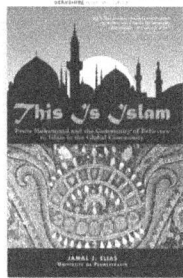

www.ingramcontent.com/pod-product-compliance
Lightning Source LLC
Chambersburg PA
CBHW082353270326
41935CB00013B/1602